The Great Philosophers

THE EASTERN WORLD

Eric Walter Frederic Tomlin is one of the best-known figures in the world of contemporary British philosophy.

Born in Surrey, England, in 1913, he entered the University of Oxford at the age of nineteen. There he made a notable mark for himself by taking Honors Degrees in Politics, Philosophy, Economics, and Modern History.

At Oxford, too, he encountered the man who was to prove probably the greatest single influence on his development. This was the distinguished philosopher and historian, R. G. Collingwood, who helped young Tomlin develop the perceptive historical approach to philosophical subjects that has been put to such brilliant use in the two-volume work on *The Great Philosophers: The Western World* (Vol. 1) and *The Eastern World* (Vol. 2).

Mr. Tomlin, who traveled extensively in the Middle East while in the service of the British Council, is an Extension Lecturer for the University of London. He is a member of the Aristotelian Society and a fellow of the Royal Asiatic Society. A contributor to numerous literary reviews in England, he is also the author of *The Approach to Metaphysics* and *Life in Modern Turkey*.

BY THE SAME AUTHOR:

Turkey, the Modern Miracle

Life in Modern Turkey

The Approach to Metaphysics

The Great Philosophers: the Western World

THE GREAT PHILOSOPHERS

THE EASTERN WORLD

E. W. F. TOMLIN

A. A. Wyn, Inc. · New York

Library of Congress Catalog Card Number: 52-11700

Printed in the United States of America

To

MY SON

ACKNOWLEDGMENTS

My thanks are due to Mr. Michael Cullis for having read through the text of this book both in manuscript and in proof. I also wish to thank Mrs. S. Sabavala for having read and commented upon the chapter on Zoroaster. My gratitude to these two experts does not involve them in any responsibility for my views or their presentation. With regard to the typing of the manuscript at various stages, I am indebted not to one or two persons but to an entire secretariat: I would mention in particular the Misses Möller, McGibney, Gunter, Beall, McDougall and Thouin. To Miss Brenda Tripp I wish to record my thanks for having introduced me to *The Secret of the Golden Flower*. Finally, I am deeply grateful to Mrs. René-Martin for having undertaken the difficult task of compiling the Index.

Acknowledgments are due to Messrs. Charles Scribner's for permission to quote extracts from J. H. Breasted's rendering of the Egyptian "Song of the Harp Player" and the Sun Hymn of Ikhnaton, and to Phoenix House, Ltd., for permission to quote extracts from the translation of the *Bhagavad-Gita* by Christopher Isherwood and Swami Prabhavananda.

E. W. F. T.

CONTENTS

LIST OF ILLUSTRATIONS

"The initiation of all wise and noble things comes and must come from individuals: generally at first from some one individual."

JOHN STUART MILL

"The men whom we call founders of religions are not really concerned with founding a religion, but wish to establish a human world that is subject to divine truth: to unite the way of the earth with that of heaven."

MARTIN BUBER: *Moses*

"One can tell for oneself whether the water is warm or cold. In the same way, a man must convince himself about these experiences, then only are they real."

I-Ching

"Like an image in a dream, the world is troubled by love, hatred, and other poisons. So long as the dream lasts, the image appears to be real, but on awakening it vanishes."

SHANKARA: *Atma Bodha*

"Truly, philosophers play a strange game. They know very well that one thing alone counts, and that all their medley of subtle discussions relates to one single question: why are we born on this earth? And they also know that they will never be able to answer it. Nevertheless, they continue sedately to amuse themselves. Do they not see that people come to them from all points of the compass, not with a desire to partake of their subtlety, but because they hope to receive from them one word of life? If they have such words, why do they not cry them from the housetops, asking their disciples to give, if necessary, their very blood for them? If they have no such words, why do they allow people to believe they will receive from them something which they cannot give?"

JACQUES MARITAIN

PREFACE

THE aim of this book is twofold: to provide a straightforward account of the life and work of the great thinkers of the Orient, and to attempt to show, in terms intelligible to the ordinary reader, with what remarkable insistence the greatest of these thinkers dwell upon common themes. The account that follows is to be regarded neither as a formal history nor as a source book, still less as a scaffolding upon which the author has attempted to erect a private system of his own. In the case of thinkers whose ideas are presented so often in abstract form, and who are sometimes in danger of being regarded almost as disembodied intellects, the approach through biography, where material for such treatment is available, has much to recommend it. While we therefore propose to maintain the general approach adopted in the companion volume,[1] we do not allow the reader to forget that the greatest thinkers, especially those of the Orient, expound their thought more effectively in their lives.

It has sometimes been maintained that philosophers, as distinct from other people, ought not to have any private lives; or if, as in the case of Peter Abelard, private life and public life were inextricably intermingled, that this was a regrettable aberration which the serious student of philosophy should either regard with amused tolerance or else ignore altogether. This is surely a mistaken attitude. Failure to "practise what they preach" is a reproach not merely frequently levelled at, but unfortunately all too often deserved by, Western philosophers. To say that the great oriental sages were too busy living their philosophy to write about it is perhaps not far from the truth. Apart from the fact that the Buddha, Christ, and Mohammed could probably neither read nor write, such accomplishments remained, we feel, irrelevant to their mission. In any case, their disciples to a great extent repaired this deficiency, and their later followers have perhaps over-compensated for it. Conversely, it might be suggested—no doubt with a certain cynicism—that more than one Western philosopher has been too busy writing about his philosophy to live it. In recent times, indeed, the situation has tended to assume a ludicrous aspect. Academic exponents of philosophy, that is to say, have derived a perverse pleasure from demonstrating, not indeed for the first time, that philosophy in its metaphysical and theological aspect is based upon a misapprehension as to the use of words. Of this trend in modern philosophy we have spoken at length elsewhere,[2] and we revert to it briefly in the Conclusion here.

Immersion in oriental philosophical writing over a period of years has led the author to believe that much of its attraction for Western readers resides first in its exotic terminology, and secondly in its apparent and to some extent inevitable vagueness. Words such as *Nirvana, Karma,*

[1] *The Great Philosophers: The Western World.*

[2] *The Approach to Metaphysics* (Routledge and Kegan Paul, 1947), Part IV.

Vedanta, and *Maya* produce, it seems, an effect very much like hypnosis, above all perhaps upon those to whom their meaning is unknown. And admittedly few ideas of this order can be rendered into English with the precision demanded by Western philosophers for their own concepts. We have therefore refrained from introducing more than an absolute minimum of technical terms, even where the temptation proved strongest, as in the sections on the *Upanishads,* the Yoga systems of Patanjali, and the Hindu doctrines or *darshanas*. And secondly, we have throughout endeavoured to bring home to the reader that ideas which need to be rendered in vague or general terms are often the reverse of vague in the original. If, as Patanjali maintained, there are thirty-six forms of consciousness, or, as Kapila maintained, twenty-five different "realities," we are bound to miss endless subtleties of meaning by rendering their thought in the half dozen terms available at most in English.

How ought we to approach oriental thought? In the case of some of the more "difficult" Western thinkers, such as St. Thomas Aquinas, Kant, or Hegel, we have formed the habit of approaching their works indirectly. We have climbed scaffolding of our own construction, and peered with awe at the immense edifices before us. Such surveys and distant scrutinies are not without their utility—or, glancing at some of the pages ahead of us, we may presume to hope as much; but it would be regrettable if, from fear of intellectual vertigo, we were to rest content with such external appraisal. This book would not have assumed its present form, nor acquired any merit that it may possess, if the author had not based his study as far as possible upon the original texts. These are now largely accessible to anyone who takes the trouble to seek them, for the translation of the Eastern scriptures has reached in our day a high pitch of excellence.

The reader must not presume to imagine that by reading the *Vedic* Hymns, a few select *Upanishads,* some of the Jataka Books, the *Analects* of Confucius, and some *suras* of the Koran, he has assimilated the chief products of oriental thought. The corpus of Eastern literature is enormous; it is said—to take a minor example—that only one ten-thousandth part of T'ang poetry has been translated.[1] What Mr. Gai Eaton calls in his recent book the "richest vein"[2] will not be quarried in our lifetime. We have so far merely scratched the surface. At the same time, it is evident that people in the Occident are becoming increasingly alive to the necessity of studying oriental thought.

The history of India, for example, sheds a flood of light upon the problem of what it is that constitutes a civilization or culture: for while India has been conquered and dominated again and again, its distinctive philosophy or metaphysics has survived not as a curiosity or what we might call a "cultural heritage" (as the classical Western philosophy has survived within our own civilization) but rather as that through which a

[1] The T'ang dynasty (618-905 A.D.) was China's most civilized epoch. (The phrase is Thoreau's.)

[2] *The Richest Vein: Eastern tradition and modern thought* (Faber, 1949).

vast community has preserved its conscious identity. The resulting unity, to quote that remarkable Orientalist, René Guénon, is a "doctrinal unity." Now that the Western domination is at an end, it is incumbent upon us to treat with respect that which we tended formerly to regard with aloof patronage. In short, we have ceased to teach; it is time that we should learn.

It is often assumed that a people may be best understood by reference to its political history and geographical situation. The efforts of modern nations to understand one another are dictated to a large extent by fear: and when international conflicts periodically break out, frantic appeals are launched for the services of missionaries, modern language teachers, historians, and archaeologists. We know only too well how, in spite of these efforts, nation can still fail to understand nation to an extent that may spell disaster. The truth is that a people consists in that in which it believes. While it may be very difficult to discover what its beliefs are—and for such investigation scepticism and infidelity are as important as faith itself—all other information or evidence as to a people's likely behaviour is insufficient, and may prove seriously misleading. It is possible that much of the turmoil associated with the "British connection" in India was due to a failure to appreciate the importance of this aspect of the Indian character, if aspect is not too slight a word: the failure in India was at bottom a religious failure.[1] Even if religion were the "illusion" that Freud declared it to be, as distinct from the oriental view that all is illusion except religion, the *fact* of belief would need still to be taken into account: for if a man thinks something to be true, this conviction, however preposterous, will inevitably influence his conduct. The words of Georges Sorel are particularly relevant to a study of the oriental mentality: "*Les religions constituent un scandale particulièrement grave pour l'intellectualiste, car il ne saurait ni les regarder comme étant sans portée historique, ni les expliquer.*"[2]

The author, while conscious of the book's many faults, must inevitably remain unconscious of many more. Those who hold the beliefs that are here outlined, or who reverence the figures that have been portrayed, will find much with which they disagree. The concluding chapter will likewise evoke criticism from thinkers in both East and West, and for this the author is not unprepared, and may even be grateful. From one sort of defect, and that perhaps the most odious of all, he believes himself to be exempt. No one can accuse him of adopting an attitude of superior flippancy towards those who, if not among the world's saints, have come nearest to attaining perfection of character; or of holding up to ridicule and derision ideas which, according to modern canons, appear to lack both reasonableness and consistency. He may even and with greater justice be chided for having taken certain doctrines too seriously, and for

[1] Cf. T. S. Eliot, *Notes Towards the Definition of Culture* (London, 1948), pp. 64-5.
[2] *Réflexions sur la Violence.*

having attempted with too great a show of earnestness to credit the earliest of thinkers with profundities which they never, could we but know their minds, sought to compass. *Adnuit.* All that can be hoped, if such be the case, is that our modern thinkers and those who succeed them will persist in being at least as frivolous as Ikhnaton, as superficial as Confucius, as shallow as Shankara, and as complacent as the Buddha.

With this brief exhortation addressed to the learned, the author commends his work to those who, like himself, feel that they have something yet to learn. He cannot claim that the book was written throughout in ideal conditions; no condition is ideal that is within reach of a modern newspaper. But if he mentions that certain chapters were written overlooking the Dents du Midi and others within sight of the Iles d'Or off the French Riviera, he may at the same time hope that something of those pleasing prospects has affected his treatment of a subject that needed all the stimulus and inspiration that he could muster.

E. W. F. TOMLIN

THE GREAT PHILOSOPHERS: THE EASTERN WORLD

INTRODUCTION

Characteristics of oriental and occidental thought

THOSE who approach the philosophers of the Orient after a deep or perhaps even a superficial study of Western thought cannot fail to be struck by one salient feature. Whereas so many Western philosophers, especially of the modern era, dwell upon minute technical problems and appear to avoid generalizations about the universe as a whole, the great philosophers of the Orient never lose sight of the fundamental problem, namely that which concerns life's meaning and purpose. From the oldest of coherent philosophical speculations in the Hindu *Vedas* and *Upanishads* to the sages of modern India, the quest not so much for certainty as for truth has continued without relaxation. Nor has this preoccupation been confined to a few men of distinction, learning, or piety in each generation; it has exercised the minds of those anonymous, patient, toiling millions with which, to the Western eye, the Orient is peopled. Hence the much-quoted and commonly accepted distinction between "Western materialism" and "Eastern mysticism".

When we come to examine closely the thought of the oriental philosophers, we find that such a generalization needs to be qualified. Eastern thought has its materialistic aspect, just as Western thought has its strong vein of mysticism. Furthermore, an extreme form of idealism such as involves the denial of the reality of matter itself is likely, by way of reaction, to turn into its opposite. For example, a theory which repudiates the existence of the human body is found upon examination to be largely concerned with the preservation of physical health. Buddhist mysticism, commonly supposed to be among the purest and most exalted forms of idealism, is linked with a theory of knowledge that would satisfy the most diehard Western materialist or positivist. Finally, in contrast to the upright and noble Confucius, the Orient can produce more than one distinguished "moralist" whose cynicism and cunning go far beyond anything preached by Machiavelli himself.[1]

Those elements common to both Eastern and Western thought should confirm us in the belief, so often repudiated, that the human

[1] E.g. Kautilya Chanakya, adviser to the Indian ruler Chandragupta (*c.* 322–298 B.C.); also Yang Chu (*c.* 390 B.C.), and Hsun-Tze (305–235 B.C.). For the latter, see Chapter VII.

mind is everywhere one and the same, or at least that it operates in the same way. We should therefore avoid overdoing distinctions. That an Andaman pigmy and a Middle West farmer in the United States should employ a different system of logic is inconceivable, though they clearly start from very different assumptions. What lends to the study of Eastern thought its particular fascination is the fact that it is not merely vastly older than Western thought but that it represents far more of a continuity. To survey the long history of human thought is to observe that Western philosophical enquiry is merely an offshoot, though a flourishing one, of the oriental parent tree, just as Europe (in the phrase of Paul Valéry) is merely a tiny cape jutting off Asia. This is no doubt the reason why European thinkers such as Schelling and Schopenhauer and also Goethe and Tolstoy have been struck, on making acquaintance with Eastern philosophy, by its amazing profundity. It is indeed profound; and its profundity is that which results from having deep roots.

Presuppositions of oriental thought

The remarkable continuity of oriental thought, the long-hallowed tradition of speculation upon ultimate values, have been responsible for a further popular notion, namely that the oriental mind is essentially static. Here again the phrase may have meaning when applied to industrial organization, or methods of hygiene, or even diplomatic practice; it requires considerable qualification when applied to the oriental conception of life. That conception is not static; it were better described as rhythmical. It does not repudiate changelessness, but rather it is obsessed with the idea of eternal recurrence. To try to determine that which originally gave rise to philosophical speculation in the world, and when first it took systematic form, is no doubt a dangerous and possibly a futile game; but as far as the Orient is concerned, the process of animal and human generation, the rhythm of sowing and reaping, and likewise the daily miracle of the sun's birth and death, would appear to have suggested at least one ancient metaphysical doctrine, namely that of the "transmigration of souls". This doctrine indeed has been preserved by Indian thought from remotest antiquity.[1] Accepting it with neither question nor proof, such innovators as Gotama Buddha merely sought to deepen its significance and to prescribe means of diminishing its terrors; for it is a doctrine at once terrible and sublime. Nor did a sceptic such as Mahavira, founder of the Jain religion (599–527 B.C.), succeed in loosening its hold on the common people. For what after all is the doctrine of transmigration

[1] Some of the reasons why it should for so long have obsessed the oriental mind are analysed in Chapter V.

save a belief that the law applying to almost everything in nature applies likewise—and perhaps pre-eminently—to the soul of man?

So thoroughly has the oriental mind been preoccupied with this notion of reincarnation, or the sempiternal rebirth of the human soul in an infinite number of guises, that the chief task of every great Eastern prophet has been to show how such intolerable recurrence might be avoided. And since so great an evil could hardly be expected to yield to an early remedy, it was felt that the annihilation of desire—if possible at all and even if possible only after repeated experiments—was not too high a price to pay for final release from consciousness. Instead of being calmed and soothed by the notion of perpetual tranquillity, the Eastern mind is merely tantalized by it. What the Eastern sage or fakir remains most clearly aware of, at least this side of the condition of *Samadhi*,[1] is the storm and stress of instinct, passion, and desire. Men do not perpetually talk of inward peace if they already have it as an inalienable possession.

In the history of Western thought there is a thing called philosophy and there is a thing called theology; and it has usually been possible, except during certain periods such as the Middle Ages, to distinguish between the two. In the history of Eastern thought there is only a thing called theology. This is true even of the humanist thought of Confucius and Mencius, which is merely an ethical doctrine become detached from the religion providing its sanction. Philosophy pursued as a secular game, a technique to be acquired at a university or extra-mural seminar, a recipe to enable the student to be formidable in argument, is not merely a Western product, but a product of quite recent date. In the Orient it is impossible to be a philosopher without being also a sage. In the Occident it is not only possible, it is highly to be recommended. For it is difficult to be a sage in Europe on an income of less than several thousand pounds a year.

Philosophy and Myth

Although we have stressed the futility of seeking to explain the origins of philosophical thought, it is not unreasonable to suppose, following the Italian philosopher Giambattista Vico, that such thought or systems of thought originated in an ambience of myth.[2] There is a logical, if not a temporal, priority of imagination to thought; and so long as philosophy remains associated with religion

[1] The state of final release from consciousness. See page 214.

[2] For further treatment of this subject the reader is referred to the extremely interesting essay entitled "Myth and Reality" in the volume *Before Philosophy*, ed. Frankfort (Penguin Books, 1949).

or with mysticism, so long will it remain wedded to myth. In Western thought the divorce between philosophy and myth took place at least as early as Aristotle's reaction against Plato; and no doubt the importance assigned to myth in Plato's philosophy has led certain commentators to suppose him to have been immersed in Eastern lore, and even to have undertaken secret journeys to Babylon and Persia. As Western philosophy developed, Christianity filled the gap created by the expulsion of the pagan deities, or at least their retreat, as it were, "underground". And when, at the close of the Middle Ages, the intellectual influence of the Christian faith began to wane, the purely mythical impulse reasserted itself, but thereafter in association with the adventures of the new scientific hero called Matter. No doubt the philosophical impulse properly so-called, i.e. the disinterested enquiry into reasons, causes, and evidence, first took its origin from the clash of tribal myth, whether as a result of conquest, natural fusion for defence against man or nature, travel, or exogamy.[1] The claims of rival deities, then as now, had to be debated and assessed in human courts. The growth and refinement of man's reasoning faculty is the consequence of divine multiplicity.

It is tempting for the historian of Western thought to attribute the peculiar mental qualities of the Ionians, their curiosity and aptitude for enquiry, to the factor of environment and environment alone. Now environment is a blanket word; we are never quite sure how much it is intended to cover. If, however, environment means simply geographical conditions, then these are never a "cause" in any orthodox sense of the word. To assert that man is the product of his surroundings is to say he is part of them, in which case there is nothing positive to be surrounded. Environment in the strict sense is the cause of that which man chooses to make out of it. When the romantic Hellenist has drawn our attention to the idyllic beauty of the Greek countryside and coast, suggesting that such firmness, clarity of outline and atmospheric "numinousness" provided direct inspiration to the early Ionian thinkers, he fails to explain how it is that only with Thales of Miletus in the 6th century B.C. did the Greeks begin to respond to this particular form of stimulation.[2] Communities living in circumstances no less propitious have been remarkable for their lethargy and lack of achievement. The mixture of races, the growth of trade, the experience of seafaring—these were presumably the decisive factors in the emergence of the Ionian spirit of enquiry: for what people having made contact successively with Egyptians, Phoenicians, Chal-

[1] i.e. compulsory marriage outside the tribe.
[2] We would refer the reader also to the chapter on Islam.

daeans and Babylonians, nations so diverse in customs, language, and type, could have failed to make comparison one with the other, and having compared, to judge, and having judged, to co-ordinate?

The Unitive Vision

We should therefore look upon Western thought as the point at which the oriental imagination became articulated into action, just as the churches of Christendom are the practical manifestation of Eastern mysticism. The growth of applied science is similarly an inevitable accompaniment of the Western philosophical approach; for we can act only in a world that we believe to be both real and worth inhabiting. Now characteristics such as reality and value are precisely those which Eastern thought, with certain exceptions, refuses to ascribe to the natural world. Similarly, the philosophers of the Occident, with even fewer exceptions (such as Schopenhauer), assume that man's primary duty is to cultivate his conscious life, to increase his awareness of the world of sense, with the object of achieving mastery over his environment. Compare the oriental attitude. So far as Hinduism and Buddhism are concerned, the aim is to effect an escape from consciousness, to obliterate awareness of the self, to doubt even to the point of negation the reality of the world of sense. An exception is that of Chinese thought, which is on the whole individualist, humanist, almost egocentric, certainly familocentric. Nor can we ignore the paradox of the Hindu sage or fakir who, by his very isolation and eccentricity, comes in time to assume that very "individuality" which he is striving so obstinately to renounce.

In the chapters that follow we shall undertake to survey the history of oriental thought from the earliest times, using as our landmarks the great figures who have deserved, more even than in the Occident, the name of leaders and sages, and of whom a great number seem more than human in their personality, and some few of almost divine-human compound. The Western mind has tended to separate the various faculties of man, just as it has separated the sciences, the literary *genres*, and the various professions. A man is a poet or an aeroplane fitter. Biology is a science in its own right. This piece of verse is a lyric. We have a category into which everything can be fitted, and knowledge is sometimes identified with the capacity merely to read the labels. The Orient has eschewed this tendency to separation. Its philosophers are at once poets, moralists, statesmen. Its religion is a blend of poetic myth and precise reasoning. Knowledge is more than a collection of information; it is a species of visionary wisdom. We in the Western world have for too long remained blind to this unitive viewpoint.

The Morning of Reason

Writing at the time of the French Revolution, Thomas Paine expressed his conviction that "a morning of reason" had dawned in Europe, and that the dark night of superstition was being finally rolled back.[1]

When was the first "morning of reason"? That is a question which has never ceased to puzzle historians, anthropologists, philosophers, and psychologists. It must have taken place, if the expression is at all accurate, long before the earliest recorded history, and possibly earlier than such pre-history as we are able to deduce from rock painting, implement, menhir, or barrow. "I want to know," said Voltaire in his *Essai sur les Moeurs*, "what were the steps by which men passed from barbarism to civilization." So indeed do we all. In spite of great progress in archaeological investigation, whereby at least half a dozen civilizations—Egyptian, Sumerian, Babylonian, Hittite, Cretan, and Dravidian—have been uncovered, we are no nearer to answering that question than was Voltaire: we merely know how much farther we have to go back—to find men already to some extent civilized.

The evidence of art is misleading. The cave pictures and even the sculpture of the Paleolithic or Old Stone Age (from *c.* 100,000 B.C.) is superior, judged on present evidence, to anything produced during the New Stone Age (*c.* 5000 B.C.), save perhaps in respect of pottery; and not merely may the cave paintings of the Dordogne and Andalusia be accounted exquisite masterpieces, but they are clearly part of a tradition already of some antiquity. We cannot imagine them as either isolated "sports" or the works of some extraordinary genius. It is possible that the works of genius have perished, and that these are merely the conventional efforts of journeymen.

Of the earliest writing we must speak with similar reservation. Whether script was used first for recording numbers, symbolized by plain strokes or fingers (digits), or was merely an abstraction from some kind of gesture-pictography such as the Chinese *Ku-wan*, we may legitimately assume that its development and perfection presupposes a considerable unwritten, unrecorded, pre-alphabet civilization. An eminent authority, Dr. David Diringer, believes that the alphabet as we now know it must have been invented in Syrio-Palestine about the middle of the Second Millenium B.C., but the Egyptians were using an alphabet as early as 3000 B.C. That writing was originally an art or craft for the few, or at least for recording recondite and select subject-matter, may be deduced from the antiquity of the word *Hieroglyph*, which means literally a "sacred

[1] Cf. *The Rights of Man* (1791).

carving". Nor has the activity of writing altogether lost its arcane significance in a society which, like that of the present day, still respects the literary as opposed to the merely literate, those who "write" as opposed to those who can write. Finally, it is misleading to draw inferences from the mental condition of tribes or peoples contemptuously labelled "savage", if only because our conception of savagery has lately undergone considerable revision: partly as a result of the emulation by some civilized peoples of methods hitherto regarded as primitive, and partly because the progress of anthropological studies has disposed of certain persistent notions concerning the "irrationality" of much primitive culture.

Moreover, the "savages" whose habits have been studied in recent times are those already undergoing corruption by contact with Western civilization: a contact that has tended first to demoralize them and then as often as not to bring about their extinction.[1] Certain practices conventionally associated with primitive culture, such as magic and even sorcery, are now regarded as by no means confined thereto, but rather as forming an element in all civilization. Indeed, their absence or neglect, or worst of all their deliberate eradication by rationalist-minded persons, may be the cause of serious harm to a civilization's stability. And that is another reason why Western readers should seek a better understanding of the thought of the Orient, where the dissociation of religion and philosophy, magic and science, has been achieved with much less violence than in Europe and America.

The Notion of a Golden Age

Sooner or later the enquirer into the origins of enquiry itself finds himself speculating upon the possibility of some kind of fall from grace, some cataclysm whereby mankind, hitherto the child of nature, was obliged to fend for himself, to "stop and think", to assume the burden of freedom. From such a moment, it would seem, philosophical speculation must have begun its limping career. The story of the Flood, regarded by our devout ancestors as a legend, has become for their sceptical successors a historical reality; and if the researches of Sir Leonard Woolley in Iraq do not prove the Biblical account of Noah and the Ark, at least they suggest its symbolic truth.[2] For our present purpose we need not ask whether the so-called Fall of Man was a historical occurrence, or whether, as the Higher Criticism tended to suggest, it was a purely spiritual one (whatever that may mean). What we need to ask is whether the

[1] Anthropologists have devoted insufficient attention to ascertaining the "savages" own definition of "savage". The results might be illuminating.

[2] For an account of the various Flood legends, see Chapter II.

society anterior to this Fall represented, as is usually assumed, a kind of Golden Age. Why the natural or uncivilized should necessarily be more peaceful, serene, or desirable than the "unnatural" or civilized is assumed more often than proved. In some very interesting books Professor Perry has stated a case for supposing there to have existed a pre-civilized condition of mankind, not too incredibly remote, in which war, even inter-tribal scrapping, was entirely unknown.

Such a theory, if true, does not necessarily entail the view that social life was one prolonged idyll and had remained in this condition from the beginning. From inspection of the earliest known (and therefore probably quite "late") legal code, that of Hammurabi, for instance, we obtain an impression not of simple dealings or straightforward human relationships, common disputes or obvious means of redress, but very much the reverse: a contentious, right-conscious, sophisticated community, in which men quarrelled and had always been known to quarrel as much as they do now, and probably took the law into their own hands more frequently. The rule of "an eye for an eye and a tooth for a tooth" was probably the common law of antiquity, though not the only law, if we may judge from the earliest known legal document (now in the Egyptian section of the British Museum), dealing with a case of disputed inheritance. The more "natural" human life may be, the more painful in many respects it becomes. If we find hints in Hesiod or even Plato of a remote Golden Age, we need not accept their implied suggestion that it was a life of undiluted bliss and serenity. The Golden Age, as H. J. Massingham finally concludes in his brilliant little study[1], is mankind's vague memory of its own youth: hence we must locate it at no particular point in time. But if we could recapture in their identity the feelings experienced in youth, we should recognize that period for what it is, namely a time of mental and physical distress from which we longed to be delivered. The Golden Age is golden only in retrospect, and merely gilded upon examination.

[1] *The Golden Age: the story of human nature* (London, 1927).

CHAPTER I

THE EGYPTIANS

A Young Science

THE insight gained during the last century into Egypt's past has altered our whole conception of history. We may also ask to what extent it has altered our conception of moral and philosophical thought. For apart from its antiquity, the civilization of Egypt differs from all other known civilizations in at least two respects: in its length and in its continuity.

As the story of Eastern philosophy begins with such speculations as have been preserved in Egyptian records, we are now in a better position to enquire how far back in the past man's efforts at ordered thought can be traced. For we are curious to know what evidence there is of *civilization*—meaning thereby an ordered system of society dominated by a coherent view of life—having antedated the existence of written records, and by what conceivable stretch of time.

In order to answer these questions, it will be useful to touch for a moment both upon the rediscovery of ancient Egypt, or in other words the history of the young science of Egyptology, and upon the reasons for the fact, now largely accepted by historians, that Egypt was the birthplace of philosophical speculation as we know it.

Apart from the extremely interesting and largely accurate account of Herodotus, the Greek historian (484–425 B.C.), and of certain other Greek and also Roman writers, very little contemporary information about Egyptian life and culture has come down to us. It is true that we may derive much valuable information from both Testaments of the Bible, and we shall later be able to observe the extent to which Hebrew civilization was based upon that of Egypt. Unlike Greece, Rome, and Israel, however, Egypt produced no great historians and few reliable chroniclers. Of the latter, an Egyptian priest named Manetho, who lived between 300 and 250 B.C., compiled a list of Egyptian kings from all but the earliest times; or rather, since his work has survived only in fragments and transcripts, this list of rulers is the one contribution to knowledge with which he may fairly be credited. It took the form of a division into *dynasties*, such as our history books and museums have made tolerably familiar; but this division, which was never very enlightening to the non-specialist, has proved misleading. In the first place it suggested, what was not necessarily true, that the kings grouped in a particular dynasty belonged invariably to the same family. Secondly, it failed to make clear that certain dynasties, instead of preceding or succeeding one another, were, in consequence of political rivalries, contemporaneous. Thirdly, being based upon incomplete evidence, it began to number the dynasties from the beginning of what historians now call the Second Union (roughly 3500–2631 B.C.), thereby omitting to take account of any previous social epoch such as that which has now come within the purview of Egyptologists as the First Union.

The modern study of Egyptology was the by-product of a venture inspired by motives far removed from those conventionally associated with research. When Napoleon invaded Egypt in 1797 he took with him a large party of *savants*, chiefly scientists and archaeologists. With whatever degree of sincerity Bonaparte himself embraced oriental ideas—at one point he proclaimed his intention of becoming a Moslem, and it appears that in spite of certain disqualifications (the authorities finally decided that circumcision was not an indispensable condition of embracing Islam) he was officially admitted to the faith—his band of research workers made good use of their time. The publication in 1809 of their learned *Description of Egypt* is evidence of this. Perhaps the most valuable result of the expedition, however, was the discovery by a French officer, who happened to be working at Rosetta in the Nile Delta, of a basalt stone bearing an inscription in three different scripts. As one of these scripts, Greek, was known, the scholars were able to translate forthwith what proved to be a decree issued by Ptolemy V Epiphanus (205–181 B.C.). The presumption, which in due course proved correct, was that the other two scripts, namely Hieroglyphics and a more popular cursive script called Demotic, carried a faithful rendering of the Greek version. Nevertheless, the process of transliteration and translation raised a variety of difficulties. Published in its entirety in the above-mentioned report, the inscription on the Rosetta Stone, which is now in the British Museum, long exercised the intelligence of scholars in every European country, particularly Germany, England, and France. But it was to a young French student of Egyptology, Jean-François Champollion (1790–1832), that we owe the inscription's final decipherment.

Something of the magnitude of Champollion's achievement may be judged from two circumstances. In the first place the text ran on without regard to division between words; and, secondly, neither Champollion nor any other contemporary scholar knew at the outset whether hieroglyphic signs represented ideas, sounds, or syllables: in short, whether they were ideographic, phonetic, or merely syllabic. Nor did the experts realize, save after prolonged deliberation, that the hieroglyphic script was in fact based upon a combination of ideographic and phonetic characters, some of the latter acting merely as aids to comprehension rather than as elements in pronunciation, a fact which Champollion originally deduced from the preponderance of hieroglyphic signs over the Greek. To mention all the problems with which Champollion was confronted is unnecessary; we may merely note that it took him fourteen years to "break" the hieroglyphic code, and another ten to acquire sufficient familiarity with the language to compile a grammar and dictionary—and incidentally to kill himself with overwork. By 1822, the learned world was put in possession of the means of understanding, however partially, the mind of ancient Egypt. Not since the closing of the Egyptian temples in the 2nd century A.D. had access to such riches been possible.

Egypt as the Cradle of Civilization

The story of Egyptian excavation, which naturally received fresh impetus from the mastery of hieroglyphics, has been a record of patience and surprise, with no small admixture of romance. Moreover, it is a story to which new chapters are being added year by year. A new discovery on the banks of the Nile seldom fails to provide material for journalists, since Egyptian archaeology has received a good press in both Europe and America; nor is any European museum regarded as complete without its painted coffin or even its tattered mummy. Beyond the fact that the Egyptians practised the art of embalming and built enormous pyramids, however, the general public is not always aware of what it is that these industrious people achieved. No doubt the origins of thought and the first awakening of a moral and social conscience are less dramatic than the unearthing of a tomb or the prising open of a sarcophagus.

For our purposes we are interested in the Egyptians as being the first people, the first nation even, to debate those moral issues—issues of good and evil as applied to life itself, and issues of right and wrong as applied to human conduct—with which we are equally concerned today. Although man had perhaps been in existence as much as a million years before the first recognizable "literature" was produced, we cannot in the present state of our knowledge conceive there to have been any similar attempt at coherent philosophizing before that of the Egyptian sages. The Babylonians, as we shall see, were in certain respects original thinkers and even more original scientists; but their religious speculations early assumed a superstitious character from which few positive or fruitful conclusions issued. Finally, the civilization of Elam probably antedates by several hundred years that of both Babylon and Egypt; but, apart from the potter's wheel, we know of no specific contribution to civilization made by that obscure people.

Why, then, Egypt? Can we explain how it was that a country so oddly endowed, if not victimized, by nature should have become the "cradle of civilization"?

Without entering into physiographical details, we may begin by pointing out that after the slow desiccation of North Africa at the beginning of the Neolithic period (*c.* 5000 B.C.) Egypt remained a comparatively protected area. That the Nile Valley has been inhabited by man from the very earliest times is now generally believed. Excavations begun as long ago—or as recently—as 1894 have furnished us with a good deal of information concerning the prehistoric inhabitants of the Nile Valley. Many of these people must have sought that fertile region as drought overtook them and their flocks. Of the characteristics of the Paleolithic[1] inhabitants of Egypt we know little, though archaeologists do not despair of finding a skeleton from which the *original* Egyptian might be known. Such cemeteries as have been unearthed suggest that the Egyptians of the Neolithic period and onwards were assured of at least one of the conditions of civilization, namely a continuity of food supply. No other people on earth had, it appears, enjoyed this privilege before. Furthermore, they had learned both to work metals and to domesticate animals; and from their burial customs it appears that they nourished that unshakable belief in an after-life for which, as their culture developed, they sought by diverse means to equip themselves. In due course we shall see how their attitude to this world and the next affected the development of moral ideas.

Ever since Herodotus called Egypt the "gift of the Nile", it has been customary to regard that country as the happy product of purely physical conditions, as if man had scarcely a hand in the matter. This is a serious misapprehension. Egypt is an oasis (itself an Egyptian word). Now anyone familiar with desert country knows that such oases, however well situated, depend for their survival as inhabited areas upon the exertions of man. Where man chooses to live, there he makes life tolerable, and where he is forced to live, there he will make life possible. That the fertility of Egypt depends upon a regular inundation, caused by rainfall upon the hills of Abyssinia swelling the White Nile from June onwards, is only a half-truth. Such a gross surcharge of water and mud, though varying in quantity from year to year, would prove as much of a

[1] i.e. the enormously long period preceding the Neolithic, and beginning about 500,000 B.C.

menace as a blessing were it permitted to reach the Nile Delta unchecked. Indeed, we know from various ancient records that the Nile, its flood assuming unusual proportions, has several times brought havoc upon the land. The ten plagues described in the Book of Exodus probably represent, as Flinders Petrie has well shown in his book *Egypt and Israel*, successive phases of such a catastrophe. In short, the survival of Egypt is due to a work of man, namely irrigation. That is as true today as it was five, ten, and perhaps a hundred thousand years ago.

Traces of the irrigation system of ancient Egypt show it to have been a highly intricate organization. And when we consider that the land, being 2,000 kilometres long and only a few kilometres wide, contains no more than 30,000 square kilometres of cultivated soil (i.e. 3·5 per cent), we perceive that the problem of irrigation is nothing but a problem of government, and *vice versa*.[1] To ensure not merely the control of the yearly inundation but its equitable distribution, the government of Egypt needed to be both strong and centralized. That is to say, the Pharaoh was obliged to use all possible means, including the assumption of divinity, to ensure his political authority. From the point of view of administration, however, the land divided itself naturally into small districts or *nomes*, of which there were forty; and more than one ancient papyrus affords us an insight into the tyranny which local rulers, believing themselves secure from governmental supervision, might occasionally wield.[2] A common danger, which in Egypt's case was the danger of extinction, is an unfailing means of unification. Thus it happened that Egypt, once the sources of its strength and weakness were understood by its people, developed not merely the first major social organization (the population of ancient Egypt was probably about seven millions), but, as we have pointed out, the most enduring human society so far known. Precisely how early the first unification of Egypt took place was not realized by those who, accepting the original order of dynasties, dated the reign of King Menes from about the year 3300 B.C. It is to modern archaeologists such as Flinders Petrie and Breasted that we owe our knowledge, such as it is, of the First Union, which is thought to date from at least 4000 B.C.[3]

It is the custom to honour the astronomer who detects a new

[1] On the narrowest part of the Nile at Kummeh (east bank) may be seen the mark of the River's level made by a 12th Dynasty Pharaoh 4000 years ago. It is about 30 feet *higher* than the level reached today.

[2] See the story of the Eloquent Peasant, page 54.

[3] On a fragment of the royal annals in the Cairo museum, Breasted discovered representations of kings of the pre-Dynastic period wearing double crowns, symbolic of this early union.

planet, the chemist who isolates a new element, the physicist who propounds a new law of nature. For reasons which are not apparent, we seldom appreciate the achievement of the archaeologist or historian who discovers a new age. This is regrettable, because nothing is at once more exhilarating and chastening to the mind than the opening of a new vista in the past. If we cannot yet say how or why civilization began, we are at least better able to tackle these questions once we know, as we now think we do, when it began.

No writer has done more to throw light upon the origins of civilization and the development of thought than the American archaeologist J. H. Breasted. A life devoted to excavation in the Middle East, and particularly in Egypt, put him in the best position to undertake that revision of historical perspective which recent discoveries, both his own and other people's, had rendered necessary. In defining what he called, not inaccurately, the New Past, Breasted drew attention to the fact that civilized life, as we understand it, must have grown up in the thousand years between 3500 B.C. and 2500 B.C., the period of the Second Union. To grasp so remote an epoch is not easy; but some idea of its uniqueness may be appreciated from the fact that Europe, at this time and for many centuries after, was still in the Stone Age. By "civilization" Breasted primarily implied two things: first a social organization based upon some measure of law and order, and secondly a conscious purpose animating that order, whereby the citizens, or at least a group of them, seem bent upon pursuing certain ideals of conduct, even if the latter should be more honoured in the breach than in the observance.

This general definition is important, because the archaeologist's spade has turned up evidence of several civilizations older than, or at least as old as, that of Egypt: for example Sumeria, Elam, and Babylon. Of these we shall have more to say in due course. In the meantime we may examine Breasted's contention that Egyptian civilization not merely outlasted and perhaps outshone every other, but substantially contributed, through its influence upon the Hebrews, to the development of our own. During this unique thousand years the civilization of Babylon was likewise developing, though with nothing like the same continuity and along much less intellectual lines. But what does our Western civilization owe to the thought of Babylon? Little enough, save that which was appropriated by the Hebrews, including the story of the great Flood, which, as we saw, was probably less of a myth than a real calamity in the Mesopotamian basin.[1] The code of Hammurabi, in spite of

[1] See also Chapter II, page 96.

its enlightened provisions, does not represent a milestone in ethical thought as do the remarkable Egyptian documents to which we are about to turn.

Civilization written and unwritten

It will be clear that the civilization to which we refer is exclusively a written civilization. Some historians have maintained, or at least assumed, that civilization began with the invention of letters. There is no reason to suppose that this was so. The impulse to collate, to compile, to record, probably finds expression at the point at which civilization, as hitherto defined, is already some way advanced, perhaps even beyond the stage of maturity, certainly many centuries after birth. If, for example, we are right in assuming that the First Union in Egypt dates from about 4000 B.C., it is hardly surprising that no written records should be found until at least 1,500 years later. Moreover, no public monuments belonging to this epoch have been discovered. But we should consider a further point: how many years of experiment, of temporary or abortive alliance, of diplomatic manœuvre, of competition for leadership, of the ousting of rivals, of the expulsion of foreigners,[1] must have passed before that first national union, so evidently precarious, was itself achieved? We possess no materials for answering these questions. All we can say is that the civilizing process, having come to so early a climax, must have started earlier than we can at present conceive, or so early as not to have had a start at all, if by that we presuppose an epoch of human life devoid of even the most elementary organization. If, however, we presuppose such a condition of mankind, we are faced with the further mystery of how man should have succeeded in issuing from it: a mystery almost as difficult to solve as that of the evolution of man from animal creation.

These matters, apart from their inherent difficulty, hardly come within the scope of our study. What is more relevant, though equally involved in difficulty, is the question as to why man, having evolved a technique for recording his thoughts, should have proceeded to develop them with such rapidity that within a few thousand years he should have acquired his present control over nature. More interesting still, if a great deal less reassuring, is the problem of why his moral vision, which apparently awakened five thousand years ago, should have failed to keep pace with his technical accomplishments: a fact so indisputable that the very

[1] The Egyptians made a distinction between "men" (i.e. themselves) and "foreigners", just as the word for the "land" of Egypt also meant the "earth" (i.e. the civilized world).

statement of it has become a platitude. It is true that material progress had enjoyed a start of several hundred thousand years, and that the development of writing was as much a stage on its journey as the development three thousand years later of printing, and the discovery five hundred years later still of radio. But, as Breasted has pointed out in his book *The Dawn of Conscience*, the evolution of moral thought in Egypt during the Second Union represents the farthest point to which such speculation can go in the absence of religious revelation. In this millenium of ethical reflection, we have something that had never taken place before. Men were systematically meditating on their destiny for the first time. To their implements, adornments, and techniques, they were now adding something totally different from any of these, namely a moral conscience.

The Memphite Drama

How old and important an oral tradition of philosophizing there must have been, at least in Egypt, can be inferred from the "oldest written thoughts" known to us. These are embodied in what is called the Memphite Drama (from Memphis, the ancient capital of Egypt), which was written, so Breasted thinks, by priests from Heliopolis in the middle of the fourth millenium B.C. We do not possess the full text of this remarkable piece of literature; and its preservation, even in mutilated fragments, is the result of happy accident. Its history is briefly as follows. The Ethiopian Pharaoh Shabaka, who reigned in the 8th century B.C. (he was a contemporary of Isaiah, and is called So in the Old Testament), ordered the ancient text to be copied from an old papyrus and inscribed on a black stone, where such a valuable "work of the ancestors" (for so he significantly called it) might the better be preserved for future generations. This block, now in the British Museum, was unfortunately used for many years as a nether mill-stone, so that along with the corn of many generations part of its message was ground away. Even so we possess enough of the text to enable us to judge to some extent of what is omitted.

That the most ancient recorded thoughts should be concerned with a discussion of Right and Wrong is a fact of very great interest. Nor is it without significance that the discussion should be conducted partly in dramatic form, thereby tending to confirm the religious origin of drama. But what, at first reading, strikes us most forcibly about this production is its extreme complexity. Here, we have to remind ourselves, is the beginning. Here is the infancy of thought. Here, more than two millenia before Thales, is the expression of an ordered view of life, yet couched in language suggestive of a tradition many centuries old. In other words, here is something very like mature philosophy: thought which, formulated by many minds, is so much a common possession as already to be anonymous. These circumstances alone prove that, long before writing was invented, organized and systematic thought had begun. What writing chiefly served to do was to establish an orthodoxy, a norm. It thus became a necessary agent of social stability, a means whereby the communal mind was informed and directed. Without writing we should view the past not as historians but as archaeologists; it is in the latter capacity, indeed, that we survey the development of man from the Paleolithic period until the age of which we speak. Writing is a means to spiritual continuity, and spiritual continuity is a condition of history.[1]

The piecing together of the text of both the Memphite Drama, and the highly abstruse philosophical discussion that follows it, has been a triumph of multi-national scholarship. We cannot here do more than summarize its contents, which, properly understood, throw light not merely upon the mentality of the Egyptian people of that distant age, but upon the development of philosophical speculation. There is something peculiarly exciting about examining a work of such extreme antiquity, the very nature of which was unknown until a few years ago. A new country of the mind is thereby revealed to us.

The piece begins with an invocation to the god Ptah. Now Ptah was the local god of Memphis. Originally, as one among many gods, he served as the patron saint of craftsmen; but eventually he assumed a pre-eminent position, no doubt as a result of being identified with making or creation in general. When King Menes subdued both Upper and Lower Egypt, it appears that he promoted Ptah to a position hitherto occupied by the Sun God himself. The reason was that Memphis had become, and was long to remain, the capital of united Egypt, in the forming of which Ptah had shown himself a master-builder.

How was it that the Sun God had traditionally wielded such influence? The question is easily answered. Egypt owed her geographical survival to two natural forces, the waters of the Nile and the rays of the sun. Consequently her people came to deify both. The Sun God, Re, whose headquarters were at Heliopolis (Greek: "Sun Town", originally called On), was traditionally represented by a falcon, the bird that was thought to fly nearest to heaven. As a convenient symbol, a winged disc was often employed. The Nile god, on the other hand, was god not merely of water but of the fertility that the river was known to produce; and as the power of

[1] Cf. "Language makes it possible for man to *be* historically" (Hölderlin, quoted in Heidegger's *Hölderlin and the Essence of Poetry*, 1936).

this god increased with the perennial evidence of his bounty, so he came to rival the Sun God, and to assume many of the latter's characteristics. The name of this rival was Osiris.

To return to the newly-promoted god of Memphis. Was the invocation addressed to Ptah merely a matter of form, a conventional reverence? It appears not. For the qualities ascribed to him are highly original. Ptah is described as "the heart and the tongue of the gods". Why, precisely, "heart" and "tongue"? Are these merely stereotyped metaphors? Scholars would suggest otherwise. By "heart" the Egyptians meant something very like "mind" or "understanding", while by "tongue" they referred to "speech" or "expression", particularly that form of expression which is official or *ex cathedra*. To be both "heart" and "tongue" is therefore to be not merely the interpreter of the gods in plenary session, but the divine mind itself engaged in the act of creation by giving concrete expression to its thoughts.

Such a notion may seem rather abstruse. It undoubtedly is. It becomes more intelligible, however, if we try to understand what the priests, in issuing such statements, had in mind. From inspection of the whole text and from what we know of early Egyptian thought, it seems clear that the priestly authors are engaged in a discussion of how the world began, i.e. what originated it. Now whatever we may think of their manner of expression, we cannot deny that they were tackling an eminently reasonable problem—a problem to which the early Greek and Hebrew thinkers likewise addressed themselves and to which we in our day have been able to give no ready answer. The beginners of thought at least began at the beginning.

It is to the nature of their answer to this question that the modern student may be inclined to take exception. Most text-books of the history of philosophy begin with the speculations of the pre-Socratic thinkers of Greece, whose object it was to discover the original element, or group of elements, from which the world of nature was derived. Thales maintained that the world was ultimately derived from water; Anaximander that it was derived from a kind of mist; Anaximenes that something even vaguer, called "the boundless", was that from which all things originated. To our sophisticated minds these answers appear elementary, far more so no doubt than they really were, for the Ionian philosophers must not be considered simple just because they put forward simple solutions. Nothing is less simple than genuine simplification. The Egyptian thinkers, who lived about thirty centuries *earlier* than the Greeks, envisaged the problem in very different terms. They maintained—and we must not dismiss the answer as absurd without giving it careful attention—that the universe originated from

W. F. Mansell

IKHNATON

thought: not so much thought in general as a particular kind of thought, a realized, objectivized, or incarnate thought.

Before commenting upon this apparently novel idea, let us look once more at the text. Here, as later, we quote from Breasted's translation. Ptah, we are informed, acting on behalf of all the other gods, "pronounced the names of all things, created the sight of the eyes, the hearing of the ears, the breathing of the nose, that they may transmit to the heart. It is he (the heart) that causes that every conclusion should come forth, it is the tongue which announces the thought of the heart . . . Every divine word came into being through that which the heart thought and the tongue commanded; and thus the stations (official positions) were made, and the functions (of government) were assigned, which furnished all nutrition and all food". And later: "Thus was it found and perceived that his (Ptah's) strength was greater than all gods, and thus was Ptah satisfied after he had made all things and every divine word".

The above extracts summarize an idea, which, like many similar notions in Egyptian literature, undergoes considerable repetition. Boldly vested with the Sun God's functions, Ptah is proclaimed the Creator and Mover of all things. His creative organs are heart and tongue, the respective seats of intelligence and expression. Everything in the world, therefore, is the embodiment of *realized intelligence*, whereby it "came into being". The world, we may note, was not created as if by magic; nor was it created merely according to an intelligent plan; it came into being and is continually sustained in being by the active operation of intelligence, which is the breath of god. Moreover, Ptah, surveying his handiwork, was "satisfied", i.e. like the God of *Genesis*, he "saw that it was good".

In order to understand ancient philosophy we need to be prepared to do two things: first we must learn to become accustomed to unfamiliar terminology and secondly we must be ready to believe that our ancestors were in most respects as adult and mature as we are. There is much heedless talk about the "childhood of the race", as if men had remained for centuries or even millenia in a condition of infancy, from which they struggled to adolescence about the time of the Renaissance and have since grown up. That the brain-power of *homo sapiens* has undergone any marked increase since the earliest times has yet to be proved. If mere size should be a reliable criterion, we have the startling fact that the cranial measurements of the Cromagnon man (about 20,000 B.C.) reveal a brain fifty per cent larger than that of his successors. We live in an age which, impressed with the power of techniques, tends to approach the problems of existence from a materialist angle; but we have only to reflect for a moment to perceive that much of our intellectual background has been formed from very different traditions. The priestly authors of the Memphite Drama are not, upon closer examination, so fantastic in their speculations as they at first appear.

An Early Version of a Familiar Idea

For nearly two thousand years the congregations of Christian churches have listened, with varying degrees of attention, to the opening of the Fourth Gospel, "In the beginning was the Word, and the Word was with God and the Word was God". How many realize the history behind these words—those particular words, that is to say, apart from the new meaning which they are given in the Gospel? For, as we know, the writer goes on to make a statement which, given the conventional philosophical ideas of the time, must have seemed both new and challenging. Having declared that in the beginning the Word was with God and indeed *was* God, he proceeds to claim that as a result of the Christian revelation the Word has become incarnate and "dwelt among us". Now although the authorship of the Fourth Gospel has been ascribed to St. John, we do not know for certain who wrote it. Nor do we know for certain when it was written. We assume, on the basis of the recent discovery of a fragment of papyrus,[1] that it was known in Egypt early in the 2nd century A.D., which is much earlier than some experts had supposed. On the other hand, we think we know for certain why it was written. Composed originally in Greek like the other gospels, the Fourth Gospel was intended primarily for Greek readers. It therefore employed the kind of terminology with which the intelligent Greek would be naturally familiar. Moreover, it invoked a particular tradition of thought into which the Christian gospel was henceforth to be integrated. In the beginning was the Logos, and the Logos was one with God. Now, however, the Logos had been made flesh and was one with man. Hence the incarnate Logos, Christ, was also Immanuel, "God with us".[2]

What meaning attaches to the term "Logos" in Greek philosophy? It occurs first in the fragmentary speculations of Heraclitus, and there it means a creative principle, a kind of fertilizing thought, an agent of divine energy. We find it later in Plato, who uses it to denote that aspect of God's creative power which results in the multiplicity of His works; the Logos is the *agent of variety*, but of ordered variety, not mere profusion. The concept of the Logos also had its parallel in Hebrew thought, sometimes personified as the Divine Wisdom. Indeed, it appears that this Wisdom idea, though reinforced by Greek thought, had already a long and

[1] Cf. *An unpublished Fragment of the Fourth Gospel.* Ed. by C. H. Roberts, 1935.

[2] This idea is discussed further in the Conclusion.

authentic Hebrew history; and this prompts us in turn to ask whether the Hebrews, who experienced so much Egyptian influence, did not owe some part of the idea to early Egyptian thinkers. In short, the authors of the Memphite Drama, being priest-metaphysicians, were probably the first elaborators of the Logos concept. What we do not find preposterous in Plato, in Philo of Alexandria, and in the Gospel according to St. John, should hardly cause us surprise and perplexity in these early Egyptians. If surprise there is, it is not so much associated with the idea itself as with its remarkably early expression. Man's first written thoughts are concerned with the power of thought itself.

If the Memphite Drama and discourse contained no more than a series of metaphysical statements, the interest of these works would be limited. But there is a great deal more to the text than that. Just as we have here the first metaphysics, so we have the first ethics, or morals. Since that is a gigantic claim to make in respect of any ancient inscription, we must remind ourselves that written words must long ago have been spoken, and longer still debated in the mind. In the case of moral questions, we must presuppose many generations of varied human experience; for men do not begin systematically to reflect upon problems of conduct until they have become aware of a conflict of loyalties, and can readily distinguish between obligation and self-interest. Even today this distinction is not always recognized, and there have been philosophers to whom its denial has been a matter of passionate concern. What strikes us as particularly interesting about the Memphite philosophers, however, is that they are seeking to establish a divine sanction for moral conduct. "Life," says the text, "is given to the peaceful and death is given to the guilty": a statement which, though ambiguous, is clarified to some extent by the later definition of the peaceful as "he who does what is loved" and of the guilty as "he who does what is hated". In endeavouring to reconstruct the message of such early thinkers we are naturally dependent upon a rendering which we trust, but do not know, to be exact. The greatest scholars, with characteristic humility, admit as much. Thus Breasted's master Erman, one of the greatest of Egyptologists, suggested that "he who does" should read "he who makes". This interpretation would alter the sense of the passage by introducing the notion, not in itself unreasonable, of a god who *created* good and evil. Sethe, another German Egyptologist, prefers to believe that the rôle of God is that of distributor of rewards and punishments, giving life to those that do his will and death to those that do not. If, as Breasted thinks likely, this interpretation is correct, we may gain some insight into the prevailing moral ideas. In the first place, it is clear that morality is already a *social* thing, and therefore susceptible of social regulation. Of two possible lines of conduct, one only is approved by the city and therefore by the city's god. Secondly, it follows that God is the kind of being to whom the conduct of human creatures is a matter of real concern. He is not simply a figurehead, a champion, a civic patron, still less a vague metaphysical entity like the God of Aristotle. He is a judge and guide, the friend of the good and the enemy of the unrighteous.

At this point we must issue a word of warning. Conduct ordained by a god, or prescribed by priests or rulers, and demanding perhaps no more than external observance, is admittedly not what we mean by morality. It is rather social custom, an outward thing. This distinction is important. The Memphite priests possessed no doubt a very strong vested interest in the maintenance of custom, or, given their status as servants of a new master, in the establishment of new custom. But what is distinguishable is not necessarily different. Features that became clear and articulate in morality are already present implicitly in custom. Like many a later ruler, the Pharaoh may have camouflaged his own personal wishes by representing them as having been ordained by God from all eternity. Hammurabi did the same. We know from the inscriptions on tombs and pyramids that the greater the Pharaoh's claim to divinity, the more intensely the people worshipped him. Whereas the Popes of a later civilization claimed to be the vicegerents of God, the Pharaohs of the early dynasties claimed to exercise powers so far-reaching that nature herself was subject to their influence. Nor need we assume that all absolute rulers, yesterday as today, are animated by motives of cynicism, cloaking their power with extravagant propaganda in which they do not personally believe. In the majority of cases the Pharaoh was as convinced of his own divinity as were his subjects. The latter were obliged to obey him; he was obliged to obey himself. To sustain his immense responsibilities, however, he needed the support of a priestly caste engaged in the perpetual assertion of his divinity. We shall see in due course how the one Pharaoh to rely exclusively on his own belief in himself was very soon deprived of power.

The Memphite Drama, if correctly interpreted, shows the world of nature or the cosmos to be the product of divine intelligence. Both agriculture and government are therefore the revelation of such intelligence. God, in fact, has not merely thought man into being, but, in thinking him, thinks through him, and thereby guides him in the acquisition of such techniques as those of cultivation and husbandry. The divine origin of arts and crafts, together with skill in exploiting natural phenomena such as fire, is reflected in the mythology of almost every known culture. But the Memphite

Drama is concerned with more than God's infinite creative powers; it is concerned likewise with the duty of man towards God. God actively thinks man; man, in turn, must actively think God. He must maintain his fellowship with God through prayer; for prayer, as the dictionary tells us, is not merely the making of a request, but a summoning to one's support.

Here it may be worth pointing out that Western philosophy, especially that of the last three hundred years, has almost completely lost sight of this communion of intelligence with intelligence, which is at the basis of so much ancient thought, even that which appears at first sight to be purely materialistic, such as the religion of the hunter of North America, with its visions and asceticism but obvious utilitarian aim.

The rôle of the Pharaoh

There are few religions, and few cultures likewise, that do not look back to some pre-eminent human figure, the founder or rather the interpreter of its faith. This figure may be a personified force of nature, like Re the Sun God; or wholly mythical, like Prometheus; or a historical figure, like Christ or Confucius; or semi-historical, like King Arthur. Similarly, he may have lived once, or he may be subject to reincarnation or palingenesis. Such a figure was the Egyptian Pharaoh. His person was doubly sacred: he was the embodiment of the Sun God and therefore a religious figure, and he was the symbol of United Egypt, and therefore a political one. Moreover, he was the object of a mythology so ancient and elaborate that even in the time of Herodotus the rites connected with his person were already shrouded in mystery. Today, although we still know very little about Egyptian religion, we understand much that puzzled former generations, whose ignorance of hieroglyphics was frequently combined with an approach best described as "positivist". That is to say, they were inclined to dismiss as ignorant superstition anything which failed to conform to their notion of what was progressive and enlightened. We now know that the so-called primitive mind was the reverse of simple and childish, just as we realize that primitive art was often more subtle and skilful than that of the so-called Western "primitives". Modern savages, if carefully interrogated, will be found to believe not that civilized mankind is cleverer than they, but that it is simply more wicked and corrupt, the slave of evil powers. If we examine the mythology that surrounded the person of the Pharaoh, we shall find much to excite curiosity but little to cause derision. This mythology will not merely shed light upon the origin of ethical thought; it will explain how such highly elaborate metaphysical systems as that of the Memphite Drama came to be formulated.

Most ancient of the gods of Egypt was Horus, the Falcon or Hawk god. Like many other gods of Egypt, he was originally a local deity, the divinity associated with the town of Edfu in Upper Egypt. Even so, he was not simply a god of provincial significance; he was the local embodiment of the Sun God himself, pictorially represented, as we have seen, first by a falcon and later by the winged sun-disc. If the falcon was the sun, then too the sun was a falcon, traversing the sky from east to west in the course of each day: an image later employed with numerous variations, the dead Pharaoh and his heavenly barque sometimes taking the falcon's place. The earliest Egyptian legends known to us are concerned with a titanic struggle between Horus and his enemy Seth or Set, who is usually portrayed as a dog or an ant-eater. This is presumably a symbolism of the struggle, renewed every twelve hours, between night and day, in which the eye of day is repeatedly put out. Hence the later myths concerning the miraculous powers which this particular member could confer, and the frequent appearance in Egyptian paintings and tomb engravings of a stylized image of an eye, the celebrated "eye of Horus".

The process of transformation—or, perhaps more strictly, transmogrification—whereby Horus became identified with the son of Osiris is as fascinating to trace as it is difficult to explain. All we can say is that Osiris, originally a god of vegetation or perhaps even a tree (his mother was Nut, the sky-goddess), seems to have come in time to symbolize the idea of fertility in general. He was associated with the underworld because of the upthrust of natural life from the nether regions, and he was on the same analogy associated with the Nile itself, as being both the source of Egypt's prosperity and, like the sun, believed to parallel its worldly course by traversing the underworld. In the earliest legends the dead Osiris was brought to life by receiving the eye of Horus, his son. In time the figure of Osiris was represented as possessing the power not merely of communicating life to others but of absorbing into himself the power of other gods, until his prestige almost exceeded that of Re. A school of theologians finally arose whose object was to impose the worship of Osiris over that of all others.

This deliberate imposition may be traced in the numerous hieroglyphic inscriptions in the pyramids of Sakkara, which are known as the "Pyramid Texts".[1] First brought to light in 1880 with the exploration of the pyramid of Pepi 1st, these texts date from about

[1] It is worth noting that, except for those at Sakkara, the Egyptian pyramids contain neither inscriptions nor diagrammatic carvings. The attempt by certain religious sects to foretell historical events from the Pyramids, especially the Great Pyramid or Pyramid of Cheops at Gizeh, is based upon measurements of passages, chambers, etc., from which wholly arbitrary deductions are made.

2600 B.C.; but Egyptologists are agreed that they contain material belonging to a much older period, for certain words and expressions are so archaic that we possess no clue to their meaning. What interests the student of Egyptian theology, however, is that certain texts originally composed in praise of the Sun God have evidently been later rewritten to praise Osiris. There is frequent evidence of actual substitution of one name for the other. In certain pictures, for instance, we find Osiris holding court and issuing judgment from a throne situated in heaven, which is frank evidence of usurpation. Nor was the elevation or apotheosis of Osiris merely the result of a theological argument in which the solar theologians of Heliopolis were temporarily defeated, as happened in the case of Ptah. Everything for which Osiris stood—the rhythm of the seasons, the reality of death and renewal, the functions of the "good" earth—was the daily experience of the common people. Consequently, Osiris was their god, a god whose habits they understood, and whose favours they might ask with some hope of requital. Osiris became in effect the god-king of Egypt, the president of a country that was itself a sort of recurrent miracle.[1]

To suggest that the worship of Osiris altogether overshadowed and excluded that of the Sun God would be to misunderstand the workings of the religious consciousness, particularly in ancient Egypt. In cases of this kind—and such parallels may be found in every civilization—there is no absolute exclusion, but merely the blending of functions and characteristics: in this instance the Osirianization of the Sun God and the solarization of Osiris. Theology lays down a terminology and believes that it has established uniformity of worship; but what is worshipped is worshipped in the freedom of the individual conscience, and few theologians have been able to withstand the pressure of popular devotion consecrated by time and responding to an instinctive need. When at a critical moment in Egyptian history an attempt was made to impose a new and purified form of Sun worship, the experiment was short-lived, not because the Pharaoh responsible for this innovation was devoid of character, but because the doctrine was too clear-cut to permit of that latitude and ambiguity whereby the common people, though nominally orthodox, are able to continue their cherished worship. The Egyptian *fellaheen* were not the only people in history, nor the most primitive, to pay lip-service to the sun, while privately propitiating a god of earth and water, virility and fecundity, darkness and terror.[2]

[1] The Egyptians were the one people who would not have accepted the statement of Jean Cocteau that "*un miracle qui dure cesse d'être considéré comme tel*".

[2] In the earliest of the Pyramid Texts Osiris is represented as being no friend to man.

If we were writing a detailed account of Egyptian mythology, we should need at this point to retell the story of Osiris's death, the floating of his corpse down the Nile, its rescue by Isis, his sister and wife, its dismemberment by his brother Seth (whose mutilation of Horus we have already described), his restoration by Isis and his consequent return to life. This story, which survived Egyptian civilization and became part of the mythology of Greece and Rome and did not perish with the Christian era, assumed various forms. In most of them, indeed, Osiris comes to life only to renounce his rights in favour of his son Horus. Having abdicated, he then descends to the underworld. But the traditional antagonism between Horus and Seth still continues; and when Horus proclaims himself Pharaoh, Seth brings what is virtually a legal action against him at a trial at which all the gods are present. This challenge is directed not so much against Horus's title as ruler over Egypt as against his claim to be the son of Osiris. The point is interesting, because early versions of this and similar legends clearly date from a time when paternity was not properly understood. Thus a son such as Horus could be born impossibly long after his father's death. When the myth came to be rationalized, the revival of Osiris was made to serve the secondary purpose of enabling him to beget Horus in the normal manner. His presence is thereafter no longer required outside his nether kingdom.

The Pharaoh, then, was Horus, and the new Pharaoh was simply Horus reincarnate. Because he was Horus incarnate, the Pharaoh was the source of national life and health; and, since the existence and prosperity of Egypt were dependent upon a seasonable rhythm, the Pharaoh was obliged to perform such ceremonies as would ensure the regularity of inundation and ebb, and even of night and day. Never, as we have said, was a ruler so weighed down with responsibility as was the Pharaoh, and never were a people so concerned with their ruler's welfare as were the Egyptians. Nor did their solicitude end with death: it merely assumed a new form. Since the dead Horus needed food, implements, means of transport, and even entertainment, the pyramids were built to ensure his preservation for as long as the world was thought likely to last. The purpose of these gigantic structures was not so much to keep the Pharaoh imprisoned as to provide him with an earthly *pied à terre* to which his soul could return at will. Every pyramid was therefore provided with vents for entrance and exit, together with a lifelike statue, which the soul on its visits to the earth could inhabit, or at least use as a means of self-identification. The entrance of the Great Pyramid points directly to the Pole Star, for the dead were supposed to inhabit that region of the sky.

From the Pyramid Texts we learn a great deal about the Egyptian conception of immortality. At first it appears that the Pharaoh alone could attain to everlasting life. Indeed, the extraordinary inscriptions on certain of the pyramids suggest not merely that the Pharaoh was regarded as deserving immortality as of right, but that the repetition of this fact must necessarily help to promote his future well-being.

As Breasted has pointed out,[1] the Pyramid Texts, though mortuary inscriptions, mention the word death only in two sorts of context: first to deny its reality as applied to the Pharaoh, and secondly to assert it as the inevitable fate of his enemies. The Pharaohs are addressed with almost frantic ejaculations, as in the case of King Pepi: "This King Pepi dies not. Have ye said that he would die? He dies not. This King Pepi lives for ever. This King Pepi has escaped his day of death. Raise thee up, O this King Pepi, thou diest not", and so on. Apart from such rhetorical phrases, which were carved in the stone with a delicacy and precision that still excites our wonder, there are graphic accounts of the manner in which the Pharaoh, having renounced human life, ascends to heaven. As Horus, this ascension may seem unexpected. Should the Pharaoh not rather descend to the nether world and become one with Osiris? He should and he does—at least in the earliest Egyptian myths. The headquarters of the Sun God was Heliopolis, and the Heliopolitan priests, the authors of the Memphite Drama, acquired increasing influence with the Pharaoh at Memphis.[2] During the Pyramid Age it became the convention to represent the deceased Pharaoh as being "ferried over and set on the east side of the sky" (i.e. the side from which the sun was born every day and whence came all similar gods), though admittedly he might also fly heavenwards or ascend upon a golden ladder. Thus one text reads: "O men and gods! Your arms under King Pepi! Raise ye him, lift ye him to the sky! To the sky! To the great seat among the gods!" And the final goal of this journey, however undertaken, was first his meeting, and, after due trial and judgment, his actual identification with the Sun God. While the Pharaohs clung to their official solar religion, however, the reputation of Osiris was growing among his people, until it gave rise to precisely that re-editing of the Pyramid Texts to which we have referred. After the close of the Pyramid Age, Osiris, being no longer confined to the nether world, is himself translated to the skies and becomes the Supreme Judge. In the latest Pyramid Texts, as Breasted shows,[3] he is sometimes represented

[1] *The Dawn of Conscience*, Chapter V.
[2] Memphis is only twenty-five miles from Heliopolis.
[3] *The Dawn of Conscience*, Chapter VIII.

as climbing the ladder to heaven. Now this is a double promotion. Not merely is Osiris about to greet his mighty rival the Sun God, but he has taken the place of the traditional climbing figure of the Pharaoh. The two faiths have telescoped.

This meeting of two streams of belief is not a mere compromise engineered by theologians. It has a more profound significance. Although we cannot hope to penetrate the innermost thoughts of those whom Herodotus called "the most religious of all men", we can refrain from extreme assumptions regarding their mentality. Partly through the influence of history primers long out of date, and partly through unwarranted inferences from surviving relics of the past, we are inclined to assume that a monarchy such as that of Egypt must have been a monstrous tyranny; that structures such as the pyramids could have been built only by a system of slave-driving of unparalleled severity; and that the evidence both in Egypt and elsewhere (such as Sumeria) of wholesale public sacrifice excludes the possibility of these communities having enjoyed the smallest degree of social liberty. Such assumptions ought to be questioned.

When we represent the pyramids as having been constructed by slaves, cowed and driven by force, we ought to ask ourselves what undertakings of this magnitude are achieved without compulsion, whether wielded by a single master, which is rare, or by a guild or union, which, though formed perhaps with the object of combating despotism, comes to exercise in course of time a measure of constraint. In such communal undertakings force is employed not so much in achieving the object directly, as in inducing men effectively to associate together for that purpose. At the one extreme there is slave-labour with its problem of association; at the other extreme there is the free group with its inevitable proportion of grumblers. Nothing great is achieved wholly voluntarily. Even the solitary worker bent upon work to which he is passionately devoted will have his moments of lassitude and discouragement when (to employ the obvious expression) he must take himself to task. Believing implicitly in the sacredness of their ruler, and regarding his dead presence among them as more significant—more beneficent even—than his living one, the people of Egypt no doubt erected the pyramids by a common effort of will, an upsurge of devotion.

And if the sound of the lash and the knout were heard to mingle with that of chant and incantation, so the building of the great Christian cathedrals cannot have been achieved without much goading and verbal blasphemy. In a conscript army there must always be many who would prefer not to fight: but such elements must experience the extremes of resentment before they start shooting their officers.[1]

We have already observed that the Pharaoh, before approaching the realm of the Sun God, was obliged to face the judgment of the gods. Earlier still, in the legends of Horus, the idea of trial and judgment was no less clearly conceived. To ascribe so great a measure of responsibility to the most powerful man in the land may seem unusual, since we find a tendency throughout later history for the strong and powerful to evade this burden. Although there have been rulers such as Marcus Aurelius, Ashoka, and Saint Louis who have taken their job extremely seriously, they are the exception rather than the rule: responsibility has been attributed lower down in the social scale. That moral obligation was early recognized at the summit of Egyptian society may have something to do with the stability and duration of that society: for if Toynbee's "challenge and response" theory of history is right, the society most morally tough will clearly be in a position to respond effectively to any challenge. What the student of thought will find particularly interesting is the easily traceable process whereby moral responsibility underwent a sort of democratization, the ordinary individual gradually becoming conscious of personal responsibility for the first time in history.

How did this moral awakening occur? No satisfactory explanation has yet been given, though we shall suggest some explanations in due course. We cannot legitimately say that human thought shows a process of development from concrete to abstract speculation. It does not follow, therefore, that ethical concepts, being abstractions, must have arisen at a certain stage in social development. The earliest recorded thought cannot have been evolved without the most thorough grasp of abstractions: nor does the fact that the Egyptians tended also to express their thought in concrete images prove that their hold upon abstract thinking was precarious. We have reason to believe that, psychologically speaking, one capacity goes hand in hand with the other. Furthermore, we have been able to trace what may be regarded as the first abstract ethical concept evolved by humanity, namely the Egyptian concept signifying "Righteousness" or "Justice". And of one thing we may be sure: when this concept first appeared it had already enjoyed a long history not merely as a vague notion or impression but, to use the terminology of David Hume, as a genuine "idea".

[1] It is interesting to note that of the three great pyramid builders, Cheops, Chefren, and Mykerinus, we know extremely little. On the basis of the statement "Happy is the country that has no history", we may venture to believe that their reigns were not eventful. This would appear to preclude any violent social upheavals or unrest.

The concept of Justice

The word employed by the Egyptians to signify Justice, Goodness, Righteousness, or Truth (probably it signified or included all four notions, like Plato's Form of the Good) was *Maat*. The word *Maat* does not occur in the surviving fragments of the Memphite Drama. There is nothing particularly mysterious about that. The concept is clearly much older than the sophisticated theological argument of the priests of Heliopolis; for moral thinking must long have antedated theological thinking. Something of the antiquity and veneration in which *Maat* was held may be judged from the fact that Justice, as thus conceived, was regarded as the daughter of the Sun God himself. Hence its diffusion from above—a further resemblance to the Platonic Form of the Good, which was compared to the sun on account of the latter's power both to lighten and to sustain life. This is sufficient to show that *Maat*, whatever its individual features, was not just a simple quality, a label to be pinned on to something worthy of praise. It was the spirit behind, or permeating, the universe: the "Way" in the sense so often employed in oriental thought. For the Hebrews, *Maat* became Wisdom; for the Christians, Love—again not merely love of one's neighbour or one's country, but the *Amore* of Dante, "the love which moves the sun and the other stars".

Some time before the beginning of the 18th Dynasty certain Egyptian scribes copied from an old manuscript a work to which they gave the title "The Instruction of Ptah-hotep". Composed most probably about 2880 B.C., so far as our present knowledge suggests, this work forms a kind of political testament. Its author, a Governor of Memphis and Prime Minister to a king of the 5th Dynasty, decided, upon relinquishing office, to compile a summary of precepts concerning not merely good government but—what interests us for the moment more—the good life. In a preface to his work, he asks permission of the king to transfer to his son the authority he can no longer exercise; and it is evidently for the new Prime Minister that the precepts are primarily intended. Addressing the king, Ptah-hotep declares his firm intention to "speak the words of them that hearken to the counsel of the men of old time, those that once heard the gods", wherein we obtain a momentary glimpse of a tradition of thought already regarded as exceedingly ancient and in need of scrupulous preservation, together with hints of a period of time in which gods and men were on terms of familiarity and even intimacy, as we see also in the early chapters of *Genesis*. The wisdom itself, or such of it as has been preserved, bears a distinct resemblance to that which Polonius imparted to his son, or Benjamin Franklin to the readers of his *Autobiography*.

It is at once shrewd, pithy, incontrovertible, worldly; and this essential worldliness, this surface brilliance or (in the literal sense) superficiality, reveals something of the nature of the civilization of the time. Whatever its corruption and its foundation in servitude, this civilization must have exhibited a good measure of stability and order, or else the precepts of the minister would have been irrelevant and even meaningless. In such precepts as "Beware of making evil with thy words . . . Overstep not the truth, neither repeat that which any man, be he prince or peasant, saith in opening the heart", or "Silence is more profitable to thee than abundance of speech", or "Consider how you mayst be opposed by an expert that speaketh in Council: it is foolish to speak in every kind of work", we obtain insight into a world not destitute of manners and social graces, a society in which the art of pleasing and gaining influence needed as careful cultivation as now. It is a society in which words and deeds are equally important, if not on occasion identical. Social vices do not differ very much from one age to another.

Save that they are the first moral statements of their kind to be preserved, though certainly not to have been uttered, the maxims of Ptah-hotep do not exhibit particular profundity. What impresses us is their urbanity. They are the fruit of the experience not of one man only but of many generations of men in office; they may even be rehashed from a commonplace book. Now it is much more interesting that the earliest recorded moral maxims should be trite than that they should be of staggering depth: for nothing suggests more forcibly that civilization is a great deal older than we ordinarily believe. Nevertheless, the "Instructions" are not without their moments of sublimity, even if such sublimity is merely an example of the conventional rhetoric of the time; witness the following phrase, which stands out from the rest with peculiar force: "Great is *Maat*: its dispensation endureth, nor has it been overthrown since the time of its maker." In short, the foundation, the ground of all these injunctions to virtue, is a power enduring through the ages, an eternal value, a force operating not merely in the individual soul, but in society itself. Now this power, though embodied in the Pharaoh,[1] is conceived as an abstract concept. Perhaps it is the first such concept to be evolved in human thought.

That the maxims of Ptah-hotep became part of the traditional wisdom of Egypt is shown by the fact that they were invoked about four hundred years later in a document of remarkable similarity. This document, a papyrus at present in the museum at Leningrad, is known as the "Instruction addressed to Merikere". Who was

[1] Cf. The Pyramid Texts, "King Unis comes forth to righteousness (*Maat*) that he may take it with him," etc., etc.

Merikere? Unfortunately we know very little about him. He was the son of a king of Heracleopolis, the town about seventy-five miles south of Memphis. One of these kings, having overthrown the ruler in Memphis, assumed the title of Pharaoh. A period of great disorder followed. The country split up into warring provinces. The Old Kingdom disintegrated. The result was the collapse of that political union of Egypt which had already endured for a thousand years. The king of Heracleopolis who drew up this particular document seems to have been the most able, or at least the wisest, in his dynasty, for the latter has no other claim to distinction; and despite the fact that the usurpation of his family had done much to destroy the traditions of the Old Kingdom, he displays a deep veneration for the wisdom of the past. Characteristically, the king begins his address with a reference to *Maat*: "Truth comes (to the wise man) well-brewed, after the manner of the ancestors. Imitate thy fathers, thy ancestors . . . for lo, their words abide in writing"—a reference to the wisdom of Ptah-hotep which is confirmed a few lines later. There follows much strictly political advice, first on the subject of foreign policy and later on internal affairs. How, asks the king, can a just system of government be preserved? He proceeds to answer his own question—by ensuring the material prosperity of those whose business is to administer justice. "He who is wealthy in his own house does not show partiality, for he is a possessor of property and is without need. But the poor man (in office) does not speak according to his righteousness (*Maat*), for he who says 'Would I had' is not impartial; he shows partiality to one who holds his reward."[1] But although the king declares "Make great thy nobles that they may execute thy laws," he is careful to add: "Increase the new generations thy followers, equipped with possessions, endowed with fields, entrusted with herds. *Exalt not the son of an important* (i.e. "*well-connected*") *man above a humble one, but take for thyself a man because of his ability.*"

Such an approach to the problems of administration might suggest that Merikere was to concentrate on the means rather than the end. But this is not so. As the admonitions unfold, we find the king anxious to drive home an important lesson. "It shall go well," he says, "with an impartially-minded sovereign, for it is the inside (of the palace) which conveys respect to the outside"; and he thereupon commits himself to what Breasted rightly calls "one of the noblest observations in ancient Egyptian moral thinking": "More

[1] The idea was shared by many others. Cf. for example the inscription on the tomb of a noble called Mentuwoser who lived in the reign of Sesostris (or Senusret) I (2192–2157 B.C.), "I was one who heard cases according to the facts, without showing partiality in favour of him who held the reward, *for I was wealthy and goodly in luxury.*"

acceptable is the virtue of the upright man than the ox of him that doeth iniquity." We may remember that his utterance, so reminiscent of a later wisdom, was written more than two thousand years before the composition of the Hebrew Psalms, i.e. a period longer than that separating us from the birth of Christ.

The immortality of the Pharaoh has already been shown, and his moral responsibility emphasized. But the assumption of immortality is not automatic; his deeds in this world must still be weighed in the balance. Whereas Ptah-hotep had not considered this fact worthy of attention, the king of Heracleopolis gives it due emphasis. No doubt this change in attitude represents a development of the moral conscience. "Set not thy mind," says the king, "on length of days, for they (the Judges) view a lifetime as an hour. A man surviveth after death and his deeds are placed beside him like mountains. For it is eternity which awaits man there and a fool is he who despises it." The idea of immortality underwent a progressive deepening of significance in Egyptian thought, until it was regarded as the reward of any man of righteous disposition. "He who comes (to the other world) without having committed sin, shall live like a god, going onward freely like the lords of eternity."

It was perhaps the gradual realization that *Maat* alone could assure eternal life to the individual that led to a popular revulsion against the values of what we have here called the Pyramid Age. The Pharaohs of that period clearly trusted to powers other than *Maat*; they built and equipped their tombs on such a scale as to ensure themselves at least permanent material habitation, almost as if they intended to rid time itself of victory over change. We have seen, too, that they caused their servants to cover the walls of these tombs with a kind of insistent verbal conjuration. The Pharoahs sought to take the kingdom of heaven by a storm of incantation and rhetoric. To us today there is something absurdly ironic in the fact that the object of all this elaborate construction of stone and chisel, musk, pigment and ambergris is the one thing that has in many cases failed to survive, namely the kingly body itself. Only the vessels, the food, the toilet requisites, the furniture—and the texts—remain.

The collapse of Materialism

The common notion that the Egyptians were people who spent all their time building pyramids and embalming their dead obscures the interesting fact that during centuries and even millenia of Egyptian history, men looked back on the great pyramids as archaic monuments, as remains of a civilization whose ideas and values had long been repudiated. It is true that Egyptian kings continued to be buried with elaborate ceremonial up to the time of the Macedonian conquest (333 B.C.); but the so-called Pyramid Age ended about 2500 B.C., and soon the enormous area covered by the pyramids (about sixty miles in length) was nothing but a waste of sand-strewn masonry. Caesar and Napoleon, looking down upon these monuments, reflected on the transience of human glory and pride. So also did the Egyptians. To them the sight was even more poignant, because it was their own history that lay in ruins before them. No wonder that such contemplation could inspire poetry of great depth and dignity. An example is the remarkable "Song of the Harp Player", which was sung both at funerals and, as a *memento mori*, at banquets. Composed some time during the Old Kingdom (2200 B.C.?), this song is not known to us in its entirety. It has survived in two fragments, one on a papyrus and the other on the walls of a tomb at Thebes:[1]

How prosperous is this good prince!
The goodly destiny has come to pass,
The Generations pass away,
While others remain,
Since the time of the ancestors,
The gods who were aforetime,
Who rest in their pyramids,
Nobles and the glorious likewise departed,
Entombed in these pyramids. . . .

Behold the places thereof
Their walls are dismantled,
Their places are no more,
As if they had never been.

None cometh from thence
That he may tell us how they fare,
That he may tell us of their fortunes
That he may content our heart,
Until we too depart
To the place whither they have gone.

Encourage thy heart to forget it,
Making it pleasant for thee to follow thy desire,
Whilst thou livest.
Put myrrh on thy head,
And garments on thee of fine linen
Imbued with marvellous luxuries,
The genuine things of the gods.

[1] The slab is now in the Leyden Museum.

Increase yet more thy delights
And let (not) thy heart languish
Follow thy desire and thy good,
Fashion thine affairs on earth
After the mandates of thy own heart.
Till that day of lamentation cometh to thee,
When the silent-hearted hears not thy lamentation,
Nor he that is in the tomb attends the mourning.

Celebrate the glad day
Be not weary therein,
Lo, no man taketh his goods with him.
Yea, none returneth again that is gone thither.

The extract here quoted fails to convey the sombre majesty of even those fragments that remain; but the reader who is sensitive to beauty of image and depth of feeling will be struck by two things. First the essential thought of the poem has survived translation from a language as far removed from English as Chinese, and secondly the thought itself (though not the primary element in any poem) anticipates that of some of the world's great poetry. To suggest that the original of this poem may compare at times with the great monologue of Hamlet, to which so much of the subject-matter is common, as the translation compares almost at times with a well-known passage in *Isaiah*, is not perhaps an exaggeration.

In the above version, which is that of the papyrus, we have the expression of a pessimism so profound that nothing save oblivion can overcome it: "Encourage thy heart to forget it." In the version preserved on the wall of the Theban tomb, which is that of Neferhotep, a priest of Amon, a more positive note creeps in. Here the living are enjoined, in addition to "following their desire wholly", to

Give bread to him who hath no field
So shall thou gain a good name
For the future for ever,

indicating the value to posterity of a good example, but not seeking to discern the ultimate sanctions of moral conduct. What we have here, in fact, is a variety of *humanism* such as usually follows the collapse of orthodox religious faith: a humanism which, while advocating sensual enjoyment of a refined kind, pays due respect to conventional morality chiefly for the "good name" that it gives a man. If we wish to find a later parallel for this attitude of mind, which is a recurring one, we may point to that of such 19th-century figures as T. H. Huxley, Matthew Arnold, and Emerson. Huxley, for example, while repudiating traditional religious belief, clung steadfastly to traditional ethical belief, chiefly perhaps for the "good name" with which it invested those who conformed to it. Such an attitude may not suggest the most profound view of morality; but it does suggest an essentially social view of morality, because a "good name" means nothing if not a "good name" among men. Moralists tend to regard the "social conscience" as something that developed only recently, with the abolition of slavery and the removal of disabilities on certain religious sects. From these fragments of Egyptian literature we see that the social conscience is as old as history. What is paradoxical about the social conscience is not so much its astonishingly early emergence as the fact of its survival among men whose instincts are predominantly anti-social.

In the light of the above, what may be said to constitute ethical or moral progress? One view held strongly until very recently was that first came a few moral men, and later, largely through their influence, a moral or semi-moral society. To say that this view was wholly mistaken would be absurd: we all know that such a thing as public opinion can be cultivated, and that nothing influences public opinion more than the eloquence (in deeds or words) of a man of vision. But the more attention we pay to the organization of primitive society, and the more we study comparative religion and culture, the clearer it becomes that social beliefs, taboos, and habits are equally things against which the individual leader rebels as things for which he is personally responsible. Both theories hold. Society needs to be influenced towards greater social responsibility, greater efforts towards mutual aid: it also needs to be shaken out of collective lethargy and public indifference. In a society like that of Egypt, with its extremely elaborate hierarchy of functions, its rigid social organization based upon material necessity, and its complex mythology and religious beliefs, the remarkable fact was not that a man should have a social conscience but that he should have an individual one. What the French sociologist Durkheim called social *pression* was felt by the ordinary Egyptian at every point. It is the inner experience, the drama in the soul, the individual at war with himself, for which philosophers in search of the origins of genuine moral perception look. Such an experience was that of Job. Another was that of the hero of the *Bhagavad-Gita*.[1] Do we find anything comparable to such dramas of conscience, at least as regards subject-matter, in the early literature of Egypt?

We certainly do. We find it, moreover, full one and a half millenia earlier than Job and Prince Krishna. The work in question, which has been preserved on a papyrus now in the Berlin Museum,

[1] See Chapter IV.

dates from as early as 2000 B.C.; but we should bear in mind that a work committed to papyrus probably needed to be of established antiquity before such permanent form would be conferred upon it. It is only modern literature that receives almost immediate imprint and distribution; the classics are almost all transcripts. The text to which we refer has no title; but Breasted, possibly having in mind Plato's definition of philosophy as "the dialogue of the soul with itself", calls this piece of "existentialist" philosophy "The Dialogue of a Misanthrope with his Own Soul", which is an appropriate description. The Misanthrope in question appears not to have been so from birth; what warped his temperament was the series of calamities that befell him. Of the precise nature of these calamities we are ignorant, because the relevant part of the papyrus has been lost: we can only infer that, like Job, he suffered accident, sickness, the loss of friends, property, and finally reputation, until it appeared to him that nothing remained but to "curse God and die". At the point at which he begins seriously to consider taking his life the papyrus resumes the story, but in a novel form. The unhappy man and his soul are made to confront each other. The soul begins to argue with the man. To die, it declares, is a misfortune; but to die in circumstances of misery and public execration is a calamity without parallel. Why is this so? Because a man deprived of means and deserted by his friends will have neither tomb nor mourner—a fate which to an Egyptian of this epoch could hardly bear contemplation.

Even so, the richest funeral is at bottom a mockery, as the neglected tombs of the Pharaohs and the nobles prove. "My soul opened its mouth and answered what I had said: If thou rememberest burial, it is mourning, it is bringing of tears; it is taking a man from his house and casting him forth upon the height.[1] Thou ascendest not up that thou mayest see the sun. Those who build in red granite, who erect the sepulchre in the pyramid, those beautiful in this beautiful structure, who have become like gods, the offering tables thereof are as empty as those of these weary ones who die on the dyke without a survivor." If, in other words, the physical death of the Pharaoh is as sordid as that of the anonymous slave who helped build the royal pyramid, no one of sound mind would willingly hasten his end. Appropriately, then, this part of the dialogue concludes with a phrase reminiscent of the "Song of the Harp Player": "Follow the glad day and forget care."

In order to appreciate both the merit and the originality of this document, we have to "think away" four thousand years of literary and philosophical achievement. This involves considerable mental

[1] The funeral plateau (Breasted).

effort. Even so, the Misanthrope, though shrewd and free from sentimentality, has advanced to no deeper spiritual insight than the author of the "Song of the Harp Player". But the manuscript does not end here. It continues in a form of even greater originality. The prose introduction is succeeded by four poems, each of which conveys a stage or phase in the writer's spiritual progress towards enlightenment. With self-loathing rather than self-pity, the first poem dwells upon the theme of loss of reputation and good name in the manner of the "Harp Player". The image of stinking fish is employed as an analogy, for the Egyptian would as naturally compare a bad name to the stench of "the catch when the sky is hot" as we today might refer to a name as "stinking in men's nostrils". The second poem stresses the Misanthrope's disgust with life from another point of view. What manner of man, it asks, can be trusted? Even brothers may prove false, while "friends of today are not of love". Wickedness abounds, but the malefactors are not brought to book. "The gentle man perishes, the bold-faced goes everywhere". Worse still, evil conduct excites not so much disgust as a tolerant amusement. Social life is a scandal, because "there are no righteous" to whom to make appeal. Monotonously, but with the kind of insistent emphasis reminiscent of the Psalms, the first line of each verse of this poem runs, "To whom do I speak today?", just as a modern prophet or artist might ask: "What public shall I address? Who will listen to my message?"

In the last two poems, which are unquestionably the best, death is contemplated first with tranquillity as the final release from care, and secondly with confidence as the source of divine justice. Thus the mood of the early part of the manuscript is dispelled, and the injunction to forget death gives place to the counsel to accept the inevitable in the hope that it may lead to something more than mere physical dissolution. Of these poems, the third is undoubtedly the most beautiful, as the citation of even a few lines will show:

> Death is before me to-day
> Like the recovery of a sick man
> Like going forth into a garden after sickness.
> Death is before me to-day
> Like the odour of myrrh,
> Like sitting under the sail on a windy day . . .

where on one of the few occasions in any literature the contemplation of death evokes images the reverse of horrific, morbid, or distressing. In contrast to the conventional ideas of this and later times, we have the approach of death compared to the recovery of a man from sickness. The entry into the unknown world is likened to stepping from the shuttered sick-room into a garden, and so on. This mood of awakening faith, conveyed in poetry at least equal to that of the "Song of the Harp Player", provides a fitting transition to the final poem, which is concerned not so much with the fact of death as with the dead themselves. In this final phase of the Misanthrope's spiritual pilgrimage the immortals "who are yonder" are regarded as judges and punishers of the wicked after death. If there is no justice on earth, then at least there is justice in heaven. Death is not the end, nor is it a passing into forgetfulness. It is rather the beginning, an entering upon a mode of living in which good and evil receive their due. Already, in other words, we have arrived at a stage at which all men are held responsible for their actions, at which conscience has become democratized, and at which a man's "dialogue with his own soul" is becoming a recognized theme for literature. Nor does the concentration upon personal experience indicate the absence of a "social conscience". It is simply a form of social conscience, man's thoughts being "driven inwards" on account of the corruption of society.

In the same way, Job was a public figure, a man of substance and reputation, who, having lost everything capable of making life worth living, was obliged to consult his own soul as to the meaning of life and suffering. What is remarkable about the experience of the Egyptian Misanthrope is not merely that it antedated that of Job, but that it forms part of the social conscience of a people lacking the profound spiritual endowment of the Hebrews. To this subject we shall return in due course. It is perhaps sufficient to remark that the Misanthrope, who no doubt died "full of years" like Job, seems to have arrived at the condition of faith entirely on his own. Unlike Job, he sought and obtained no interview with God. There was no whirlwind conference. Nor, at the conclusion of his trials, was he "blessed more than his beginning" with material possessions. For him, faith was literally "the substance of things hoped for, the evidence of things not seen"; for we must remember that with all his belief in the supernatural and in tutelary deities, the Egyptian of this epoch had no conception of a religious revelation open to all mankind. Faith had nothing but itself to stand upon.

The Defence of Maat

That other documents surviving from this age should reveal a similar mood of disillusion cannot be accident. The student of modern literature, intent upon tracing a particular line of thought or trend of feeling, succeeds by judicious selection in finding all the evidence he needs; but the selection must necessarily be rigorous and it may sometimes be arbitrary. Hence the reversal in each generation of the judgments and valuations of the immediate past. In this section of our study the situation is totally different. No arbitrary selection need be made. The corpus of Egyptian literature, though much bigger than is usually supposed, is manageable, uniform, and now for the most part accessible. We need not juggle about with it to prove our theories. We may accept it as it is. A progressive deepening of moral and spiritual awareness crystallizes out of all the writings from the Memphite Drama to the time of *The Book of the Dead*. Since almost all these fragments of literature were preserved by the court and the priesthood, a good deal of careful editing was no doubt undertaken. Even so, the body of writing to have survived is still remarkable, and perhaps all the more so for its evidence of increasing spiritual insight on the part of both authors and editors: material which, so far as we can tell, had been assembled for the first time in history.

Two very interesting examples of this increasing insight unto the nature of morality date from roughly the period of the Misanthrope. The first is a meditation by a priest at Heliopolis called Khekheperre-soneb. This text was copied by a scribe of the 18th Dynasty on to a board which is now in the British Museum. To this shrewd observer of his fellow-men, the old standards of morality have broken down. Unlike the Misanthrope, he appears to nourish no personal grievance, but merely a professional concern for the neglect of *Maat* and the wisdom of the ancestors. "I am meditating," he writes, "on what has happened (i.e. his is no imaginary denunciation). Calamities come to pass today, tomorrow afflictions are not past. All men are silent concerning it (although) the whole land is in great disturbance. . . . Long and heavy is my malady. The poor man has no strength to save himself from him that is stronger than he." And so he proceeds in the same vein for many lines, expressing social disillusionment all the more bitter and dark because it appeared to be without precedent. The rise and fall of empires and civilizations is a theme to which our modern historians increasingly address themselves, until we have come to regard the dissolution of our own civilization as merely a matter of time, so convinced are we of its inherent weaknesses. Khekheperre-soneb and his companions were facing the hitherto unthinkable: the disintegration of a social system regarded as ordained by God from all eternity and sustained by His living representative the Pharaoh and the power of *Maat*. The phrase "I am meditating on what has happened" evidently refers to the contemplation of what had never happened before.

The second example is altogether more original. This is the story of the "Eloquent Peasant", a lengthy piece of writing preserved on a papyrus roll now in the Berlin Museum. At first sight this tale, together with the moral which it points, provide a most damaging criticism of the upper and especially the official classes; for the story relates how a poor peasant, driving his mules one day near the estates of the king's Grand Steward, was tricked by a wily official into trespassing and permitting the beasts to nibble the master's corn. The peasant's goods and chattels are seized and he is arrested, but he determines to plead his cause before the Grand Steward himself. He does so in a series of nine lengthy speeches, each more eloquent and bold than the last, in which the high officials and even the king are reminded of their duties. To the earlier speeches the Grand Steward either lends a deaf ear, or, goaded to fury by the impertinence of the suppliant, replies by ordering him to be soundly beaten. Such chastisement merely prompts the peasant to greater feats of eloquence. Addressing the Grand Steward in impassioned phrases, he brings his argument to a climax with these words:

> Be not light, for thou art weighty,
> Speak not falsehood, for thou art the balances,[1]
> Swerve not, for thou art uprightness.

To drive home his point, he stresses the fact that justice is not dependent upon human inclination or whim, but, being eternal, survives neglect, defiance, and corruption: "Justice (*Maat*)," he declares, "is from all eternity: it descendeth with him that doeth it into the grave." After this series of lessons from the least of his subjects, the Grand Steward becomes convinced that justice has after all been abused. He therefore arrests the guilty official and restores the peasant his property.

Whether or not this story was originally intended as propaganda, it sheds a vivid light upon the common notions of the time. What impresses us most forcibly is the fact that, in spite of its central theme of justice, there is at no point the smallest suggestion that the social order should be *subverted*. Unjust officials should be replaced by just officials, but peasants aspire to be nothing more than peasants: that is the underlying assumption of a story not devoid of wit and something often approaching humour. Secondly, and perhaps in consequence of this acceptance of an immutable social hierarchy, there is nothing inherently absurd in a peasant either reminding his masters of their social obligations or in possessing sufficient education to do so. In a country in which responsibility had rested upon the ruler for so many centuries, there must

[1] In Egypt the balances were always the symbol of Justice. Justice is still usually represented as carrying them.

have been considerable force in the peasant's arguments. Throughout later history there is much denunciation of the rich and powerful merely on account of their riches and power: the preservation of the story of the Eloquent Peasant suggests that it was regarded less as subversive literature than as a reminder of what an enlightened king expected of his officials. We have here one of the few social documents in which the duties of masters to servants are regarded as the primary source of social stability. Almost every other civilization, having assumed the duties of servants to masters, proceeds to demonstrate its humanitarianism by making "concessions" to the lower orders. The only concession for which the Eloquent Peasant made plea was that justice should be done him as a man performing his duty in his particular station. He makes the distinction between that which may be conceded as a result of power and that which should be granted as a result of obligation. We concede what we must, but we grant what we ought.

Those who caused the story of the Eloquent Peasant to be preserved and transcribed had evidently perceived the insufficiency of the maxim laid down in the "Instruction to Merikere", that an official will tend to do justice provided he is well paid. If, as it now seemed, the only guarantee of just action was the existence of a just ruler, the problem of how to find a just ruler admitted of no clear-cut solution. It was a matter of chance. Moreover, with the collapse of the old order and the neglect of the traditional wisdom, there was an increasing danger that even the best-intentioned ruler or official would be corrupted. The traditional wisdom had been a bulwark against the grosser abuses of power. Now that such a guarantee was removed or weakened, what could take its place?

The men who sought to answer this question, or whose answers happen to have been preserved, were very different in outlook from those whose thoughts we have been considering. There was good reason why they should be. Ptah-hotep and the authors of the "Instruction to Merikere", the "Song of the Harp Player" and the testament of the Misanthrope were either worldly commentators on life or stoic contemplators of death. Finding mankind full of iniquity, they look to the after-world to redress the balance of good and evil. After the collapse of the Old Kingdom, however, we find certain thinkers whose disillusionment, though extreme, is nevertheless tempered with hope in a new social order: not an order to be obtained by the dispossession of the ruling classes or the accession to power of new social elements, but an order to be established by a ruler divinely guided to restore the power of *Maat*. This is more than "social idealism" in the modern sense; it is, as Breasted has pointed out, the first hint in history of *messianism*. While the greatest of the Prophets were those to appear in Israel—greatest by reason perhaps of their continuity of message, for which there exists no parallel—the ancient world did not lack prophets of another order, whose utterances strike us as less impressive only because of the absence of some evident fulfilment.

When we read the sombre pronouncements of the Egyptian sage called Ipuwer we are driven to wonder how many other men equal in insight have missed the accident of record: for a man who voices a feeling common to many in the same generation must do so in a language that has already expressed much in the same tenor. You can initiate thought; you cannot initiate the language in which it is expressed. Ipuwer is more than a shrewd commentator on society; he is concerned, as every great philosopher is concerned, with the human condition, then as now hardly conducive to optimism. In what are called his "Admonitions", he refers to the social evils of his time in terms not of political propaganda but of philosophic disillusion. He is in fact the first philosopher to identify the decline of civilization with what Gilbert Murray has called, in connection with a similar moment in Greek history, the "failure of nerve": that is to say, a collapse of the will to believe, issuing in doubt concerning the benevolence and even the reality of the gods.

The sages before Ipuwer lament the decay of standards, and wring their hands over the impending collapse of their culture. Ipuwer probes deeper. For he perceives very clearly that once such doubts become widespread, once they eat into the soul, the very nature of life becomes abhorrent: not perhaps life itself but rather that characteristic of life which is least open to explanation, namely the vain and wearisome repetition of its functions. "Would," he exclaims at one point, "that there might be an end of men, that there might be no conception, no birth!" This, indeed, is the first recorded note of a theme which is to run through Eastern thought to this day; but it is followed by a passage of strangely reminiscent beauty, composed, like the rest of Ipuwer's "Admonitions", in a metre later made familiar in the Hebrew Psalms, and hinting at the advent of a saviour or benevolent conqueror to whom, as we shall see, almost all ancient literatures make reference: for men had not yet discovered any science upon which they could nourish their illusions, or any art with which to beguile them. "He"—and this can refer only to some such deliverer as we have mentioned—"brings cooling to the flame. It is said he is the shepherd of all men. There is no evil in his heart. When his herds are few he passes the day to gather them together, their hearts being fevered." So he continues in lines that remind us of Isaiah and Ezekiel, prophets for whom the theme assumes a greater significance fifteen hundred years later.

Faced with utterances such as the above, certain historians seek hastily for a materialistic explanation of its prophetic content. At all costs, it seems, these ancient sages must be shown not to mean what they say. It is not at all impossible that Ipuwer, like the priest Neferrohu,[1] had in mind a real person. Observing that the men of his day were accustomed "to go ploughing bearing a shield", and being horrified at the thought of civil war (which, as he shrewdly says, "pays no taxes"), Ipuwer may well have placed his hopes in a foreign ruler, probably from the south, whose spokesman he chose or was persuaded to become; or he may have invented an imaginary figure in the hope that it might later become incarnate. The attitude is none the less messianic. For we know that the people most possessed with messianic ideas, the Jews, were always divided, and are so to this day, as to the exact form which their deliverer should take.

Decadence

To the Eloquent Peasant, *Maat* was a spiritual possession to which all men had access. The fact that this story enjoyed official approval, as we cannot doubt that it did, shows that the spiritual growth observable in the sages had been accompanied by relative popular enlightenment. If the peasant was more than usually eloquent, he was in other respects typical of his class. But this democratization of *Maat* had its attendant dangers: first, because the exalted "solar" theology became increasingly blended with the cult of Osiris, the people's natural faith; and secondly, because the admission of the Pharaoh's subjects to the heaven originally reserved for the king conferred greatly increased powers upon the priesthood. The priestly caste in Egypt—for caste it was—had enjoyed an immense reputation from the earliest times.

Herodotus, who learnt most of what he knew about the mind of the Egyptians from the priests he questioned, speaks well of this branch of the theocratic government. According to him, the priests were for the most part both highly skilled and upright in character. The "mysteries" they supervised were in one sense as mysterious as the Nile inundation; and in another sense as practical as the control of this overflow by irrigation and the timely harvesting of crops. A lofty, metaphysical religion without any immediate

[1] Neferrohu writes in terms of disillusion similar to Khekheperre-soneb, but the saviour to whom he looks forward is almost certainly Amenemhet I, founder of the 12th Dynasty about 2000 B.C. The latter did not achieve what was expected of him. He left a testament to his son Sesostris, in the course of which he said: "I gave to the beggar, I nourished the orphan; I admitted the insignificant as well as him who was of great account. But he who ate my food made insurrection: he to whom I gave my land aroused fear therein."

connection with practical life would have been unintelligible to an Egyptian, who at certain seasons of the year was obliged to do overtime for his faith. Such powers and responsibilities were naturally a source of great temptation. It might even be suggested that the chief cause of corruption in the priesthood was not so much idleness, sloth, indulgence—the usual breeders of decadence—as too great pressure of work. The elaborate ceremonial connected with a royal tomb might occupy the lifetime of groups of priests over a period of centuries. Temples needed to be staffed and maintained. Property accumulated by purchase or pious bequest had to be managed. Archives, more precious and revered then than now, required careful storage and occasional editing. Schools for scribes and catechumens were a condition of the profession's continuity. Above all, the people's needs, requests, and superstitions had to be attended to with patience, and perhaps with guile. If the people were to be satisfied they must be given that in which they were prepared to trust, whether it took the form of a charm, or an incantation, or a sacred scroll of unintelligible script. And if they sought help to cast out demons in this world and the next, the most reasonable reaction was not to deride their credulity but to furnish them with the necessary spells at the appropriate price.

It would be totally inaccurate to say that such methods worked only among the people: credulity of this kind is found among all classes of *Homo credens*. During the so-called Middle Kingdom (2065–1580 B.C.) powerful and wealthy officials used to arrange for their coffins to be covered inside with texts and inscriptions, mostly setting forth spells and magical formulae.[1] Studied carefully, such inscriptions betray evidence of having been used not for the sake of their intellectual content, which is in most cases small, but as a kind of verbal protection for the body against demons and spirits. Consequently there is a great deal of repetition and error in their composition, and many passages are left incomplete, suggesting the rapid and mechanical work of funerary scribes whose task was to adorn the entire interior of the wooden box with writing.

In addition to these magical clichés — which, as Seth pointed out, were evidently intended to "read themselves"—there were a large number of papyrus rolls of similar character[2] which could be purchased from the priests and deposited in tombs. These texts form what has come to be called *The Book of the Dead*. Assembled officially during the period of the Ptolemies about 400 B.C., *The Book of the Dead* has sometimes been mistakenly termed the "Bible

[1] These inscriptions have been collected and published under the title of "Coffin Texts", by Breasted chiefly.

[2] About 2,000 of these have been discovered.

of the Egyptians", whereas it is in large part a Demonology of a particularly gruesome kind. Here we find such odd official spells as those for "refusing serpents", for "repulsing crocodiles" and other beasts of prey, and also a variety of formulae of a negative and (to us) ludicrous kind such as "for not walking head downwards", to "avoid losing one's mouth or heart", to "prevent drinking-water turning into flame", etc. The latter category of spell evidently provided a harassed priesthood with infinite possibilities of magical prescription; for if both the dying or the companions of the deceased wished to make provision against the remotest as well as the most obvious contingencies, there was bound to be a sale for almost any formula whatever.

Less grotesque but equally negative in spirit are a series of written acts of personal contrition to be found not merely among the Coffin Texts in *The Book of the Dead*, but also as inscriptions on the walls of tombs. These so-called "negative confessions" sometimes assume a wheedling form, as if the soul had hopes of coming to terms with the judge Osiris by a kind of settlement out of court. At other times they reveal a depth of moral understanding which not merely disposes of the view that the sense of sin is something instilled into man by his rulers, but shows that eternal life was regarded as a prize to be earned by rightous conduct in this world. The tomb of Ameni, Baron of Benihason, is inscribed with the following typical phrase, "There was no citizen's daughter whom I misused, there was no widow whom I afflicted, there was no peasant whom I evicted." Likewise the mortuary texts contain statement after statement of the following nature: "Hail to Thee, Great God, Lord of Truth and Justice! I have come before Thee, My Master . . . I have not committed iniquity against men. I have not oppressed the poor . . . I have not defaulted, I have not committed that which is abomination to the gods. I have not caused the slave to be ill-treated of his master. I have not starved any man, I have not made any to weep, I have not assassinated any man," and so on in an endless protest of innocence, culminating in the repeated phrase, "I am pure, I am pure, I am pure." We employ other people to write our obituary notices.

Ikhnaton: the "Great Schismatic"

In referring to the worship of Osiris, we mentioned the later imposition of a new and purified religion by an Egyptian ruler of more than usual distinction of character. The brief reign of this Pharaoh, who came to the throne under the name of Amenhotep IV in the year 1380 B.C., has attracted more attention from historians and ordinary people than that of any Egyptian king save, for more accidental reasons, his son-in-law Tutankhamen. Deservedly so; for Amenhotep was not merely one of the most remarkable men that has ever lived, but, as historians have pointed out, the first real *individual* known to history. (Some have reserved this title for the earlier Imhotep, the doctor and architect to King Zoser, who lived about 3150 B.C.; but Imhotep, who is incidentally mentioned in the "Song of the Harp Player", is too obscure a figure to qualify for this distinction. Indeed, he was later worshipped as a god of knowledge, like another "individual" whose personality has become blurred by veneration, Pythagoras.) Much of what we know about the "heretic king", as he was later called, is derived from the works of art and literature associated with his reign, all of which are remarkable for their innovations in form, style, and content. What remains less explicable to the point of mystery is why this revolution, which was by no means confined to art, should have taken place at all.

When the Egyptian capital was established at Thebes by the Pharaohs of the New Empire (1580 B.C. onwards), the priests of Amon, the Theban equivalent of Re, began steadily to acquire power in the land. Possibly because he regarded such influence as a threat to his political authority, or because he abhorred the corruption of the Amon cult, Amenhotep IV seems to have lost no opportunity of showing his hostility to the orthodox priests. Such a policy of opposition to the most powerful caste in the country was attended by great risk. The high priest of Amon was chief among all Egyptian priests, and, given the excuse, he could mobilize more wealth than the Pharaoh himself, and also if necessary summon substantial aid from abroad. Indeed, at the end of the 19th Dynasty (*c.* 1200 B.C.), a High Priest of Amon actually usurped the throne. Such considerations did not deter the young Pharaoh. With amazing self-confidence he resolved upon a course of action which, instead of simply purging or reforming the Amon cult, put the entire priesthood out of work. He declared Amon to be a divine impostor and proclaimed his worship blasphemy. Although the motives animating the young reformer have remained obscure, we can suggest various explanations of his extraordinary conduct. In the first place, his attack upon Amon was not simply iconoclastic. In abolishing one form of worship, he was ready to replace it with another. The cult of his choice was that of Aton, the Sun God, whose worship he declared himself to have embraced as the result of a personal revelation. How true this is we shall never know. If he did not actually experience such a revelation, his conduct suggests that he believed himself to have done so on frequent occasions throughout life. In such cases, as William James pointed out in his *Varieties of Religious Experience*, the distinction between a man's claim to have felt something and his having actually done so, disappears: the claim may be the form that the feeling took. But is this all we can say? Perhaps the circumstances of the King's life serve to throw light upon this crucial phase of his development. Now that we have for the first time in this book a life to study, the question assumes particular interest.

From the vivid pictorial records that survive from this period, we observe that the young devotee of Aton was accustomed to appear in public accompanied by his wife and his mother. Such a practice, novel at the time, possessed an added significance on account of the personality of these two women. Both were evidently remarkable, particularly the wife. Nofretete, for such was her name, differed from most other royal consorts in that she was a foreigner, an "asiatic". From early times it had been the custom for the Pharaoh to marry his sister, just as Osiris married Isis. In ancient Egyptian, the words "brother and sister" may also be used to imply the relationship of love. Ikhnaton was one of the first to depart from this ancient tradition. His wife came from Syria, which, though part of the Egyptian Empire, was a land of mystery and strange cults, which it remains to this day. Now the Syrians, too, worshipped the sun; and it is not impossible that Nofretete, in becoming the Pharaoh's wife, brought with her the particular form of sun worship to which she had been accustomed. Of her great influence over her husband we have abundant evidence. Her exquisitely beautiful face was everywhere reproduced in painting, carving, and sculpture; and if, as we may suppose, the new realistic tendency in art dealt with her as faithfully as it did with others, as well as with animals and natural objects, she may be accounted the most beautiful queen in history, not excluding Cleopatra or some of the Circassian slave-women whom the Ottoman Sultans took to wife. She was invoked in reverent and affectionate terms in the Sun Hymn, reputedly composed by her husband: she is therefore the only wife of a founder of a religion to be associated on equal terms in the routine worship of the cult. Finally she became her husband's partner not merely in private life but in public life. Not merely was she the first lady in the land, but she became the protagonist of her sex in general, encouraging her seven daughters to adopt a similar rôle in society, and remaining, as far as we can tell, on the best of terms with her mother-in-law. Even allowing for rhetorical exaggeration, it is possible to impute something approaching domestic perfection to one who could be described by her husband as "Mistress of his happiness, at hearing whose voice the king's heart rejoices." That Ikhnaton should have been attracted and finally converted to her faith is more than probable.

Since Nofretete brought personal happiness to her husband, though not a son and heir, and since he must have acquired from her a particular respect for women, nothing was more likely to rouse his antipathy to the Amon cult than its practice of sacred prostitution. At the great temple at Karnak, not far from his own palace, special quarters were set aside for the priestesses appointed to minister to the needs of the god. It is unlikely that the king would have objected to this practice, which was common throughout the world and, in sublimated form, has been a feature of most religions, including Christianity. But it was an open secret that the vestal virgins were also employed upon secular duties, in which the priests of Amon were associated. No doubt the manner in which the god was worshipped, rather than the nature of the deity himself (who was, after all, the Sun God too), induced the young king, already encouraged by his wife, to declare the cult an abomination. Another reason may be found in the nature of the new cult of Aton.

In suggesting that Nofretete imported the faith which her husband was persuaded to embrace along with herself, we do not mean to imply that Aton was an alien god. He was an Egyptian god. His name, together with the symbol of the sun disc,[1] appears in the earliest Egyptian records, including the Pyramid Texts. Moreover, he had been worshipped for generations as a Sun God. How was it, then, that the substitution of a Sun God (Aton) for a Sun God (Amon), leaving the supreme Sun God (Re) apparently unchallenged, produced such a complete revolution in social life?

The answer to this question lies in the form taken by the worship of Aton. This, for Egypt, was thoroughly original. In the first place, the devotee of Aton was obliged to renounce all other gods; Aton alone was to be worshipped. Secondly, the worship of Aton consisted not simply of sun worship; it was worship of the sun's life-giving properties, as the great Hymns make abundantly plain:

> Creator of the germ in woman
> Maker of the seed in man
> Giving life to the sun in the body of its mother . . .
> Nurse even in the womb
> Giver of breath to animate every one that he maketh.

The word Aton, indeed, means strictly "heat which is in the sun", and the sun disc was intended to represent, as it is sometimes accompanied by, the sun's rays, the life-distributing antennae. That sun worshippers had hitherto stressed this aspect of the solar deity is not certain: a hot climate may not persuade men that the sun's

[1] One of the signs representing Horus. See *infra*, page 31.

influence is uniquely beneficial, still less the source of life. But it is clear that the worshippers of Aton were chiefly preoccupied by the beneficence of solar energy. Thirdly, and this was so marked a departure from Egyptian religious custom as to point to an Asiatic origin, the true temple of Aton was the open air itself. Dispensing with statues and shrines, the devotees of the new faith adored Aton in person and basked themselves in his bounty. God was to be worshipped in spirit and in truth.

Although the young king seems to have shown a marked preference for dreams as opposed to realities, poetry to diplomacy, he was well aware that the religion he had established could not be made to flourish without material support. Nor did he ignore, though he evidently grossly underestimated, the latent opposition of the devotees and priests of Amon, most of whom were unemployed, though a few of them apparently rallied to the new faith. He therefore took stern practical measures to prevent a resumption of Amon worship. He ordered that the name Amon should be erased from every public inscription in the country. Such inscriptions ran into thousands. And since the new faith was monotheistic, a similar campaign was launched against all public references to "gods" as opposed to "god".[1]

That the name Amenhotep, his own, contained the hated syllable naturally did not escape his notice. Accordingly it was changed to one embodying the name of the new god. Henceforth the king called himself Ikhnaton, meaning "Aton is satisfied". As the same objection applied to the name of his dead and revered father, the royal tomb was reinscribed along with the rest. Most of these erasures and alterations are still visible.

In order to complete his dissociation from the cult of Amon, Ikhnaton finally decided to abandon Karnak, which was too closely identified with the past, and to establish himself in a town specially dedicated to his god. He chose for his new capital the site now known as Tel el-Amarna, which was several hundred miles down the River Nile and roughly half-way between Thebes and Memphis. Upon it, as upon everything else, he conferred an Aton-name. Akhet-aton, which means literally "Horizon of Aton". From this site archaeologists have unearthed most of the written testimony concerning Ikhnaton's reign. Not content with one Aton town, however, Ikhnaton decided to build two others, one in Nubia and the other in Asia: for he was resolved to demonstrate that Aton was the god not merely of Egypt but of all the world, or at least the Egyptian empire. There would likewise be a special significance

[1] It is interesting to note that, apart from this, no gods except Amon were officially declared impostors.

in establishing such a town in that part of the empire from which the queen herself came.

In the enthusiam of the new faith, life at Akhet-aton seems to have been both prosperous and contented. As Egyptian society had always been accustomed to look upon its Pharaoh as the fount of blessings, the presence of a royal family so united and devout must have been regarded as a special mark of God's favour, a sign of Aton's appreciation of the new respect he had acquired among men. In the sphere of art, as we have said, the freedom of the Aton faith produced a remarkable liberating effect. Men and women are portrayed naturalistically as never before. The king permits the scenes of his domestic life to be recorded with almost photographic exactitude, including one which represents him embracing his queen. The delicate and somewhat effeminate portrait that has survived suggests that Ikhnaton, scorning the conventional flattery of court artists, wished to be portrayed exactly as he was—not as a warrior or even a man of authority but rather as a poet or seer. (The only puzzling feature about this human portraiture, suggesting perhaps a subtle flattery, is the fact that most of the figures appear to have deformed legs, which, as this cannot have been the case with so many, may possibly have been the case with one, whose feelings were in this way respected.) But perhaps the most beautiful survival from this other-worldly interlude is the great Sun Hymn itself, with its passages reminiscent of the 104th Psalm ("O Lord, how manifold are thy works! in wisdom has thou made them all"):

> How manifold are thy works!
> They are hidden from before us,
> O sole god, whose power no other possesseth,
> Thou who didst create the world according to thy heart,

and with its direct references to the royal pair:

> Thou didst establish the world
> And raised them up for thy son . . .
> Ikhnaton whose life is long;
> And for the chief royal wife, his beloved
> Mistress of the two lands,
> Nefer-nefru-aton, Nofretete,
> Living and flourishing for ever and ever.

Unique in literature, and probably more beautiful in the original than we can easily imagine, this hymn may provide us with a clue to the strength and weakness of Ikhnaton's revolution. Composed in everyday language, it was simple, ecstatic, and intellectual. That it can ever have been popular, as hymns should be popular, is extremely doubtful. If the faith which it expressed was intended as a universal faith, its poetic expression was that of a solitary, almost a recluse, like the author of certain of the Hebrew psalms:

> Thou art in my heart,
> There is no other that knoweth thee
> Save thy son Ikhnaton.
> Thou hast made him wise
> In thy designs and in thy might.

So he thought. However great his sincerity and the depth of his spiritual experience, this tendency to seek God in the quiet of his bedchamber, this extreme subjectivism, was probably the cause of the lack of hold which the new faith had on his people. For, whatever their respect for Ikhnaton and his family, the ordinary man neither abandoned his old beliefs nor in most cases imagined that he was required to do so. A change of name meant very little to him, as little as the new theology itself. Curiously enough, the literature produced during Ikhnaton's reign makes no mention whatever of Osiris. Was this because the ban on Amon worship was assumed automatically to refer to Osiris too? Or was it because no innovator, not even Ikhnaton, would have been foolish enough to forbid the public devotion to Osiris, which was less a religion than an inveterate social habit? At any rate, the cult of Aton, being (so to speak) too free from superstition to compel the attention of the masses, made no headway in displacing the great Judge of the Underworld. The public must have its underworld, and the lofty realm of Aton proved no substitute for it. Finally, the Aton cult was primarily one of adoration, of sheer worship; whereas a religion cannot take root, cannot be practised, unless it is practical. Just as morals must be buttressed by religion, so religion must become incarnate in morals.

The immediate threat to Ikhnaton and to the new social gospel came not from the discontented priests of Amon and their followers, still less from the common people, to whom social revolt was unthinkable, but from outside the country. Ikhnaton had hoped to govern Egypt by an idea, a dream; but an empire, however benevolently administered, must be defended and protected by force. Certain historians have maintained that Ikhnaton, though not a warrior like Thutmos III, sought to further the imperial interests of Egypt by the more subtle method of conquering the minds of his subjects: hence the cult of Aton was a form of propaganda. The winged sun disc was certainly a more easily exportable symbol than any other Egyptian insignia, and the Sun Hymns could be accepted anywhere, though it was a novelty for a national or imperial anthem to be at the same time ravishing poetry. The province of Syria was the first to raise the signal of alarm. The enemy came originally from Asia Minor—a fierce, hardy, dour people, though, as we are rapidly discovering, not without culture. Those people, the Hittites, had acquired numerous allies on the borders of the Egyptian empire. The first incursion into the imperial territory was made by the King of Kadesh, who occupied northern Syria. This attack was followed swiftly by an advance of the King of the Amorites to the wealthy and strategically vital ports on the Phoenician coast, including Byblos. Frantic appeals for aid were sent to Ikhnaton from his distracted but loyal political officers. Reluctant to use open force, the Pharaoh sent a trusted official to Phoenicia on a fact-finding commission. This emissary, who no doubt acted in the spirit of the instructions given him by Ikhnaton, informed the King of the Amorites that he might stay where he was. It was hoped that he would later come to regard himself as a vassal to Egypt. The invader, agreeing to this arrangement for the time being, held his ground.

But the attacks continued from other quarters. The Bedouins, rising in revolt, seized the town of Megiddo (Armageddon) near Jerusalem. The Assyrians came down like a wolf on the fold. Finally, the King of the Amorites, who had hoped to turn vassalage into independence by discontinuing his nominal tribute to Egypt, was confronted with his old allies the Hittites, and obliged to sign away his nearly-won freedom. His governors deposed, his envoys insulted, his coffers empty of tribute, Ikhnaton suddenly found himself powerless abroad and friendless at home; for the opposition party had naturally become bolder in its protests as the situation abroad deteriorated. Much of the *débâcle* must be put down, it seems, to sheer political and diplomatic ineptitude on the Pharaoh's part. From the hundreds of cuneiform tablets discovered between 1855 and 1893 by Flinders Petrie at Tel el-Amarna (the "Tel el-Amarna Letters"), we know that Ikhnaton's foreign representatives not merely kept him fully informed of what was happening but begged him earnestly to send them military aid.[1] Disloyalty there may sometimes have been; but such desperate appeals suggest that many of the provincial governors, though not always Egyptians by nationality, were willing to stick to their posts. In the end, Ikhnaton lost nearly the whole of his empire without a fight.

A man can survive defeat, but a national god cannot. Of the end of Ikhnaton's life and reign we know little, because the evidence is

[1] Cuneiform was still the language of diplomacy, a relic of the traditional power of Babylon.

obscure. Still less than thirty years of age, he appears to have broken down under the strain and humiliation of the national reverses: an older man might have borne these trials more philosophically, if he had had a more realistic philosophy upon which to rely. Whether, as is suggested, the king renounced the worship of Aton and returned to that of Amon, and if so whether he did so voluntarily, as a condition perhaps of being able to retain the throne, we cannot say. As for Nofretete, we gather that she remained at Akhet-aton but refused to renounce the Aton cult: a further indication that she had been brought up in its spirit. Had she borne a son, the latter would now have ascended the throne. Instead, Ikhnaton appointed the husband of his eldest daughter Semenkhare to rule jointly with him, perhaps at Thebes and perhaps as nominally repentant devotees of Amon. If so, the two must have died within a short while of each other, for the next Pharaoh to be proclaimed was the boy-husband of the second daughter.

This lad, who had remained with Nofretete at Akhet-aton, was called Tutankhaton. After three years' reign he abandoned the Aton capital, returned to Thebes, declared the Aton cult illegal, restored the Amon priests in their former offices, and, ridding himself of all vestiges of the old regime, changed his name to Tutankhamen.

Both Aton and his prophet received the same treatment at the hands of Tutankhamen as the Amon priests and their god had done under Ikhnaton. Inscriptions were once more changed, and the name of the late Pharaoh was banned even from conversation. If reference to him became necessary, it was as the "great criminal", or the "great schismatic". By what luck or cunning Nofretete succeeded in remaining at Tel el-Amarna we do not know. Her enemies accused her of seeking the support of the Hittites against her own son-in-law If this was the case, the wonder is not that she did so but that her activities, known to be directed against the new regime, were not more carefully watched. It is possible that, in her isolation, she was considered incapable of doing much harm.

Meanwhile the political misfortunes of Ikhnaton's reign were being repaired, not indeed by his successor, who seems to have lacked initiative, but by one of the latter's generals, Horemheb. In a series of remarkable campaigns, the latter not merely restored Egypt's fortunes but successfully made his own. Married to one of Ikhnaton's daughters, Horemheb finally ascended the throne as the last ruler of the Dynasty he had done so much to preserve; but with extraordinary arrogance and some ingratitude he insisted upon dating the beginning of his reign from the death of Amenhotep III, thus effacing from record the reigns of Ikhnaton, Tutankhamen, and Ai (married to Tutankhamen's widow), who were considered to have brought disgrace upon their ancient line. As a restorer of his country's fortunes, however, he was no doubt justified in his claim, otherwise with little basis, to be the real founder of the 19th Dynasty; for, having grown old in ceaseless military action, he decided to consolidate his achievements by arranging for the throne to be occupied by a comrade-in-arms, Rameses I (1320 B.C.), the immediate successors of whom, above all Ramases II,[1] justified his foresight by their immense achievements in building and foreign conquest. Nevertheless, these triumphs were the prelude to disaster. The Amon priesthood, now more firmly in the seat of power, succeeded during the reign of the last of the Rameses in putting one of their number on the throne itself. There was now no check upon corruption. Political decisions were determined as much by omen as by reasonable argument. Superstition, instead of being a creeping and inevitable growth of the spiritual underworld, was allowed freely to proliferate. The maxims and charms of *The Book of the Dead* invaded the sphere of the living, until a condition of mind was reached in which it was not considered preposterous that a sorcerer, bent upon extracting some favour from the gods, should threaten not merely to betray their names to the demons but to tear out their hair "as lotus blossoms are pulled from a pond". This mentality was neither blasphemous nor foolish; it was simply decadent—a state of credulity in which the devout are persuaded that God can be mocked at will.

The new insight: conclusion

Although the reign of Ikhnaton was a comparatively brief interlude—and, according to Horemheb, an interlude that disgraced the national annals—it would be a mistake to assume that the worship of Aton did nothing to affect the life and thought of Egypt, still less that its official interdiction erased it altogether from men's memories. Whatever their political naivety, Ikhnaton and his wife had unquestionably influenced the people by their example of personal devotion to a god, or at least to an ideal. There is evidence too strong to discount that after this golden moment of delight in life—for realism of the kind displayed in art was as genuine a reflection of such delight as realism of another kind is a reflection of disgust—strength and beauty of character was increasingly recognized to be a value in itself, perhaps for the first time in history. That is the reason why Ikhnaton, despite the fact that we know much less about him than we should wish, stands out as an indi-

[1] Considered by some to have been the Pharaoh who figures in *Exodus*. Apart from this, he was a man of character. Reputed to have had several hundred wives, he assembled a family so large that it became for the next few centuries a clan of its own.

vidual in a world of types and figureheads, or mere shadows. The great sages who preceded him—ministers, governors, and priests, men wise in their generation—were content to expound the wisdom of the ancients, enjoining others, usually their sons, to follow it.

In contrast to these venerable figures, Ikhnaton, having received wisdom into his soul, lived it. On that account alone the Aton interlude is a significant moment in history. Like the few other interludes with which it may be compared, such as the reign of Ashoka,[1] its chief value is to have shown that the effort towards human perfection can be made in any age and simply by the power of human aspiration. And if such interludes appear to belong to poetry rather than to history, to imagination rather than to action, that is because history is merely the material that fills in the tedious gaps between such bright periods: which explains why all histories, including that of the Western world, begin with an interlude of poetry which is consequently also a prelude to a new kind of life.

Such a new life is perceptible only at certain levels and always at rare intervals. It is interesting to notice, however, that coupled with the dawning appreciation of human character went a new attitude towards human imperfection or sin. *The Book of the Dead* was largely composed of recipes for avoiding judgment hereafter, for concealing one's shortcomings, for cheating the gods. In spite of the orgy of sorcery, magic, and thaumaturgy to which we have already referred as heralding the collapse of Egyptian culture, we notice here and there a new note. This is a note not of protest of innocence but of admission of guilt, a genuinely expressed mood of contrition, a humility wholly absent from the conventional obituary inscriptions of rulers and governors, intent upon self-justification even in death.

This attitude, which is the sense of the Christian gospel, is nowhere more clearly expressed than in the works of the sage Amenemope, who lived about 1000 B.C. and whose work has survived in a papyrus now in the British Museum. Of all the works of the Egyptian sages, those of Amenemope are the most striking and the closest to us in spirit. Indeed, they provide us with the most fitting transition to the wisdom of the Hebrews, whose recorded thought, though dating from a later period, bears numerous traces of Egyptian influence. In places, fragments of Egyptian wisdom appear in the Hebrew scriptures in word for word translation. Some of Amenemope's writing, for instance, is reproduced, as Breasted demonstrated so convincingly, in at least one place in the Old Testament, namely *Proverbs*, Chapter xxiv. We know that Amenemope's wisdom was translated into Hebrew and was presumably circulated throughout the Middle East along with other

[1] See Chapter V, page 201.

Egyptian writings. We know likewise that Hebrew leaders and prophets were familiar with such writings, among them Moses, whose opportunities for making their acquaintance were obviously great, and no doubt also Amos and Hosea.

When Ptah-hotep and Merikere enjoin their children to revere *Maat*, we are in the presence of the wisdom of a civilization considered to be both unique and everlasting: wisdom, to use the definition of a Western philosopher, was a "settled habit", since the laws of social life in Egypt were supposed to have been established by Thoth for ever and ever.[1] When Amenemope observes that "God is in his Perfection, and man is in his insufficiency", however, we are in the presence of the wisdom of a civilization the very reverse of settled, a civilization in course of formation in bondage, a civilization on the march. In short, we are in the world of the Psalmist, whose insufficiency is his daily preoccupation, and for whom insight into the majesty of God is to be attained not through enlightened maxims but through anguish of soul.[2]

We now take our leave of the civilization of Egypt. In most books dealing with philosophy it is the custom to begin with the pre-Socratic philosophers and to proceed to the great thinkers of Greece: after which, if the author happens to be interested in theology, he turns to a consideration of the ideas of the early Christian Fathers, leading through St. Augustine to the great mediaeval thinkers. In the preceding volume of this series such an orthodox approach was adopted, for our concern was to trace the development of a westward-moving tradition of thought. The present volume gives us an opportunity of studying a philosophical tradition starting from a somewhat similar point but moving in another direction. In observing this contrary movement, however, we shall be covering certain ground common to both traditions, while in these first few chapters we have been studying a culture not merely older and more lasting than any that is yet known, but more important as a cultural influence than has been recognized. Throughout the journey already accomplished we have constantly been obliged to remind the reader that what he is faced with is, if not the beginning of wisdom, then at least its beginnings; that these brief

[1] Thoth was god of Wisdom. His reign, lasting 3000 years, was supposed to have begun about 18,000 B.C.

[2] It is perhaps worth pointing out for the benefit of those who are interested in Existentialism, a collective name for a variety of different and often conflicting theories, that the Hebrew Psalms reveal a point of view distinctly existentialist. There is the same consciousness of man's utter helplessness before powers outside his control, the same realization that his freedom comes through action and service, the same preoccupation with degradation and death. The theme of the Psalms, or at least the great majority of them, is *Angst*. In fact, by a paradox, the Psalms approximate in spirit less to the religious existentialism of Gabriel Marcel than to the nihilistic or atheistic existentialism of Jean-Paul Sartre. We revert to this subject in the Conclusion.

specimens of thought about God, man, immortality and the good life are the first of their kind to be recorded; that the earliest metaphysical treatise known to us, the Memphite Drama, would seem to presuppose a tradition of thought already ancient by 2500 B.C.; and that we cannot yet attempt to say why, at a moment to which no accurate date can be assigned (but at least a million years from man's first appearance on the earth), civilization should have arisen at all.

In an age in which the idea of progress has been dismissed as an illusion it is refreshing to observe that an advance in moral and spiritual apprehension is not merely hinted at, but, on the material available, incontestable.[1] Naturally, this does not mean that as time went on men behaved better and better. Unfortunately conduct lags behind precept in a way that secular moralists must find wholly baffling. Such progress is the result, we may suppose, of man's beginning to reflect systematically upon questions to which, for material reasons, he had not addressed himself before: he was too busy keeping alive. If moral insight is a faculty to be attained, man's first attempts to acquire it are likely to have been made along the logical stages of its acquisition. Hence the steps of his progress from mere obedience to divine law, to a sense of duty to society, and finally to the exploration of his own conscience, entailing the acceptance of moral responsibility—a progress which, in the Pyramid Age, seems nearly to have taken a wrong turning, as kings endeavoured to build enormous bulwarks against death—have become visible landmarks on this distant rim of history. Such a development is remarkable for yet another reason: it was virtually completed before any other civilization, including that of the Hebrews, took up the theme on its own. And if no civilization of a later age exhibits a comparable development, this is simply because none other started, as it were, from scratch.

We must conclude this section upon a note of warning. Impressed by the wealth of material made available by excavation in Egypt, and its extreme antiquity, certain able thinkers—above all Flinders Petrie, Elliot-Smith, and to some extent Breasted himself—arrived at what has been termed the "diffusionist" theory of culture, according to which all civilization in the world originated from developments in the Nile Valley. That Western civilization owes an immense debt to Egyptian influence is incontestable; there is likewise a good deal of evidence to suggest that Egyptian influence extended to parts of the world where it might least have been

[1] "Progress is real if discontinuous. The upward curve resolves itself into a series of troughs and crests. But in those domains where archaeology as well as written history can survey, no trough ever declines to the low level of the preceding one, each crest out-tops its last precursor" (Gordon Childe, *What Happened in History*).

expected.[1] But while acknowledging that Egyptian civilization must have exerted profound influence in every quarter which it penetrated, we can hardly accept the "diffusionist" theory until it can be supported by more definite proof and less pure guesswork.

We might also point out that the Egyptians, though an imperialist nation for several centuries, made little serious attempt to export their culture. On the contrary, they guarded that culture with extreme care, resenting the intrusion upon their soil of anyone likely to threaten its existence. As early as the second millenium they had erected what they called the Wall of the Ruler, "in order to prevent the foreign herds from coming down again to Egypt, so that they should beg after their fashion for their cattle to drink". The Egyptian gods, likewise, were not merely ultra-nationalist but inhabitants of a realm which, save for the obvious disadvantages attendant upon terrestrial life, bore the closest resemblance to the Land-of-the-Nile. There was a sacred Nile in the sky, and upon this river the deified Pharaoh sailed in his barque. There was also a Nile in the nether regions upon which Osiris sailed. All the descriptions of immortal life represent such existence as merely a heightened form of life in everyday Egypt. It is almost as true to say that heaven was a replica of life on earth as to say that earth was at least in intention modelled upon life in heaven. When an attempt was made by Ikhnaton to export Egyptian culture in the only effective way in which a culture can be exported, namely by diffusing its religion, the faith in question was a highly abstract version of the god-crowded, mystery-ridden religion of Egypt, having been deliberately denationalized for the purpose. Hence the Nile itself becomes for the first and only time in theory what it was later to become in fact, namely an international highway. In Ikhnaton's Sun Hymn the alteration in spirit is quite evident:

> There is a Nile in the sky *for the strangers*
> And for the cattle *of every country* that go upon their feet.

But we know that the mission of Ikhnaton was as much a failure abroad as it was at home. What the world owed to the genius of Egypt was what the world borrowed from Egypt; but the borrower must possess another kind of genius in order to put to good use the things he has appropriated. Henceforth civilization is a shared possession.

[1] To go no farther than Cornwall, the late Dr. T. F. G. Dexter maintained with some plausibility that the ancient form of Cornish Cross is not merely of pagan origin but a development of the form of the Egyptian "Ankh", symbol of fertility, and that certain customs still preserved reveal Egyptian ritualistic influence. These theories were developed not as a result of any *parti pris* but in consequence of extensive archaeological research in Cornwall. See his *Cornish Crosses, Christian and Pagan* (Longmans, 1938).

CHAPTER II

BABYLONIA AND ISRAEL

Hammurabi

IN the section of the Louvre in Paris containing antiquities from the countries of the Middle East, the visitor's attention will be struck by a glass case situated in a central position which contains an object of curious shape and somewhat forbidding appearance. This object is a shard of black diorite standing about eight feet high and two feet in diameter. On closer inspection, the stele, though in places smooth and polished and even emitting a faint gleam, is seen to be striated with notches and wedge-shape marks arranged in long vertical columns. Forty-four in number, these columns, bearing here and there evidence of deliberate defacement, consist of cuneiform script of remarkable legibility, seeing that it was cut nearly four thousand years ago. At the top of the pillar some carving is visible. A bearded and seated figure, presumably that of a god, is presenting a gift to another, who, though portrayed standing in an attitude of respect, possesses the bearing and wears the robes and helmet of a king. What is this gift? It is evidently something intangible but of surpassing importance. It is in fact the substance of that which is written on the lower flank of the column. For the seated figure is the Babylonian sun deity Shamash, the recipient of his gift is Hammurabi, King of Babylon, and the gift itself is the oldest legal code in the world.

It is a far cry in both space and time from that glass mausoleum in the Louvre to the site where the shard was first erected. When Hammurabi caused it to be fashioned, about 1910 B.C., he decided that it should be set up in a spot where everyone might be able to inspect it. Such a place was the temple at Sippara, a town not far from Baghdad, the capital of modern Iraq. Temples in Babylon were built to command a view of the surrounding buildings, their foundations being level with the roofs, and were used also as law courts. There the admonitory pillar remained for nearly a thousand years, during which time the laws inscribed upon it still continued to command the respect and obedience of the Babylonians—as indeed was the case for another five hundred years: a period of authority equalled by few other legal codes promulgated by a single individual. About 1100 B.C. it was captured and removed by a king of the neighbouring region of Elam, who was responsible for the wanton defacement of five of its columns. We say wanton, because whereas it was customary for Egyptian kings to deface monuments with the object of inscribing them afresh,[1] the damage to Hammurabi's code was apparently purposeless. The cylinder then disappeared for nearly three thousand years, concealing from men's minds almost everything there was to know about Hammurabi and his contemporaries. Finally, in 1902, a French archaeologist, de Morgan, discovered it when digging at the Aeropolis at Susa in modern Persia. In turning up this block of stone he helped to bridge a void in our historical knowledge measuring over a thousand years.

It might be maintained that the development of law, being a branch of politics or economics, should have no place in a book concerned with philosophy. In a sense this is perfectly correct, especially with regard to modern legislation. But a book on the history of thought can no more neglect the earliest attempts to frame a legal code than it can neglect the rudiments of medicine or art. Law implies a law-giver; and it is not an accident that around the personalities of most of the great law-givers of history there has been woven a fabric of myth, almost a religious aura. Whoever imparted wisdom to mankind must likewise have imparted law, the wisdom of living the good life in community: or, if this important item of knowledge had been omitted, someone responsible and of trust in the tribe was obliged, like Moses, to go and fetch it. The apparent sacred origins of law, or the fact that law-givers such as Hammurabi considered it necessary to invest their codes with divine authority, are of considerable interest to the philosopher, who, being concerned with questions of value, wishes to ascertain what it is in particular that men hold sacred.

There is a further reason why the student of philosophy should take special interest in the nature of law. Law is a matter of words—or perhaps it would be more accurate to say, a form of words. Once written, it becomes identified with and resolves itself into the words in which it is expounded. If you introduce the smallest alteration in the wording you simultaneously alter the law. (The legal quibble is therefore an inescapable and even indispensable element in all jurisprudence, to the exasperation of the laity, who, in resenting the fact that law cannot be made to mean what they want it to mean, demonstrate the absolute necessity for law.) Now the only effective means of bringing home to people that law could not be changed without ceasing to be law was to write it down; and this act of committing law to stone or potsherd, or whatever was likely

[1] Sometimes an old or execrated name was deliberately carved on a monument only to be crossed out and over-written with another. Horemheb, like our modern hoarding scribblers, was accustomed to assert his authority in this way.

to prove most durable, was another way of reinforcing its sacredness, since writing was itself a sacred art.

As an arcane and difficult acquirement, such writing was understood only by a privileged few, though probably by no fewer than those who understand our present legal codes. To say that law had to await the invention of writing before being recorded would be to suggest that law was originally nothing but unwritten custom. Of certain elements in law this may be true, but it is not true of law in general. The laws that are written down are usually those for which custom has made no provision. Hammurabi caused to be written down 285 such laws. Conversely, if custom has long held certain actions in abhorrence, such prohibitions need not necessarily be mentioned in the legal code. Among those crimes not specially mentioned in the code of Hammurabi, for instance, is that of murder.

Now apart from its concern with value, philosophy is preoccupied with the relation of thought to expression and in consequence with the definition and interpretation of words. What the lawyer undertakes in the course of a juridical enquiry into a particular set of circumstances, the philosopher undertakes in the course of a philosophical enquiry into a particular set of problems. Philosophy is a form of intellectual jurisprudence.[1]

A short motor trip from modern Baghdad takes the sightseer to what remains of ancient Babylon. Surrounded by arid desert, the capital of Hammurabi and later Nebuchadnezzar has now shrunk to a few crumbling mud-brick ruins and mounds. Less traces remain of its former opulence than have been unearthed at the more ancient site of Ur of the Chaldees, once the home of Abraham, which is situated several hundred miles to the south. Who were the Babylonians? They were a blend of two neighbouring peoples: the Sumerians, a non-Semitic tribe, who inhabited the extreme south of Mesopotamia in such towns as Ur, Urak (called Erech in the Bible), Larsa (Ellasar), Lagash, and Nippur, and the Akkadians, the inhabitants of Agade farther up the river Euphrates, a distinctly Semitic people.

The blending of these two peoples, whose existence was practically unknown before the middle of the 19th century, was achieved as the result of a struggle from which the Akkadians appear to have emerged victorious. As a language, Babylonian was inevitably a composite formation. It contained Sumerian and Akkadian words written chiefly in Sumerian script, which represented not letters but

[1] For a development of this line of thought, whereby the methods of philosophy and history are shown to form in combination what is known as *metaphysical* enquiry, the reader is referred to the author's *Approach to Metaphysics*.

syllables; but gradually the Sumerian element gave place to a vocabulary predominantly Semitic, and Sumerian itself became a classical language studied only by scholars and priests. In subduing both Sumeria and Akkad, Hammurabi was faced with the task of welding these nations—themselves composed of numerous petty princedoms—into a unity. From the evidence of seals and various inscriptions that have been deciphered we gather that Hammurabi was primarily a man of action; but although he freely boasted of his military exploits he was no less anxious that posterity should learn of his civil achievements in building and irrigation. Whether because he lacked the callous streak so easily acquired by victors, or because he considered himself strong enough to dispense with such means of arousing terror in his enemies, he left no catalogue of massacre and destruction such as has survived from the reigns of other ancient conquerors. Boasting of his destruction of Elam, Ashurbanipal, who ruled in Assyria several centuries later, declared: "For a period of one month and twenty-five days I devastated the districts of Elam. . . . Sons of the kings, sisters of the kings, members of Elam's royal family, young and old, prefects, governors, knights, artisans, as many as there were, inhabitants male and female, big and little, horses, mules, asses, flocks and herds more numerous than a swarm of locusts—I carried them off as booty to Assyria. . . . The voice of men, the steps of flocks and herds, the happy shouts of mirth—I put an end to them in its fields, which I left for the asses, the gazelles, and all manner of wild beasts to people."[1]

Hammurabi, on the other hand, put the following on record: "When Anu and Enil (gods of Unek and Nippur) gave me the lands of Sumer and Akkad to rule, and they entrusted this sceptre to me, I dug the canal Hammurabi-nukhush-nishi (Hammurabi-the-wealth-of-the-people), which brings copious water to the land of Sumer and Akkad. Its banks on both sides I turned into cultivated ground: I heaped up piles of grain, I provided unfailing water for the lands. . . . The scattered people I gathered: with pasturage and water I provided them: I pastured them with abundance, and settled them in peaceful dwellings." Indeed, his reign of forty-two years (he died in 2081 B.C.) seems to have been one of comparative prosperity, progress, and—once he had eliminated his rivals—peace.

It is easy to interpret a statement such as the above in more ways than one. In declaring that the gods Anu and Enil "gave" him both Sumer and Akkad and "entrusted" him with the royal sceptre, Hammurabi may simply have been conveying with subtlety what

[1] This, by the way, is a comparatively mild example of the claims of Ashurbanipal (Sardanapalus, as the Greeks called him) to be remembered by posterity.

other conquerors preferred to announce with perfect frankness, namely that he seized by force what he proposed to hold by the same means. Hammurabi introduces his Code with a no less pious claim: "When the lofty Anu, King of Anunaki, and Bel,[1] Lord of Heaven and Earth, he who determines the destiny of the land, committed the rule of all mankind to Marduk,[2] when they pronounced the lofty name of Babylon; when they made it famous among the quarters of the world and in its midst established an everlasting kingdom whose foundations were firm as heaven and earth—at that time Anu and Bel called me, Hammurabi, the excellent prince, the worshipper of the gods, to cause justice to prevail in the land, to destroy the wicked and the evil, to prevent the strong from oppressing the weak . . . to enlighten the land and further the welfare of the people. Hammurabi, the governor named by Bel, am I, who brought about plenty and abundance . . . the governor of the people, the servant, whose deeds are pleasing to Anunit."

While mankind is accustomed to fine phrases, especially in manifestoes or as a prologue to constitutions, and is no doubt also accustomed to their remaining a dead letter, we need not suppose that these words of Hammurabi were simply a cloak for the violence and cupidity characteristic of the actions of absolute rulers. Accustomed to survey the outcrops of violence that jumble the territory of the past, historians adopt often enough a cynical attitude towards human motive, whereby all great men are branded as either scoundrels or hypocrites. Possibly, if such were the case, our dealings with our fellow-men would be greatly simplified. But clearly the assumption goes beyond the bounds of common sense, because if all motives were suspect there would be no such thing as suspicion, just as if all men were hypocrites the masks would automatically fall from their faces as being no longer of use. The significance of Hammurabi's claim to have established justice and peace in Babylon lies not so much in whether he actually did so, though he seems to have done, but in the fact that he considered it a commendable thing to have attempted. Nor would he have taken the trouble to place the fact on record had he not believed that his people and his successors would have registered approval. Consider, again, the manner in which he ends his Code: "I am the guardian governor. . . . In my bosom I carried the people of the land of Sumer and Akkad . . . in my wisdom I restrained them, that the strong might not oppress

[1] Baal, god of the earth.

[2] The national god of Babylon. Originally a Sun God, like Shamash: later called Bel-Marduk to signify that he had assumed the deities of the other gods. Originally there were thousands of these gods, many lacking all personality and receiving no individual worship. As they almost outnumbered men, Babylonian religion represents the farthest remove from Monotheism in history.

the weak, and that they should give justice to the orphan and the widow. . . . Let any oppressed man who has a cause, come before my image as king of righteousness! Let him read the inscription on my monument! let him give heed to my weighty words! And may my monument enlighten him as to his cause, and may he understand his case! May he set his heart at ease (saying): Hammurabi indeed is a ruler who is like a real father to his people . . . he has established prosperity for his people for all time and given a pure government to the land. . . . In the days that are yet to come, may the king who is in the land observe the words of righteousness which I have written upon my monument!"[1]

This passage, it will no doubt be agreed, is even more significant than that with which the Code opens, because it not merely makes claim to have established justice, but it invites any man to put this claim to the test. Wisely enough, Hammurabi is careful to specify that the man must have a *prima facie* case. If a suitor was found to be wasting the court's time he was likely to suffer severe penalties, especially in the case of a felony. "If a man brings an accusation against another," the first item of the code reads, "and charges him with a presumably capital crime, but cannot prove it, the accuser shall be put to death." Thus one of the chief curses of a society in which legal redress is within reach of all, namely excessive litigation, was removed by a somewhat more drastic method than the imposition of high costs, the usual modern deterrent.

If Hammurabi is to be taken at his word it would follow that he was the originator not merely of the first legal code but, in certain respects, of the most enlightened and liberal code that the world has known. Before arriving at such a remarkable conclusion concerning a system created nearly four thousand years ago, we must examine some more of its detailed provisions. These are at once primitive and progressive. Savage punishments and reasonable fines (varying sometimes according to the status of the plaintiff: it cost more to strike a patrician than a plebeian) are imposed for crimes of greater or less seriousness. Both the *lex talionis* of Rome and the Mosaic Code of "an eye for an eye and a tooth for a tooth"[2] are not merely anticipated but worked out with anatomical scrupulousness. By insisting that the criminal should suffer the precise equivalent of the harm inflicted upon his victim, a man who killed a boy was punished by the execution not of himself but of his son, and so forth. Nevertheless, among these startling edicts there stand out ordinances

[1] The Code of Hammurabi may be studied in the edition of R. F. Harper, University of Chicago Press, 1904, from which the above rendering is taken, or in C. H. W. John's *The Oldest Code of Law*, 1903.

[2] For the influence of Hammurabi's Code on the Mosaic Code, see page 98.

which are in advance of anything that has yet been given legislative form: for example, the law that a man who has fallen victim to unidentified robbers shall, upon making "an itemized statement of his loss" and swearing a suitably solemn affidavit, be recompensed from public funds. Clearly, Hammurabi did not think out all these measures *in vacuo*. Being a clever conqueror, he most certainly arrived at his system by careful compilation and co-ordination of the laws of provinces recently subdued.

While the Code of Hammurabi contains many enlightened measures, it betrays not the least concern for the rights of the individual against the state. Admittedly, the absence of such provision is probably due not so much to conscious despotism as to the fact that neither Hammurabi nor his subjects had envisaged a situation in which such rights could be exercised. Babylon, like Sumeria, was a theocracy. The king, though not himself a priest, donned priestly robes at his coronation, thereby signifying the absolute unity or identity of church and state. Taxation was imposed not in the name of the king but in the name of Marduk, who was considered owner of the soil of Babylon; and most of the money went to the priests. If the king needed financial help, and was not engaged in warfare that seemed likely to yield loot, he was obliged to apply for help to the Temple treasuries, though he was usually reluctant to do so unless in extreme difficulties. Moreover, in this country of law and order, no professional lawyers existed. Legal business was discharged by priests, who used the temples as assizes. The courts of the Lord—an expression made familiar to us by the Bible—were therefore also the courts of men. While the kings of Babylon were not regarded as actuating the course of nature as well as the processes of government, they remained divinely appointed governors, fathers of their people, distinguished from mere magistrates by being vested with ancestral authority, against whom rebellion or even contention was an act of impiety.

Thus, if Hammurabi's people possessed no means of asserting their rights against the system of government in force, they enjoyed within that system a considerable measure of material advantage and protection against molestation. Property, marriage, business, trade, and labour were regulated in a manner that suggests a busy, almost sophisticated, social life: for it is obvious that Hammurabi's regulations must have been formulated at an epoch when commerce and industry, though often controlled by priests, had reached a high stage of development. Nor have we any reason to suppose that Hammurabi was interested exclusively in promoting the material welfare of his people. To the Babylonians we probably owe the beginnings of astronomy, mathematics, and medicine; and we know

W. F. Mansell

HAMMURABI

Diorite shard now in the Louvre, Paris

from the literary remains that have been found that they were assiduous scholars and, to use a slight anachronism, bibliophiles. Every temple of importance contained its library, which consisted of brick tablets stored in jars as in a columbarium. On a series of such tablets, found in the library of King Ashurbanipal at Nineveh in 1854,[1] is engraved the Babylonian story of the Creation. These tablets form but seven of 30,000 others which, copied by the Assyrians from originals now lost, have provided us with more detail concerning Babylonian society than we possess of nations much closer to us in time. The majority of these tablets represent routine business correspondence, including contracts, receipts, and even I O Us.

To most people, a glance at history a few hundred years B.C. induces a kind of chronological vertigo. The sense of proportion is deranged for want of landmarks in time, or fixed stars in the historical firmament. Roughly contemporary with Hammurabi was that lonely priest Neferrohu, who, having lamented the collapse of moral standards in the Egypt of his day, hailed the advent of a saviour-monarch whom we have presumed to be Amenemhet I (2061–2013 B.C.). We have referred to the dispute among historians of ancient civilization concerning the relative moral advancement of such countries as Egypt and Babylonia. In many ways the development of the sciences and the arts run roughly parallel: the problems of writing, mathematics, and government are worked out as necessity engenders invention. While the Egyptian conception of life, and above all the good life, matured earlier by perhaps a millenium than that of Babylon, and developed with greater continuity and consistency, we should not underestimate the enlightenment of a society of which the ruler freely undertook, without indulging in an idle boast, to "prevent the strong from oppressing the weak, to enlighten the land and further the welfare of the people". For there is evident here a sense of *abstract justice* upon which later pronouncements of this kind do not present a conspicuous improvement. Our own century, to exclude the past altogether, has seen the open advocacy of theories of government in which the rights of the weak against the strong—or, what comes to the same thing, of the minority against the majority—have been not so much ignored as derided. Once again, it may be argued that practice does not always conform to theory. This is true: but if we are interested in estimating moral or ethical growth, a man's moral standards must be judged by what he thinks he ought to do as well as by what he does. It is the "spirit of the laws", to use the phrase made famous by Montesquieu, that counts. By this standard

[1] Sennacherib sacked Babylon in 689 B.C. Ashurbanipal reigned from 669–626 B.C.

Hammurabi and his associates stand out among the early champions of justice.

Just as we knew little of Hammurabi before the discovery of the potsherds or *ostraka* and the Code itself, so it is possible that archaeologists will one day unearth evidence of mature legislation belonging to a much earlier age. Perhaps they have already done so. Nearly a thousand years before Hammurabi (about 2903 B.C.), Yrukagina, King of Lagash, introduced a series of reforms into his country, the general aim of which was to "protect the weak against the strong". In the view of many archaeologists, an investigation of the Mesopotamian region as intensive as that made in Egypt during the last century would reveal a civilization older in origin, though not necessarily more mature, than that of ancient Egypt. Unless supported by a series of discoveries in the cultural sphere, however, the opening of such a new perspective would not therefore invalidate the general point of view here maintained. As in evolution we observe creatures which, though possessed of human characteristics, have remained inexplicably undeveloped, so in history the intimations of civilization are constantly surprising us by their early appearance. This is especially true in art, the frontiers of which are being thrust farther and farther back in time. What counts in history, however, is continuity united with fecundity. Hammurabi's claim to attention is not merely that he compiled the first great legal code, but that his work exerted a profound influence upon later peoples. One such people was to accomplish a historical mission far greater than that of either Egypt or Babylon. It is to this people that we now turn; and we begin by turning south.

Abraham

The final stage of Hammurabi's conquest of the Mesopotamian region was his overthrow in 1910 B.C. of his powerful rival Rim-Sin, King of Larsa, a town south-east of Lagash and north of Ur. Rim-Sin, who had been a capable and munificent ruler in his day, was now an old man. Hammurabi, on the other hand, had proved himself an energetic young commander of marked administrative capacity. Unable to retain the loyalty of the princedoms under his control, Rim-Sin suffered the first defeat of his career. The Sumerian kingdoms surrendered. Ur, a Semitic city and no doubt sympathetic to Hammurabi, did not even put an army in the field. She quietly declared herself under the protection of the king of Babylon. The Semitic influence in both culture and commerce was now dominant throughout Babylonia.

We now enter, though with much greater confidence than would have been possible fifty or even thirty years ago, upon the realm of conjecture. Among the subjects of Rim-Sin was a man to whom three of the great world religions still look back as their Patriarch, the father of their faith. Abraham, for such was his name, inhabited the town of Ur, known in the Bible as "Ur of the Chaldees"[1]; and it was from here that, according to *Genesis*, Chapter xi, verse 31, he "went forth", accompanied by his entire family, "to go into the land of Canaan". That journey, for reasons that we shall show, was one of the most momentous ever to be undertaken.

The so-called Higher Criticism of the Bible did not arise, as many suppose, in the 19th century. It was initiated by the Jewish philosopher Spinoza (1632–77), who was ousted by the local synagogue for criticizing, though not necessarily rejecting as false, certain claims made by Holy Scripture.[2] In the last century, however, critical scholarship of biblical sources, together with the archaeological investigation of sites associated with the Bible, made considerable progress. The revelation of inconsistency, though bewildering to the pious, need not injure faith: for if faith can move mountains—which it may do, as on a journey the resolute traveller puts them one by one behind him—it can no doubt also overcome logical contradiction. *Credo quia impossibile est.* But to the sceptic the revelation of inconsistency is conclusive evidence of error. When, therefore, the critics drew attention to contradictions and anachronisms in scripture, the biblical narratives, though remaining "magnificent literature", were frequently dismissed as fiction.

By clearing away irrelevances and exposing slipshod scholarship, the Higher Criticism achieved much that was of value. To say that it has been largely superseded is true. It has given place to what, consistently enough, is a still higher criticism. This higher criticism seeks not merely to arrive at facts through a haze of myth; it also seeks to examine and analyse the mythical element itself. To the old criticism, for instance, the fact that such figures as Abraham or Moses are surrounded by a penumbra of legend was sufficient to prove that these figures were themselves legendary, as if greatness of reputation and posthumous fame were sufficient to cast doubt upon the reality of the person to whom they attached. This attitude had certain odd consequences. Denying the reality of the man but being obliged to accept that of the myth, such critics—among whom are some distinguished psychologists—proceeded to evolve a theory whereby myths, especially those relating to leaders of men, played a part in history best described as organic or catalytic. Such myths

[1] The title "of the Chaldees" is an anachronism. The Chaldeans belong to a later epoch. Visitors to Urfa in south Turkey, a town difficult of access, are shown a cave reputed to be Abraham's birthplace. The claim is due to a confusion of names. Urfa was known as Edessa in the early Christian epoch.

[2] See the author's companion volume, Chapter VIII.

either set history going or enabled it to restart. Of certain figures associated with early civilization this interpretation is plausible, though it is still the persons concerned with originating the myth that provide the dynamic elements in history, not anything impersonal or "archetypal". In the case of men whose reputed deeds have been handed down by oral tradition over a period of centuries, and then recorded by scribes, a different approach is necessary, especially if archaeology can meanwhile establish the veracity of circumstantial detail. According to this approach, a penumbra of legend is regarded as likely to surround historical personalities whose achievements, because they were authentic, invite such embellishment. When enthusiastic members of the Academy circulated the story that Plato was the son of Apollo, and that bees had settled on his infant lips in anticipation of his honeyed words, they were not striving to show that Plato did not exist; they were striving to show, in the fashion of the time, what a great man he was.

Although excavations began at Ur under the direction of the British at Basra in 1854, and were resumed systematically in 1922 under Sir Leonard Woolley, not a single inscription among the great wealth of material brought to light has been found to contain a reference to Abraham. When we consider the meagre references to be found to persons living thousands of years later—Shakespeare, for instance—this absence of direct testimony need not greatly disturb us. What leads us to suppose that the Abraham of the Bible really existed is the fact that the biblical account is consistent with our knowledge, most of it very recently acquired, of the people to whom he is said to belong.

Who were these people? The first-known mention of the Habiru, whom scholars now agree to be identical with the Hebrews, is to be found in the reign of Rim-Sin, Hammurabi's old rival. The reference is not casual. The Habiru are accorded a vivid, if terse, description. In the Sumerian script they are represented by an ideogram which, translated broadly, means nomads, brigands, or cut-throats. Now although in *Genesis* xiv, 13, Abraham himself is described as a Hebrew, his nephew Laban (xxv, 20) and, later on, Jacob,are referred to as Syrians or as Aramaeans, a tribe undoubtedly identical with, or related to, the Amorites. That the Amorites enjoyed the same reputation as the Habiru of Rim-Sin's reign is proved by a variety of references. A Sumerian hymn praising the "gods of the west", of which the date is about 2000 B.C., makes direct reference to these Amorites who roamed the Western hills. This tribe, says the hymn, "knows no submission, eats raw flesh, has no home in its lifetime, and does not bury its dead kinsfolk". According to a later Egyptian source, the Amorite is described no less vividly as "the miserable stranger . . . He does not dwell in the same spot, his feet are always wandering. From the days of Horus, he battles, he does not conquer, and is not conquered". With this we may compare the prophecy of Balaam in *Numbers* xxiii, 9, "Behold a people that dwells alone, and amid the nations is not accounted." The construction by the Babylonians of the so-called Wall of the West as early as the third millenium B.C. had been due to a desire to prevent the infiltration of these unruly folk. Where such measures proved ineffective, local governors did their best to put the nomads to useful work. Either they were employed at stock-raising[1] or, to exploit their warlike qualities, they were enlisted in the army, though in special battalions in the manner of mercenaries or minorities. Rim-Sin, himself a soldier, seems to have preferred the latter method of discipline.

In that repository of odd information, the "Tel el-Amarna Letters", to which we have already referred in connection with Ikhnaton's imperial problems, we read of a people called the Habiri. Their sporadic raids into Palestine from the desert were causing concern to the local governors holding office under Pharaoh. For a time scholars were in doubt as to whether to identify Habiru and Habiri. Now they are inclined to do so. For if we recognize that the Habiru were not necessarily an ethnic group but simply one of a variety of tribes united by love of wandering, the identity is more easily acceptable. But the "Tel el-Amarna Letters" disclose a fact more interesting still. Mention is made therein of both Habiri and Aramaeans: but the ideogram here employed for Habiri is precisely that which conveys the notion of cut-throats and brigands. Now it is possible, and even likely, that a governor reporting to his superiors an attack by foreigners upon imperial territory would lump the whole band together as brigands, just as we used to talk of Huns; but what emerges is that the Habiri were associated with a group of people to whom the general name Aramaean attached, and that this group led a life similar to that of the modern Bedouin.

According to the account in *Genesis*, Abraham's first halting-place on his journey to the land of Canaan was Harran, a town now situated in the south of Turkey near the Syrian frontier. That such a northward movement of a Habiri family was usual at this period does not destroy the uniqueness of Abraham's journey: the uniqueness lies in that to which it gave rise. A northward migration had in fact been going on for some time: tablets of the 15th century B.C. found not long ago at Kirkuk, the oil-town in the north of Iraq, refer to the Habiri as frequently to be met with in the upper regions of Mesopotamia. Now there are two possible causes to which these

[1] Apart from forced labour, this was the main occupation of the Jews during the Egyptian captivity.

migrations can be ascribed. In the first place, it is nothing surprising in a nomad people to betray evidence that they wandered. In the second place, they may have had reason to believe that their services, whether military or civil, might be better employed elsewhere than in the south. We have seen that large numbers of Amorites served in the Sumerian army. Being mercenaries, their primary reason for changing their allegiance would presumably have been a mercenary one: better pay and conditions were reported to be obtainable up north. Not merely did Hammurabi appear to offer immediate benefit. As potential master of the whole of Mesopotamia, he offered as good a chance of permanent employment as any mercenary troops could desire. We have no particular reason to suppose that Abraham's family belonged to the military caste, though *Genesis*, Chapter xiv, reports a desert scrap in which Abraham and his men clashed with the forces of "Amraphel King of Shinar", who is thought by some to have been Hammurabi. But such an incident, even if isolated, would not be unusual in a nomadic body, especially as the story mentions that substantial booty was secured. It is more likely that Abraham's family were rich camel-owners, and that Harran—a town with which they were probably already in touch[1]—seemed, for reasons shortly to be mentioned, to offer better trading prospects than Ur.

On this point negative information is almost as valuable as positive. The *Genesis* narrative later refers to the large number of camels Abraham had at his disposal: but none of the thousands of business records found at Ur mention the camel. A probable explanation, upon which modern conditions shed considerable light, is that the camel business was altogether outside the normal affairs of the town. Populated by as many as a quarter of a million people, Ur had for years been a thriving centre of business. The society that thronged its narrow streets was, to quote Sir Leonard Woolley,[2] "highly individualistic, enjoying a great measure of personal liberty, materialistic and money-making, hard-working and most appreciative of comfort and the good things of life": in short, a sophisticated, urban society in violent contrast to the tribal society outside its confines. While a camel-owner might be both extremely rich and as familiar with urban life as any other merchant, the source of his wealth would be, as it were, extra-mural, and might even be expressly concealed. Even today the use of camels within inhabited areas in some Middle East countries is subject to restriction, and the passage of these animals through the streets is limited to night-time.

[1] The name Harran means "way" or "caravan", indicating a place or junction where caravans met and parted.

[2] Woolley: *Abraham*, p. 131.

To complete the picture, which must be drawn with precision if we would understand the revolution in thought for which Abraham was responsible, let us revert to the point from which we began: namely the collapse of Rim-Sin's Sumerian empire. While the ordinary inhabitant of Ur or Larsa cannot have realized how critical the situation was, the simultaneous surrender of all the great Sumerian towns must have seemed to him a disaster greater even than the ruthless sack of Ur by the Elamites in 2170 B.C. If he did not judge it to be the end of Sumerian political hegemony, his confidence in the national powers of recovery must have been put to severe strain. But supposing that this anonymous citizen of four thousand years ago was not a Sumerian but a Semitic nomad, his attitude might have been very different. He had never really been wanted. That was clear enough from the epithets customarily applied to him. He, in turn, had never really "belonged". That was a consequence of his race, his habits, and the trade in which he was engaged. Furthermore, it is the custom, as we know, for nations in defeat to seek scapegoats among the minorities to which they have formerly given protection. The nomadic Habiru, whose loyalty may often have been in doubt, would be only too likely to incur some portion of blame and recrimination. In these circumstances, his decision to leave, even if already taken for economic reasons, would no doubt have been hastened.

All this may account satisfactorily for the journey of Abraham's family from Ur to Harran. It does not yet throw light upon the circumstances in which we are chiefly interested. If Abraham is still looked upon as the father[1] of three out of the half-dozen great religions of the world, at what point in his career and simultaneously with what spiritual experience did he abandon the beliefs of his forefathers and render homage to the One God? Such a change in outlook cannot have been effected without some kind of spiritual crisis, perhaps a family crisis; because a conversion in the conditions of a theocratic state, with its enormous pantheon of national, local, family, and nature gods, all demanding due allegiance, would be a much more drastic affair than its equivalent today. Without informing us of the religion in which Abraham originally believed, the Bible asserts (*Joshua* xxiv, 2) that his family "served other gods". What other gods? Surely the gods of Sumeria, and in particular the gods of Ur. Now the civic god of Ur was Nannar, a moon god. Another town dedicated to a goddess of the moon was, curiously enough, Harran. This latter goddess was named Terah. So was Abraham's father. Is it possible, perhaps, that Terah, coming of a family of moon worshippers, was named after the deity of a town

[1] Though not the founder. See p. 103.

with which the family, or at least the roaming tribes to which the family belonged, had established close associations? If so, that might explain why he set out in time of adversity for the place most likely to afford him protection.

That Terah and his son should have left one "moon" town to live in another suggests not a weakening of belief in the family god but the determination to continue the same form of worship. The choice of a place to live, which today is dictated by economic rather than sentimental reasons, meant a great deal to our forefathers. At every level, even that of business and trade, religious considerations would be given their due weight, as no doubt they were by the leader of the party. But while the family would be dominated by the father, nothing would prevent Abraham from professing other beliefs once he succeeded Terah as head of the clan. Now we know that Terah died and was buried at Harran. And it was after his decease that, according to the biblical account, Abraham received his first direct message from "the Lord". The message, in this case, took the form of a command. Abraham was to lead his people to Canaan and there to establish a new community.

What happened at Harran after the death of Terah? For it was then, if at all, that the conversion must have taken place. Of its nature the Bible affords no direct clue. We do not even know the exact name of the God who, without apparent warning, issued the command to strike camp. Nor did Abraham's family know Him by any other title than that of the "God of Abraham" or (as the family acquired other heads) the "God of Abraham, Isaac and Jacob". This anonymity was preserved for much longer than is generally realized. It continued for several centuries, perhaps for as long as a thousand years, until, at a dramatic moment in the history of the same clan, God disclosed His identity to Moses. In an age when the names of gods, and indeed the names of anything, were of particular significance, this deliberate reticence on the part of Abraham's god seems to us as strange as Abraham's own acquiescence in it.

If we approach this problem from a somewhat different point of view, we may be able to explain not merely its baffling aspects but the nature of the conversion which Abraham must have experienced. Although the conversion assumed a drastic form by reason of the complicated polytheistic faith against which it was a reaction, such an experience might have been less obtrusive at Harran than at Ur. It might even be a consequence of deciding to leave Harran, a place known to the clan, for Canaan, a place unknown but promised.

As we have seen in the case of Aton, gods do not usually survive the political defeat of their worshippers. To affirm as much is not to adopt the condescending attitude of the rationalist historian to "primitive" beliefs. A god to whom a town looks for protection, encouragement, and defence cannot dissociate himself, unless he is a special kind of god, from public misfortune or disaster. Just as the citizen of Sumer must have witnessed the national reverses with foreboding, so his confidence in the civic gods must have undergone corresponding deflation. If he was by nature devout, the one form of pessimism would have been impossible to distinguish from the other. Experience in other epochs and at similar times of stress leads us to believe that minorities, even if of different religious persuasion, may be no less attached to the gods or, as we might say, principles of the country of their adoption than the nationals themselves. Their attachment or respect may be particularly strong, witness the feats of agents of non-British origin during the late war. Thus the Habiru clans, though treated as outcasts, may have contained cultivated individuals, who, priding themselves on being good citizens, shared to the full the disillusionment following Sumer's fall. Among these the family of Terah would be numbered. In abandoning Ur, and in seeking a town of better omen, we may well imagine a fundamental difference in attitude between the old, conservative father, seeking a place of retirement under the protection of his personal god, and the son, eager to rebuild his fortunes. Pursuing our conjectures to the limit, we can picture Abraham at the death of his father as a man who, conscious of the great responsibilities that had fallen upon him, considers what he can salvage from the past to sustain him in his future wanderings.

Although the biblical narrative withholds until the appropriate moment all direct information about the "God of Abraham", we know that He possessed a characteristic that distinguished Him from others. This characteristic was that He moved about. Almost all other gods were stationary or attached. This applied especially to the gods of Sumeria. At Ur the Moon God, Nannar, had his own private apartments in the Temple; while his wife, Nin Gal, had her own bedchamber. The couple lived at Ur, nor did they leave the capital except under compulsion, as happened when the Elamites "captured" them by removing their statues to Susa. Likewise, all nature gods were rooted in the soil, or in groves, mountains, or rivers; they could not move, unless for some reason the natural objects did themselves, as when a river overflowed or a volcano erupted. From some interesting Hittite inscriptions of a later period we learn of certain gods called *Iani Habiri*, which may be translated either as "gods of the Habiru" or, more likely, "Habiru gods". By referring to Habiru gods in this fashion the authorities were no doubt emphasizing a characteristic for which such gods were well known, namely their habit of *accompanying the clan in its wanderings.*

Of the God of Abraham, two features now stand out: (*a*) that He was nameless, and (*b*) that He was peripatetic. With regard to the latter characteristic, we know that, though unattached, He still had His temple in the tent-tabernacle set up at every major halting-place; but no proper temple was erected in His honour until the time of Solomon (974–937 B.C.).

In describing the God of Abraham as an unattached God, we have been understanding the word attached in the sense of fastened to something static. But naturally it is possible to be attached to something non-static, to something that moves. The God of Abraham was attached to Abraham and his family. Why, then, should He not have been a family god? Given Abraham's situation at Harran, family considerations would inevitably have been uppermost in his mind. The civic gods of Ur, the national gods of Sumeria, had been left behind; but whether they had failed him or not, such local civic gods could not be removed or, being removed, retain their power. Nor, after Terah's death, was there much inducement to test the beneficence of the civic gods of Harran: a place to die in for the father was not necessarily a satisfactory abode for the son. When at this moment the Lord said to Abraham (*Genesis* xii, 1), "Get thee out of thy country," meaning Mesopotamia, the Lord who thereby attached Himself to Abraham may, for all that is said to the contrary, have been stressing an attachment of long standing. The conversion may have been a form of reversion.

If the family god hypothesis is to be sustained, we must be able to show not merely that such gods were cultivated in Sumeria but upon what grounds, in this instance, the god remained nameless. To Sir Leonard Woolley we owe some valuable information on this as on most other points in the history of Abraham. From the researches made by the Joint Expedition of the British Museum and the University of Pennsylvania, it became abundantly clear that the Sumerians, while paying respect to an immense number of official gods, were accustomed also to worshipping tutelary deities, like the *lars* and *penates* of the Romans. These "household gods" were usually represented by figurines or, as the Bible calls them, *teraphim*. But such representation differed from that of other gods by being purely conventional; the god itself exhibited no particular characteristics.[1] Another custom of universal observance, as the excavations testify, was that of burying the bodies of ancestors directly beneath the little chapel attached to every private house.[2] In this domestic chapel, therefore, reverence for ancestors would be com-

[1] The prohibition of representing God has remained permanent among the Jews. Likewise the word Jehovah is always read "Adonai".

[2] Woolley, *Abraham*, p. 220.

bined with worship of the household god who watched over the family, both living and dead. Prayers, led by the head of the household, would be said regularly and offerings made, usually in the form of food; but it is an interesting fact that none of these chapels contains any inscription or sign whereby the domestic god can be named.[1] He was evidently regarded as a power whose identification other than as god of the family, past, present, and to come, was considered unnecessary. That he was identified *with* the family was all that mattered. If, as we may suppose, these ancient people, with their pronounced religious sense, derived genuine consolation from some at least of the innumerable forms of worship at their disposal, we may conclude that it was in the domestic chapel rather than in the public temple that such emotions were most often stirred.

The family god lives with the family, moves with the family, does not desert the family in its vicissitudes. It is the one god whose reputation undergoes no change when misfortune visits the little group, so intimately is it identified with its life through many generations. To a Habiri clan such as that of Abraham it would no doubt be much dearer than to more settled families; but not until the break with Ur and its gods effected by the death of Terah did it appear to Abraham, perhaps in a flash of insight or perhaps as something very simple (the Bible suggests the latter), that it was the one stay left. Forsaking all others, the family should allow itself to be guided by the god who had steadfastly accompanied it up to that moment. At that realization, God spoke.

To have followed the account in Chapter I of Egyptian religion and thought, followed by the outline of ideas current in Babylon four thousand years ago, will be to have confirmed our initial observation, namely that in studying the mind of the Orient we are unable to separate, if not to distinguish, religion and philosophy. There has sometimes been a tendency, not unrelated to the school of Higher Criticism, to suggest that the two not merely can but must be distinguished if we are to isolate what ancient man "really thought" from the tissue of "beliefs" with which, for reasons left to be explained, he encumbered himself. A more scientific approach is that which regards the beliefs themselves as what he "really thought", and proceeds to enquire how such beliefs came to be entertained. This is history; the rest is prejudice thinly disguised as scientific impartiality. To endeavour to peel off the belief, whether supernatural or merely "numinous", as if it formed a kind of chrysalis concealing and constricting the butterfly of fact, is to do

[1] Cf. Martin Buber: *Moses* (1946), p. 205. But Buber, following Kaufmann (*History of the Hebrew Religion*, I, p. 675), says that these gods received no worship. This would seem to be incompatible with the existence of domestic chapels and votive offerings.

violence to the state of mind of men not necessarily more irrational than ourselves, and to render our understanding of them much more difficult than it need be. Hence our attempt to reconstruct from the available evidence what Abraham, in initiating a new development in the outlook of man, thought he was doing.

To trace the process whereby the family god of Abraham became the "Most High God" of Israel is to show, first of all, that there is no obvious contradiction between a private god becoming a public one if the public group is simply an expansion, as in the present case, of a private unit. The family of Abraham was already a clan; it developed into a tribe in the natural process of moving as a unit across vast stretches of desert. Naturally, Abraham and his near relations would still form a kind of central nucleus, as it was the custom for the elders to remain an inner clan of their own. Thus in the 14th chapter of *Genesis* we learn that among Abraham's followers there were a number of "bondsmen", men presumably who had agreed to bind themselves to him as a natural leader. Such stray adherents, who attached themselves casually and finally decided to throw in their lot with the chief, were common enough in desert life. Even the "stranger within their gates" is in Moses' time permitted to enjoy all the communal privileges, such as resting on the Sabbath. The tribe must be prepared against attack—"And when Abraham heard that his brother was taken captive, he armed his trained servants, born in his own house, three hundred and eighteen, and pursued them into Dan" (*Genesis* xiv, 14). And with every desert encounter the tribal unity was strengthened, the reputation of Abraham enhanced, the God of Abraham magnified.[1]

To conceive of the family God of Abraham on the analogy of the diminutive modern family, conditioned by the semi-detached house, hire-purchase and state allowances, is to form a grotesquely inaccurate picture of its size and complexity. The God of such a "snowball" band was already god of a community, hence a God of potentially universal appeal. The transition was both natural and inevitable. Above all it was historical. The cathedrals of Europe, the parish churches of England, the chapels and meeting houses of America, the missionary huts of Africa and Asia, represent the gigantic projection of that process in time.

Abraham the bearer of civilization

This is not the place to enter into biblical controversy by debating the relative importance or antiquity of this or that passage in the Old Testament. In view of recent archaeological discoveries,

[1] Abraham would not accept payment for military aid rendered to others. See *Genesis* xiv, 23.

the subject is of great fascination; but our object is to trace man's early ideas about life and death, good and evil, and in pursuance of this task we must now turn to another aspect of Abraham's character of which little was suspected until the beginning of the present century. In short, we must study Abraham as the transmitter of civilization in the form of both myth (using that word in no derogatory sense) and law. Woolley has pointed out that not until the story of Abraham begins to unfold does the Bible truly become alive. What precedes this story is mere chronicle, a hotchpotch of legend and imaginative speculation thrown together with little regard for consistency. Much of this material owes its origin to pre-Hebraic sources; and, where an indubitable Babylonian source can be proved, we are inevitably led to enquire how such accounts can have been handed on from one civilization to another.

The seven tablets discovered at Nineveh in 1854 record one by one the days of the creation of the world according to Babylonian tradition. On the first of these tablets it is related how Apsu, the Ocean, father of all things, and Tiamat, Chaos, the mother, mingled together. At a time when

> No field was formed, no marsh was to be seen,
> When of the gods none had been called into being
> And none bore a name and no destinies were ordained,
> Then were created the gods in the midst of heaven.

As a result of this huge gestation, order began slowly to form as the gods assumed control of their respective spheres. But before much progress could be made, Tiamat, suddenly resolving to make an end of her progeny, engulfed all the gods save one, Marduk. According to the fourth tablet, Marduk "stood upon Tiamat's hinder parts and with his merciless club he smashed her skull". Then, intent upon rendering her for ever innocuous, he "devised a cunning plan; he split her up like a flat fish into two halves". Having thus splatched and divided her, "one half of her he established as a covering for heaven", and the other half "he spread out under his feet to form the earth". Then, so the fifth tablet relates, he resumed the task of setting the universe in order:

> He made the stations for the great gods,
> The stars, their images,[1] as the stars of the Zodiac he fixed.
> He ordained the year and into sections he divided it,
> For the twelve months he fixed three stars . . .
> The moon-god he caused to shine forth, and night he entrusted to him.

[1] An idea to be found also in Plato.

Finally, deciding to make a creature who should not merely enjoy this stupendous work, but give thanks to the gods who fashioned and sustained it, Marduk proceeded to create man. This achievement is the burden of the sixth tablet: "My blood will I take and (presumably by mixing it with earth) bone will I fashion . . . I will create man who shall inhabit the earth."

According to Babylonian tradition, the early condition of mankind was the reverse of simple and idyllic. Man was a creature as yet uninstructed in the arts and crafts of life. Just as the Egyptians, who held a similar view, regarded Thoth as the first teacher of man and in particular the inventor of writing, so the Babylonians attributed man's capacity to fend for himself in a hostile world to the instruction of a creature called Oannes, a kind of enormous fish-man. Even so, since man did not prove an amenable creature, the gods resolved in due course to destroy him. A flood of unprecedented dimensions, overwhelming the entire earth, promised to annihilate all natural creatures. But Ea, goddess of Wisdom, whom Marduk had consulted before making man ("He opened his mouth and unto Ea he spoke"—sixth tablet), seems to have regretted the god's decision. She decided to save a man called Shamash-napishtim and his family, who under her guidance set to work to build an ark.

The story of Shamash-napishtim is told in a remarkable epic poem which was inscribed on twelve tablets found in the same library as that from which the Creation story was recovered. This is the *Epic of Gilgamesh*, a poem which some experts believe to date from as early as 3000 B.C. Gilgamesh, King of Unek, was a descendant of Shamash-napishtim, whose adventures are related in the course of the poem. As in the Biblical account with which we are familiar, the most precise details are first given of the size of the ark under construction. Shamash speaks in the first person:

> On the fifth day I drew its design
> In its plan 120 cubits high on each of its sides.
> By 120 cubits it corresponded on each edge of its roof.
> I laid down its form, I enclosed it,
> I constructed it in six storeys,
> Dividing it into seven parts . . .
> Three sars of bitumen I poured over the outside,
> Three sars of bitumen I poured over the inside.

Having finished the vessel, "I put on board my family and relatives, the cattle of the field, the beasts of the field," and when "the appointed time arrived and the ruler of darkness at eventide sent a heavy rain, I entered the ship and shut my door". For seven nights the storm continued:

The wind blew, the flood, the tempest overwhelmed the land.
When the seventh day drew near, the tempest, the flood,
Ceased from the battle in which it had fought like a host.
Then the sea rested and was still, and the wind storm and the flood ceased,
I opened the window and daylight fell upon my face.

Soon land was sighted, and "the mountain of the land of Nisir held fast the ship and suffered it not to stir"; whereupon

> I sent forth a dove and let her go,
> The dove went to and fro,
> But there was no resting place and she returned.

So Shamash tried first a swallow and then a raven. The latter, "beholding the abatement of the water, came near, wading and croaking, but did not return". Shamash then gave the order to disembark, and, camping on the peak of the mountain, made sacrifice and offered a libation. Apparently the recession of the flood was due to the fact that the gods, once having decided to destroy man, realized that they would now cease to be worshipped and thus be deprived of burnt offerings. For when Shamash makes it his first duty to offer thanksgiving, "the gods smelt the sweet savour, the gods gathered like flies about him that offered up the sacrifice".

What is remarkable about this account, which we know to have already been *in writing* during the time of Abraham, is its resemblance not merely in outline but in actual phrasing to that given in *Genesis*, Chapters vii, viii, and ix. Even the offer of sacrifice(ix, XX)is reproduced, with the comment that God "smelt the sweet savour", though the entire theological aspect has been subject to revision in conformity with Hebrew monotheism. That the "mountain of Nisir" should have been changed to that of Ararat is natural, as the latter would be the highest peak in the "world" known to inhabitants of Palestine and northern Syria.

Now the story as related in the *Epic of Gilgamesh*, which records incidentally how Shamesh-napishtim was made immortal for assisting the preservation of man and other forms of life, is not a pure essay in imaginative writing. Whereas the main story of the *Epic*, of which we possess only a fragment, is concerned with the adventures in love, battle, and the search for truth of the hero Gilgamesh, it is no more completely a work of fiction than the *Odyssey* or the *Iliad*. Just as Troy was a real place and its siege an historical engagement, so we have reason to believe that the flood described in the *Epic* forms the memory, however vague and distorted, of an historic episode. In the course of their excavations at Ur, Woolley and his colleagues succeeded, by sinking deep shafts into the soil, in exposing the levels at which the town was successively rebuilt in the four thousand years of its history. At a certain level the layers were found to be interrupted by an immense quantity of silt. This could be explained only by the onset of a catastrophic inundation (milder forms of which were as common in this area as in the Nile Valley); for lying immediately beneath the deposit were further ruins in layers similar to those nearer the surface. Woolley has also drawn attention to the authenticity of much of the local colour of the story: the comparative shallowness of the inundation, so familiar and welcome at other times, the caulking of the ark with bitumen, a local product of proved utility, and so on. Nor need we suppose that this flood, though very likely to have been the Flood, was the first of its kind: such disasters represented a recurrent threat to a land dependent for its fertility upon a highly complicated, man-devised system of irrigation, traces of which remain over much of modern Iraq.

In the Creation Myth we have something entirely different. This is not the story of a historical episode, but a plain allegory. As an allegory, it is admittedly a great deal cruder than the Memphite Drama, with its remarkable excursion into metaphysics; but the reader will no doubt have observed in it a gleam, however faint, of something more profound, something that lifts it above being a mere blood-and-thunder myth. Tiamat and Apsu are monsters. And the product of their union so closely resembles a monstrous-birth that the chaos-mother is moved to destroy it in self-loathing. She in turn is killed, not without brutality, by Marduk, who is himself a kind of monster. Before Marduk creates man, however, he consults, not another monster like himself, but the goddess Ea, the embodiment of Wisdom. It is likewise Ea who, observing the imminent return of chaos, intercedes for man and ensures his preservation. According to these early bardic-philosophers, therefore, man's existence and survival have something to do with the power of an intelligence comparable to the Egyptian *Maat*, the Chinese *Tao*, and the Greek *Logos*: a power perpetually at war with the forces of disorder, barbarism, and chaos.

This perception of the divine principle at work both in the world and in man is apparent in other parts of the *Epic of Gilgamesh*, overlaid as the poem is with much extravagant fantasy and grotesque adventure. At the conclusion of the fragment, Gilgamesh, mourning the death of his friend Engidu, is driven to reflect upon the nature of life and death. Having sought out and communed with Shamash-napishtim, his immortal ancestor, he finally decides to seek a personal interview with Engidu. Although this must naturally entail the latter's emergence from the underworld, Gilgamesh prays fervently to the appropriate gods and Engidu finally appears. When he is asked by Gilgamesh to unfold the secrets of death, however, he replies, "If I were to tell thee that which I have seen, terror would overthrow thee, thou wouldst faint away." Gilgamesh's answer, which in effect concludes the fragment, is as follows, "Though terror should overwhelm me and I should faint away, yet tell me." This spirit of obstinate enquiry, apparent in a folk-tale five thousand years old, is perhaps the sole power capable of carrying man through the next five thousand years, if in the meantime he does not unlock the secrets of nature to his own destruction.

When, we may now ask, did the Hebrews first learn of these legends? Was it not during their Captivity, which dated from about 586–538 B.C.? So it has often been surmised. But there are a number of grounds for rejecting this view. We know from the biblical account—and we would in any case assume—that the Babylonian Captivity was a time of great heart-searching and recall to the basic principles of faith. There had been a marked tendency to compromise with the rulers, and even to neglect the traditional worship. At such a time the compilers and guardians of the sacred lore would have taken steps to see that nothing but orthodox and accredited material were placed on record. While they might well have corrected and rewritten the story of the Creation and the Flood, it is unlikely that they would have chosen that particular moment to incorporate such stories from outside. In view of the extreme exclusiveness of Hebrew tradition, the contemporary popularity of such stories in their original form would have been a reason for rejecting rather than for accepting them. The fact that they are embodied in the Old Testament at all suggests that they were already part of the traditional sacred writings. Biblical scholars now hold that the early books of the Bible are based upon sources which not merely date from as early as 1000–900 B.C., but represent the first written record of an oral tradition of greater antiquity. These sources, three in number, are known as P., J., and E. Source P. hardly concerns us. It is so-called because it forms a kind of Priest's Code, with details of ritual and ecclesiastical law as practised at the end of the Babylonian captivity. The other sources are distinguished one from the other by the different words they employ for God: J. calls Him Yahve and E. Elohim, a word in the plural number. Both represent accounts of Hebrew history and religion from the point of view of what we may call the common man. As both J. and E. contain distinct versions of the Creation and the Flood stories, and as both are thought to date from a period prior to the Babylonian exile (J. certainly does in the opinion of most scholars), the case may be considered proved.[1]

What we may further suggest, though without the same show of proof, is that these particular stories were among the elements of Sumerian and Babylonian tradition brought to Palestine by Abraham and his followers. There exists incidentally a tablet in the dialect known as Harrian, which was that spoken at Harran, recording a version of the Flood story in which the hero is called not Shamash-napishtim but Nah-molet. Now the name Noah, which bears a resemblance to no other name in the Bible, may well have been derived from at least the first syllable of the "Harrian" name.[2] We have at least proof here that the story was circulating in a place with which Abraham and his family were closely identified over many years. Nor, on this basis, would the insertion of Ararat—the nearest high mountain after the Taurus peaks—be difficult to explain.

Code and Covenant

We have spoken of Abraham as the transmitter of some of the world's great myths; we have now to speak of him as the transmitter of some of the great legislative principles in history. The Code of Hammurabi formed, as we suggested above, a compilation of various legal codes or customs in force among the peoples whom the great king of Babylon wished, after subduing, to unite. The task of co-ordination and collation must have engaged the attention of a large number of experts, working first in the field and later in groups. Whenever the ancient world speaks of an achievement as due to one man, we may suspect the united labour of a number of expert assistants.

The Code of Hammurabi represents a great triumph of committee-work. Among the legal systems to which particular attention must have been paid was that of Sumeria, where law and litigation had already reached a high degree of development and complexity. Every plea and counter-plea was scrupulously recorded on tablets, and judicial procedure was established on a rigid basis. Now when the Code of Hammurabi was rediscovered and translated early in the present century, the extraordinary resemblance between its provisions and those of the Mosaic Code or Book of the Covenant became immediately apparent. Many of the individual items were identical, while the wording of many more was similar. In view of the notoriety acquired by the Mosaic edict of "an eye for an eye and a tooth for a tooth", which Christ singled out expressly as summing up the spirit of the Old Dispensation, it is interesting to quote the

[1] The isolation of the three accounts from the material available has been a triumph of analytical scholarship.

[2] See an article in the *Journal of the Royal Asiatic Society*, 1925, by Father Burrows.

literal rendering of Hammurabi's law on the subject: "If a man destroy the eye of another man, they shall destroy his eye. If the man knock out the tooth of a man of his own rank, they shall knock out his tooth." That the Mosaic Code should owe nothing to that of Hammurabi on the ritualistic side is hardly surprising. It is on the social side that the resemblance is most impressive.

These indisputable similarities dispose of the view that the Code was invented by Moses. No legal code was "invented" by anyone. Moses himself must have gone to a good deal of trouble to co-ordinate the laws already in force among the tribes under his leadership. His work did not stop there, nor was such co-ordination its most important aspect. What he chiefly sought to do was to put his followers in mind of their old traditions, which their prolonged sojourn in Egypt had rendered dim.[1] He himself had already had a taste of desert life among the Midianites. Much of his efforts, therefore, would have been directed to a revival, compatible with the new conditions, of the legal customs of that period in Hebrew history in which the tribes were, as then, on the march. During his journey from Ur to Harran, and from Harran to Palestine, Abraham had maintained order by means of the legal customs in which he had been brought up. Changes appropriate to a desert life must naturally have been introduced: nevertheless "there is in the Old Testament concrete evidence for the fact that the tent-law of (Abraham's) family was actually the law of Sumer".[2] If, in other words, Moses had drawn up his Code of Laws before reaching the Promised Land, he—a man "learned in the wisdom of the Egyptians"—could not possibly have compiled the Book of the Covenant, as described in *Exodus*, in language reminiscent of the laws of Hammurabi: he would more likely have been tempted to introduce elements from Egyptian law.[3] In bringing the tribes to a better understanding of the God of Abraham—a task which, in spite of the miracles of preservation already experienced by them, he apparently found extremely difficult, judging from their inherent tendency to idolatry—Moses would have sought to revive as much as possible the law to which Abraham had conformed all his life.[4] The law in question was that of Hammurabi. Although Hammurabi's Code remained authoritative in Mesopotamia for several centuries

[1] See especially Martin Buber's *Moses*, chapter on "The Sabbath". It must be remembered likewise that the stay in Egypt lasted probably about 400 years.

[2] Woolley: *Abraham*, p. 183.

[3] The same argument disposes of the view that the Hebrews acquired their law from the inhabitants of Palestine among whom they had come to settle. Palestine had long been part of the Egyptian empire.

[4] For further evidence that Abraham acted according to Sumerian law, particularly in the case of Hagar, see Woolley: *Abraham*, Chapter V.

after the death of Moses, we cannot imagine that it was assimilated by the Hebrews at a later period. As in the case of the Creation and Flood legends, a later borrowing was incompatible with the desire of devout editors to preserve, not to say insulate, authentic Patriarchal traditions from those likely to exert a direct threat to their purity.[1]

Earlier in this chapter we showed that as the domination of Babylon by Hammurabi and his successors became complete, the old Sumerian culture gave place to that of the conquering people. Thus the language of Sumeria gradually assumed the status of a classical language, to be studied in schools for its "cultural" value, as we study Greek and Latin. In one sphere only it remained alive. The temple services of Babylonia were performed not in contemporary speech but in Sumerian: a practice resembling that adopted by the Roman Church in its performance of the Mass, and also by the Moslem use of classical Arabic for religious practice. Such Sumerian religious literature as has survived suggests that its *corpus* must originally have been immense, perhaps as great in proportion as that of the Hindus, who are quantitatively the most religious of peoples. Much of the Sumerian scriptures consist of magical lore and treatises on demonology: there is a great deal of such matter on the tablets from the library of Ashurbanipal. Of all the literature that has survived, nothing is more interesting than the series of poems best described as penitential psalms. Composed in Sumerian, as was to be expected, these psalms might well be included in the Christian biblical canon without exciting the least suspicion as to their origin. In form they exhibit that "parallelism of numbers", peculiar to hymnography, which seems to have first been employed in the hymns of the early Pyramid Texts. Breasted maintains that the Hebrews borrowed this technique (which suggests an antiphonal mode of performance) direct from the Egyptians. It is equally possible that the Hebrews derived it from the Babylonians, whose religious temperament was much closer in spirit. Although not all these psalms are strictly penitential, the themes of abasement before God and the weight of sinfulness are those which prompt the psalmist to most eloquent expression:

> Mankind is perverted and has no judgment:
> Of all men who are alive, who knows anything? . . .
> O Lord, do not cast aside thy servant:
> He is cast into the mire, take his hand!

[1] An example of a prohibition all the more necessary in view of the influence of foreign practice was that concerning images. The Egyptian practice of representing their gods must have been a perpetual temptation to the Hebrews: hence the second commandment of the Decalogue with its absolute ban upon image-making.

The sin which I have sinned, turn to mercy!
The iniquity which I have committed, let the wind carry away!
My many transgressions tear off like a garment!
My god, my sins are seven times seven . . . etc.

Such utterances, even in a bald translation, are perceived to differ radically from the "mock" penitential rhymes from *The Book of the Dead*. The mood prevailing is one of spiritual anguish. Except in rare instances, *The Book of the Dead* is an anthology of religious humbug, like the rules of a celestial game of forfeits. From what we know of Babylonian social life we may also be reassured on another point: these psalms were not simply a verbal channel for the off-loading of the individual's emotions. Babylonian "sin catalogues", wherewith the individual worshipper took regular soundings of his spiritual condition, have survived. Moreover, the theme of penitence was carried into everyday life. Certain days in the year, for instance, were set aside for the purposes of penitential reflection. The word *shabattu*, which applied to these particular days, was also applied to the middle of the month. Four other days, the 7th, 14th, 21st, and 28th, significantly separated by intervals of seven,[1] were regarded as *dies irae* on which the high officials from the king downwards refrained from carrying out their normal duties. The word *shabattu*, from which is derived Sabbath, carries the meaning of "calming of the heart". The notion survives, with a difference in orientation, in the statement in *Genesis* that "God rested the seventh day and hallowed it". In *Exodus* xxxi, 17, we find a phrase suggesting that, after the creation of the world, God "rested and breathed freely". "Calming of the heart" may also mean propitiating the regularly-incurred anger of the gods, as if every so often they called to mind their remorse at having created man. In borrowing the word *shabattu*, the Hebrews proceeded to apply it to precisely those days of the week which the Babylonians regarded as "cursed". Significantly enough, the Hebrew conception of the Sabbath was altogether more serene than the Babylonian; and this may explain why, in seeking a word for it, they took over (perhaps unconsciously) that which applied in Babylon to a specially holy day. For the mid-month festival was that of the full moon, the day on which Nannar or Terah appeared in the highest perfection of beauty.

Whether we shall ever possess enough insight into Babylonian psychology to discover why, and how early, certain days were regarded as of bad omen (or, to use our modern shirking word, unlucky) is more than doubtful. Like many other peoples, the

[1] Cf. also the term "sabbatical year". A relic of the same notion may perhaps be found in the expression "seventh heaven".

Babylonians held seven to be a sacred number. If, as is possible, they were the first to believe the world to have been created in seven days, whatever they may have meant by "day", the isolation of every seventh day in the month as an occasion for national humiliation suggests the commemoration of an event of cosmic significance. Nor would this hypothesis be nullified if it were proved, as has often been suggested, that the idea of seven-day creation was the consequence rather than the cause of the universal veneration for this number.

As the Babylonians were the originators, so far as we know, of the lunar month of twenty-eight days,[1] it seems clear that the black days were those connected with the phases of the moon. But we should need to penetrate the depths of their minds, as we have succeeded in penetrating the ruins of their houses, in order to understand why they insisted upon punctuating their lives with such intervals of self-castigation.[2] Such a tendency may be the result of the growing rigidity of custom, which seems to cast an atmosphere of solemnity over that which it no longer, or only half, understands. Certain persons, in England at least, deplore the tendency towards the "continental Sunday", forgetting that there has likewise been a tendency towards something equally removed in spirit from the original "Sunday", namely the kind of dismal festival represented on occasion by the Scottish Sabbath. Thus the Babylonian days of abasement may be as much a perversion of early moon festivals, as the Hebrew Sabbath of the New Testament—for the violation of which Christ was reproached by the Jews—was a perversion of the original Sabbath introduced or revived by Moses. For we cannot help observing the oddity of the situation described in *John* v, where, so far as healing the sick is concerned, it is apparently permissible for the angel to "trouble the waters", but blasphemy for Christ to trouble the Sabbath.

Just as it is impossible to invent a legal code, so it is impossible to invent a religion. We constantly hear of new religions, especially in countries like the United States where there is a good deal of unexpended female mental energy, but such gospels are sure to reveal, upon examination, familiar and even banal characteristics. A man may decide to worship a colour, but that was done long ago in Syria, where a sect still worships the colour blue; or himself, but that was done by a Roman Emperor. In our account of Abraham we have failed of our purpose if we have given the impression that

[1] They were also the first to divide the day into twelve hours, and the hour into sixty minutes, though they also experimented with an hour divided into thirty minutes.

[2] Mircea Eliade, in his book *Le Mythe de l'Eternel Retour*, maintains that "*la durée des nations exigeait la répétition périodique d'actes cosmogoniques et que tout sacrifice répete le sacrifice initial et coïncide avec lui*".

he personally invented the faith which, for the next two thousand years, goes by the name of Judaism. He did nothing of the kind. "The men whom we call founders of religions are not really concerned with founding a religion, but wish to establish a human world that is subject to divine truth: to unite the way of the earth with that of heaven."[1] That is a statement the importance of which, for reasons at which we hinted in our first chapter, has tended to be obscured in the Western world. It remains the plain truth about the oriental world, the key to its spiritual mentality. Except in very rare instances, the oriental mind does not argue about the existence of a divine realm. Such a realm is accepted as a fact. If there is any argument at all, it is concerned with the degree to which the natural or material world falls short of this realm in respect of truth and reality.

In the light of these considerations, it is no less misleading to describe Moses as the true founder of Judaism than so to describe Abraham. Like Zoroaster or Buddha, both Abraham and Moses were engaged in establishing or re-establishing the "divine connection". Connection, in both their cases, involved also connection with the past. They innovated to conserve; the one to keep his family, the other his tribe, together. This is the explanation of the so-called Covenants (*berith*) which Abraham and Moses, and later Josiah, are reported to have concluded with Yahve. Such covenants are sometimes described on the analogy of contracts or even political agreements. The Jews were free at last from the authority of Pharaoh. In the desert they began to exhibit a tendency towards anarchy, as people suddenly released from political despotism are inclined to do. The other form of rule available to them was that of the desert wanderer, the Bedouin, whom they had already encountered in their brush with the Amalekites, kept at bay so long as held Moses aloft his staff (*Exodus* xvii, 8).

The object of the Covenant was to assert the authority of a different form of rule, that of Yahve Himself. In another of its aspects the Covenant was a way of establishing that permanent relationship between God and man first announced in *Genesis* after the survival of Noah, and of which the symbol was the bow in the clouds. If the Covenant needed later to be renewed, as was often the case, that was due to man's repeated failure to realize the implications of such a relationship. Such a human-divine pledge was not unique. The more we study the Archaic culture the more we discover that Covenants between man and God form part of the traditional mythology of ancient races. Covenants can be made with the devil too; we have yet to see whether the modern world's

[1] Martin Buber: *Moses* (1946), p. 82.

covenant with science and technology is not of this diabolical character.[1]

A study of man's early conceptions of good and evil cannot ignore, in discussing the history of Israel,[2] certain arguments tending to diminish the spiritual insight attributed to the Old Testament Jews. In philosophy we cannot slur over difficulties or ignore criticism: these must resolutely be faced. It has been said that Yahve, instead of being the invisible, unrepresentable God who first disclosed His true identity to Moses, was in fact a god already well known in the district where He was first encountered. The Sinai peninsula, it is true, shows evidence of volcanic activity of, geologically speaking, recent occurrence. Such phenomena inevitably gave rise to notions of the presence of spirits or local deities. Yahve, it is held, was a fire or volcano god. And Moses' first genuine encounter with Yahve took place on the mountain where He permanently resided.

This theory is extremely plausible. Even if true, it is not necessarily damaging. The naming of a god may originally have been as accidental, or as little to the purpose, as the naming of a person, though admittedly this is not likely among people to whom naming was a serious matter. But, as far as we know, the name Yahve was not attached to any god honoured on Sinai.[3] Like most volcanic regions, Sinai could presumably boast of a volcano god, and such a god was bound to receive homage from local inhabitants. The Hebrews were neither local inhabitants nor, according to our argument so far, did they regard Yahve as an "attached" god. He temporarily inhabited Sinai as he temporarily inhabited the Burning Bush, which, because of its momentary inmate, "was not consumed"—and indeed as He had temporarily inhabited the desert spring perceived by Abraham's maid Hagar (*Genesis* xvi, 7, 13). This momentary investment of natural objects proved not so much His kinship with ordinary nature gods, whose essence was to remain in one place, as His absolute difference from them. By taking up positions all along the line, as it were, He made mock of their fixity.

If Mount Sinai harboured a god, as we have suggested, what was he called? We do not know. But we do know that a tribe called the Kenites inhabited this region, or, since they may have been a wandering people, frequently visited it. This tribe probably helped to work the neighbouring copper mines; some of them were ore-

[1] It is worth remarking that the outstanding characters of the Bible do not mix with the gods. Humanity and divinity are always separate. The reference to giants on earth in *Genesis* vi, 4, is obviously an interpolation.

[2] The meaning of Israel is "God rules". Cf. Islam, "submission (to God)".

[3] See Montgomery: *Arabia and the Bible* (1934), p. 10, and Buber: *The Prophetic Faith* (1949), p. 25.

smelters or travelling smiths. Their god may well have been that of Sinai, whose activity on a grand scale so closely resembled their own. We cannot suppose that Moses' wife, a Midianite, had not spoken to him of the mountain god of this district. The subject is bound to have arisen in a household in which theological discussions must have been frequent. And when her father Jethro visits Moses at Sinai and is informed (*Exodus* xviii) of what Yahve had done for the people of Israel, his exclamation, "Now I know that Yahve is greater than all the gods," resembles the episode in *Genesis* (xiv), in which Melchizedek makes a similar declaration to Abraham. In the first case, the god is called El'Elyon, the name of Melchizedek's god, for which Abraham deliberately substitutes the "Most High God" of his fathers. In the second episode, the word Elohim is used, which, as explained above, is a word meaning gods as well as God. Now the statement of Jethro (who is here described as a priest) is sometimes taken to suggest not merely that he attributed Israel's fortune to the bounty of his own god, before whose sanctuary the company were encamped, but that thereafter Moses and his people were converted to this same god, whose name was Yahve. What happened was precisely the contrary, as the later history of Israel proved. Both incidents describe the kind of Covenant, human as well as divine, whereby Yahve became through His representative the God of peoples other than Israel, until in the time of the prophets He was pronounced a God universal in both power and appeal: in short, a God not of Nature but of History.

The Prophets

After wandering in the desert for as long as forty years—a period which, though apparently excessive even for a heterogeneous group, might well have elapsed in the case of nomads—Canaan was finally conquered, and an era of settlement followed. The history of this settlement, with its disturbances and upheavals no less serious than those of the desert trek, must briefly be passed over. Israel was governed first by judges and then by kings, of whom Saul, David, and Solomon were the most distinguished, the last two being men of unusual vision and wisdom. Nothing is recorded of either Saul or David outside the Bible, but part of the *Book of Kings* has been confirmed from inscriptions found in 1935 at Tel Ad-Duweir. After Solomon's death in or about 937 B.C., Israel was convulsed with civil war. As a result, the country split into two kingdoms, a northern kingdom of Ephraim with its capital at Samaria, and a southern kingdom of Judah of which the capital remained at Jerusalem. That such social unrest was partly due to the extravagance of the great kings, particularly Solomon, is very probable.

We learn that the Temple took seven years and immense quantities of material to erect, and that Solomon thereafter devoted thirteen years to building himself a palace. Public works of this kind are usually either an attempted palliative for labour troubles or a very potent cause of them. When finally the Egyptian Pharaoh Sheshante invaded Judah, sacked the capital, and seized most of Solomon's accumulated gold, it may well have seemed that God was executing divine judgment on His people.

At this critical stage in Israel's history, something of the old guidance was required. The religion of the Patriarchs stood in need of preaching afresh. Under the kings there had been wealth, wisdom, and (if we accept David as the author of some at least of the Psalms) art. But neither David nor Solomon had been disinterested followers of Yahve. Their reputation had been immense, their personal example less impressive.[1] Only their great power had enabled them to maintain their position as leaders. Such power was evident in the case of Saul and Solomon, but in the case of David there was something more than power, namely genius. After Ikhnaton, and much more vividly, David is the ancient world's great "individual". His character is too subtly and yet frankly depicted to be that of any but a living person. (To cast doubt upon his authenticity by pointing to the lack of evidence for it outside the Bible is to forget what an important testimony the Bible itself provided, as archaeologists are discovering; it is like questioning a series of facts because it is nowhere mentioned outside the *Encyclopædia Britannica*.) Who, then, were to be the keepers of the moral conscience of Israel? In whom, to put the question in the form appropriate to our enquiry, did the development of the moral sense in man seem most clearly perceptible?

The word Prophet or *Nabi* does not necessarily mean one who foretells the future. It means one who "announces", a spokesman of news. Such is likewise the meaning of the Greek word *prophetes*. If we bear this sense of the word in mind, we perceive the error of asserting that at a moment of disruption in Israel's life the prophets appeared. They did not appear. They reappeared. Naturally, like everything else that reappears, they did so in a new form, a form appropriate to the time. Instead of being accredited leaders of men, they were usually persons who, with nothing but a burning conviction to sustain them, arraigned the authorities for their wickedness and blindness to facts. Sometimes they were men of family and substance. Sometimes, poor to the point of destitution, they roamed the wilderness, where the reverberation of their cries

[1] Solomon, for example, did not scruple to build altars and temples to alien gods, such as Astarte and Chemosh.

symbolized the heedlessness that so often greeted their message. Sometimes they were men whose personalities we can easily understand: occasionally they remain mere mouthpieces of vatic denunciation. For in their message we observe a resumption of the theme of oppression of the weak by the strong at a point where the Egyptian sages and such isolated figures as Hammurabi tended to leave off. These men are neither intellectual critics nor the earliest preachers of doctrinal socialism. They are self-elevated public figures enraged by social injustice. With no men earlier and possibly only with Socrates later can they bear comparison.

The most important fact about the prophets, and one which tends to be obscured if we regard them simply as radical spokesmen for the proletariat, is that they claimed divine inspiration: "The spirit of the Lord is upon me." In the ancient and to a great extent in the modern oriental world, the idea of possession by spirits is nothing remarkable. It does not happen to everyone, but to some it may happen by nature. The Holy Man is not a curiosity; the village idiot or his equivalent must be accepted as such. At what point in the history of the Western world the capacity for "seeing visions" and speaking with tongues (i.e. permitting another to speak on one's behalf) became atrophied, only manifesting itself during religious revivals or in attenuated form as aesthetic inspiration, we cannot say. If T. S. Eliot is right to suppose that a certain form of disciplined dreaming common in Dante's time has ceased within the last six or seven hundred years,[1] we cannot wonder that the last few thousand years should have witnessed a decline in susceptibility to other forms of visionary experience, disciplined or otherwise. No study of the oriental mind can ignore the fact of supra-sensible experience. To some thinkers—and Aldous Huxley in his distinguished book *The Perennial Philosophy* counts himself among them—the norm of oriental speculation is simply the mystical grasp of a transcendent order of being, leaving "philosophy" in the Western sense to explore the foothills of knowledge. If you deny the possibility of such knowledge you must at least take upon yourself to explain how the oriental mind, which does not lack subtlety, should have expended so much energy towards its attainment. Even if the oriental mystic, or any mystic for that matter, is under a misapprehension concerning the nature of this form of communion, it would be interesting to lay bare the causes of such a radical departure from common reason. Without pursuing this question, which we shall treat in detail later, we must accept the fact not merely that the prophets claimed to be divine spokesmen,

[1] See *Dante* (1925).

but that they were the most distinguished, judging from contemporary records, of a group of persons gifted with similar insight.

In almost every language the word for "spirit" and the word for "breath" are, if not identical, related: *pneuma*, *spiritus*, and in Hebrew *ruah*. A prophet—or prophetess, for there are women spokesmen or announcers too, especially in Israel—is one through whom the breath of divine knowledge blows, and whose words are consequently "inspired", or drawn from the reservoir of spirit which is God. From the earliest times we have evidence that such inspiration can be of several kinds, only one being truly authentic: for falsity and fraud are often to be distinguished by variety. There is the prophet uniquely and consciously persuaded of his vocation to deliver a message. There is the man who, without proper understanding, is made a vehicle for such information: Balaam was evidently such a person. And finally there is the "false prophet", common enough in Israel, whose message, whether understood or not, is wholly mischievous. Common to all is the breath, the afflatus, that upon which the message is borne. A true prophet breathes weighted eloquence. A false prophet is merely a windbag.

According to Mohammed, no great prophet has ever lived who did not begin life as a shepherd. Amos was a shepherd. Living in the days of Uzziah, King of Judah, he described how, though "neither a prophet nor a prophet's son but a herdman and a gatherer of sycamore fruit", the Lord "took him as he followed the flock", and said to him, "Go prophesy unto my people Israel." Having visited the town of Bethel, he there "sat at the gate" and poured forth a fierce denunciation of its citizens and of all Israel for its extravagance, exploitation, and neglect of God. His words are all the more effective in that he preserves the imagery of his original calling, "Woe to them that are at ease in Zion . . . that lie upon beds of ivory, and stretch themselves upon their couches, and eat the lambs out of the flock, and the calves out of the midst of the stall: that chant to the sound of the viol and invent to themselves instruments of music, like David." And later, more bitterly and to the point, "Thus saith the Lord, As the shepherd taketh out of the mouth of the lion two legs or a piece of an ear, so shall the children of Israel be taken out that dwell in Samaria in the corner of a bed in Damascus on a couch."

This attack upon those who "swallow up the needy, want to make the poor of the land to fast", and who "falsify the balances by deceit", is a great deal more violent in its effect than the only other surviving piece of denunciatory literature with which it may be compared, namely the Egyptian story of the Eloquent Peasant. The peasant reminds the authorities of their duties. "Thou art the balances," he cries to the Grand Vizier; but he does not suggest that this instrument shall be struck from the ruler's hand. He wishes it to remain there. Speaking on behalf of Yahve, Amos threatens with utter destruction the society that has always understood itself to be the "peculiar people" or "treasure" of the Lord. Two remarks in *Amos*, viii, make this abundantly clear. "The end is come upon my people Israel," God is made to say. "I will not again pass by them any more." Thus the very hymns and psalms of the temple "shall be howlings in that day", and, more dreadful still, the means whereby Israel's deliverance was originally effected shall be turned against an ungrateful and heedless people. "It shall rise up wholly as a flood, and it shall be cast out and drowned as by the flood of Egypt."[1]

If the message of Amos were purely destructive, it would deserve no more than passing attention. But his prophecy, together with that of another prophet roughly contemporary with him, Hosea, seemed to have been justified in the event. "They that sow the wind shall reap the whirlwind," Hosea proclaimed. Ephraim and Judah were soon at war one with the other. Feeling herself threatened, Judah sought aid from Assyria. The latter country sent an army which not merely routed Judah's enemies, but, determined to exploit its success, turned upon Judah herself and swept up to the gates of Jerusalem, almost capturing the city. Even so, such apparent fulfilment of the words of the prophets was not the most important part of their mission. In the work of Amos we observe a development of thought concerning God which reveals the prophets as initiators of a new stage in the moral consciousness of mankind. Having denounced Israel and threatened its virtual extinction as a nation, Amos reminds his people of something which, in their conceit, they had tended to ignore. By establishing a Covenant with Israel, God had singled them out as His chosen people. At the same time this choice laid upon them particular responsibilities. Not merely must they deserve the trust placed in them, but they must realize that they are not the only people in whom God is interested. "The whole earth," He declares, "is mine." He even taunts them for supposing that, by delivering Israel from the house of bondage, He was undertaking something absolutely unique: "Are you not as children of the Ethiopians unto me, O children of Israel?" saith the Lord. "Have not I brought up Israel out of the land of Egypt? And"—to drive home the irony—"the Philistines from Caphtor, and the Syrians from Kir? . . . For, lo, . . . I will sift the house of Israel among all nations, like as corn is sifted in a sieve" (ix, 7, 9).

[1] A threat repeated in ix, 5.

Such is the climax of a story which, beginning with the compact with Melchizedek and Jethro, ends only with the Christ's injunction to preach the gospel to every creature. The gradual development and widening vision to which the Old Testament, with all its inconsistencies, bears steady and convincing witness, has appeared to some critics to suggest a series of accidents from which the world faith of Christianity emerged more by chance than by design. Leaving aside the question of the "truth" of this or any other system of belief, the onus rests upon such critics to suggest some other way in which a universal faith can emerge than by its gradual dissemination from small beginnings. The kingdom of heaven is not to be advertised by a mailed circular: its origin is a grain of mustard seed.

The point of view of Amos and Hosea was further developed by a remarkable man who personally witnessed the Assyrian assault on Jerusalem. This was Isaiah, the author of at least thirty-nine chapters of the book bearing that title. Sharing the opinion of his fellow-prophets concerning the unworthiness of Israel, he sees in her possible destruction or defeat a means whereby her iniquities may be chastened. If the God of Israel is a universal God, He will "use" Assyria and indeed any other nation to work out His purpose. Thus a new attitude to history is born. To the Egyptians, Pharaoh's enemies not merely deserve defeat but are doomed inevitably to suffer it. Death and destruction, which we saw to exist only for the enemy, were invented expressly for such as challenged the power of the sacred descendant of Horus. To Isaiah, who is the first of a series of such seers, this attitude is one of childish pride. The children of Israel must resist the national enemy within as well as without. Justice at home is an obligation no less than resistance to foreign enemies, whose cupidity has usually been inflamed by the prospect of looting a disordered and unruly kingdom. So Isaiah, having advised King Hezekiah to resist Sennacherib to the best of his ability, forthwith turns upon his own nation with words that express for all time the *saeva indignatio* of a just man. "What mean ye that ye beat my people to pieces and grind the faces of the poor? . . . Woe unto them that join house to house, that lay field to field, till there be no place. . . . Woe unto them that decree unrighteous decrees to turn aside the needy from judgment, and to take away the right from the poor of my people, that widows may be their prey and that they may rob the fatherless!" The traditional worship, the regular offering up of sacrifice, even the orthodox prayers, are not sufficient. "I am full of the burnt offerings of rams and the fat of fed beasts. Your appointed feasts my soul hateth. . . . And when ye spread forth your hands (in prayer) I will hide mine eyes from you; yea, when ye make many prayers I will not hear; your hands are full of blood."

Although he was the most eloquent of the prophets and perhaps of all his eloquent race, Isaiah did not exhaust his listeners with mere diatribes. He issued them with precise instructions as to what to do to be saved. "Seek judgment (meaning, see that justice is done), relieve the oppressed, judge the fatherless, plead for the widow." But these precepts, vigorous though they are, do not form the most original part of his message. Like his attitude to the political struggles of his day, this message is essentially historical. Suddenly switching his attention from the present, he peers into a future which, though distant, is not to be regarded as inconceivably remote. The troubles of Israel and of Israel's neighbours, which occupy the whole of his attention, are realized to be too deep-seated for any immediate cure. Only the "gathering up" of history in an event both in and out of time would herald the end of discord, lust, and war. Such an event is the inconceivable (and therefore unconceived) birth in human form of the hitherto imageless, unrepresentable, God of the Fathers. The climax of the "shewings" of God from that at Sinai onwards would logically be His actual appearance upon earth, his taking human flesh, His Incarnation. And as the successive revelations had hitherto been made to the holy and privileged people, so the birth of this Saviour would naturally spring from the "stem of Jesse". Except for the brief passage of Ipuwer, the meaning of which must always remain obscure, the following words are the first of their kind to be uttered:

"Behold, a virgin shall conceive, and bear a son, and shall call his name Immanuel. . . .[1] For unto us a child is born, and the government shall be upon his shoulder, and his name shall be called Wonderful, Counsellor, the Mighty God, the Everlasting Father, the Prince of Peace. . . . And there shall come forth a rod out of the stem of Jesse. . . . And the spirit of the Lord shall rest upon him, the spirit of wisdom and understanding, the spirit and might, the spirit of knowledge and the fear of the Lord. . . . With righteousness shall he judge the poor, and reprove with equity for the meek of the earth. . . . And righteousness shall be the girdle of his loins, and faithfulness the girdle of his reins. The wolf also shall dwell with the lamb, and the leopard shall lie down with the kid, and the calf and the young lion and the fatling together; and a little child shall lead them. . . . And they shall beat their swords into ploughshares and their spears into pruning-hooks. Nation shall not lift up sword against nation, neither shall they learn war any more."

It is difficult to judge with what measure of understanding the

[1] See p. 34.

Israeli royal house, the priesthood, and finally the people, whose needs were here for the first time declared, received this impassioned prophecy. The Bible—and in some generations such as Puritan England the Old Testament in particular—has become a sacred book for millions, as well as a book respected by millions more. Yet orthodox Christians would do well to reflect upon the explosive material assembled within that richly-bound volume, which, reposing so often in the quiet of a church or on an obscure bookshelf, assumes an outward appearance of innocuousness. If we were to bind together the most violent political denunciations of the rich and powerful, the fiercest satires upon conventional morality, the most penetrating commentaries upon the vanity of life, together with the best poetic expressions of our civilization and its wittiest maxims, we should not have collected an anthology one-tenth part as disrupting of complacency as that eclectic handbook of the Old Dispensation. We may wonder how the prophets managed to escape with their lives, and how their message, with its inflammable content, did not meet with drastic censorship or even total suppression.

The wonder is increased by a reading of the message of Jeremiah. In 639 Josiah had ascended to the throne of Judah. His reign is of particular importance for two reasons. As a result of the preaching of the prophets the priesthood was becoming gravely concerned about the condition of the orthodox faith, which was in danger of both pollution and neglect. It was time to return to first principles, or in other words to renew the Covenant of Moses. The discovery in the Temple either by chance or of set purpose of a scroll purporting to have been written by Moses himself caused a profound sensation throughout the country, and marks the beginning of the deliberate putting together of the sacred writings that now form the Pentateuch.[1] But, in spite of Josiah's reforming zeal, the political fortunes of Israel reached an extremely low ebb. The power of Assyria admittedly disappeared with the fall of Nineveh in 612 B.C.; but one enemy soon gave place to another, and Josiah himself was killed at Megiddo in an attempt to stem an Egyptian invasion. The next threat came from Babylon, whose king, Nebuchadnezzar, twice attacked Jerusalem, first placing a puppet king called Zedekiah on the throne, and later, when the puppet sought to be something more by pulling strings on his own, deposed Zedekiah, reduced Jerusalem to ruins, and deported most of its inhabitants to Babylon. The so-called Babylonian Captivity followed.[2]

[1] Greek: "Five Rolls", the first five books of the Old Testament.

[2] This deportation had been preceded by a transfer of 10,000 Jews to Babylon after Nebuchadnezzar's first attack on Jerusalem.

This was Jeremiah's opportunity. His mission had begun immediately prior to the Exile. Declining to sustain public morale in the orthodox sense, he set himself up as the scourge of an incorrigibly idolatrous people. Like the first Isaiah, he declared that the domination of Babylon must not merely come about but should be endured as the will of Yahve. The Jews, he maintained, had brought this terrible fate upon themselves. If the rules of justice had been observed, if internal oppression and corruption had not increased, Yahve would surely have come to the aid of His Holy People; but (the passage reminds one of God's attitude to the inhabitants of Sodom) "Run ye to and fro through the streets of Jerusalem, and see now, and know, and seek in the broad places thereof, if ye can find a man, if there be any that executeth judgment, that seeketh the truth, and I will pardon it." At a time of acute national crisis, when futile recrimination is usually silenced, Jeremiah insisted upon the priority of justice and righteousness even over national safety. As a reward for his frankness he was pilloried on a high gate, consigned to a filthy dungeon, and all but put to death; but the king, reluctant to add the reputation of martyr to that of prophet, stayed his execution. On forcing the gates of Jerusalem, Nebuchadnezzar found this reluctant ally under protective arrest in the king's palace. Zedekiah he executed; but he spared Jeremiah, nor did the latter follow his people into exile.

In the days before the siege, as part of his stock-in-trade, Jeremiah had worn a wooden yoke round his neck, symbolizing the fate due to overtake Jerusalem. In old age he wrote a series of *Lamentations* in which that fate was mourned in sombre, though magnificent, poetry. Just as his exiled countrymen were required by their taskmasters to "sing one of the songs of 'Sion'," which they did in the superb psalm beginning "By the waters of Babylon", so Jeremiah, an exile in the ruins of his own home, was prompted to dwell upon the same theme, but with even greater penetration and therefore increased disillusion. The question of the Egyptian Misanthrope is here raised afresh, as it is raised by the discerning in every age: "Righteous thou art, O Lord, when I plead with thee, but"—and this is the fundamental issue between man and God—"*let us talk of thy judgments: Wherefore doth the way of the wicked prosper?* Wherefore are all they happy that deal treacherously?" This theme receives its most profound treatment in the *Book of Job*, which must have been composed about 450 B.C.[1]

"If I forget thee, O Jerusalem, let my right hand forget her cunning," was the burden of the earliest among the exiles. But the

[1] Some fragments of Babylonian literature on the same subject are thought to have influenced this composition. The protagonist is Tabi-utal-Enlil, a ruler of Nippur.

conditions that made it difficult "to sing the Lord's Song in a strange land" made it easy to grow lax in religious observance, or, more destructive of communal morale, to "go whoring after strange gods". Of the latter, Babylon had a large variety. The Babylonian Exile, though shorter and on the whole less burdensome than the Egyptian, proved in many ways more damaging to a people united by a faith born of bondage and persecution, yet gifted with powers of assimilation above that of any other people. In these circumstances the mission of the prophet proved more important than ever. Ezekiel, one of the few prophets to have been a priest (or so he declares), set out to continue the work of Jeremiah. Unlike the latter, he knew in direct fashion the bitterness and demoralization of exile, having been among the first of the Jewish deportees to Babylon. True to the *Nabi* character, he describes how he was "among the captives by the river of Chebar in the land of the Chaldeans" when the hand of the Lord was set upon him, and he saw, through the opening of the heavens, "visions of God". These visions assumed many strange forms. Anyone who has visited the country in which Ezekiel was obliged to toil can detect in much that he wrote a hallucinatory quality born of long spells of exposure to intense heat, whereby an impression is obtained of the sky giving forth images as he records them in the opening verses.[1]

Unlike Jeremiah, Ezekiel concludes upon a message of hope. If the children of Israel will renounce their politicial divisions (especially that into the two kingdoms of Ephraim and Judah), if they will cease "defiling themselves with their idols", and other "detestable things", Yahve will cleanse them, and they shall once again be His people.

If, as the Jewish people have thought, the prophetic books of the Old Testament do not reach fulfilment in the New Testament, their successive message—for it is one message delivered by many mouths—reveals a progress in spiritual discernment, a deepening grasp of the nature of God, to which no other tradition, religious, literary, or historical, can be compared. If they do not anticipate a Saviour, or at least the Saviour who was Jesus of Nazareth, they may well anticipate each other: the torch of enlightenment is not merely handed on but, as it is grasped afresh, seems to grow brighter. They may not, if you like, prophesy the supreme Prophet; but, in the person of the so-called Second or Deutero Isaiah, they prophesy the consummation of Prophecy. For it is in the work of

[1] A later writer can often bring to life a passage of past literature, or at least render it still more moving. This is the case with T. S. Eliot's poem *Ash Wednesday*, in Part II of which the valley of Ezekiel forms the background. Ezekiel is said to have been an epileptic: but the suggestion may be based upon the modern assumption that the capacity to see visions is usually the result of illness.

this latter writer, whose identity we do not know, that the true nature of the God of the Fathers is apprehended in the purest light. Ezekiel, as we have seen, concluded on a note rarely struck by his predecessors (whose obsession with the vengeance of Yahve could be described in our modern jargon as pathological): "I will make a Covenant of Peace." In the same way, the second Isaiah begins his message with almost startling mildness, like a sudden calm after a storm of unparalleled severity, "Comfort ye, comfort ye, my people, saith your God." Declaiming in the traditional manner that the spirit of the Lord is upon him, he thus announces the terms of his mission, "The Lord has appointed me to preach *good tidings* unto the meek: he hath sent me to bind up the broken-hearted, to proclaim to the captives, and the opening of the prison to them that are bound." No one in Israel or anywhere else had spoken quite like this before.

The mood of exaltation which is sustained throughout almost the whole of the second part of *Isaiah* loses its force if we regard it merely as fine literature. Fine literature in the sense of ringing words without content, or with a content that is pronounced unacceptable to educated readers, is mere sounding brass and tinkling cymbal. "The Bible to be Read as Literature", to quote the title of a much-heralded publication, is the Bible to be left largely unread and finally neglected, as all literature severed from its living message deserves to be. The second *Isaiah* is fine literature because its message of hope and forgiveness, even if nourished upon an imaginary historical consummation, is the noblest message that man had hitherto delivered to his contemporaries in the few thousand years of civilized life. If its proclamation at that epoch is not to be regarded as a matter of history, as part of the achievement of the human mind in its slow evolution, then the matter of history is assuredly dead matter, and all our civilized values would seem to be based upon illusion.

The literature of hope and the literature of messianism go hand in hand. We have observed an occasional note of hope in the literature of Egypt: in the literature of Babylon practically none. Oppressed by a stern theocratic society without and by the pressure of "sin consciousness" within, the men of the mid-oriental archaic world seem to us to have lacked almost everything that makes life worth living. In fact we know that as far as day-to-day happiness is concerned the men of one age are hardly better off than those of another. Historical records, being by necessity abbreviations, do not record *la vie quotidienne*. Yet there is another form of happiness, that which not only makes life worth living but also death worth dying. This is the product of faith in the meaningfulness of life itself, and if of human life then of all life. Such a faith, for reasons beyond our present understanding, seems to have been communicated to, or evolved by, man within historical memory, but even so gradually and step by step. That the second Isaiah should have recorded his messianic vision perhaps contemporaneously with the Buddha in India may suggest either a similar, though unrelated, preoccupation in several regions of the world at the same time, or, since such preoccupation is permanent, a more than usual series of attempts to meet it. To the Christian the following passage must naturally appear to make more sense than to those who reject Revelation, but it is still not senseless: "The voice of him that crieth in the wilderness, Prepare ye the way of the Lord, make straight in the desert a highway for our God. Every valley shall be exalted and every valley or hill shall be made low, and the crooked shall be made straight and the rough places plain. And the glory of the Lord shall be revealed, and all flesh shall see it together. . . . O Jerusalem that bringest good tidings, lift up thy voice with strength. . . . Behold the Lord God will come with a strong hand, and his arm shall rule for him, behold, his reward is with him and his work before him. He shall feed his flock *like a shepherd*: he shall gather the lambs with his arm and carry them in his bosom, and shall gently lead those that are with young."

Here we have three invocations: the promise of the originally nameless and imageless God of the Fathers being finally revealed to his people, the invocation of Jerusalem not in the scarlet terms of Jeremiah and even Ezekiel but as a bride awaiting her husband, and finally the metaphors of the early shepherd prophets brought to a climax of pastoral beauty.

Although Isaiah speaks in the loftiest strains, he possesses as acute a political sense as his namesake. The delivery of the Jews from Babylon was not simply a matter for messianic hope. It was a practical matter. Introducing the passage in which he makes one of his most important theological statements, he declares boldly, "Thus saith the Lord to his appointed, to Cyrus, whose right hand I have holden, to subdue nations before him, and I will loose the loins of the kings." Cyrus, King of Persia, seemed to Isaiah to be the only man capable of overthrowing Babylon and of securing the passage back to Jerusalem of the exiles. He proved to be right. Cyrus not merely entered Babylon in 539 B.C., but restored to the Jews all the money that Nebuchadnezzar had appropriated from the Temple. For the journey home he ordered the Babylonian families who had employed Hebrew slaves to provide them with food and money, including a subscription towards rebuilding the Temple. "Whosoever remaineth in any place where he sojourneth," said

Cyrus, "let the men of his place help him with silver and with gold and with goods and with beasts, besides a freewill offering for the house of God which is in Jerusalem." The exiles were soon organizing their departure; but on returning to Jerusalem they found an alien and hostile people awaiting them. A generation passed before the Temple was rebuilt, and another century before national life was consolidated on the principles of the Law of Moses. This Law was re-edited and reaffirmed in 444 B.C., by the priest Ezra, who entertained the people to a reading of the sacred scrolls lasting seven days.

What is the consummation of prophecy of which we spoke? It is the vision expressed by the second Isaiah of a God not merely of Israel but of all mankind, and secondly of a God claiming absolute allegiance. In the Decalogue, God is made to refer to "other gods" whose relative power by claiming superiority He implicitly acknowledges: "Thou shalt have none other gods but me." In *Isaiah* He is made to declare: "I am the Lord and there is no one else, there is no God beside me. . . . I have made the earth and created man upon it . . . I have raised him up in righteousness and I have directed all his ways." And again: "Behold the nations are as a drop of a bucket, and are counted as the small dust of the balance. . . . And Lebanon is not sufficient to burn, nor the beasts thereof sufficient for a burnt offering. All nations before him are as nothing, and they are counted to him less than nothing and vanity. . . . Hast thou not known that the everlasting God, the Lord, the Creator of the ends of the earth, fainteth not, neither is weary? There is no searching of his understanding. Even the youths shall faint and be weary, and the young men shall utterly fall. But they that wait upon the Lord shall renew their strength; they shall mount up with wings as eagles, they shall run and not be weary, and they shall walk and not faint." Furthermore, the consciousness of sin and death, which runs like a swollen vein through the archaic mind, an inexplicable dread,[1] is accorded for the first time some prospect of relief: "Surely he hath borne our griefs and carried our sorrows. . . . The Lord hath laid on him the iniquity of us all." This is already the sense of the Christian Gospel.

Conclusion

If, turning our backs upon the events of the next three or four centuries (the second Isaiah wrote about five hundred years before the birth of Jesus), we contemplate the archaic world, we observe two supreme efforts at self-knowledge, like the mounting curves of

[1] Cf. "When the gods created mankind they determined death for mankind. Life they kept in their own hands" (*Epic of Gilgamesh*).

a graph. There is the Egyptian challenge to death, first in the materialism of the Pyramid Builders and later in the perception of the absolute value of *Maat* as reflected in individual conduct; and secondly there is the Hebrew challenge to the nature gods of antiquity by the vision of a God of righteousness, justice, and mercy, originally conceived on a family and tribal basis and finally as a God supreme over all men. Between these upward thrusts of moral aspiration there are thoughts equally debased and degraded: the gross trafficking in indulgences of *The Book of the Dead* and of the Babylonian manuals of theurgy, the incurable idolatry of the Israelites, the worship of Baal and Moloch, and so forth.[1] There are also such blind alleys as the sun worship of Ikhnaton, and the myths of Tammuz and Ishtar, touched with a strange beauty which suggests that no religion can dispense with an element of poetry.

Cyrus, the king who had supervised the return of the Jews from Babylon, showed the greatest respect for the religion of these ex-captives. He even seems to have acknowledged the God of Israel as the true God. "The Lord God of Heaven," he declared in a royal proclamation, "hath given me all the kingdoms of the earth, and he hath charged me to build him a house at Jerusalem, which is in Judah. . . . He is the God." One would suspect that, like Napoleon in Egypt, he professed beliefs that served his political ambitions. To the Babylonian priesthood he was equally respectful. A conqueror in those days was obliged to admit, as Alexander in turn soon discovered, that peoples will not change their religion so easily as kings. In 334 B.C., this young Achilles,[2] arriving in Palestine, accepted the surrender of Jerusalem from its High Priest and continued Cyrus's policy of toleration. Three years later, after capturing Babylon, he became master of the entire Middle East. Judea, midway between Egypt and Persia and therefore a perpetual invitation to foreign conquest, next came under the domination of Rome. In the reign of Caesar Augustus, at a time when the Roman world was stable enough to warrant the taking of a census of the population, Jesus was born in the outhouse of a crowded *hahn* in Bethlehem, in the province of Galilee, when Herod was King of Judea.

The origin and diffusion of that extension and to many minds completion of Judaism, called the Christian faith, does not come within the scope of this book, which halts upon the threshold of revelation. The preaching of the gospel of Jesus Christ and the foundation of his church are matters to which neither philosophy

[1] "Then they came to Baal Peer and dedicated themselves unto that shame-idol, and became (the same) beings of abomination as that which they loved" (*Hosea* ix, 10).

[2] Alexander's conception of himself.

nor history can remain indifferent. The birth was a registerable fact, the death a consequence of juridical proceedings, and the foundation of the church a reality, as we know not so much from its survival in history as from its being in great measure the history that has survived. This projection of a new scale of values, a *vita nuova*, into the historical process raises philosophical considerations of great importance; but the working out of the new philosophy was undertaken chiefly in the Roman and Byzantine worlds, first by an isolated figure such as Philo of Alexandria (a contemporary of Christ but not a Christian), then by the early Christian Fathers of both East and West, and finally by the great mediaeval theologians. To affirm that the Christian faith exerted negligible influence upon the oriental world, however, would be both a serious and, from the point of view of understanding Zoroastrianism and Islam, a disastrous error. Few religions are self-enclosed. All great faiths interpenetrate. Church may persecute church, and every so often a church is obliged to expel from its orbit an element of danger and disaffection, as the Catholic Church expelled the Catharist heresy, and Islam that of the Mu'tazilites. But the impulse behind every faith—even the most crude and primitive, such as the furtively cultivated worship of luck and fortune which will survive as long as human nature—is, as we have hinted, identical. We may therefore find it convenient, during the rest of our survey, to drop the world religion altogether as too much enveloped in vague and misleading associations, and to adhere to the more illuminating definition. Religion will thus be viewed not as the competitor or even the extension of philosophy, but as the basic element in the Perennial Philosophy.

CHAPTER III

ZOROASTER

A figure shrouded in legend

THE king of Persia who displayed such toleration of the faiths of his subject peoples was officially a Zoroastrian. The three wise men of the East who, according to Gospel tradition, arrived at Bethlehem saying "Who is he that is born king of the Jews? for we have seen his star in the East and are come to worship him," were possibly priests of the same faith. Who was Zoroaster?

As with most other religions, one school of thought maintains that he did not exist at all. We certainly know less concerning his life than about the founder of almost any other faith, though the legends of his birth, upbringing, and conversations with God are numerous. Modern scholars, no less than ancient devotees and historians, are equally divided as to the date of his birth. The earliest date to which he has been assigned is 6000 B.C. We need not for a moment suppose him to have lived as early as that. To have preached a gospel three thousand years before the earliest known kings of Egypt, when most of the world was no further advanced than the Bronze Age, would have been to preach into a kind of historical void. (There is no reason why men of wisdom should not have lived much earlier, but we are unlikely ever to learn what they said.) Berosus, the Babylonian historian who lived in the 4th century B.C., committed himself to the opinion that Zoroaster lived about 2000 B.C.; but we are never sure with early historians, even with the great Herodotus, upon what basis they are calculating time. This is true even of such original and painstaking mathematicians as the Babylonians. Today, scholars are inclined to believe that Zoroaster was born no earlier than 660 B.C., which brings him to within a few years of some of the greatest thinkers of the world.

Whereas we possess the means of verifying certain events in the lives of such figures as Ikhnaton, Abraham, Buddha, and Christ, we enjoy no such facilities in the case of Zoroaster. There are no known or credible events to verify. The career of Zoroaster is shrouded in a tissue of legend so fantastic, and to Western minds so preposterous, that he appears at first sight to belong to the order not of human beings but of mythical heroes. But we must not be too hasty in making inferences. Let us consider first of all the marvellous stories connected with his birth. Such stories seem invariably to attach themselves to religious leaders, and also to those who are regarded with something approaching religious awe—Plato, for instance; for the world is reluctant to allow men of outstanding personality to have come to birth in the manner of normal human beings. These legends do not prove a man never to have existed; but while they certainly do not prove the contrary their existence and persistence may, as we have said, be accounted for by there having been some outstanding personality to eulogize. Oral tradition is not necessarily less reliable than written record. Today, with our dependence upon written testimony, we underestimate the power of communication by word of mouth, which served mankind for perhaps as much as a thousand times as long as writing. We can justifiably assume that where there is legendary smoke there is a spark at least of factual fire.

The name Zoroaster is the Greek rendering (Zoroastres) of Zarathustra, which Nietzsche adopted in his famous poetic fantasy *Also sprach Zarathustra*. He was born in Persia. To unravel from the Pahlavi Texts the precise details of his birth is extremely difficult, as the discourse has a habit of running on like a kind of divine gossip. We gather that some archangels "framed together on a stem of Hom (the *haoma* plant), the height of a man, excellent in colour, and juicy when fresh", which Zoroaster's guardian chose to enter. Six white cows were then led up to the plant, and two of them, though virgin, became full of milk. These two cows ate the *haoma* plant, so that "the nature of Zarathustra came from that plant to these cows, and mingled with the cow's milk". Then a young girl of noble birth called Dukdaub was persuaded by the priest Porushaspo to milk the cows, whereupon Porushaspo pounded the *haoma* plant and mixed it with the cow's milk. Both he and the girl "drank up that Hom and milk, when they were mingled together and announced to Ahura Mazda; and here occurred a combination of the glory, guardian spirit, and bodily nature of Zarathustra into a manchild". Even so the evil spirits did their best to prevent the normal gestation of the child in his mother's womb; but she prayed to Ahura Mazda and became well. On the day Zarathustra was born the village of Porushaspo was suffused with a kind of divine illumination, "the fire being in every crevice"; but the greatest marvel of all was that "on being born he laughed outright. The seven midwives who sat round him were quite frightened thereby; and those terrified ones spoke thus: 'What is this, on account of grandeur or contempt, when, like a worthy man whose pleasure is due to activity, the manchild so laughs at the birth owing to him?' But Porushaspo replied proudly: 'Bring out this manchild to the sheepskin clothing which is soft. The affair was owing to thee, owing to the virtue of thee who art Dukdaub, that the advent of glory and the coming of radiance to this manchild was openly seen when he laughed outright at this birth.' "

The events attendant upon Zoroaster's birth were nothing to the trials and adventures that beset his boyhood. The demons and evil spirits sought by every means to destroy him. They tried to strangle him by appointing a nurse to perform this act on their behalf, to throw him under galloping horses, to burn him to death by placing him on a pile of ignited firewood, to have him seized and eaten by wolves. In each case he was rescued unharmed. On the last occasion, this was due to the fact that "Vohumano and Srosh the righteous brought a woolly sheep with an udder full of milk into the den, and it gave milk to Zarathustra, in digestible draughts, until daylight".

As a very young child, likewise, he was reported to have "looked a long while upwards, downwards, and on all sides round".[1] On being asked what he was doing, he replied that he was seeing visions of the blessed ascending to heaven, and the wicked descending to hell, while at the same time he prophesied the dissemination of a new gospel throughout the earth.

The divine mission

Like Jesus, Zoroaster began his mission about the age of thirty years. This mission opened with a kind of spiritual examination undertaken by the good spirit Vohumano. Having challenged Zoroaster one day to declare "what was his foremost distress, about what was his foremost endeavour, and for what was the tendency of his desire", the young man replied, "About righteousness I consider my foremost distress; about righteousness my foremost endeavour; and for righteousness the tendency of my desire." Being in due course admitted to the company of spirits, Zoroaster was able to put questions to Ahura Mazda himself. "In the embodied world," he asked, "which is the first of the perfect ones, which the second, and which the third?" To which Ahura Mazda replied, "The first perfection is good thoughts, the second good words, and the third good deeds."

At the outset of his mission, Zoroaster seems to have lived the life of a recluse. Like John the Baptist, he took to the wilderness and subsisted upon nothing but cheese and roots. Then came temptation. Whereas Christ's tempter was Satan, Zoroaster's was a female demon, Spendarmad. The meeting took place not in the wilderness but among ordinary men, whose habits Zoroaster had resolved to study: "Zarathustra proceeded to the habitable and friendly world, for the purpose of fully observing that beaten track of the embodied existence. Then the fiend came forward—a female,

[1] The same was reported of the young Buddha at birth.

golden-bodied and full-bosomed. Companionship, conversation, and co-operation were requested by her from him." Being aware that her charms were utterly deceptive, he requested her to turn her back. She replied, "O Zarathustra of the Spitamas, where we are, those who are females are handsome in front but frightfully hideous behind, so do not make a demand for my back." He insisted, and after she had protested a third time she consented to turn, upon which there issued from her a loathsome progeny of serpents, toads, lizards, centipedes, and frogs. The real ordeal, however, came later in the form of devilish assaults upon him, among which was the injection of molten lead into his stomach. But nothing succeeded in shaking his faith in the righteousness of the god with whom he had enjoyed communion, Ahura Mazda. Finally, as a reward for his stoic devotion, Ahura Mazda presented him personally with a Book of Heavenly Wisdom later called the *Avesta*. This was the gospel of which he had dreamed as a boy. The missionary now had his Bible.

Although his preaching fell at first upon deaf ears—for the Persians already had their gods and nature cults—Zoroaster gradually began to make converts. When finally a Persian prince called Vishtaspa or Hystaspes decided to embrace the new faith, a powerful movement of religious conversion began; for this prince at once declared his intention of spreading the Zoroastrian religion throughout his kingdom. The usurping successor of Cambyses, a devotee of the old Magian gods, endeavoured to stamp it out; but, with the accession to the throne of Darius 1st in 521 B.C., Zoroastrianism was officially proclaimed the religion of Persia. Some historians believe that Hystaspes, the prince who first befriended Zoroaster, was none other than the father of Darius. If so, that would prove Zoroaster to have been born at the latest date claimed for him.

According to tradition, the death of Zoroaster, which is supposed to have taken place in his seventy-eighth year, was accomplished with as much drama as his birth, though more quickly. A flash of lightning enveloped him, and he was borne up to heaven.

Such a brief account of Zoroaster's life, despite its picturesque anecdotes, may not strike the Western reader as either particularly convincing or particularly edifying. Of the personality of Zoroaster we learn next to nothing. He is without doubt the most shadowy of all the spiritual leaders whose lives we shall have occasion to study. The marvels attributed to him, or associated with various phases of his life, verge often upon the grotesque. Whatever their effect upon the people of his time and upon his later devotees, they tend not so much to magnify him in our eyes as almost to exclude him from the front rank of men of superhuman vision. That is our first impression.

It is true that if you know little enough about a man you can make him into any sort of person you wish. Whatever our ignorance of Zoroaster, we can be certain that he was a very different person from the genial sage, the German professor on holiday, that Nietzsche made him out to be. Indeed, the figure of Zarathustra presented in the work already mentioned is merely a prop upon which to hang samples of the Nietzschean philosophy of the Superman. For no other great figure of antiquity was sufficiently free from historical trappings. Our only hope of attaining to understanding, however modest, of the significance of Zoroaster is to view him against the background of his time. We are dimly aware of a great change in the spirit of the civilization to which he belonged—a change that is associated with the evangelistic work of a great teacher. To examine the new teaching is to approach as far as it is possible to an understanding of the man. The result may be surmise, but what history beyond a certain era is not? This line of enquiry would seem worth pursuing.

The pre-Zoroastrian gods of Persia bear a striking resemblance to those of the Hindu *Vedas*. Indeed, it has often been maintained by Indian scholars that the *Avesta* owes almost all its essential teaching to the *Vedas*, including its name. The pantheon contained two major deities: Mithra, god of the sun, and Anaita, goddess of the earth and of fertility. The importance of the cult of fertility was further emphasized by the worship of the bull-deity Haoma, whose blood was supposed to confer immortality upon those who drank it. The *haoma* herb, as we have already seen, was that into which the spirit of Zoroaster first entered on its devious journey towards birth. Found chiefly in the mountains, *haoma* possesses intoxicating properties: the worship of the bull-god consisted of drinking the plant's juice as being equivalent to the life-giving blood. The Hindu god Soma is probably the same as Haoma. Among these early peoples we also find distinct traces of ancestor worship: a religion whose disappearance in civilized times has left a void which is filled by such abstract substitutes as nationalism, the only religion that the West has presented to the East.

We have mentioned that the Zoroastrian scriptures to have survived, namely the *Avesta* and the Pahlavi Texts,[1] make difficult reading for the Western student. No doubt this is because there is almost nothing in Western literature with which they may be compared. In fact, the surviving texts are but fragments of a much larger body of scripture, some of which perished when Alexander the Great destroyed the royal palace at Persepolis, while other parts

[1] The *Avesta* were written in Zend (hence the title *Zend-Avesta*), and the Texts in a dialect of Hindu origin from which the modern Persian language is derived.

were lost during the Moslem conquests in the 7th century A.D. The *Avesta*, with its collection of stories, hymns, and prayers, bears a certain resemblance to the Old Testament: what it appears to lack is a continuous theme, which is one of the most remarkable characteristics of at least the Pentateuch. Nevertheless, once the repetitions, obscurities, and unusual terminology of the Zoroastrian writings are discounted, a general message begins slowly to emerge, and the reader who has approached them determined to be baffled remains to surrender to their spell. Nor is the word spell employed without deliberation. The prose literature operates upon the imagination with the force of incantation. To look for logic is to look for something that was apparently never meant to be there (or at least that is not apparent in translation), except in passages of epigrammatic wisdom such as we associate with the Chinese sages. Curiously enough, the Western reader may find proportionately more content in the poetry. The Zoroastrian Hymns or *Gathas*, with their moral and sometimes metaphysical argument, contain a good deal more substance than the Sun Hymn of Ikhnaton and the exquisite hymns of the *Rig-Veda*.

Content of the faith

What general impression do we derive from these miscellaneous essays on righteousness and justice, these reports upon interviews with the Lord of Light, these accounts of the creation of the world and the propagation of the human species, and finally these outbursts of ecstatic poetry? It is an impression of delight in life and nature, a faith not so much of a materialist as of a vitalist character, but shot through with a sense of awe and dread of the power of evil.

In other words, the old fertility worship is still there, exercising its powerful and not-to-be-denied pressure, much as the worship of Osiris continued to maintain its hold in Egypt side by side with that of Re. In an agricultural nation, this was no doubt natural. "Unhappy is the land that has long lain unsown with the seed of the sower and wants a good husbandman, like a well-shapen maiden who has long gone childless and wants a good husband."[1]

What Zoroaster seems to have done was to purify the fertility cult of its grosser aspects. Similarly, Moses had tried to stem the inherent tendency of the children of Israel to engage in extravagant rites. From the biblical narrative it is possible to infer (though the inference has been hotly disputed) that Yahve's refusal to allow Moses to enter the promised land may have been due to his failure, particularly at the last moment, to keep these demoralizing instincts

[1] *Vendidad, Fargard* III.

in check.[1] We are told that at the very threshold of their new home, which merely to have sighted ought to have convinced the ordinary individual that Yahve was the true God, large numbers of the men entered into illicit relations with the women of Moab, whom we assume to have solicited their co-operation in the performance, not in itself "immoral", of a fertility rite. No doubt Zoroaster endeavoured to wean his countrymen from the worship of Haoma for the same reason that Moses strove, though often in vain, to suppress the worship of the Golden Calf: not for what it was, namely a graven or molten image, but for what it stood for, namely a bull, the most obvious fertility totem. For the same reason Zoroaster's emphasis upon the transcendent character of Ahura Mazda may have derived from a conviction, which was entertained equally by Abraham and Moses in respect of Yahve,[2] that such elevation would place Him "above sexuality". Ahura Mazda and Yahve were, and remain, masculine only for grammatical purposes. They inhabit a different level from that of the ancient god-goddess pantheon, which is likewise invaded by animal or half-animal deities, whose sex is interchangeable.

One of the most interesting passages in the *Vendidad* (Chapter II), which is that part of the *Avesta* forming the priestly code of the modern Parsees, contains an account given by Ahura Mazda to Zoroaster of the first "holy man". His name is Yima.[3] "The fair Yima" was a shepherd with whom Ahura Mazda had conversed before he revealed himself to Zoroaster. When Ahura Mazda invited Yima to be "the preacher and bearer of my religion", the latter declined on account of his rudimentary education. To this Ahura Mazda replies, "Since thou dost not consent to be the preacher and bearer of my religion, then make thou my world increase, make my world grow: consent thou to nourish, to rule, to watch over my world." Yima agreed, promising that as long as he ruled the world there should be "neither cold wind nor hot wind, neither disease nor death". He was true to his word. After the passage of three hundred winters the abundance of "flocks and herds, with men and dogs and birds and blazing red fires" was so great that the earth could not hold them all. When Ahura Mazda drew Yima's attention to this crisis, the young king proceeded to press the earth with a golden seal and to bore it with a poniard (the insignia of his office), whereupon it miraculously increased in size by one third. This process was repeated every three hundred years, the

[1] The refusal was clearly on account of some omission of duty. See *Deuteronomy* xxxii, 51.

[2] Cf. Buber: *Moses*, p. 194.

[3] Cf. the Hindu Yama.

earth being enlarged correspondingly on each occasion. We observe here a preoccupation, even an obsession, with natural abundance and increase, either reflecting the territorial expansions of a tribe of herdsmen and tillers of the soil, or depicting in language of exaggeration the condition of the world before some disaster equivalent to the Babylonian Flood.

The same theme reappears in the Zoroastrian accounts, two in number, of the Flood itself. In the first of these, Yima the shepherd reappears in the rôle of Noah or Shamash-napishtim. The flood is caused on this occasion by the melting of mountain snows. "Upon the material world," Ahura Mazda informs Yima, "the evil winters are about to fall, that shall make snowflakes fall thick on the highest tops of the mountains. . . . Before that winter, the country will bear plenty of grass for cattle, before the waters have flooded it. Now after the melting of the snow, O Yima, a place wherein the footprint of a sheep may be seen will be a wonder of the world." Accordingly, Ahura Mazda bids Yima lay out a garden "long as a riding ground on every side of the square, and thither bring the seeds of sheep and oxen, of men, of dogs, of birds and of red blazing fires". Within this enclosure or compound (*Vara*), presumably raised to a certain level, Yima is instructed to undertake the cultivation and procreation of men, beasts, and plants in such manner as to eliminate all imperfection. In the case of men, "there shall be no humpbacked, none bulged forward there; no impotent, no lunatic, no one malicious, no liar, no one spiteful, none jealous, none with decayed tooth, no leprous to be pent up, nor any of the brands wherewith Angra Mainyu stampt the bodies of mortals". All this was accordingly done, and the episode, which we have here shorn of its repetitions, closes with the observation that "the men in the *Vara* which Yima made live the happiest life; since they conform in every detail to the precepts of the religion of Ahura Mazda as interpreted by Zarathustra". Like every earthly paradise, however, it is doomed to interference and destruction by the powers of evil.

Whereas the first Flood story accounts simply for the preservation of the species and provides an opportunity for mankind's improvement, the second from the *Bundahis*[1] strikes a note of greater profundity. Here we find stated in relief the essence of the Zoroastrian theology, which is the world-wide conflict between the forces of good and evil, light and darkness, Ahura Mazda and Ahriman, the Evil One. Instead of the Flood being sent by God as a punitive measure, as it is in both the *Epic of Gilgamesh* and in *Genesis*, the Zoroastrian catastrophe was deliberately engineered by the powers of darkness for the overthrow of Ahura Mazda. The conflict

[1] A surviving fragment of the *Avesta*.

of wind and water forms merely a background to a gigantic duel between Ahura Mazda and his allies, and Ahriman. Only by endowing Tistar, the star-god, with "the strength of ten vigorous horses, ten vigorous camels, ten vigorous bulls, ten mountains, and ten rivers", did the powers of Good manage to prevail.

If we now turn to the Zoroastrian legends concerning the origin of mankind, we observe this same conflict at work in the Zoroastrian equivalent to Adam and Eve, who are called Mashya and Mashyoi or Matro and Matroyao. We may note in passing that, as in *Genesis*, man was sixth in order of creation. According to the *Dadistan-i-Dinik*, Ahura Mazda produced the material of man from light, but for the space of three thousand years this creature neither spoke nor ate, existing only for the purpose of reflecting upon "the righteousness of the perfect and true religion, the desire for the pure glorification of the creator". Birth, as we know it, was the consequence of an evil design on the part of "the contentious promise-breaker", but we are not told how this misfortune came about. All we know is that "a burdensome mortality" was conferred upon the person of Gayomard, who, with the co-operation of an angel, transmitted at his death the seed from which Mashya and Mashyoi, "brother and sister of mankind", were born. The story is now taken up by the *Bundahis*. The brother and sister, here called Matro and Matrayao, were physically united, the waists of both being "brought close and so connected together that it was not clear which was the male and which the female".

To this twin-individual Ahura Mazda issued a solemn warning. "You are," he said, "a man, you are the ancestry of the world." He thereupon enjoined "them" to obey the laws of his religion, and to remain pure in thought, word, and deed. Above all they were to worship no demons. For a time all went well. They enjoyed the delights of nature, and worshipped Ahura Mazda as the Lord of Creation. Then the demons decided to act. "Antagonism rushed into their minds and their minds were thoroughly corrupted", so much so that they began to attribute creation not to Ahura Mazda but to the evil spirits themselves. For this wickedness their souls were later consigned to hell "until the future existence". Gradually their bodily appetites asserted themselves. They milked a white-haired goat by applying their mouths to its udder, and they relished the taste for its own sake, not attributing its deliciousness to the Creator. Next they killed a sheep. By blowing upon the wood of the Lote-plum and the boxtree, they produced fire and set the sheep to roast. On this occasion, being more thoughtful of the gods, they threw three handfuls of the meat into the fire, as its share: three handfuls at the sky, as the share of the angels. Meanwhile a vulture appro-

W. F. Mansell

ZOROASTER

From a bas relief at Persepolis

priated a share for itself. Later they acquired skill in weaving cloth and sewing garments. They dug a pit in the earth, obtained iron, smelted it, and made an axe to cut wood. They even set up a wooden shelter.

With increase in skill came contention. They had their first quarrel. Being attached one to the other, their disputes were unusually violent. They cuffed each other, scratched each other's cheeks, and tore out each other's hair. This was the demons' opportunity. They called upon Mashya and Mashyoi to surrender their souls completely to Ahriman. In this way, it was promised, their "demon of malice" would be quietened.

In consequence of this steady falling away from God, the pair soon became unbearably conscious of carnal desires. For fifty years such instincts had lain dormant. Now they became imperious. The couple entered into union. After nine months twins were born, but the parents promptly devoured them, a practice that might have continued but for Ahura Mazda's intervention. Hence man was born in sin and lived thereafter on divine sufferance.

That the first man and woman were either one creature or very closely connected is an idea by no means peculiar to Zoroastrianism. It is found, as we shall see, in the *Rig-Veda*, where Yama and Yami, children of Vivasat, are represented as twin brother and sister. Likewise in *Genesis* Eve is made by God from the rib of Adam. In the *Symposium*, Plato puts into the mouth of Aristophanes a legend concerning the origin of mankind from a two-headed creature which was later split in half: from this division he explained the passion of love, which is the desire of either creature to find the complement from which it had been severed. This aspect of the subject, however, is trivial. What is more significant is the fact that each story, save that of Aristophanes (which is intended to be fanciful), describes the origin of the sexual impulse as being associated with sin, or with some kind of fall from grace. Even the conception of Zoroaster was associated with guilt: the couple Porushaspo and Dukdaub "start up ashamed" when their "embrace with desire for a son" is interrupted by the evil spirits. For the moment it would be unwise even to speculate as to why this idea should have such widespread currency, or how it has come to be so deep-seated. That is a subject to which we shall revert after studying the profound notions of the Indian sages, whose preoccupation with generation and birth assumes primacy over all other interests.

Good and Evil

It is idle to seek an explanation as to why Ahura Mazda, though nominally supreme, should have been subject through all eternity to the challenge of Ahriman. Zoroastrianism has no legend of Lucifer, though its equivalent to Satan must certainly have influenced Christian thought. We notice that Satan figures more frequently in the later books of the Old Testament, while in the New Testament he is an accredited member of the *Dramatis Personae*. Yahve's early competitors are not emissaries of Satan but simply other gods. In the Zoroastrian theology we are merely told that Ahriman "preferred the practice which is iniquitous".

In the *Zad-Sparam*, an extremely vague allegorical account is given of the original antagonism between Ahura Mazda and Ahriman. We are told in terms reminiscent of early *Genesis* that at the beginning of time "light was above and darkness was below, and between those two was open space". Ahura Mazda inhabited the light realm, Ahriman the dark. Whereas Ahura Mazda "was aware of the existence of Ahriman and his coming for strife", however, Ahriman was not aware of the realm of light overhead. One day, loitering along in the gloom, Ahriman by chance emerged from the nether regions and "a ray of light was seen by him", and because of its antagonistic nature to him "he strove to reach it, so that it might also be within his absolute power". At this point Ahura Mazda approached the boundary. What then occurred was not a struggle, such as took place between the Herculean Tistar and the powers of darkness, but the expulsion of Ahriman by "pure words" (cf. Zoroaster's first interview with Ahura Mazda), whereby his witchcraft was "confounded". Again, in the *Vendidad*, Ahura Mazda is made to explain to Zoroaster how the evils and defects of life have originated. He begins by pointing out that he has made every land, "even though it had no charms whatever in it", dear to its people; otherwise the whole world of men would have long ago invaded the *Airyana Vaejo*, the Aryan land, or home of the race from which both Persians and Indians are descended.[1] After the creation of this most beautiful of lands, Angro Mainyu (Ahriman's other name) proceeded to "countercreate" all the unpleasant aspects of it. The list is prolonged to include sixteen lands or districts, in each of which Angra Mainyu has wrought such evils as serpents, ants, locusts, pride, tears, witchcraft, burial,[2] unbelief, oppression, monstrous births, excessive heat, and above all winter—the latter being described at each mention as "the very devil" ("a work of the *daevas*").

Such allegories are clearly invented to satisfy the minds of a

[1] Herodotus observed that the Persians regarded nations as inferior according to their distance from Persia.

[2] Described as "the sin for which there is no atonement". The modern Parsees strictly refuse to bury their dead; the corpse is exposed on what is called a "Tower of Silence" for birds to consume.

simple people. We need not thereby belittle their importance. All religions have recourse to such allegories, which have the supreme advantage of keeping a faith concrete. Metaphysical religions, such as that of Aristotle, are not intended for popular consumption. Just as the national religion of Egypt was kept before the minds of both the young and the mentally young by allegories of the dead Pharaoh and his golden barque, or the adventures of Osiris, so the religion of Zoroaster was brought home to the humblest peasant or nomad (Iran has always been a land of tribes) by means of stories of the strife of ogres and the mischief of *daevas*: terms in which the teaching could enter into the living tissue of everyday experience. There may be a good deal to be said for the view that theological truths, having an inherent tendency to fly off into remote abstractions, are better rendered in allegory than in any other medium. To express them at all is to express them as myth. Myth, in other words, is not false religion, but rather its particular way of being true.[1]

In speaking of the faith of Ikhnaton we emphasized the necessity for every religion to have as a complement to its theology a clear-cut system of ethics. You may teach men in general terms what is good and what is evil; but if you would hold their allegiance you must make absolutely clear to them what is right and what is wrong. Most religions find it necessary to couch these ethical maxims in negative terms. This was so in Babylon. Of the Hebrew Decalogue eight of the items are negative. The Zoroastrian teaching, though shot through with negations and antagonisms in its theology, is on the whole positive in its injunctions. The ethical system is outlined most succinctly in the *Zad-Sparam*, one of the Pahlavi Texts, which consists of two parts, one concerned with "Dispositions" and the other with "Admonitions". The five Dispositions, which are described as specially for the attention of priests, lay down rules of ceremonial and of right conduct in office. The Admonitions, of which there are ten, are applicable to all. The first is to maintain what is called good repute, so that you may win respect not merely for yourself but for your teachers or guardians. The second is to refrain, for the same reasons, from acquiring the least element of evil repute. The third is not to beat your teacher, or to annoy him by repeating that which he has not taught you. The fourth is to accept the best of your teacher's instructions humbly, as if they were a loan instead of a gift.[2] The fifth is to see that the law of punishing malefactors and rewarding the righteous is kept for the sake of

[1] Cf. Schelling: "The myth is not based on a thought, as the children of an artificial education suppose; but is itself a kind of thinking, which imparts a conception of the world, but imparts it in a sequence of events, acts and sufferings."

[2] Certain of these maxims are obscure. We have tried to bring out what we consider to be the essential meaning.

progress. The sixth is to keep open house to all men of righteousness and goodwill. The seventh is freely to confess the sins you have committed, so that by expelling what is evil you will keep your mind pure. The eighth, which resembles the former, is to keep away all occasions for sin. The ninth is to do your utmost to spread the true religion, and to help restore its authority should it be subject to reverses. The tenth and last is to give due obedience to the ecclesiastical hierarchy.

From this list of Admonitions it is easy to see in what the whole duty of man consists. It consists in being devout and pious, obedient to both teacher and priest, and an example to all. Nor is the least duty that of propagating the gospel.[1] In an account of the Resurrection given in the *Bundahis* the faithful are warned that it is their special duty to see that the erring friends are given every chance of amendment. If, for example, a wicked man complains on the judgment day that his righteous friend "did not make him acquainted with the good deeds that he practised himself", then the righteous friend will receive appropriate punishment. Moreover, although in the last day the "wicked man becomes as conspicuous as a white (*sic*) sheep among those which are black", the good will not be able to escape grief. "They suffer," the account goes on, "everyone for his own deeds, and weep, the righteous for the wicked, and the wicked about himself"; for though the father may be good, the son may be bad, and so forth. Nor is the experience of hell anything to make light of. For the fear of most other things is more than the thing itself, but "hell is a thing worse than the fear of it". We are told that at the Resurrection all those judged righteous will have the sensation of walking perpetually in warm milk, while the wicked will have the sensation of walking in molten metal.

Such scrupulous piety implies the regular worship of God according to consecrated rites. As the centuries passed, the simple ceremonies of the Zoroastrian faith became complicated, just as its lofty monotheism became studded with polytheistic ornaments. A god is accorded sole worship. He is endowed with every perfection. In due course these virtuous characteristics become detached and receive special veneration. God is nowhere. Therefore He is everywhere. So He is in everything, and everything contains God, and therefore becomes a god. Hence the original unity gives place to a granular polytheism. The *daevas*, expelled, return as *fravashis*, or guardian spirits.

That Zoroaster's chief object was to purify rather than to overthrow the traditional faith of his countrymen is suggested from many

[1] It is curious, however, that the modern Parsees admit no converts to their faith, and therefore do not proselytize.

sources. Mithra, the Sun God, far from being expelled, was both worshipped as a Celestial Fire and praised in most of the Zoroastrian hymns. Haoma the Bull may be excluded from the Pantheon; but the plant in which his power was worshipped plays its part in the prophet's creation.[1]

The early followers of the new faith built neither temples nor idols, but they erected altars upon which fires were lit in honour of Ahura Mazda. Fire, to which so frequent mention is made in Zoroastrian literature, soon came to be worshipped as a god, as did the sun itself, until these deities almost usurped the place of Ahura Mazda.[2] The custom of maintaining a perpetual fire in the home became part of a man's daily religious observance: for the hearth was especially sacred in a faith that glorified family life. Incidentally, the rainbow, that substitute for the sun, was regarded by the Zoroastrians in much the same way as it was in *Genesis*, as "a sign above from spiritual to earthly beings".

Just as the followers of Zoroaster were allowed no temples, so they were forbidden to have idols. Something of the power which idol worship and belief in demons exerted over the common people may be judged from the elaborate Mazdayasnian creed which is to be found in the *Yasna* (the liturgy of the Zoroastrian priests). Here we have a lengthy formula of abjuration directed chiefly at expelling the influence of the *daevas*, "Off, off, do I abjure the *daevas* and all possessed by them, the sorcerers and all that hold to their devices, and every existing being of the sort; their sorts do I abjure, their words and actions, and their seed that propagate their sin; away do I abjure their shelter and their headship." Such repudiation of the enemies of "the most imposing, best, and most beautiful religion that exists" is extended throughout much repetition, but its drift, especially in the mouth of a priest, is clear. It is sometimes maintained that Zoroaster, in asserting the supremacy of Ahura Mazda, intended to deny the reality of the demons or *daevas*. Whatever he may personally have believed, it is clear that his followers were loth to abandon such cherished notions. The Pahlavi Texts introduce the personified powers of evil into every phase of the life of Zoroaster, as in that of the good angels his confederates.

Evolution of the faith

Some idea of the quality of the faith preached by Zoroaster may be gained by considering the vicissitudes of its history. Any religion whatever, indeed any political creed, will prevail for a time

[1] The juice was also drunk as a religious act even after Zoroaster's time.

[2] It is incorrect, however, to describe the modern Parsees as "fire-worshippers" The lighting of fires is merely a rite.

if it is imposed by order of an authoritarian ruler. In this respect the edict of Darius 1st resembles that of Ikhnaton. The religion became law, impiety being equivalent to treason. One suspects that the creed of Zoroaster, as originally preached, imposed too great or too sudden a strain upon a people not yet educated up to the level of pure monotheism.[1] The old gods crept back; the demons were already there. Gradually the pre-Zoroastrian priesthood, the Magi, who had been excluded from favour as rigorously as the priests of Amon, returned to power. Mithra, as we have seen, shone more brightly: indeed the cult of Mithra became, in due course, so popular with the conquering Roman legions that it spread to countries so inferior to, by reason of their distance from, Persia as Britain. Although the Sassanid kings of Persia (A.D. 226–651) tried to restore Zoroastrianism as the state religion, the impetus of the once pure faith was exhausted. Small groups continued to maintain the old worship; but today, except for a tiny group of adherents in Fars, Zoroastrianism as a faith is extinct in the country of its origin. It survives, however, as the religion of the Parsee inhabitants of the Bombay Presidency. This people has done its best to keep the faith pure, and their present enlightenment may afford some idea of the impact of the founder's personality upon his contemporaries.[2]

Zoroastrianism was given the *coup de grâce* by Islam. The militant faith drives out the less belligerent, less missionizing, religion of the elements. Nevertheless it would be wrong to assume that the religion of Zoroaster left no permanent traces either in Persia or elsewhere. We have already drawn attention to the possible influence upon the Old Testament of Zoroastrian ideas concerning the personified evil spirit. Similarly, the Zoroastrian conception of life after death may well have exerted influence in the same quarter, because we find little or nothing of such a notion in the early part of the Bible. The ideas of a seven-day creation, of an earthly paradise, of the fall of man from grace, and of a "prehistoric" catastrophe threatening the existence of the human race, are common to more faiths than Judaism, Christianity, and Zoroastrianism, though in the latter we find some interesting and original modifications. If there is nowhere reason to suggest that Zoroastrian religious practices directly influenced those of the Hebrews, we can legitimately assume that such practices were among those with which the Hebrews, ever prone to religious flirtations,[3] were instructed to have nothing

[1] There has been no later development of the *theology* of Zoroastrianism.

[2] During the last ten years a new Mazdayasni creed has been started in Bombay by an American millionairess. The faithful, it appears, are occupied chiefly with special breathing exercises and *la cuisine*.

[3] Even as late as Joshua's assumption of leadership, the children of Israel had to be asked to make up their minds whether they wished to worship Yahve or "other gods".

to do. Indeed, if it is not to the practice of fire-worship by disciples of Zoroaster that the following passage from *Ezekiel* refers, then it is difficult to see the point of the vision so meticulously described: "It came to pass . . . as I sat in my house . . . that the hand of the Lord God fell upon me. Then I beheld, and lo a likeness as the appearance of fire; from the appearance of his loins even downward, fire; and from his loins even upward, as the appearance of brightness, as the colour of amber. And he put forth the form of a hand, and took me by a lock of mine head; and the spirit lifted me up between earth and heaven, and brought me in the vision of God to Jerusalem, to the door of the inner gate that looketh towards the north. . . . And he brought me to the inner court of the Lord's House, and behold, at the door of the temple of the Lord, between the porch and the altar, were about five and twenty men, with their backs towards the temple of the Lord and their faces towards the east: and they worshipped the sun towards the east. Then he said unto me, Hast thou seen this, O son of man? Is it a light thing to the house of Judah that they commit the abominations which they commit here?" If Zoroaster lived at the end of the 7th centruy B.C. we can well imagine that the enthusiastic practice of his doctrine in countries bordering Persia, such as Mesopotamia, may have been common in the time of Ezekiel (*c.* 580 B.C.).

A credible figure

To appreciate the full nature of Zoroaster's faith, with the object of comparing it with the few others that have achieved at least comparable success among men, a prolonged treatment of the surviving scriptures against the background of their composition would be required. In this chapter we have naturally done little more than sketch the essentials of the creed. Even so, the impression with which we started may well have undergone a degree of modification. A not altogether incredible figure seems to advance through the shadows. The grotesque elements fall away, become inessentials, froth. The creed that was passionately preached, energetically practised for a period, and then allowed to fall into relative neglect, was the creed of an individual to whom an experience similar to that of the Prophets must surely have been vouchsafed. The 19th-century theory of the importance of the individual, which was so aptly summed up by Emerson in his statement that "history is the lengthening shadows of great men", may have been exaggerated; but there is a point beyond which it cannot be scaled down without producing an opposite error. And those who deny the possibility of that which has been so unfortunately named "religious experience" (as if it were possible to entertain religious belief without experiencing it) need not suppose that what has never happened to them cannot in any circumstance happen to other people. We perceive at the origin of the worship of the Lord of Light one of those great leaders of the spirit of whom we have spoken; a master of simplification, like all such leaders, who pictured the struggle in the individual soul as mirroring *in parvo* a great cosmic struggle between Good and Evil; who was essentially a lover of nature not in the superficial scenic sense popularized by the Romantics but in the deeper sense which sees in the fundamental instincts of the body something holy, since they were implanted there by God and are turned to evil only because dark powers seek to appropriate that which belongs to the world of light; who consequently conceived a particular tenderness towards the young, the fecund and the new-born,[1] and not least the animal creation;[2] who saw in the family the most precious safeguard of the unity of society, and who conceived the unity of the family to be impossible without respect for the household gods and the souls of the ancestors (*Fravashis*); and who evidently envisaged a time, albeit distant by three thousand years and in consequence of the work of other prophets, when the forces of evil should be utterly overthrown, and mankind should be restored to its ancient paradise. Few men, it seems, and few religious leaders, have been so completely free from the unwholesome and the morbid.

Of the Christian mystics, no one save perhaps St. Francis and Thomas Traherne approaches Zoroaster in his adoration of creation: "He who recites the praise of Holiness, in the fullness of faith and with a devoted heart, praises me, Ahura Mazda. He praises the waters, he praises the cattle, he praises the plants, he praises all good things made by Mazda, all things that are offspring of the good principles" (*Yast* fragment). Finally, we detect in the faith of Zoroaster an element overshadowed, but by no means superseded by emphasis upon personal repute and obedience to authority, namely a stress upon inner experience manifested above all in the priority given to "good thoughts" and a righteous disposition:[3] There is no surer sign of spiritual enlightenment. Nor is this preoccupation with the interior state of sanctity a mere temptation to quietism. The true faith demands constant exertion both in the form of self-discipline and in the form of social action. Above all there must be an end to bigotry, the most obvious danger to which an

[1] "It lies with the faithful to look after every pregnant female, either two-footed or four-footed, two-footed woman or four-footed bitch" (*Vendidad*).

[2] This was particularly true of cattle and dogs. Cf. the *Vendidad*: "Whosoever shall kill the dog kills his own soul for nine generations."

[3] See especially the *Prayer for Guidance*: "Tell us how you may come to us with good disposition."

official creed is subject. There are few passages in the scriptures of the world's faiths at once so dignified and inspired as this from the hymn called the *Farvardin Yast*: "We worship this earth, we worship those heavens: we worship those good things which stand between the earth and the heavens and that are worthy of sacrifice and prayer, and are to be worshipped by the faithful man. We worship the souls of the wild beasts and the tame. We worship the souls of the holy men and women, born at any time, whose consciences struggle, or will struggle, or have struggled, for the good."

CHAPTER IV

HINDUISM

The Vedas

AT the conclusion of the chapter on Babylon and Israel we made, as the reader will remember, a resolution. This resolution was to drop the word religion in so far as religion was to be distinguished from philosophy. We now approach the study of a philosophy in which the purpose of this repudiation of a distinction so dear to the Western mind will become clear. Hindu thought, in practically all its aspects and throughout its long history, has remained indifferent to the distinction between religion and philosophy.

To eliminate a superfluous term from our intellectual vocabulary is no doubt a matter for congratulation. The human mind has too many terms that accomplish too few significant operations. Unfortunately, the study of Hindu thought makes it abundantly clear that in identifying religion and philosophy the Indian sages were not prompted by any marked economy in the use of terms. On the contrary, the philosophical terms in their vocabulary exceed in number those of any other form of intellectual belief. No language of ancient or modern times contains more philosophical terms than Sanskrit. Similarly, in "pricking" the distinction between religion and philosophy, the Hindu sages show no corresponding reluctance to draw distinctions in other fields. Indian thought arrives at subtleties of distinction so varied and acute that the uninitiated and unprepared reader may well receive the impression that Indian philosophers enjoy the use of half a dozen intellects instead of one. We are accustomed to the idea of scientists constructing artificial brains to effect calculations which neither a single individual, nor a team of individuals devoting a lifetime to the task, could hope to achieve. The elaborate system of certain Indian philosophers sometimes appear to be the product of such socially-constructed intellects. This impression is deceptive. Just as the electronic brain is made by men to do what lies beyond man's power, so the great systems of Eastern thought were evolved by thinkers trained in a tradition of speculation that seems to overshadow but in fact enhances their individual contributions. "Hercules had not more muscles than we," said Paul Valéry; "they were only larger muscles."

While we need not allow these gigantic thought-structures to overawe us, it would be foolish to pretend that merely by taking thought we can understand in them all there is to be known. According to authoritative Indian scholars, there are certain terms and therefore arguments in Hindu and oriental philosophy in general which remain virtually untranslatable into European languages. A thorough acquaintance with oriental tongues, therefore, would be a condition of our being able fully to understand Eastern thought: added to which we must presuppose a marked talent for speculation. Such a combination of talents has appeared in a William Jones, an Edwin Arnold, a Rhys Davies, but we must admit that it is an occurrence of once or twice in a century. Meanwhile, men of high intelligence have confessed, after devoting much time to oriental research, that if they were to arrive at complete understanding of Eastern philosophy they would need to abandon Europe altogether and begin life again as an oriental. It is possible that the reverse is also true, though the spectacle of so many Indians, Chinese, and Japanese adapting themselves successfully to the life of the Western hemisphere would seem to disprove it.

What may well enable us to pursue a middle course between arrogance and helpless inferiority is the consciousness of the great movement of understanding and sympathy that seems to be uniting Orient and Occident. Of this movement, with its attendant dangers, we shall have more to say in the sequel. That the East has in the past borrowed some of the least desirable features of Western civilization is a commonplace. While deliberate borrowings from the East by the West have been rare, Eastern influences have percolated unconsciously into the Western mind for centuries. Today we are witnessing something to which the past offers no parallel: that is to say, a sudden awakening on the part of Western scholars, including poets and artists, to the infinite riches of oriental and especially Indian culture. Like several others of its kind, this movement has been going on for some time without attracting much notice; for political events and prejudices have often obscured its real nature. Attempting to raid unfamiliar material in search of "new thought" or "secret wisdom", cranks have tended to bring discredit upon it. But it advances. And the ordinary man may find, to his surprise, that the thought thus made accessible not merely enables him to understand aspects of the oriental mentality about which he has entertained the most superficial notions, but throws much light upon questions that have long perplexed him.

Exponents of Indian philosophy are usually anxious to draw attention first to its profundity and secondly to its antiquity. Concerning the former there has never been any doubt. If India has not ascertained the secret of life, it has probably framed by far the most searching questions on the subject. When precisely it began asking such questions is a matter about which experts disagree. The oldest known Indian religious literature is the series of hymns that form the *Rig-Veda*. As far as we can tell, these were written between 1500 and 1200 B.C. That lends them sufficient antiquity: we need hardly repeat what we have stressed so often, that the *impulse* from which they originate must date from a much earlier time. But let us look for a moment at the history of Egypt. By 1500 B.C. two long and eventful civilized epochs had passed away, the Old Kingdom and the Middle Kingdom. A profound and extensive philosophical and religious literature had been composed. By 1200, to take the later date, Ikhnaton's revolution had come and gone, and the great moral effort of which we have spoken at length had been almost completed. Or let us take the civilization of Western Asia. By 1500 Babylon had produced all the literature and art that it was to produce, the Code of Hammurabi was established over the whole of what is now the Middle East, Abraham had turned a family into a tribal nation or "portable fatherland", as Heine called it, and the Hittites had developed the civilization that begins only now to yield its secrets. By 1200, again, the Jews had conquered Canaan. For the present (and this qualification must be stressed for reasons that will soon appear) it seems beyond question that Egyptian and also Babylonian religious and philosophical speculation of an advanced kind antedates that of India by many centuries.

We must hasten to add that such priority in time does not mean that Egyptian thought necessarily exhibits greater profundity or indeed enjoys any other intellectual advantage over that of India: but in a survey such as the present we must maintain our historical bearings, and above all we should be on our guard against the chauvinism of scholars, which can sometimes assume unexpected intensity.

It is one thing to correct misleading impressions about the antiquity of Indian speculative thought; it is another thing to compare the relative antiquity of Indian and other traditions of social life. On this subject recent archaeological investigations have thrown a most interesting and even startling light. If in due course the earth could be made to surrender all its archaeological treasures, we may envisage a series of revolutions in historical perspective necessitating the scrapping every few years of hundreds of authoritative text-books. That might be all to the good. If a work is to remain useful for as long as most works of exposition can expect to remain, it must seek to avoid too close an identification with any contemporary school of archaeological doctrine. On the other hand, it must not omit to report the latest conjectures: one of the difficulties of such reporting is precisely that these may have shifted and been replaced by others during the composition of the book itself.[1]

The archaeological discoveries to which we refer are those undertaken since 1924 by Sir John Marshall and some Indian colleagues at Mohenjo-daro and Harappa on the lower Indus. These investigations brought to light the remains of a series of cities —the word is used deliberately—built one upon the ruins of the others. Five such cities have so far been unearthed, and it is possible that more will in due course be found.[2] The buildings show every evidence of having been several storeys in height. There are hundreds of them, suggesting a thriving city life very similar to that which flourished at Ur. What has been recovered from the buildings themselves is more interesting still. Pottery, jewellery, furniture, inscribed seals, weapons, tools, and toys; these have been found not merely in great quantity but of a quality which is often unsurpassed. Curiously enough, the lower levels of excavation have revealed a number of objects superior, judging by artistic canons, to those found higher up. But for the fact that some of the weapons are of stone, others of copper, and still others of bronze, we should be led to doubt whether our conventional prehistoric categories any longer applied. Sir John Marshall believes that the cities of Mohenjo-daro belong at least to the third millenium B.C., and perhaps even to the fourth. How long they took to grow into flourishing cities we cannot tell: the presumption is that their origin must belong to a period to which we have so far denied the title of civilized. It seems certain, in other words, that Mohenjo-daro was the scene of brisk commerce, trafficking, and gracious living at a period assigned by the Egyptians to mythical kings such as Scorpion. This places Mohenjo-daro, for the present, at the head of all the civilizations of the world.

The more we know about archaic culture the more we become aware of links, borrowings, and influences. The fact that many of the seals and some of the pottery found at Mohenjo-daro resemble those found in Sumeria cannot be an accident. What is more remarkable is that these particular seals belong to different phases of their respective civilizations: the products of the very earliest phase of Sumerian culture match those found in the later epochs of Mohenjo-daro. This presumably suggests not merely that the Indus

[1] We mention this circumstance because it happens that during the writing of the present volume two extremely interesting discoveries have been made: first, the finding of the earliest Old Testament manuscripts near Jericho, and secondly the unearthing at Kara Tepe in Cilicia of the inscribed Hittite bas-reliefs. The past is a great deal more fluid than the present.

[2] The lowest foundations are unfortunately waterlogged.

civilization was in touch with that at Sumeria, but that the latter owed a great deal—perhaps even its existence—to the former. Or, perhaps, as some archaeologists believe, both civilizations owed their existence to a third situated somewhere between. Possibly when we learn to read, if we ever do, the pictographic writing adorning some of the pottery found at Mohenjo-daro, we shall become aware of something else, even if only indirectly: the existence of a tradition of thought taking us back to and even beyond that of the Memphite Drama. And that will mean another drastic revision of current preconceptions.

Reference to these early civilized settlements in the Sind region was necessary even if only to dispel the impression, derived inevitably from history books, of a sudden and therefore inexplicable arrival of thought, art, and science in India. Such things do not arrive suddenly, though they may be suddenly extinguished. They must be viewed against their own receding background. Their apparent isolation in time must be discounted. When the so-called Aryan invaders descended upon north India they found the country occupied by a people of whose existence traces have been found at Mohenjo-daro itself. These people are known as Magas and they worshipped the serpent. Now the serpent symbol is found upon seals unearthed from Mohenjo-daro. It is likewise found upon some of the seals that we have mentioned as belonging to the earliest Sumerian (or pre-Sumerian) civilization. Today it remains the symbol of that strange devil-worshipping people, the Yezidis, who inhabit the region of Arbil in northern Iraq. Another people, of whose civilization we have evidence, were met by the Aryans in their invasion of the Deccan region to the south. These were the Dravidians.

Where did the Aryans come from? It seems almost certain that their home country was precisely that *Airyana Vaejo* (Aryan Home) of which we have already heard in Zoroastrian scriptures, particularly the area of Persia bordering the Caspian Sea. Possibly this area is the cradle of civilization. Entering India about 1600 B.C., they took a long time penetrating so vast a country; but, by following the great rivers, they finally mastered a very large part of it.[1] In calling themselves Aryans they meant to convey the impression, reinforced by success, of racial or class superiority: for Aryan derives from the Sanskrit term meaning "noble". Being likewise a small if powerful minority, they were evidently determined to preserve their purity of race. Intermarriage between Aryan and Naga or Dravidian was rigorously forbidden. This measure was the origin,

[1] i.e. the area known as Hindustan, from the Persian word *Hindu*. This meant the whole of the north.

at first purely ethnographic, of that system of social discrimination which is known as Caste.[1]

Although the "Vedic Age" is usually considered to have started about 2000 B.C., the world of the *Vedas* is that of the early Aryan conquerors. For this reason they reflect two worlds at once: that into which Aryans had ventured, with its strange and sometimes uncouth gods, and that which the conquerors themselves introduced. The word *Veda* means in Sanskrit "knowledge". Of the original number of these Books of Knowledge we are ignorant. Judging from the four that have survived they must have formed a very considerable body of sacred literature, which was the transcript of a still greater volume of memorized lore. Like all religious scriptural material of any antiquity, the *Vedas* contained a great deal of purely ecclesiastical data and the inevitable portion of *arcana*, magical and hermetic lore, etc. In the history of human thought, only one of the *Vedas* is of importance, namely the *Rig-Veda*, a collection of 1,028 religious hymns or *mantras*. *Rig* means "verse"; *Rig-Veda* may therefore be rendered by some such title as "Songs of Spiritual Knowledge".

The *Vedas* were intended to be committed to memory. Recitation from memory was originally a religious act. Even today we speak of "learning by *heart*", and not by mind or brain: no child was ever taught to read his prayers. So important was it that the *Vedas* should be transmitted orally (and learning by heart depends upon oral practice) that they were not committed to paper until long after writing became widespread in India. As this transcription took place perhaps as late as the 9th century B.C., we can judge to what extent early Indian religious thought depended upon communal memory. Some critics have suggested that this long dependence upon oral tradition makes nonsense of the claim that the *Vedas*, being supposedly communicated to man by God, have been preserved without modification from time immemorial. Without subscribing to the divine authorship of the *Vedas* (unless by that we mean authorship dictated from "above", such as that which produced the Decalogue and, if we are to attach any significant meaning to "above", every other piece of inspired writing), we may still accept the view that they have undergone comparatively little change. For, as we remarked in connection with the *Zend-Avesta*, oral transmission in days when this was either the sole or the most revered method of communication was probably as reliable as written. Even today the things that for convenience we commit to memory—the alphabet, for instance—are not observed to suffer

[1] The only mention of such social division—very elementary at this stage—is in the *Vedic* "Hymn to Perusha" (Book X, 90).

appreciable corruption in the process. Alterations and interpolations in tales and sagas are another matter. These are due, as Aristotle remarked, to the idea entertained by all story-tellers that exaggeration renders a tale more exciting.

Like the great poetic works that succeeded them, the *Vedas* are composed in Sanskrit, the most ancient of the group of languages from which English is itself derived. But the Sanskrit that we study today was not the language of the early Aryan invaders of India. Arriving in groups or tribes, these invaders probably spoke a variety of dialects. It is possible that Sanskrit may not originally have been a vernacular tongue at all: the word itself conveys the notion of something which is reserved for special purposes, probably sacred ones. Just as Hieroglyphic means "sacred writing", so Sanskrit means "sacred speaking". The composition of the *Vedas* in Sanskrit is another indication of their antiquity; it is also an indication of the esteem in which they were held. The classical, sacral language would be used only for that which was considered holy and worthy of preservation.

Of the religion of the pre-*vedic* age we know extremely little; all we can do is to make inferences about it. We know that the worship of animals, including the serpent, was prevalent, and from this we can assume the practice of fertility cults. There were also gods of trees (*yakshas*) and plants. One such tree, the *Bodhi* tree, seems to have been regarded as sacred from remotest time. When Buddha, sitting under it, received the sense of his mission, he was stationed at a spot at which such experiences, though less remarkable, were regarded as natural and appropriate.[1] One such plant, the *soma*, and in particular its intoxicating juice, had long been revered in both Persia and Hindustan. When Zoroaster was said to have been brought into the world through its agency, his sacrosanct nature was thereby demonstrated or confirmed. A new religion is rendered the more holy by having chosen to avail itself, in its formative years, of the salient features of the old; for repudiation is a political rather than a religious weapon. In the *Vedas* we find hymns addressed to almost every aspect of nature, and particularly to those objects whose influence could directly be felt by man; the sun, wind, water, fire, light, and that imperative force that resides in men themselves, ensuring their increase. Addressed directly as personalities, the gods of the *Rig-Veda* form a kind of ordered hierarchy: which suggests that the hymns are approved elements of a canon established by priests. We may therefore assume that they are concerned with a selection rather than a collection of gods. What may strike the European as a crude, polytheistic attitude

[1] See Chapter V.

Picture Post Library

THE CHILD KRISHNA AND HIS FOSTER-MOTHER YASHODA

by Asil Kumar Haldar

to life is no doubt the most refined abstraction from popular animism and totemism.

Like the compilers of the Old Testament, the editors of the *Rig-Veda* anthology were careful to preserve intact material belonging to different epochs. We are thus able to trace the development of the early Aryan religious consciousness, just as a reading of early and later parts of the Bible affords us an enlarged conception of the nature of the Hebrew Yahve. There is wisdom in this refusal on the part of priestly guardians to suppress the primitive elements of their faith; for these are better kept well before the eye than allowed to fester, as the result of excision, in that uneasy corner to be found in the most devout conscience. Some of the *Vedic* hymns are merely satirical, such as that addressed "To Frogs", which is considered to be a satire on the priesthood; or straightforward *vers de société*—such as that on "The Gambler", of whose dice ("dearer than *soma*") it is said:

> Downward they roll, and then spring quickly upward, and, handless, force
> The man with hands to serve them.
> Cast on the board, like lumps of magic charcoal, though cold themselves, they burn
> The heart to ashes.

Others consist of fanciful or naive speculations, such as why the sun travels through the heavens without falling down, or imaginary dialogues such as that between the first man and woman, Yama and Yami (cf. Yima of the Zoroastrian scriptures), debating whether or not to start the human race, an initiative for which Yama shows some reluctance. If the *Rig-Veda* contained nothing but verse of this kind, it would still be a curiosity of great interest and a historical document of a period otherwise obscure; but its value would be on a level with that of the *Atharva-Veda*, with its charms and formulae to grow hair, cure sterility, confound witchcraft, and encourage the crops.

The great value of the *Rig-Veda* lies in those *mantras*, mostly to be found in the tenth book, which deal with philosophic themes. Let us take first the great Creation Hymn, which Max Müller described as the "first word spoken by Aryan man". (That may be true; but if so, Aryan man must have thought a good deal before he spoke.) The hymn begins with an attempt to represent the world or universe as it was before creation started. At that time, says the poet, only "That One Thing, breathless, breathed by its own nature: apart from it was nothing whatsoever." The notion of That One Thing is further illuminated, or obscured, by a line further on which states that "the gods are later than this world's production". What, we may ask, is meant by That One Thing? The Sanskrit word for it is *Tatekam*. Now *Ekam* means "The One" or "Unity", and *tat* is the neuter personal pronoun. The concept of a Power beyond, behind and yet between all things, and finally before all things, is fundamental to the understanding of Indian thought. Sometimes called *Perusha*, but more frequently *Brahman*, this Power is nameless, beyond our mental grasp, because infinite, and also the origin of all things human and divine, because creative. The first description of it in this early hymn may give an impression of extreme vagueness, to which the poetic content no doubt lends colour; for poetry in the Western word has been regarded since the Romantic Revival as a medium in which accuracy and precision are obstacles to enjoyment. In our study of Indian thought we need to remind ourselves that the *Vedic* hymns, the *Upanishads*, and indeed all the important sacred writings of Hinduism, are in point of fact striving after an accuracy beyond that of normal everyday experience. Vagueness is neither the aim nor the result; it is the enemy. The difficulty with a concept such as That One Thing is not that it is vague, but that it represents the extreme of *abstraction*. Unfortunately the word "abstraction" is used often in two senses: the sense in which a notion is stripped of its qualities, and the sense in which a notion is freed from error or adulteration. To strip a thing of its qualities is like peeling an onion; you end up with nothing, no hidden nucleus. To free a notion from imperfection, error, and illusion is less an intellectual than a spiritual operation; and that is what the Indian mystics attempted to undertake on a scale never before practised.

The hymn in which this primary concept is first promulgated does not content itself with mere statement. It ponders how creation started. First of all, there was "desire, the primal seed and germ of spirit". This idea, to which Buddha and later Plato devoted so much attention, is not here elaborated, for the poet is concerned primarily with the awe and wonder of creation, not with its detailed mechanism. Indeed, he concludes with questions that are deliberately rhetorical:

> Who verily knows and who can here declare it, whence it was born and whence comes this creation?
> The gods are later than this world's production. Who knows then whence it first came into being?
> He, the first origin of this creation, whether he formed it all or did not form it,
> Whose eye controls this world in highest heaven, he verily knows it, or perhaps he knows it not.[1]

[1] Cf. the Zoroastrian *Prayer for Guidance*, which contains a similar series of questions.

Although this hymn and the others of the same nature are concerned to illuminate philosophic themes, we must bear in mind that, being poems intended for declamation, their primary purpose is to put the devout listener in the correct frame of mind. They form elements in a liturgy, which is none the less intellectual for having an overtly emotional purpose: people do not go to church to learn to worship. This may throw light upon an element of apparent scepticism in some of the most profound of the hymns, such as that addressed to Prajapati (X, 121), the Lord of all Living Things, who long enjoyed an immense reputation among the people. This hymn, for which the title *To the Unknown God* was suggested by Max Müller, sings of the "giver of vital breath, of power and vigour, he whose commandments all gods acknowledge", but concludes nine of its ten verses with the tantalizing phrase "What god shall we adore with our oblation?" There is an apparent contradiction here; but if we realize that the same distinction is being made as in the Creation Hymn, between the ultimate Unity (with which Prajapati was later associated) and individual deities, the point of the repeated question becomes clearer. The emphasis, as always, is on the inadequacy of the human mind to comprehend the meaning of life. In the last verse we have a clue to the general argument: "Prajapati! Thou only comprehendest all these created things and none beside thee. Grant us our hearts' desire when we invoke thee." The hymn is designed to produce a condition of mind not of scepticism but of intellectual humility.

The gods whose power and bounty are hymned with particular fervour in the *Rig-Veda* are Agni, god of fire in all forms, and Indra, the "Heaven pervading" storm god. To the latter, a quarter of the hymns are dedicated. Towards the end of the collection the reputation of both these gods suffers something of an eclipse, which suggests that they were gods associated with the days of the original conquest of India rather than with the period of consolidation and settlement. In the powerful *Hymn to Indra* in Book II (12), we may note the phrase "without whose help our people never conquer", and also the remark in verse 5 to the effect that Indra's existence and power have lately been subject to doubt. A most interesting light upon the relations between Persia and India is shed by the reputation enjoyed in the two countries by both Indra and that other important god, Varuna. Indra, the god of storm and thunder, becomes in Persia a demon. Recollecting the low repute in which winter was held among the followers of Zoroaster, we can scarcely wonder that the god whose activities contributed so largely to the defects of that season should have been pronounced diabolical. Varuna, however, the god of the heavens—"who, standing in the firmament, hath meted the earth out with the sun as with a measure"—was a figure to undergo marked development in both India and Persia. In Persia, for reasons that will appear, he was regarded as identical with no less a figure than Ahura Mazda himself. In India, from being a god of the high heavens, "the universal encompasser", he gradually came to be associated with the universality of moral and ethical order in the world. This order went by the name of *Rita*. *Rita* began by being a kind of moral thread or current running through the universe, keeping it not merely harmonious but suffused with the radiance of goodness. In due time *Rita* was conceived as also weaving its path through the souls of men, being present to the individual as a kind of throb at the depth of his self, which, duly attended to, indicated his oneness with the universe. We shall see to what length the Indian thinkers pushed this conception of ultimate selfhood when we come to discuss the *Upanishads*, with their concept of *Atman*. As guardian of this precious law—the Hindu equivalent of *Maat* and *Tao*—Varuna is thus described in an early hymn (V, 85):

> In the tree-tops the air he hath extended, put milk in kine and vigorous speed in horses,
> Set intellect in hearts, fire in the waters, the sun in the sky and Soma on the mountain.

In precisely such terms the Zoroastrians sang the majesty of Ahura Mazda.

The Upanishads

At one end of the *Rig-Veda* we have the terrible might and fury of Indra—"impetuous as a bull" (I, 32). At the other end we have a world of personified abstractions: Creativity, Liberality, Speech, Faith, to each of which at least one hymn is devoted. We seem to be moving forward to a sphere of thought in which the sonorous verse and emotional intensity of the *Vedas* will need to be sacrificed, as too much of a luxury, later to return in the elevated poetry of the *Bhagavad-Gita*. What is to happen in the meantime? The intervening period is to be filled with the deep speculations of which we have already hinted, those of *Upanishads*.

That it is misleading to regard the *Vedas* as having been composed at a kind of "morning of the world", as the phrase of Max Müller would suggest, we have duly emphasized. What is more probable is that they reflect, like most other creative movements, a renewal of vitality, one of those sudden renaissances of the spirit, the regular succession of which in the past makes history an intelligible story instead of a mere log-book. To what causes such movements can be ascribed we can hazard only guesses. Possibly soil erosion accounts for a good many of the major displacements of population in history, or the lure of more temperate climates, or the decline of an established trade. Such material causes do not determine the nature or quality of the results. Just as the movement of a tribe through Mesopotamia started a religion of righteousness, so the advance of a race through Baluchistan started a religion of knowledge. Needless to say, such invasions or penetrations may be completely sterile: the Turks and the Germans do not seem to have possessed the gift of fruitful invasion.[1]

In one of the last of the *Rig-Veda* hymns (X, 151), it is asserted that "man winneth faith by yearnings of the heart", and the same poem concludes with the words "O Faith, endow us with belief". The *Vedas* are rich not merely in faith—for the mere perception of beauty is a token of faith: faith in the value of that which is seen—but in the kind of enquiry which, by endeavouring to penetrate behind that which is seen, leads to belief in a profounder sense. In the *Upanishads* the "yearnings of the heart" assume an intellectual guise. From a sweeping contemplation of the world the sages turned to an inward scrutiny. In so doing they withdrew from all publicity and contact with men. Retiring to the forests and jungles for the sake of secrecy, they engaged in deep discussion; sage and saints in solitude, like the later Desert Fathers in Egypt, sage with sage exchanging the results of their meditations, master and pupil in the work of initiation and instruction. For the "highest mystery in the *Vedanta*, delivered in a former age", as the *Svetasvatara Upanishad* says, "should not be given to one whose passions have not been subdued, nor to one who is not a son, or who is not a pupil". The element of debate and exchange of view has been preserved in the word *Upanishad* itself, which is made up of *upa*, near, and *shad*, to sit. To "sit at the feet of" is still the phrase we use to convey the notion of receiving wisdom, as opposed to mere information, from a teacher of high repute. The *Upanishads* are the confidential reports of such secret sessions.

To contemplate is ultimately to become aware of the distinction between oneself and the object. The self here and the world there: the self with its egoistic desires, and the world with its apparently unrelated and impersonal laws: and thus arises the need to establish some relation between the one sphere and the other. This is the strategy of the *Upanishads*. Upon these problems the forest saints and sages devoted their lives to reflecting. We would give much to know about the men (and women) who were thus addicted to a

[1] See the interesting analysis of this failure in R. G. Collingwood's *New Leviathan* (1943), section on "Barbarism".

passion for thought. Of some we know the bare names. As for their daily life, this was devoted entirely to meditation, leaving no time for the "action" with which other people, terrified of being left to their own reflections, cram their waking hours. Nevertheless, as we shall see, such mental labour does not deprive them of vitality and character. In due time they come alive and acquire a reality greater than that of more strenuous individuals.

How did the sages work out the "problem" that we have stated? To answer this question is to plunge directly into that celebrated argument concerning the Self and the Divine Ground of existence—*Atman* and *Brahman*—which was first raised in the creation hymn of the *Rig-Veda*. To some people, this argument represents the highest point to which human intelligence has ascended. It forms the crux of all philosophical enquiry. Not to grasp its meaning and import is to fall short of the kind of experience that renders life significant and meaningful. There is no choice, such people maintain, between living according to this fundamental truth and living according to a "simpler" or more "comfortable" doctrine. The choice is between living according to this doctrine and not living at all. This only is reality. This only is truth, wholeness, *it*.

We may add in parenthesis that this celebrated problem is not merely a philosophical, still less an academic, one. Bearing in mind what we have said about the identity in Indian thought between philosophy and religion, we perceive that it is concerned precisely with the establishment of that "divine connection", that uniting of the way of earth with that of heaven, which is the essence of the religious quest. Moreover, it is accorded a solution to which all the great religions subscribe. A faith which refuses to accept it in general terms is one that has failed to realize the implications of its own claims to truth.

The proposition with which the sages start is as follows. Our ordinary world, with its material objects and its individual minds or consciousnesses, is a world of imprecision, incompleteness, finitude. Being incomplete and unstable, it is neither self-reliant, nor self-supporting: in other words, it depends for such reality as it possesses upon a realm of totally different character. This other realm is the Ground of all existence. It is the That One Being of which the *Vedic* hymn speaks. The "things" of which our existence and experiences are composed form manifestations of this Ground. Their "thinghood" is precisely that which, rendering them separate and distinct one from another, gives rise to their imperfection. "Wise men only," says the *Katha Upanishad*, "knowing the nature of what is immortal, do not look for anything stable here among things unstable."

An important fact to which students of the *Upanishads* do not always pay sufficient attention is that among the individual things in the universe deriving their reality from the ultimate and Divine Ground are the gods themselves, or at least the gods as conceived in the limited way characteristic of human beings. This is true even of the notion of *Brahma*, which, in contrast to *Brahman*, means God as creator.[1]

This first proposition, which resembles distinctly that of Plato in defining the world of phenomenon as only partially real, is not stated without some show of proof. The proof lies in our own experience. This does not mean that to most people such a statement appears immediately obvious. What is immediately obvious differs according to the level to which the individual's experience has attained. Part of the grounds for supposing the statement to be true is derived from the manner in which its truth comes at length to be perceived. In other words, the fuller our experience—the older we are in knowledge of life—the better equipped we shall be to acknowledge that statement as a true statement. Now what sort of knowledge is it that we acquire from ripening experience? Surely it is an increased perception of the unsatisfactory character of everything belonging to the natural plane. Only maturing experience could disclose such knowledge, such progressive *disillusion*. Nor, unless the maturing mind were simultaneously in process of acquiring a new form of apprehension, could the disclosure have been vouchsafed. The new form of apprehension is that relating to a sphere of reality from which defect, error, and illusion are absent. Without some such insight into perfection we should be unable to perceive the extent to which our everyday experience fell short of it. This ideal sphere of reality is the Divine Ground of existence. A "Ground", on this basis, is that by which ultimately everything is what it is, just as the ground (or grounds) of an argument is that upon which the argument hinges, its *raison d'être*.

Such knowledge is acquired by the process known as inference. From one condition we argue logically to the existence of another. But the sages of the *Upanishads* believe that knowledge of the Divine Ground can be acquired in a more direct fashion. This is due to the nature of the Ground itself, which is necessarily difficult to define. Although it is beyond the reach of our intellectual faculties, it is nevertheless sufficiently akin to the soul to be within its grasp. By the faculty of intuition the human mind may apprehend the Ground as something with which it enjoys a special relationship.

[1] Cf. The *Bhagavad-Gita*: "All the worlds, and even the heavenly realm of *Brahma*, are subject to the laws of rebirth. But for the man who comes to me (Krishna), there is no returning" (Book VIII). Shankara later developed this view.

And this act of intuitive apprehension, if pure and direct, effects an immediate union between the mind and that which it apprehends. Even so, as the Ground is in its wholeness beyond human grasp, the sages have a special term, *Ishwara*, to denote that much of the Ground which the intellect can know. *Ishwara* may be regarded in much the same light as the "personal" God of Christianity.

Such an act of union would be impossible if the self consisted simply of the phenomenal self, the natural ego. But every individual, even the most corrupt and self-obsessed, possesses another and deeper self, the Eternal Self. It is by discovering within himself this deeper Self that man is able, if he chooses, to apprehend the Divine Ground. And as this deeper or Eternal Self is simply the divine Ground immanent in human beings,[1] the union of one with the other is simply the recognition of Identity. Such state of union, which the sages call *Nirvana*, is not to be reached without discipline, renunciation, and indeed complete self-surrender.

Granted the existence of the Divine Ground, and assuming that in every individual there exists a deeper, inner or noumenal Self which partakes of the nature of this Ground, then it must necessarily follow that the duty of all men here on earth consists in entering into the state of divine union. Not to render themselves fit for such union is to frustrate the purpose for which they were put into the world. Worse than that: it is to condemn themselves to a prolongation of their state of separation and misery, and perhaps to an intensification of it in another existence or series of existences. "For them who depart from hence without having discovered the Self and those true desires, for them there is no freedom in all the worlds. But those who depart from hence, after having discovered the Self and those true desires, for them there is freedom in all the worlds" (*Chandogya Upanishad*).

To the Divine Ground the sages give the name of *Brahman*. Now *Brahman* cannot be translated exactly as God. It is rather a kind of undifferentiated Godhead. The inner Self is called *Atman*, which is *Brahman* immanent in man. The *Upanishads* employ a particular phrase to describe the fundamental identity between the self and the Ground of existence, between *Brahman* and *Atman*. This is the tense, startling observation upon which the whole argument hinges, "Thou art that." In other words, the "inner" Thou is not merely equivalent to, but identical with, the objective That. The eternal Ground flows under both the phenomenal world and the phenomenal self, uniting in reality that which is considered separate in the world of opaque experience; for that which is of the surface does not

[1] "When we consider *Brahman* as lodged within the individual being, we call him the *Atman*" (*Bhagavad-Gita*).

know itself to be superficial unless irradiated by wisdom. "He (the Ground) is the beginning, producing the causes which unite the soul with the body, being above the three kinds of time, past, present, future, he is seen as without parts, after we have first worshipped that adorable god, who has many forms, and who is the true source of all things, as dwelling in our mind. He is beyond all the forms of the world and of time, he is the other, from whom this world moves round, when one has known him who brings good and removes evil, the lord of bliss, as dwelling within the self, the immortal, the support of all" (*Svetasvatara Upanishad*).

To illustrate the doctrine of the *Upanishads* by introducing here and there a brief quotation, however carefully chosen, must inevitably give a false impression of both their profundity and even their charm. We must not imagine them simply as consisting of a series of aloof, dogmatic, and sometimes highly disputable utterances, delivered by those who considered themselves already to have achieved the measure of renunciation necessary to sanctity. Much of the interest of the *Upanishads* is that of following the stages of the argument: equally impressive is to observe the intellectual humility of both teacher and pupil. What they claim to have achieved is not sanctity or deliverance but the knowledge of the way to these things. Some scholars have maintained that "it is not for the systems they build or for the truths that they can be said to have discovered that these scriptures are to be so greatly prized, but rather for the simplicity and earnestness with which great problems are approached".[1] Such an approach is certainly to be recommended in preference to the arid disputation with which philosophical discussion has so often come to be associated, especially in academic life; but this attitude to the *Upanishads* remains open to the same objection as that which withholds praise from the Bible except as "fine literature". The disciples of the sages, both contemporary and in later times, regard the *Upanishads* not as exercises in thinking but as repositories of divine thought. The truth of the identification of *Brahman* and *Atman* is regarded as a fact, even a revelation. To the student whose philosophical knowledge is confined to the Western world the tendency is to accept as normal in a professional philosopher the famous doctrine of Kant, who claimed that he taught his pupils not philosophy but how to philosophize. The logical conclusion to such an attitude, at least in less capable hands, is the cultivation of philosophy as a superior kind of game, played in the lecture-room or at meetings of learned societies, where the intrusion of truth or wisdom as a guide to right conduct is considered almost a scandal. We make a great mistake if we suppose that such a

[1] Dr. Nichol MacNichol: Introduction to *Hindu Scriptures* (Dent, 1943).

superficial attitude is characteristic of the mind of India. Nor have we any reason to think that the new India will in this respect differ from the old.

Perhaps the most illuminating of these discourses, from the point of view of human interest, is that which is entitled the *Brihadaranyaka Upanishad*. The story is there related of the departure from home of the sage Yajnavalkya, the so-called "Lord of Sacrifice", who is reputed to have written some of the most revered Hindu scriptures. Before leaving to adopt a hermit life, he announces that he wishes to make a settlement between his two wives, Maitreyi and Katyayani. We are told that one of these wives "possessed such knowledge only as women possess", whereas the other, Maitreyi, was a woman of fine perceptions with an understanding, if not direct experience, of *Brahman*. Maitreyi, to whom he announces his intention of departing, takes the opportunity of asking him whether in his opinion wealth, such as perhaps she may one day possess, will bring immortal happiness. He assures her that it will not. Still detaining him, she then solicits his views upon immortality. As "thou art truly dear to me," he replies, "and speakest dear words, come sit down and I will explain it to thee". He then embarks upon an exposition of the doctrine of human love according to the meditations in which he has engaged. Human beings and natural things cannot, he maintains, be direct objects of love. When we love them, our love is directed not at but through them. Love being of the Self (*Atman*), it seeks in its activity that which will bring it once more in contact with eternity (*Brahman*); and this it does by embracing the Self in another. Such an activity, being possible only if it renounces all commerce with the world of *Maya* or illusion, is the reverse of selfish or sensual. Love on the natural plane seeks only to possess, to multiply and cultivate illusions. Love on the eternal plane seeks only to renounce, and, having renounced, to merge with the Godhead. The complete union sought by lovers on the natural plane increases their separation both from each other and from the Divine Ground. Such union is possible only in the mutual recognition of the true Self in each individual, which results in the possession of lasting happiness in the shape of release from desire (*Moksha*).[1]

Yajnavalkya illustrates his argument by a long series of statements of which the following are typical: "Verily a husband is not dear, that you may love the husband; but that you may love the Self through the husband, therefore a husband is dear. Verily a wife is not dear, that you may love the wife, but that you may love the

[1] Cf. "Love between persons means that each wants the other to be more himself" (*The Mind and Heart of Love*, by M. C. D'Arcy, S.J. (1945), p. 166).

Self through the wife, therefore a wife is dear. . . . Verily creatures are not dear, that you may love the creatures; but that you may love the Self through the creatures, therefore are creatures dear. . . . Verily, everything is not dear, that you may love everything; but that you may love the Self through everything, therefore everything is dear." He then proceeds to illustrate by means of analogy the nature of the Godhead or *Brahman* to which he would direct the attention. Here, again, we observe how such analogies serve to keep concrete and full-blooded a doctrine that must otherwise remain dim and remote. "As all waters find their centre in the sea, all touches in the skin, all tastes in the tongue, all smells in the nose, all colours in the eye, all sounds in the ear, all percepts in the mind, all knowledge in the heart, all actions in the hands, and all *Vedas* in speech; as a lump of sugar, when thrown into water, becomes dissolved into water, and could not be taken out again, but whenever we taste (the water) it is sweet—thus verily, O Maitreyi, does this great Being, endless, unlimited, consisting of nothing but knowledge, rise from out their elements and vanish again in them. When he has departed there is no more knowledge."

But Maitreyi is still puzzled. "Here thou has bewildered me, sir," she protests, "when thou sayest that having departed, there is no more knowledge." To which the husband replies: "O Maitreyi, I say nothing that is bewildering. This is enough, O beloved, for wisdom. For when there is as it were duality, then one sees the other, one smells the other, one hears the other, one salutes the other, one perceives the other, one knows the other; but when the Self only is all this, how should he smell another, how should he see another, how should he hear another, how should he salute another, how should he perceive another, how should he know another? How should he know him by whom he knows all this? The self is to be described by No, no![1] He is incomprehensible, for he cannot be comprehended. He is imperishable, because he cannot perish. He is unattached, for he does not attach himself; unfettered, he does not suffer, he does not fail. How, O beloved, should he know the knower? Thus, O Maitreyi, thou hast been instructed. Thus far goes immortality."

In the above passage, with its repetitions characteristic of an age of oral tradition, Yajnavalkya is seeking to emphasize three points of capital importance for the *Upanishad* doctrine. The first is one to which Plato later (but not so very much later) gave expression in his statement, never perhaps surpassed in pregnancy of meaning, that "Love is the desire and pursuit of the Whole"—

[1] Sanskrit *Neti, neti,* "Not this, not that": in other words the Self cannot be defined in ordinary terms.

i.e. The All, the *Brahman*. The second point is that human values, such as love and beauty, are important not in themselves but in their revelation, however intermittent, of a more fundamental and eternal love and beauty. Their reality resides in that which they "let through" from the eternal source of value which is *Brahman*. The third point is that the object of knowledge is attained not through vain learning and academic study, but through a kind of willed-for ignorance, a draining of the mind of the conceit of worldly erudition. "Not by learning is the *Atman* attained, not by genius and much knowledge of books . . . Let a Brahman[1] renounce learning and become as a child." The whole world, suggests Yajnavalkya by his similes, is as it were suffused with *Brahman*, dissolved in Spirit; but only those whose taste is not corrupted and jaded can become aware of the fact. The same truth is conveyed in another brilliant simile from the *Svetasvatara Upanishad*, namely that *Brahman* is "like a fire that had consumed its fuel". When the individual has disciplined his soul sufficiently and attained to a knowledge of truth, he will issue forth in the childlike state defined by another faith as a condition of entering the Kingdom of Heaven. When the individual is one with Reality, the inherent division of ordinary existence, with its mind-body and pleasure-pain duality, will have been healed, as the wake of a ship closes up without trace. If, to preserve the marine metaphor, we think of Being as an ocean, the waves are creatures that assert a momentary individuality and are then drawn down once more into the depths.

How, it may be asked at this point, can we suppose any husband to have addressed his wife in such terms as these, even though the husband was one of the world's great sages and the wife a woman of more than ordinary intellect? What couple can be imagined as having devoted the last hour of their domestic life together to such high-flown discourse? Naturally, the *Upanishads* as they have come down to us are stylized, formalistic documents; they are more rigid in their composition even than the *Dialogues* of Plato. Nevertheless, they transmit across all these centuries an experience that we recognize to be at bottom authentic. To the Western mind, such an experience may not come alive without violent imaginative readjustment. We have to put ourselves in the place of men and women whose conditions of life brought them face to face with naked reality, almost with essences; whereas the machine-punctuated life of the modern man shows him reality several times removed.[2] Had they been accessible, the reports of these elemental experiences would have been more easily appreciated by the pre-industrial

[1] The word here means a member of the caste of priests.
[2] We return to this point in the Conclusion.

generations, for whom the rhythm of life had undergone negligible change since the Neolithic epoch. Our modern lives are notched with such intervals as pay-day, the year's holiday, the receipt of a government pension. We find it hard to conceive of a life controlled by the more plastic but apparently endless rhythm of the seasons: a life brooded over by an eternity of natural recurrence, and alternately drenched by heat and torrent. Such materially sheltered existence has rendered us correspondingly less exposed to those spiritual truths which stare the oriental in the face—namely the vanity of egoism, desire, and attachment to objects of sense.

Granted this thoroughly disillusioned view of the nature of existence—"this patched-together hiding-place", as Yajnavalkya describes it—we find it hardly surprising that the origin of mankind should have been regarded by early Hindu philosophers as an event of shame and evil. In the hymn of the *Rig-Veda*, to which we have already referred, Yama and Yami's mating is concluded in an atmosphere of guilt. "Shall we not do," says Yami, "what we never did aforetime? we who spoke righteously now talk impurely?" Since Yama and Yami were brother and sister, the feeling of guilt may partly be accounted for by horror of incest; but in the first of the *Upanishads* (fourth *Brahman*) we find a story of the Creation which is equally coloured by feelings of guilt. In the beginning, according to this account, was the Self, the *Atman*, which, feeling no delight in a solitary existence, "made his Self fall into two, and thence arose husband and wife". After the first embrace, however, the woman, experiencing a sudden feeling of shame, feels she must hide herself. This she does by becoming successively most of the animals of creation, down to the ant. Each time, the husband, following suit, became the male animal, with the result that the entire fauna of the world were brought into existence. Even allowing for the latitude of allegory, this particular story borders on the ludicrous; but we may observe that it exhibits two points in common with most of the other Creation stories. The first is that woman is born from part of man. The second is that the act whereby mankind is begotten produces an immediate sense of shame. We are here dealing with a feeling deeply implanted within the human mind. Consciousness of sex and consciousness of sin are somehow interrelated, no man knows why: but particularly is this the case with the act from which sprang humankind. It is interesting to note that modern psychology has no more succeeded in explaining this human obsession than any other science; indeed, what modern psychology has done is merely to confirm its existence at every mental level. Undoubtedly the Hindu attitude, which received impressive confirmation at the hands of Buddha, was the result of its horror of rebirth. To be born was forthwith to step into the realm of desire and attachment—to enter upon a career that might last for ages, if not for all eternity. In these circumstances, the act from which such infinite evil might spring must itself be evil, while most evil of all would be the initial act of our first ancestors. Upon the latter (as they apparently recognized) a terrible responsibility rested.

If life, and in particular birth, represented so great an evil, however, why did not the sages recommend either the prevention of the continuation of the race or the universal practice of suicide upon attaining years of discretion? We shall see in due course that a certain school of thinkers, more logical perhaps than the forest sages, advocated and adopted precisely these measures.

The Bhagavad-Gita

The ancient hymns of the *Rig-Veda* were considered, as we saw, to have been communicated to man by God Himself. Although such divine origins were not ascribed to the *Upanishads*, the latter were, and still are, regarded as sacred writings or *Sruti*. Today they remain as precious to the devout as they were in the centuries of their composition and compilation, which was probably between 800 and 500 B.C. If the Western reader finds the *Upanishads* dull or remote he can usually assume that he has failed, even though he may have tried, to make the imaginative readjustment of which we have spoken. He may be reassured, however, by the knowledge that even the most orthodox Hindus regard the *Upanishads* as, if not deficient, then at least in need of completion by a less purely intellectual doctrine. Just as they benefit from being preceded by the imaginatively rich *Rig-Veda*, so they gain immeasurably by being followed by the far richer *Bhagavad-Gita*. "The *Upanishads*," wrote Rabindranath Tagore, "though they measured the highest reaches of the philosophic imagination of our people, were yet incomplete in their answer to the complex longing of the human soul. Their emphasis was too intellectual, and did not sufficiently explore the approach to Reality through love and devotion."[1]

Indian philosophical tradition has fully recognized the different degrees in wisdom to which the three great elements of Hindu scripture approximate. In the first place there is the so-called Path of Activity, or *Karmamarga*. To this path belongs the *Vedas*, songs to be chanted in public as a stimulus to effort: the anthems of a people

[1] Tagore's verdict, always worthy of the greatest respect, is in this case indisputable; but his view of the *Vedas* as being the product of a "childlike" approach to reality seems to be based upon assumptions about human progress learnt from the West: a danger to which lesser intellects of the Orient are the more obviously exposed.

engaged in a communal exploit needing for its accomplishment a burning faith in its mission. In the second place there is the so-called Path of Knowledge, or *Inanamarga*. To this path belong the *Upanishads*, explorations by the mind in secret conclave of that which is permanently knowable behind the world of appearances and illusion. In the third place there is the so-called Path of Devotion, or *Bhaktimarga*. To this path belong the *Bhagavad-Gita*. This epic within an epic retails the story not of the Philosopher King but of someone rarer still, the Philosopher Hero. It demonstrates for all time the possibility of serving *Brahman* wholeheartedly in a situation very different from that chosen by the authors of the *Upanishads*. Obsessed by their problems, the forest sages often failed to see the wood for the trees. Arjuna, the hero of the *Gita*, makes the great reconciliation between immediate duty, dictated by material and political considerations, and the ultimate obligations of a devotee of *Brahman*. It is perhaps the only convincing *solution* to a problem that faces sometimes a whole generation, but of which few perceive the true nature.

The *Bhagavad-Gita* is a poem unique in the world's literature. In the first place it belongs as much to philosophy as to literature, and as much to the social life of India as to its spiritual heritage. As a document revered as sacred or *Smriti*[1] by all Hindus, it is still employed for taking oaths. As a work of literature, it forms an acknowledged masterpiece; the best translations convey enough of its beauty of expression to suggest something of the perfection of the original. And compared with the scriptures of any other religion, it excels all except the New Testament in its sustained exposition of spiritual truth.

The title *Bhagavad-Gita* is best rendered in English as *The Lord's Song*. Although it forms an epic poem in itself, it is in point of fact a digression of considerable length in another epic of much greater dimensions. The *Mahabharata*, as this gigantic 200,000-line poem was called, dates from about 500 B.C. We do not know who wrote it. All we know is that it was added to and elaborated over a period of many centuries; that it received its present form about A.D. 400 under the great Gupta kings, and that at some point in its compilation the *Bhagavad-Gita* was included within it, forming what is now Book VI. No wonder that the only author to be associated, if not credited, with its composition should have borne the name of *Vyasa*, which means literally compiler or editor. The *Mahabharata* (or "Great Bharata") is the last place in which one would expect to find a piece of writing such as the *Bhagavad-Gita*. Bharata, son of the

[1] *Smriti*, as opposed to *Sruti*, means writing or teaching of saints or prophets. It amounts to "indirect" *Sruti*.

great Indian heroine Shakuntala, is the father of two tribes, the Kurus and the Pandavas. The rambling story opens with an account of the jealousy of the Kurus for the more enlightened and god-fearing Pandavas, culminating in a gambling match in which Yudishthira, king of the Pandavas (whose only weakness was love of the dice), lost the whole of his kingdom, including his wife Draupadi, to his rival. The latter, who has employed loaded dice, now decides to eliminate the Pandavas for good and all. He is restrained by the pleas of his blind father, Dhritarashtra, under whose roof the Pandavas had themselves been educated, and agrees finally to banish them for a period of twelve years. At the conclusion of this term, which the Pandavas have spent in the forest acquiring wisdom, Duryodhana, breaking his word, refuses to restore the Pandavas their kingdom. The exiled clan have by this time acquired numerous sympathizers throughout northern India. War is declared. Among the Pandavas is the warrior Arjuna, a kind of Hindu Achilles. He chooses as his charioteer Krishna, the incarnation or *avatar* of the God *Vishnu*. Realizing that he is about to fight his own kinsmen, Arjuna hesitates on the field of battle whether to proceed to the attack. Krishna, whose identity is disclosed, argues with him, and the *Bhagavad-Gita* is the record of their remarkable conversation together. Stationed at the side of the old king Dhritarashtra, the courtier Sanjaya is specially endowed with extra-sensory perception in order to provide a running commentary upon the proceedings.

The gospel of Krishna, the Lord whose Song it is, marks the culmination of Hindu thought starting with the *Vedas*. Those for whom the *Upanishads* are cold intellectual documents will find warmth and sublimity in the *Gita*. Its general point of view, though less consistent, is more acceptable to the Western mind. Furthermore, Krishna's arguments dispose of the view that the Orient lacks a doctrine of action. Of the passive resistance or *Satyagraha*,[1] preached at a later date, there is here no hint. Even pacifism itself, of which Arjuna is at first the spokesman, meets with rejection by Krishna as incompatible with the doctrine of *Brahman*. In its day the poem no doubt provided an answer to those who feared that the *Upanishads*, with their quietist doctrines, might tend to demoralize the people. Thus although the *Gita* forms perhaps the loftiest religious epic in the world, infused with the spirit of renunciation and contemplation, it is at the same time a shrewd and noble apology for action. Whereas it probably began as a heroic poem of the *Kshatriya*, or warrior caste,[2] it was gradually moulded under Brahman influence into a "high

[1] The doctrine espoused in particular by Mahatma Gandhi.
[2] To which the Buddha and Mahavira belonged.

history", like the somewhat similar legend of the Holy Grail. The highest virtue required by the *Upanishads* is to be saintly. In the *Gita* the highest virtue enjoined upon Arjuna is devotion (*Bhakti*). Now devotion is best exemplified in selfless attachment to a person. It is Arjuna's devotion to Krishna that places the *Gita* above the *Upanishads* in point of realism and humanity. Seeing that the *Brahman* of the *Upanishads* represented an entity beyond human understanding, it was impossible that such a Supreme Being should command devotion of the personal kind lauded in the *Gita*. "The path of the Unmanifested," says Krishna in the poem, "is hard for the embodied to reach." Men talk of dedicating themselves to honour, virtue, and even love; what it is to which they declare themselves attached is always something endowed, or at least credited, with personality. Men cannot adore an abstraction. The evolution of the impersonal *Brahman* of the *Vedas*, which is often referred to as "It", into the God-Man Krishna of the *Gita*, represents a natural and inevitable process. The desire to see the human incarnation of God has been a feature of every religion, above all of Christianity. Allowing for obvious differences of message, no person in history—not even the Buddha himself—spoke more in the manner of Christ than Krishna.

Although the profound wisdom of the *Gita* is discernable to us only by studying the poem as a whole in good translation, we can follow the gist of the argument by citing certain salient passages. In his first mood of dejection, Arjuna, turning to Krishna, exclaims: "Seeing these my kinsmen, O Krishna, annoyed, eager to fight, my limbs fail and my mouth is parched, my body quivers, and my hair stands on end, Gardiva [his bow] slips from my hand, and my skin burns all over, I am not able to stand, my mind is whirling, and I see adverse omens, O Kesave ['enlightened one']. Nor do I see any advantage from slaying kinsmen in battle . . . killing these desperadoes, sin will but take hold of us . . . Although these, with intelligence overpowered by greed, see no guilt in the destruction of a family, no crime in hostility to friends, why should we not learn to turn away from such a sin, O Krishna, who see evils in destruction of a family?" Krishna does not reprove Arjuna for this natural reluctance to engage in slaughter. He even applauds his wisdom, but he goes on to point out that his grief is misplaced. To be truly wise, he says, is to grieve for neither the living nor the dead. The present evils are both temporary and ephemeral. The human soul will outlast these and every other occurrence in this world. Therefore the evils of life must be borne with equanimity. To be moved and cast down by human sorrow is to display conduct the reverse of that which deserves immortality. The immediate duty, which is resistance to the enemy, must be squarely faced. Arjuna must fight. The true Self, the *Atman*, being birthless, deathless, and changeless, will thereby come to no harm. In any case, as Krishna later points out (Book XI), Arjuna, in fighting his enemies, will only "seem to slay". In point of fact these men are already dead, having been ordained to be killed by Krishna himself. No man really kills or is killed by another, for such actions have no real significance. Regret at what is unavoidable is misplaced. If death is the outcome, heaven will be the reward; if victory, a kingdom to which Arjuna is legally entitled. Victory and defeat amount in the end to the same thing. To engage in battle in a mood of holy indifference is to rid oneself of sin.[1]

Having expounded to Arjuna the true nature of the Self, according to orthodox *Upanishad* teaching, Krishna proceeds to elaborate a doctrine which, though frequently misunderstood, has perhaps enjoyed more popularity in the Western world than any other of oriental origin. This is the doctrine known as *Karma Yoga*. Although we shall discuss Yoga in detail later, it is important to understand at the outset what is meant by these two terms. *Karma*, a word to which reference is increasingly made, is not easy to translate into English. It means primarily "deed" or "work"; but it can also mean both the results of a particular deed and the chain of causes and effects that links various deeds together. It is in the latter sense that the word is now most frequently employed. *Karma* is the law which is brought into operation by our least act in this life; for what we do in the present world is not merely the result of what we did in some past existence but the cause of what we shall do in another. The meaning of Yoga is less simple. Literally a "Yoke", it can mean the state of union with *Brahman* which is the end or goal of life. Another and more usual meaning is that of rule or path whereby this union is achieved. As there is more than one path to such union, so there are several kinds of *Yoga*. That Krishna should expound to Arjuna the principles of *Karma Yoga* is appropriate, since *Karma Yoga* is concerned with action that results from self-dedication to a personal God such as Krishna represents.

At this point in the *Gita* we become aware of a tendency to humanize the rather stringent asceticism advocated by the *Upanishads*. To approach the latter in a mood of humility, which is the correct attitude, is to be overwhelmed by the demands made upon a human nature easily tired by two minutes' concentrated thought. Salvation, it may seem, is to be acquired at a price not merely too big but beyond anything ordinary men can afford. In the *Gita*, on the

[1] One calls to mind a line of a war poem written in 1940 by Herbert Read: "To fight without hope is to fight with grace."

other hand, Krishna repeatedly stresses the value of even a brave show of effort and will. "In this Yoga," he says, "even the abortive attempt is not wasted. Nor can it produce a contrary result. Even a little practice of this Yoga will save you from the terrible wheel of rebirth and death." The first requisite is to despise and ignore the fruits of action. "You have the right to work but for the work's sake only. You have no right to the fruits of work. . . .[1] Perform every action with your heart fixed on the Supreme Lord. Renounce attachment to the fruits. Be even-tempered in success or failure; for it is this evenness of temper which is meant by Yoga." Then follows a shrewd analysis of that form of conduct which, being attached to the fruits of action, lands a person in frustration and discontent. "Thinking about sense-objects will attach you to sense objects; Grow attached, and you become addicted; Thwart your addiction, it turns to anger; Be angry and you confuse your mind; Confuse your mind, you forget the lesson of experience; Forget experience, you lose discrimination; Lose discrimination, and you miss life's only purpose." Those immersed in the life of the senses naturally believe they are enjoying the richest experience that life has to offer. To such people, the detachment of the seer appears as a kind of befuddlement. The truth is quite otherwise. "The recollected mind is awake In the knowledge of the *Atman*, Which is dark night to the ignorant: The ignorant are awake in their sense-life, Which they think is daylight: To the seer it is darkness."

It is in the third section or "lesson" of the *Gita*, specially concerned with *Karma Yoga*, that the new doctrine of action is most clearly expounded. Arjuna draws Krishna's attention to an apparent contradiction in the philosophy of *Brahman*. If, as the *Upanishads* suggest, knowledge is the highest goal of man, and if the contemplative is the highest type of human being, how can action be justified at all, let alone action involving both violence and slaughter? To this question Krishna replies that the distinction between knowledge and action is at bottom a false one. Knowledge is a form of action, because action can include the operations of the mind. In other words, we never cease to act for one moment, even in sleep.[2] Hence "freedom from action is never achieved by abstaining from action". What is required of the true devotee is not passiveness but selfless action. It is that to which *Karma Yoga*, properly followed, will lead.

The exposition of the principles of *Karma Yoga* leads Krishna to explain how so great a wisdom, though preached from the

[1] Cf. T. S. Eliot, *Four Quartets* (a work much influenced by the *Gita*): "For us there is only the trying. The rest is not our business."

[2] Arjuna incidentally was supposed never to indulge in this relaxation.

beginning of time, has been neglected. The evil instincts of men, by mistaking the senses for organs of true knowledge, have obscured the knowledge of *Brahman*. For this reason Krishna is obliged from time to time to visit the world in bodily form. But unlike Arjuna, who has also experienced many forms of existence, Krishna is endowed with the capacity to remember each of his incarnations. "I seem to be born," he says, "but it is only seeming." Only when evil appears to be gaining the upper hand, "I make myself a body." (We are given to understand that Krishna's human embodiment at this time represented the eighth incarnation of Vishnu.) He then issues his first clear statement of his mission as the saviour of mankind: "He who knows the nature of my task and my holy birth Is not reborn. When he leaves this body he comes to me. Flying from fear, From lust and anger, He hides in me, His refuge, his safety: Burnt clean in the blaze of my being, In me many find home. Whatever wish men bring me in worship, That wish I grant them. Whatever path men travel Is my path: No matter where they walk It leads to me." He then sums up his teaching about action in a fashion that, though paradoxical, contains truth even on a lower level than that of which he speaks, "He who sees the inaction that is in action, and the action that is in inaction, is wise indeed."

After some detailed instructions concerning the practice of Yoga, which we shall study in connection with the philosophy of Patanjali, the *Gita* returns to the question of the weakness of human nature, for which these practices entail such rigorous discipline. Arjuna asks what becomes of those whose will-power is too feeble to enable them to follow the proper directions. For if a man fails to attain a knowledge of *Brahman*, does he not in effect miss both lives: the present which he has renounced in favour of the future life of the spirit, and the future life of the spirit which he has not attained? On both these points Krishna reassures him. Such a man, who must on no account be confused with the backslider, is lost to neither world, because "no one who seeks Brahman ever comes to an evil end".[1] Those who, having embarked upon the practice of Yoga, cannot sustain the effort of self-discipline, will still reach "the heaven of good deeds", where they will remain for a considerable time. Then, being reborn by the so-called *Pitri-Jana*[2] into a good and enlightened home, they will strive towards perfection from the point at which they left off. They may even have the good fortune—but

[1] Cf. Socrates: "No harm can come to a good man in this or the next world" (Plato: *Apology*).

[2] The "path of the fathers", as opposed to the *Deva-Jana*, the "path of the bright ones", who attain direct to a state of *Nirvana*.

this is not very common—to be born into a family of enlightened Yogis (practitioners of Yoga). Through a series of births they will finally succeed in escaping from further rebirths by attaining to knowledge of *Brahman*.

In the seventh section of the poem, where Krishna further enlightens Arjuna on the subject of who is to be saved, we observe a marked widening of outlook, a universal vision of faith, such as occurred in Judaism only with the second Isaiah. Krishna accepts the fact that men of different ages, countries, and temperament will adopt different rituals and even worship different gods. This does not greatly matter. So long as a man has faith, even if he is wicked, he is worthy to be admitted to the number of the devout. By an act which Christian theology was later to describe as one of grace, God will in due time make that faith, however misplaced, unwavering, so that "endowed with the faith I give him, he worships that deity, and gets from it everything he prays for. In reality, I alone am the giver."

Perhaps the climax of the *Gita's* teaching is reached in the eighth Book, in which Krishna answers Arjuna's question as to how, at the hour of death, God reveals Himself to those who have been faithful to Him. Introduced at a similar point in one of the greatest of modern religious poems,[1] this sublime passage alone would make the *Gita* a work of surpassing value. "Whatever a man remembers at the last, when he is leaving the body, will be realized by him in the hereafter: because that will be what his mind has most constantly dwelt on during life." We may venture to say that all the bitter and tortuous arguments concerning "faith" and "works" that were to darken the next two thousand years, especially in Europe, are here exposed as vanity. Both forms of argument are to be rejected simply because they are arguments; for there is no arguing oneself at the last moment into salvation. It is the spiritual level upon which a man is accustomed to live that will determine at the moment of mortal interruption his fate hereafter. Admittedly this level is not always easy to assess from external observation. One suspects that much overt piety, much insistence upon outward performance of duty, serve to conceal a mind unused to higher aspiration. And here we may appreciate once more the convenience of defining "religion" as the maintenance of the "divine connection": for it is this connection which, as Krishna says, the soul not merely establishes but, if deserving of salvation, maintains within himself. Thus the summit of each world faith is on a level with that of the others. At the highest point to which the Hindu spirit attained we observe that insistence upon the spiritual disposition

[1] T. S. Eliot's *East Coker*, the second of the *Four Quartets*.

which is found equally in Zoroastrianism, in Buddhism, and in Judeo-Christianity. The same insistence upon inner sanctity, distinguished, as we saw, the apex of Egyptian moral speculation. We are beginning to learn something of the mind not of one or two nations or peoples, but of mankind as a whole.

The majesty of the *Gita's* message is to be discerned likewise in its view of the nature of Knowledge. The knowledge of God for which the forest sages sought was an intellectual thing. It resembled the supreme knowledge spoken of by the great European philosopher whose "God-intoxicated" spirit most nearly resembled that of the forest sages, Benedict Spinoza. It was in fact an *amor intellectualis Dei*, an "intellectual love of God". The knowledge of God of which we learn in the *Gita* is more than that. It is devotional love. Hence the literal meaning of *Bakhti*, Devotion, is "loving faith". A modern English philosopher[1] has well remarked that true knowledge is to be distinguished from mere belief "by being vision". This visionary quality, though not always sustained to the degree apparent in the *Gita*, is that which places a work of literature in the category of inspired utterances, the work of the *Nebiim* among mankind, who are the only leaders that matter because their message is of permanent validity. In the light of such prophetic testimony, even theology reveals its inadequacy. "To the *Brahmana*, the knower of Faith, all the *Vedas* are of as little use as a small water-tank during the time of a flood, when water is everywhere."

A *précis* of a poem may, by a modest aim, do less harm than a more ambitious attempt to convey its excellences. In the brief account given above of the *Gita* we have been concerned solely to distil its message, a legitimate endeavour in a poem which, in addition to being a work of art, possesses an evident didactic purpose. We have refrained from entering into explanations of difficult philosophical terminology; the *Gita*, like *The Divine Comedy*, has its technical vocabulary and requires a sheaf of notes and an occasional diagram. Similarly, we have omitted, as outside the scope of this book, all detailed comment upon its dramatic qualities. A literary approach would certainly need to dwell upon the magnificence of Book X, in which Krishna, ceasing momentarily to act as Arjuna's charioteer, assumes the aspect of an omnipotent god, magnificent and terrifying, like the apparition in the *Book of Revelation*, and having a voice like that which addressed Job from the whirlwind.

What is the outcome of Krishna's counsel and revelation to Arjuna? Arjuna, calm but heartened, resolves to fight. Indeed his own nature, however reluctant at the outset, dictates this course

[1] The late A. E. Taylor.

of action. "If, in your vanity, you say: 'I will not fight', your resolve is vain. Your own nature will drive you to the act. For you yourself have created the Karma that binds you. You are helpless in its power. And you will do that very thing which your ignorance seeks to avoid." And the poem ends with Krishna's bidding to Arjuna to renounce all fear of life or death, all expectation of reward, all attachment except to God. Here, again, the message is addressed not simply to Arjuna but to all. "If any man meditated on this sacred discourse of ours, I shall consider that he has worshipped me in spirit."

Thus concludes the work which Wilhelm von Humboldt, to quote but one spokesman from many, described as "the most beautiful, perhaps the only true, philosophical song existing in any known tongue". That verdict may possibly be exaggerated; but there is clearly something remarkable about a poem which, during the centuries in which it has been accessible to Europe, has prompted to exaggeration so many thinkers whose views are entitled to respect.

The sceptical backwash

India has often been contrasted with China by saying that India has too much religion, China too great an obsession with ethics.[1] The preoccupation of India with the meaning of existence has admittedly been more intense than that of any other country: it has certainly been more prolonged. Preoccupation with the meaning of existence, however, does not always make for "belief" as commonly understood. It may make equally, or at least periodically, for scepticism. From too great a concentration upon ultimate problems the mind may spring back in exhaustion or even disgust. The divine connection, however passionately sought, may appear as either beyond man's capacity to discern, or else as something that in the nature of things cannot be established. The first conclusion, though not in itself productive of scepticism, may easily collapse into one that is. In the composure of the faculties to despair there is experienced a kind of tranquillity (we talk of "happy agnosticism"), whereas the realization of a basis for belief opens up bewildering vistas of effort and concentration, at least until the final attainment of union. The very fury of resolve displayed by the forest sages, their itch to arrive at certainty, their hunger for explanation, even of trivial matters—and there is triviality in certain of the *Upanishads*—indicate a state of mental turmoil persisting not for a lifetime, an "age of transition", but for several centuries. If the secret of life had been known to them, there

[1] See for example *The Wisdom of India*, edited by Lin Yutang, p. 17.

would have been no need for "secret doctrine", nor would the mystery of *Brahman* and *Atman* have needed unravelling in solitude by men with "hair grown white and having seen their son's son". The gospel of Krishna would have amounted to the revelation of banality. In short the *philosophia perennis* is shadowed by its opposite, an *anti-philosophia*, equally perennial and with the greater fecundity of the weed over the flower.

In point of fact we become aware of scepticism not only as shadowing the fluorescent doctrine of the *Upanishads*, but also as growing up in its midst. The *Chandogya Upanishad*, for instance, consists of a long meditation on the significance of the sacred syllable *OM*.[1] Employed at the beginning and end of the *Vedas*, and considered as an aid to meditation if repeated or meditated upon, *OM* may be rendered as "peace" or even as *Brahman*. We very soon come to perceive how it can be abused. When the sage Glava Maitreya went to repeat the *Veda*, we learn that a white dog appeared before him, and other dogs followed, saying, "Sing and get us food, for we are hungry." The dogs later "came on, holding together, each dog keeping the tail of the preceding dog in its mouth, *as the priests do when they are going to sing praises*. . . . After they had settled down, they began to say *Hin* (Prajapati). *OM*, let us eat! *OM*, let us drink! *OM*, may the divine Varuna, Prajapati, Savitri, bring us food! Lord of Food, bring hither food, bring it, *OM*!" Other *Upanishads* reveal not merely a critical attitude to the priesthood, but a frank scepticism about all the higher values, the gods, and the scriptures. Similarly, in the *Gita*, Krishna warns Arjuna against those "demoniacal men" who contend that "the universe is without truth, without basis, without a god, brought about by mutual union, and caused by lust and nothing else".[2] There is no doubt that this passage refers to ideas current at the time. Moreover, we can be reasonably sure of the school of thinkers to which it refers. These were the *Nastiks*, or those who "said no" —Nihilists, as we should call them. Such a negative attitude can manifest itself in a number of ways, ranging from conventional agnosticism, which does not know "either way"—whether there is a God or whether there is not—to complete materialism, which, proclaiming no law save that of chance, reduces the world to a fortuitous assemblage of bits of matter: a point of view to which the puzzling *Swasanved Upanishad* approaches. Downright materialism

[1] Compressed from the letters AUM, which symbolize the three chief *Vedas*.

[2] Attention may perhaps be drawn here to the fact that Krishna directly relates bad conduct to a false view of the world: "Holding evil ideas through delusion, they engage in action with impure resolves." Today, such is the divorce between metaphysics and ethics, we rarely regard a man's conduct, good or bad, as having anything much to do with his conception of the nature of the universe.

of the latter kind is admittedly rare in philosophy, and rarer still in life. The mind cannot easily be made to entertain, except for polemical purposes, a theory which, like a boomerang, returns to shatter to pieces the instrument that launched it: for the mind on such a theory is as chance a concentration as anything else, with the result that its conclusions are equally accidental. A genial agnosticism, especially if combined with a talent for logic-chopping, is both more common and more socially acceptable. Nothing in the modern world can be compared with the practice, as common in ancient India as in Greece, of holding public philosophical contests, sometimes under official and even royal auspices, and sometimes purely free-lance.[1] We learn of such debates in the *Upanishads*.

Likewise there existed a number of philosophical "pedlars" or *Paribbajaka*, who, like the Greek Sophists, made a profession of engaging in argument for the sake of argument, or sometimes of purveying a specious kind of wisdom, mental cures or sedatives, like quack psychologists: for every community contains its mental as well as its physical hypochondriacs. Sometimes the cure prescribed was that which entailed purging the mind of the illusion of faith, for, as we pointed out above, men are not necessarily more happy as believers than otherwise. Such a denouncer of the "opium of the people" was Brihaspati, who ridiculed the sanctity of the *Vedas* and preached a philosophy of "Eat, drink and be merry". Of his life and work we have little direct knowledge; but his influence was great enough to start a school of sceptical materialists, the Charvakas (so-called after one of the most distinguished of their number), who anticipated and outdid the sceptics of the modern world in the rigour of their destructive analysis. Whereas the faith of the *Vedas*, the *Upanishads*, and the *Bhagavad-Gita* repudiated the evidence of the senses as productive of illusion, these *Nastiks* (to resume the general term for the sceptical school) contended that men, having nothing but their senses upon which to rely, were foolish to seek a sphere of experience behind or beyond that of momentary sensation. Both *Atman* and *Brahman* were figments: their identity in that respect was unquestioned. Furthermore, the discipline of Yoga represented an outrage against nature, the invention of a twisted mentality. Not the renunciation or uprooting but the acceptance of instinct should be regarded as the true law of life. Everything that would delude men into thinking otherwise, above all the domination of the Brahman caste, was a

[1] The B.B.C. Brains Trust is our nearest equivalent. The great success of this institution, especially in its initial stages, revealed an obvious interest in serious public disputation. Possibly the gradual evolution of the Trust into an entertainment deprived it of its attraction for many people.

menace to society. There was no "divine connection". The world was maintained by a nexus of atoms. Soul and body were therefore composed of the same material.

Mahavira

Orthodox belief is supposed to induce social torpor; but, as we have shown, there is also a quietism that comes from the profession of certain forms of scepticism, mild rather than bitter. The communal mind can be roused and quickened by two quite opposite influences: that of a revolutionary and transcendental faith such as that of Ikhnaton or Zoroaster, or that of a ferociously ascetic belief such as that which, without warning, captured the minds of a small group of zealots in 5th-century India, not many years before the more profound but less stringent faith of Gotama Buddha. The faith of Mahavira, the founder of Jainism, is perhaps the most perplexing of all that we shall study in this book. That anyone should have devised such an extravagant belief is as remarkable as that anyone should have followed it, for at first glance it appears not merely incredible but impracticable. Like most other extreme faiths, it has modified itself in course of time into something in which it is possible to believe. The faith of the Jains, which denies life to the extent of regarding suicide as the most sacred act of which man is capable, has survived and even prospered for over two thousand years.

Mahavira, who probably lived from 549–477 B.C.,[1] came of a family belonging to the *Kshatriya* or Warrior caste, which for centuries was regarded as superior to all others, including that of the Brahmans or priests.[2] He was born in the town of Vaishali in modern Bihar. From the beginning his upbringing was unusual. His father, one of the leaders of the *Lichchavi* tribe and a man of considerable wealth, was an adherent of a religious sect which professed a doctrine staunchly opposed to that of the *Vedas*. If the beliefs of this sect were not exactly materialist, they were certainly nihilist or *Nastik*. Sharing the common Vedic horror of rebirth, they enjoined a particular method of avoiding it. This was by voluntary suicide. The aim was not to induce a violent end, but, by preference, slowly to drain away vitality by means of starvation. Only thus would the life-force be reduced to a degree of inanition rendering it incapable of further transmigration. It appears that Mahavira's father converted his wife to the same belief, and in due course shared with her the martydom to which they were thereby

[1] This date has been questioned.

[2] It was in fact the second caste in the Hindu hierarchy. The first, that of the Brahmans, was exempt from all taxation.

committed. Possibly they may be pronounced guilty of a certain measure of procrastination or sloth, for at the time of their fast unto death their son was already in his thirty-second year.

The death of his father and mother reduced the young man to a state of extreme dejection. Being in his prime, he instinctively clung to life while at the same time sensing and suspecting its futility. Before following the parental example, however, he determined to embark upon a quest for wisdom more thorough than that undertaken by any of his contemporaries or predecessors. Rejecting current orthodoxy and heterodoxy alike, but subscribing at least to the principle of self-purification and renunciation, he left home and adopted the life of a vagrant. To demonstrate his complete withdrawal from civilized life he dispensed with every amenity and property, including clothing. For thirteen years he roamed the country of western Bengal practising austerities of the most extreme variety. In a land of strange sects and practices, such conduct would not at first have attracted undue attention; but such was the powerful personality of this young man that he soon began to acquire followers and disciples. A tradition dating from remote time held that mankind, plunged in corruption and sin, was periodically afforded enlightenment by the appearance of Saviours, Redeemers or, as they were called, *Jinas* ("Conquerors").[1] Upon the small group of disciples of the naked wanderer there gradually dawned the conviction that their master was none other than the latest of these *Jinas*. Accordingly they gave him the new name of Mahavira, which means "Great Hero". As followers of this new leader they called themselves Jains, hero-worshippers.

In spite of the asceticism of his life, Mahavira lived to the age of seventy-two. At the time of his death there were about 14,000 Jains, some of whom had formed themselves into monastic communities, male and female. Nor did the death of the *Jina* halt the spread of his doctrine. On the contrary, the faith won converts rapidly, attracting rather than repelling by the severity of its impositions. That it should ever become a world faith was impossible; but whereas many a belief of less rigour has run into the sand, Jainism, despite schisms and fierce controversies, can still claim almost a million and a half followers.

The original beliefs of the Jains have undergone a good deal of development since their first formulation by Mahavira. Sharing the family belief that the *Vedas* were not the word of God, Mahavira was one of the first men on earth to proclaim a faith nominally without an Object. In his view, the search for absolute knowledge of *Brahman*, as for absolute union with that infinite Being, was futile.

[1] Or Jainas.

The universe was not created or started by a god: it was self-subsistent and always had been so.[1] Far from men presuming to know the ultimate truth, their very finitude renders this impossible. Just as six blind men might consider an elephant to be half a dozen totally different things by touching different parts of its body, so individual men, reflecting upon their own little facet of experience, arrive inevitably at different conclusions about the nature of the world. Truth is indeed revealed to men, but only by the *Jinas* whose appearance is recognized by the faithful. Free from the chain of Karma and rebirth, these *Jinas* win for the truth in each generation a minority of saints or *Arahats*, who remain for ever exempt from reincarnation. Of lesser though substantial merit were the "high souls" or *Paramatmans*, whose blameless conduct permitted them a temporary interruption of the birth-cycle.

Although Mahavira denied the existence of a god and even of a god-pool, he was unquestionably one of those whose mission in life was to unite the way of earth with the way of heaven. His repudiation of *Vedic* beliefs did not lead him to materialism, nor did it prevent his later disciples from constructing an entirely new pantheon composed of the saints of Jainism. It is difficult to know whether the oriental mind is capable of subscribing to a creed of absolute brute materialism. Even where the claim is made, we cannot be sure that it is being carried out in practice. Clearly, the doctrine of the transmigration of souls is incompatible with materialism even of a refined or dialectical kind. And without the doctrine of the transmigration of souls the whole point of Mahavira's self-laceration is lost. For even if your primary wish is to avoid the cycle of rebirth, you must steadfastly believe in the reality of that process in order to justify your precautions.

From the so-called *Jaina Sutras*[2] that have been preserved for the enlightenment of the faithful it becomes clear that the most striking feature of the Jain faith, its advocacy of suicide, is hedged round with certain conditions. It is not an act to be undertaken lightly. Defined as "the incomparable religious death", it cannot be achieved by mere forthright self-immolation. The proper frame of mind for such a sacred act must be induced, and this may paradoxically require a lifetime's cultivation. Among the emotions that need severely to be disciplined is that of desire or longing. Therefore you must not long for death or release. You must manage to bring about your extinction in a mood beyond both desire and aversion.

[1] Such a view, as we shall see, is not necessarily "materialistic". Aristotle held a somewhat similar view, as do our Emergent Evolutionists.

[2] *Sutra:* literally a string or thread, i.e. a series of verses or maxims on recurrent themes.

Among the instincts of life to be eradicated, therefore, is the instinct to leave it. In the *Bhagavad-Gita* there are passages to suggest that the sages were not unaware of the dangers of exaggerated self-discipline. They had observed, possibly among the Jains themselves and their related sects, a too great—almost a voluptuous—indulgence in asceticism. "Yoga is not for him who eats too much or for him who fasts excessively. It is not for him who sleeps too much, or for the keeper of exaggerated vigils, etc." (Book VI). In the *Akaranga Sutra* of the Jains, however, we read that "there are no degrees in control". This is followed by a terse summary of the kind of mental discipline expected of the devout Jain: "He who knows wrath, knows pride. He who knows pride, knows deceit. He who knows deceit, knows greed. He who knows greed, knows love. He who knows love, knows conception. He who knows conception, knows birth. He who knows birth, knows death. He who knows death, knows hell. He who knows hell, knows animal existence. He who knows animal existence, knows pain. Therefore, a wise man should avoid wrath, pride, deceit, greed, love, hate, delusion, conception, birth, hell, animal existence, and pain."

The admonition to avoid pain may appear a trifle incongruous in a creed prescribing the extremes of bodily suffering; but the emphasis here, as always, is upon the word "avoid". Nothing must deliberately be either sought or desired. Thus, in the instructions given in the same *Sutra* for the attention of "the wise ones who attain in due order to one of the unerring states in which suicide is prescribed", we are given details of three methods by which the monk or fakir should compose himself for death. The first method is to spread out straw upon a piece of ground free from living beings of every kind. Without food the Jain should lie down and endure such pains as attack him. "When crawling animals, or such as live on high or below, feed on his flesh and blood, he should neither kill them nor rub the wound: though these animals destroy the body, he should not stir from his position." The second and "more exalted method" is to lie on the bare ground and, without any comfort or food, "strive after calmness", being unattached both internally and externally. While this method permits movement if absolutely essential, the third method, or that which conforms to "the highest law", is to lie down flat and "not to stir from one's place while checking *all* motions of the body". By this means the holy man will gradually, inevitably, and mindlessly—except in so far as to reflect that patience is the highest good—permit his physical dissolution. Such an end, in other words, must not be contrived; it must be the incidental consequence of having drained the mind of all forms of volition. The will, utterly deflated, sinks, dragging the body down with it. Thus the soul passes serenely into *Nirvana*.

The reference in the above rules to the avoidance of causing death to living creatures introduces another important tenet of Jain belief. The Jain was obliged to take five vows. The first of these vows was that of *Ahimsa*. No living creature, except the first person singular, was ever to be deprived of life. To fulfil this vow effectively it was necessary to consider not occasionally but perpetually the five ways in which it might be broken: namely in thought, word, deed, eating, and drinking. In other words, nothing must be thought, no intention formulated, that might lead to an act involving the death of living beings. Nothing must likewise be said leading to the same result. Nothing, such as thoughtless walking or carelessly laying down the begging bowl, must be done directly to destroy living creatures. This means also that no Jain can engage in agricultural pursuits. Finally, before eating or drinking vegetarian food—for no other was permissible—the Jain must examine it carefully to see that he does not destroy life in the process.[1] This strict general prohibition became also a feature of Buddhism. The other four rules of conduct laid down for the Jains were the prohibition of lying, of taking that which is not a gift (this applied in particular to the ground upon which he sat begging), of all sensual pleasures, particularly those of sex, and of all forms of attachment, even if it be the attachment of the ear to beautiful sounds or the eye to a lovely sight.

Literal fulfilment of such rules would clearly restrict the number of the faithful below the limit necessary to maintain a sect intact. No faith has survived in its original purity, for survival inevitably means compromise and adaptation. The great schism in the ranks of the Jains occurred in the 1st century A.D., when a dispute arose concerning the necessity or propriety of going about naked. Those who insisted upon the latter principle were thence on called *Digambaras* or "sky-clad". Those who chose to wear clothes were called *Shwetambaras* or "white-robed". Further schismatic movements later divided these sects into numerous others. Nevertheless, the major principles of Jainism, having been stated and on more than one occasion lived to their logical conclusion, will probably continue to haunt the imagination of a minority of mankind for whom the great world religions leave too much room for the practice of the extremes of *askesis*. There is a spiritual athleticism which requires restriction rather than freedom for its exercise. Nor, as we know, has the figure of the emaciated naked fakir, periodically threatening starvation and defying the authorities to stop him, ceased to fascinate and to disturb modern India.

[1] The Jains were some of the first to set up veterinary hospitals.

CHAPTER V

THE BUDDHA

The Birth Story

WITHIN a few years of Mahavira there was born at the foot of the Himalayas, on the frontiers of Oudh and Nepal, a man whose life and personality have left a more lasting impression on the oriental world than any other. Gotama Buddha was one of those great innovators of thought whose career has become so encompassed with legend and poetry that he appears, at a remove of more than two thousand years, to be more than mortal. At the same time, this superhuman figure seems not merely to have preached but to have possessed to a degree without precedent the qualities which, no doubt with a certain irony, we call human: gentleness, kindness, tolerance, humility. Like most other apostles of the divine connection, his birth has been made the subject of elaborate and, to our minds, unnecessarily complicated legend. And like all the *Nebiim*, his mission was the result of a supposedly divine revelation. Like them all, except Christ, he was regarded by his disciples as merely one among a number of other saviours of mankind, or Buddhas. Finally, and in this respect resembling only Mahavira, he preached a faith in which there is nominally no place for a God. It is as difficult to account for the appearance on earth of a man such as Gotama Buddha as it is to imagine what would have filled the historical void if, instead of forsaking the world, he had assumed the high office for which his inheritance had prepared him.

Like Mahavira, Gotama Buddha was a man of high birth. He, too, was a member of the *Kshatriya* caste. But he was more than that. His father, Suddhodana, was a king, the ruler of Kapilavastu, a town a hundred miles north of Benares, and member of a tribe renowned for its independence and spirit, the Shakya. From the particular clan to which he belonged, the Gotama, his son Siddhartha was later known. The exact date of Gotama's birth is the subject of dispute. Most scholars now believe it to have been 563 B.C. As to the manner of his birth, this was the subject of the most extraordinary legends.

In writing the life of Buddha it is impossible, even if it were desirable, to omit these legendary accretions. While we may find it difficult to imagine a devout Buddhist of reasonable education literally believing the account of Buddha's conception as given in the first of the Jataka Books, we should be foolish to ignore even the most preposterous of the various "Birth Stories". In the first place it is extremely interesting to observe, in stories primarily intended for the common people (like the Egyptian legends), what kind of fact or fancy was thought most likely to stimulate popular wonder and awe. And in the second place it is important to realize that such stories, which characterize every world faith, were intended to be accepted in a mood not so much of credulity as of suspended belief and disbelief. To say that these legends amount simply to poetry is not therefore to suggest that they are false; they are no more false than the hyperbolic utterances of a lover to his mistress. In a situation of this kind, both sides are in a conspiracy to regard such utterances as a means of expressing that which would otherwise remain unsaid or unsayable. We exaggerate the intellectual level of mankind, just as we no doubt overrate the capacity of intellect, if we suppose that belief can be sustained purely upon the basis of fact. In inviting the common man to believe in the supernatural, the leaders of a faith must accustom him to ideas in which the laws of nature are liable to frequent suspension. If art and poetry are the religion of the natural, religion is the poetry of the supernatural.

About seven hundred years after the birth of the Buddha, the various legends concerning his conception and birth were first written down. In the introduction to the Jataka Books we learn that history is divided into three great cycles separated from one another by varying stretches of time. The renewal of a cycle of time is heralded by an event which can best be translated by the word disturbance or, literally, "uproar". The first of these disturbances, which took place after the world had been in existence for a hundred thousand years, entailed the complete destruction by fire of the earth "as far up as the Brahma heavens". The third and final disturbance would be the establishment on earth of a universal monarchy. Between these great historical disturbances, and occurring about a thousand years after the cataclysm precipitated by the first, the central fact of history took place: namely the birth of an omniscient saviour or Buddha ("Blessed" or "Enlightened One"), whose task was the salvation of the world.

When the time came for the guardian angels of the world to proclaim "The Buddha uproar", we are told that the "gods of all ten thousand worlds came together in one place", and, having ascertained who was to be the Buddha, publicly acclaimed him as such. After announcing the circumstances in which he proposed to be born, and apprising the gods of his successor, Maitreya, the Buddha thereupon died and was conceived on earth in the womb

W. F. Mansell

THE ENLIGHTENMENT

Buddha assailed and tempted by Mara, Prince of Demons

of Queen Maha-Maya, the eldest of Suddhodana's two consorts. The chronicle then enters into the following details: "At that time the midsummer festival had been proclaimed in the city of Kapilavastu, and the multitude were enjoying the feast. And Queen Maha-Maya, abstaining from strong drink, and brilliant with garlands and perfumes, took part in the festivities for six days previous to the day of full-moon. And when it came to be the day of full-moon, she rose early, bathed in perfumed water, and dispensed four hundred thousand pieces of money in great largesse. And decked in full gala attire, she ate of the choicest food, after which she took the eight vows, and entered her elegantly furnished chamber of state. And lying down on the royal couch, she fell asleep and dreamed the following dream: The four guardian angels came and lifted her up, together with her couch, and took her away to the Himalaya Mountains. There, in the Manosila tableland . . . they laid her under a prodigious sal-tree, seven leagues in height, and took up their positions respectfully at one side. . . . Not far off was Silver Hill, and on it a golden mansion. There they spread a divine couch with its head towards the east, and laid her down upon it. Now the future Buddha had become a superb white elephant, and was wandering about at no great distance, on Gold Hill. Descending thence, he ascended Silver Hill, and approaching from the north, he plucked a white lotus with his silvery trunk, and trumpeting loudly, went into the golden mansion. And three times he walked round his mother's couch, with his right side towards it, and striking her on her right side, he seemed to enter her womb. Thus the conception took place in the midsummer festival."

According to the story, the queen did not awake until the next day, when she at once recounted her dream to the king. He was naturally concerned to discover its significance. Accordingly he summoned in council sixty-four of the most learned Brahmanas (Brahmans) in his kingdom, and having both entertained them to a sumptuous feast and made them costly presents, he recounted the queen's dream and asked for an explanation of it. After due deliberation, the Brahmanas came to a unanimous conclusion. "Be not anxious, great king," they said: "a child has planted itself in the womb of your queen, and it is a male child and not a female. You will have a son. And he, if he continue to live the household life, will become a universal monarch; but if he leave the household life and retire from the world, he will become a Buddha, and roll back the clouds of sin and folly of this world."

Directly the earthly conception of the Buddha became known in heaven, an immense commotion took place. Thirty-two manifestations and prognostics were enumerated. The ten thousand worlds were suffused with a radiance never before seen. Cripples and invalids were suddenly healed. In all the hells of the universe the fires were extinguished. Horses neighed and elephants trumpeted "in a manner sweet to the ear". Musical instruments, without the intervention of an executant, played celestial tunes. The ocean turned sweet. Lotuses grew in the air. And so on. Although the queen was forty-five years old, the period of gestation passed in the most satisfactory manner. Not only did she feel unusually well, but she remained perpetually aware of the presence of the future Buddha in her womb, "like a white thread passed through a transparent jewel". When the birth was nearly due, she experienced a strong desire that the child should be born in the home of her family in the city of Devadada. The king, who was anxious to grant her every wish, ordered that a special highway should be constructed for her to pass along. Borne on a magnificent palanquin and accompanied by a thousand courtiers, she reached in due course a point in the road which was called Lumbini Grove, just outside the city gates. The sight of so beautiful a scene—for "the grove was one mass of flowers from the ground to the topmost branches"—captivated her. She expressed a desire to halt there. Wandering through the sylvan loveliness, she approached a great sal-tree in the middle of the grove. As she reached out her hand towards it, one of the branches inclined towards her, and, to her surprise, the moment she touched it the birth-pangs started. Thus it came about that, still holding the branch of the sal-tree, she brought forth the young Buddha "flashing pure and spotless, like a jewel thrown upon a vesture of Benares cloth"; for as he emerged from the womb, four angels, arriving opportunely from heaven, received him upon a golden net, while two jets of water from the sky performed the office of the ritual bath. This scene has frequently been depicted in Buddhist art. As to the queen herself, she died on the seventh day of her son's life, since "the womb that has been occupied by a Buddha is like the shrine of a temple and can never be occupied or used again". The boy was therefore brought up by his aunt, Maya-Prajapati.

It is reported that upon entering the world the young Buddha, facing east, surveyed the entire universe as if it were spread out before him "like a great open court". Like the young Zoroaster he turned his gaze deliberately and solemnly in every direction with the object apparently of ascertaining whether anyone in the world could equal him. No rival being found, he took seven strides forward and proclaimed himself, in a noble voice, the lord of creation. This infant "shout of victory" may be compared with the loud laugh which was uttered by Zoroaster at his birth. The scripture informs us at this point that simultaneously with the birth of the Buddha there came into existence the famous *Bodhi* or Bo-tree, which was to play so important a part in Gotama's career.

The Four Signs

The Buddha's birth, like his conception, was hailed by both gods and men as an event without parallel in history. A heavenly chorus resembling that which greeted the birth of Jesus sang the praises of the young child. Buddhist tradition likewise records an event very similar to that of the visit to Bethlehem of the Three Wise Men. A saintly man called Kaladevala, well known to King Suddhodana, was accustomed after his daily meal to engage in a period of rapt meditation. On the day of the Buddha's birth he noticed that the gods with whom he was holding communion were in a state of unusual excitement. Upon his enquiring the reason, he was told that their merry-making was due to the fact that "a son had been born to King Suddhodana, who shall sit at the foot of the Bo-tree and become a Buddha and cause the wheel of doctrine to roll". On receiving this information, Kaladevala, who was the Simeon of Buddhism, hurried to the royal palace and asked to see the baby. Delighted to comply with this request, the king ordered that the young prince should be dressed in his best clothes and brought in. It seemed appropriate that the baby should be made to do reverence to so holy a man, but this was not to be. No sooner was the Buddha carried up to Kaladevala than he planted his feet firmly among the matted locks of the venerable ascetic, thus showing that there was no one on earth before whom he was prepared to do obeisance. Kaladevala at once realized that he was in the presence of a divine creature, and noticing certain sacred marks on the child's body, such as that of the "wheel of the Law" on his foot, the old man made haste to genuflect. The king was astounded. Never had he observed such a reversal of the rules of etiquette as that a saint should pay homage to a new-born child. But his eyes now being opened, he made haste to follow Kaladevala's example.

The king thereupon called to mind the prophecy of the Brahmanas whom he had consulted about the queen's dream. How would it be revealed, he asked Kaladevala, whether the boy was to become a universal monarch or a Buddha? In reply, Kaladevala declared that the child's future destiny would be determined by four signs. If the boy were to see in due order a decrepit old man, a diseased man, a dead man, and finally a monk, then he assuredly would become a Buddha. The king reflected. He was privately resolved that his son, instead of retiring from the world, should become the ruler of a great kingdom. This young prince, he felt, was destined to rule the world. Accordingly, so as to ensure that he should not be thwarted in his design, the king ordered that guards should be posted in every direction with explicit instructions to refuse admittance to any suspicious visitor, but especially to the four types of men of whom Kaladevala had spoken.

For some years the prince lived a happy, heedless life at the royal palace. The elaborate precautions taken by his father appeared to have been effective. There was nothing that the boy lacked, no enjoyment of which his young life was deprived, no cloud of grief to overshadow an existence that came near to being idyllic. Even so, legend records that, while still a schoolboy, the prince, observing labourers at work in the fields, was suddenly overcome by the sight of human drudgery, and also of the destruction of insect life caused by the disturbance of the soil. At the age of nineteen it was decided that he should marry. The choice of a bride for such a prince was a matter of great importance; but in conformity with his upbringing he was given an opportunity of exercising his own judgment. Out of five thousand exquisitely beautiful young women he selected one who happened to be his cousin, the lovely princess Gopa. Fearing lest a prince so accustomed to luxury might lack the virility expected of a satisfactory husband, Gopa's father invited him to undergo certain tests of strength and manliness, which he passed without difficulty. The match proved a very happy one. King Suddhodana breathed more freely. It seemed that by this new and firm attachment, which was supplemented by a number of concubines, the prince was assured a future of worldly power and prosperity. The dreaded signs had not appeared. The auspices, such as they were, pointed to a happier destiny.

One day the prince decided to go on an excursion through the immense royal estate. This was the moment for which the gods had been waiting. For they had decided that the prince's enlightenment must now begin. One of the gods, disguising himself as an old man, crippled and shaking, stationed himself on the path along which the prince and Chauna, his charioteer, were due to pass. No sooner did he catch sight of this grotesque and pitiful figure than the prince was shocked beyond measure. Never in his young life had such an object come within his view. Chauna, to whom the visitation was also vouchsafed, thereupon explained to him the nature of old age and decrepitude. For the first time the prince experienced a feeling of intense revulsion at human life and at birth in particular, to which such a horrible outcome must be attributed. Abandoning all thought of further pleasure that day, he hurried home.

The king, who was surprised at this early return, enquired of the prince's charioteer what had happened. On learning that the prince had met an old and decrepit man, he was filled with a mixture of fear and rage: emotions that were further aggravated when he learned to what depths of despondency the prince had been moved. Orders were at once given that the guard round the palace should be strengthened, and that everything should be done to prevent the prince from indulging in morbid reflections. Unfortunately, although the king watched over his son with great care and solicitude, the first ominous sign was followed in due course by the other three. In short, the prince and his charioteer encountered in succession a man riddled with disease, a corpse, and finally a monk. On each occasion Chauna was obliged to explain to his young master the nature and meaning of disease, death, and, most significant of all, renunciation. Although familiar with the first two, the charioteer knew nothing of the life of monks, for such a mode of existence was to derive its significance from the mission of the future Buddha. Nevertheless, the gods, who had impersonated the four figures in question, put it into Chauna's head to acquaint the prince with the true meaning of retirement from the world, and also to recommend it as the life of greatest merit.

Perplexed and almost in despair, the king could think of nothing but how to continue to beguile the prince with amusements, distractions, and other pleasures. He realized too late that such artifices merely served to feed the young man's discontent. The proximity of a world of pain, disease, and death had wholly alienated his thoughts from common enjoyments. His past and even his present happiness had suddenly become meaningless. Gradually the attraction of a different mode of life began to assert itself: a life not of attachment to things and people but of detachment and contemplation, in which the true meaning of existence might become clear.

The Great Retirement

The crisis occurred soon after the birth of his first child. Devoted as he was to his young wife, the news of the birth of their son prompted him to bitter reflections. "An impediment has been born, a fetter has been born," was his only comment on first hearing news that filled the whole kingdom with joy. The king, who set great store by all that his son said, pondered this remark. "Let my grandson be called Rahula (impediment)," he declared, in a mood half of fun and half of apprehension. And the boy was so named. Nevertheless there were celebrations in the city, not merely to greet the birth of the boy, but to hail his father as the most fortunate of mortals. Such frivolous jollity only made the prince's heart more heavy. The sight of a troupe of dancing girls, sprawling at rest on the floor, filled him with sudden disgust. Weary of such meretricious allurements, he had fallen asleep during the performance. Now he awoke with the feeling of one who is told that his house is on fire. He realized it was time to make what he called "the great retirement".

Of the prince's silent leave-taking of his family, the Jataka contains a record of moving simplicity. We can well understand how this and other episodes in the life of Buddha have come to assume a place as sacred and memorable in the mind of orthodox Buddhists as the Gospel story in the mind of Christians. There is nothing in Hindu scripture, except perhaps certain episodes in the *Bhagavad-Gita*, to compare with it in respect of unaffectedness and grace of expression. Even allowing for differences in intention, the famous leave-taking of Yajnavalkya and Maitreyi in the *Upanishads* strikes the reader in contrast as absurdly intellectual and formal. "Now the future Buddha, after he had sent Chauna on his errand (to saddle his horse Kanthaka), thought to himself, 'I will just take one look at my son,' and, rising from the couch on which he was sitting, he went to the suite of apartments occupied by the mother of Rahula, and opened the door of her chamber. Within the chamber was burning a lamp fed with sweet-smelling oil, and the mother of Rahula lay sleeping on a couch strewn deep with jasmine and other flowers, her hand resting on the head of her son. When the future Buddha reached the threshold, he paused and gazed at the two from where he stood. 'If I were to raise my wife's hand from off the child's head, and take him up, she would awake, and thus prevent my departure. I will first become a Buddha, and then come back and see my son.' So saying he descended from the palace."

Mounting his great steed Kanthaka, and instructing Chauna to hang on to its tail, the prince left the city. In order to muffle the noise of the horse's progress and of the sound of its neighing, the gods took special measures; "at every step he took they placed the palms of their hands under his feet". On arriving at the gates of the city a formidable obstacle presented itself. The gates, which had been specially constructed to prevent the prince from leaving the city unknown to his father, required a thousand men to move them. The scriptural account informs us that the future Buddha, being providentially endowed with "strength that was equal when reckoned in elephant-power to ten thousand million elephants", could without difficulty have either opened the great leaves of the doors, or lifted himself, his horse and his faithful charioteer collectively over them. This feat proved unnecessary, for the god who inhabited the gates, realizing that the future Buddha wished to leave the city, opened the portals to let him pass. Scarcely had the prince ventured into open country when he was assailed by a formidable temptation. The Prince of Darkness, Mara,[1] assuming visible shape, informed him that within seven days he was due to become the great ruler of whom the Brahmanas had spoken. Renouncing all intention to seek enlightenment in the forest, he must turn back and prepare to govern an empire. The prince scorned such advice, declaring that he did not covet earthly sovereignty. "I am about to cause the ten thousand worlds," he said, "to thunder with my becoming a Buddha." Mara was not deterred. "I shall catch you," he threatened, "the very first time you have a lustful, malicious or unkind thought." Accordingly, like a shadow, Mara followed the young prince on his wanderings, never despairing of winning him from the sacred mission to which he was dedicated. Thus, at the outset of his career as the saviour of men, the Buddha, like Zoroaster and Jesus, was assailed by forces of evil intent not so much on destroying as on corrupting him. And in each case the bait offered was that of temporal power.

When the prince had reached the forest to which so many holy men and ascetics had retired, he dismissed his faithful charioteer, after presenting him with the now unwanted ornaments and rich clothes. A god, disguised as a hermit, provided the young man with rags appropriate to a beggar. Chauna had also expressed a wish to retire from the world, but his master insisted that such was not his vocation. Then Gotama, professing ignorance of their way of life, asked the forest sages to instruct him in the various methods of acquiring wisdom and sanctity. He had already heard vague stories of their rigorous discipline: how some lived on a few grains of corn, others on grass, others still, like the snakes, apparently off air.[2] By submitting to various degrees of pain, the ascetics believed themselves near to attaining moral perfection: "pain," they declared, "is the root of merit". This attitude towards life and suffering, while impressing the future Buddha, failed to satisfy him. He saw in such striving after merit a powerful impulse of attachment, a covert hope of being reborn, a subtle clinging to life; whereas since his first glimpse of the aged man, the cripple and the corpse, he had nourished the conviction that birth itself was evil, a thing to be brought to an end. Action bred life. And however near they came to snapping the last vital thread, these ascetics were still men of action. The ascetic path, it seemed, was a road

[1] The English night-*mare* is a derivative of this word.
[2] An ancient superstition.

leading not to *Nirvana* but back again to the world of illusion and rebirth.

With courteous expressions of appreciation on both sides, Gotama quietly left the sage Arata and his community of ascetics and embarked once more upon his wanderings. Meanwhile, when Chauna arrived home with Kanthaka, the news of Gotama's departure for the great retirement spread rapidly among the courtiers. Most inconsolable of all was the young prince's wife, who called to mind the very different conduct of former seekers after truth. "If," she declared, "he wishes to practise a religious life after abandoning me, his lawful wife, widowed—what is his religion, who wishes to follow practices without his lawful wife to share them with him? He has surely never heard of the monks of olden times, his own ancestor, Mahasudarsa and the rest—how they went with their wives into the forest—that he thus wishes to follow a religious life without me. . . . Surely it must be that this fond lover of religion, knowing that my mind was secretly quarrelling even with my beloved, lightly and without fear has deserted me thus angry, in the hope of obtaining heavenly nymphs in Indra's world." Her thoughts then turned impulsively to the young baby Rahula, and it seemed as if her lord had committed a double outrage in thus deserting both mother and son.

On arriving at a place of great beauty called Uruvela, about fifty miles south of Patna, the future Buddha decided to resume his meditations. To divest his mind of distracting thoughts, he resolved to begin a fast of steadily increasing rigour. He tried the experiment of living on jujube fruits or a few grains of sesame and rice, steadily diminishing his daily diet until he confined it to a single grain. His flesh sagged and wasted until it scarcely stretched over his protruding bones. "The mark of my seat," he later confessed, "was like a camel's footprint, through the little food. The bones of my spine, when bent and straightened, were like a row of spindles, through the little food. And as, in a deep well, the deep low-lying sparkling of the water was seen, so in my eye-sockets was seen the deep, low-lying sparkle of my eyes through the little food. And as a bitter gourd, cut off raw, is cracked and withered through rain and sun, so was my skin withered through the little food. When I thought I would touch the skin of my stomach, I actually took hold of my spine." In order that no one should accuse him of having failed to practise self-mortification in earnest, he pursued these austerities to a point just short of suicide.

Living thus scarcely above subsistence-level, Gotama spent as long as six years seeking to arrive at sanctity by way of absorption in self-denial. Finally it occurred to him that, despite his feats of

Picture Post Library

JAPANESE BUDDHA

mental concentration, he was following a course little better than that of the ascetics for whom he had expressed such contempt. His very absorption in the practice of self-denial was nothing but a form of absorption in the self. Moreover, the fury of his efforts at mortification, far from inducing a mood of composure, bred instability and irritation. As long as he continued to toy with life, or to flirt with death, by following the path of extreme asceticism, the goal he sought eluded him. He must recover his balance. To do so, however, he must recover his strength. Mental calm must be sought along a path midway between extreme self-denial and self-indulgence. "True meditation," he concluded, "is produced in him whose mind is self-possessed and at rest." A young peasant girl, Sujata, opportunely brought him milk and rice. By resuming a normal, if still frugal, diet, he at length acquired the robustness of the prince to whom nothing had been denied. But his change of attitude alienated the five disciples who had gathered round him.

Enlightenment

In abandoning the spectacular austerities of the hermits and sages of his day, Gotama did not renounce his spiritual exercises. With the return of bodily vigour, he embarked upon a further course of meditation. On this occasion he realized that his search must either bring him within sight of his objective, or end in futility and disillusion. An unshakable decision must be made. "Then he sat down," records the *Buddha-Charita* (Book XII), "on his hams in a posture immovably firm and with his limbs gathered into a mass like a sleeping serpent's hood, exclaiming, 'I will not rise from this position on the earth until I have obtained my utmost aim.' "

The tree under which Gotama sat was the famous *Bodhi* or Bo-tree which had come to life at the moment of the prince's birth. The word *Bodhi* means literally knowledge: the tree itself was a fig-tree to which the people gave the name of Pipal. This revered spot is now called Bodh Gaya, situated in Bihar, where about 500 A.D. an immense temple was built. Nearby stands a fig-tree, possibly a descendant of the sacred Bo-tree itself. While sitting at this spot, Gotama experienced the second and most violent of the series of temptations by Mara. The god of evil and darkness had mobilized all his friends throughout the universe. There came demons of every conceivable shape, all of equal horror, whirling in the air, at once threatening and cajoling: for after the assault of the demons, with their volley of projectiles, came a host of aerial temptresses, hoping by contrast to stir his sensuality. So vivid and yet horrifying is the description of this host from hell that we are made to realize its symbolic purpose: Gotama, on the point of making up his mind, is assailed for the last time by the doubts and uncertainties, as well as the pleasures and allurements, of human existence. It was the last step, the mountaineer's final heave to safety, when for a moment all seems in danger of being lost. True to his vow, Gotama refused to be distracted. The compass of his will trembled, but was not deflected. As his mind gathered itself for a supreme effort of concentration, suddenly, at the first hint of dawn, "the shell of ignorance was broken", and he attained to perfect knowledge. He became "the perfectly wise, the Bhagavat (Lord), the Arahat, the king of the law, the Yathagata, he who has attained the knowledge of all forms, the Lord of all Science". This insight followed close upon a vision of all eternity in a single flash, with the entire chain of births at every level of existence strung out before his eyes.

Gotama's experience beneath the Bo-tree represents the authentic—to some millions of mankind the most authentic—moment of illumination of the *Nabi*, the prophet of divine connection. To the Western mind, the curious feature of this particular vision is that it appears to illuminate a void: there is no God to hold, as it were, the other end of the string.[1] It is true that there is no God. On the other hand there is such a thing as divinity, and by the law of *Karma* there is divine punishment and retribution. This amazingly complicated law is operated from a realm outside time and beyond human scrutiny. Gotama did not invent it; he accepted it without question as the most important fact of experience. Like all prophets, Gotama's mission was not so much to introduce a new law as to reaffirm, to recall, to re-establish old communications.

Believing himself at last to have found the secret of man's deliverance from illusion, Gotama forthwith became conscious of his Buddhahood. Such consciousness did not entail the belief that he was the first "Enlightened One" to be born among men. There had been former Buddhas or Jainas. There would be others, such as Maitreya. Like Mahavira and Zoroaster, Gotama embarked upon his mission in the belief that enlightenment had been conferred upon him at a particular time for a particular purpose. To his disciples and their successors may be traced the conviction that his mission, though one among others, was unique.[2] Of the great religious prophets, only Jesus seems deliberately to have excluded a later incarnation of God, except in so far as he hinted at his own return to supervise the liquidation of history.

According to the scriptures, Gotama's assumption of Buddha-

[1] This point is discussed again in the Conclusion.

[2] He is sometimes declared to be the ninth incarnation of Vishnu (by the Brahmans who succeeded Buddhism).

hood cast the evil powers of the universe into utter dejection. It is said that Mara, feeling his power to be on the point of extinction, snatched at a last expedient for frustrating the Buddha's mission. This was to persuade him to ascend at once to heaven. "O holy one," he accordingly addressed Gotama, "be pleased to enter Nirvana, thy desires are accomplished." By refusing this subtle invitation Gotama became in the eyes of one school of Buddhists not merely a Buddha in the orthodox sense but a Bodhisattva, or one who for the sake of saving the world abstains voluntarily from entering Nirvana. "I will first establish in perfect wisdom," he said, "worlds as numerous as the sand, and then I will enter Nirvana." Thus the forces of evil were permanently held in check by the Buddha, who deferred by eighty years his passage to extinction.

A few weeks after receiving Enlightenment, the Buddha left for the holy city of Benares, making several converts on the journey. While orthodox theology conceives of the Buddha as a majestic and kingly figure, the man who was to change the outlook of so many millions went about in his lifetime as a beggar living on alms. Moreover, the assumption of Buddhahood conferred upon Gotama no particular gift for influencing his fellow-men, save that of example and eloquence. His mission possessed nothing in common with that of the magician or medicine-man. Instead of curing suffering, he merely preached the truth about it. The disciple, having been enlightened, needed to achieve his own salvation. Nor did enlightenment involve any particular exercise of the intellect: none of the great prophets or *Nebiim* have been metaphysicians, except perhaps Krishna (whose arguments in the *Bhagavad-Gita* may have received later elaboration). "The assurance of Nirvana," said the Buddha on one occasion, "is not an assurance of numbers nor logic; it is not the mind that is to be assured but the heart" (*Lankavatara Sutra*). The Buddha not merely despised metaphysical speculation; he regarded it at best as a distraction, an unnecessary refinement, like acrobatics, and at worst as an obstacle to the apprehension of simple, if unpalatable, truths. The prophet of divine connection does not need metaphysics to convey the nature of divinity. Metaphysics is the product of a disputatious discipleship.[1]

In the north of Benares is a Deer Park which, like Bodh Gaya, remains a place of sacred associations for Buddhists. It was to this quarter that the Buddha, having crossed the Ganges by a form of

[1] We do not agree with Bishop Gore when he says in his *Philosophy of the Good Life* that Buddha's "appeal was in the highest degree intellectual, and such as the uneducated or those who were unversed in abstract speculation could not have understood". Buddha eschewed abstract speculation.

levitation, directed his steps. Perhaps he knew that there he would find the disciples whom he had recently alienated. When they saw him approaching, they felt a common resentment. "This is Gotama," they said one to another, "the ascetic who has abandoned his self-control. He wanders about now, greedy, of impure soul, unstable, and with his senses under no firm control, devoted to enquiries regarding the frying-pan. We will not ask after his health, nor rise to meet him, nor address him, nor offer him a welcome, nor a seat, nor bid him enter into our dwelling." The Buddha perceived their hostility but ignored it. The simplicity of his approach, begging-bowl in hand, disarmed them. They found themselves rising to their feet. "Know that I am Jaina," he said quietly, "and that I have come to give the first wheel of the law to you." And having received the five men into a new mendicant order, he proceeded to preach to them the first of his great sermons, that which is entitled the "Discourse of setting in motion the Wheel of the Doctrine", sometimes regarded as the Buddhist equivalent of the Sermon on the Mount.

First teaching

The Wheel of the Doctrine or the Law was so-called because it is concerned with the Wheel of human life and rebirth. Without enlightenment, existence is nothing but a succession of futile lives, a treadmill of mortality, *samsara*. How, then, was enlightenment to be attained? The Buddha's sermon opens with an exposition of the two extremes to be avoided. The first and obvious extreme is that of sensual pleasure. Nothing causes the Wheel to turn so much as indulgence. For pleasure increases our dissatisfaction not merely with everything else but with itself: faced with this void, we need more of the same kind to fill it, so that we proceed to engage in a process akin to borrowing ourselves out of debt. The other extreme to be avoided is that of excessive mortification. According to the Buddha, this extreme was no more profitable than the first, for it not merely results in the increase of agitation but leads logically to extinction before any real merit has been acquired. Such was the objection that the Buddha, had he known it (and it is possible that he did), would have preferred against the teaching of Mahavira. The true object to be attained is that of calmness and composure, the condition and usually the sign of wisdom. Following the great sages of whom we have written, the Buddha defines the means of inducing this frame of mind as the cultivation of an attitude of "rightness"—a rightness which derives its exactitude by being the product of a "middle path" between extremes. The "noble eightfold path", as it is called, consists of right views, right intent, right speech, right conduct, right means of livelihood, right endeavour, right mindedness, right meditation. By the cultivation of this balanced attitude we shall attain to the cessation of that pervasive suffering which is the inevitable result and accompaniment of *craving*. Craving, as the Buddha remarks with characteristic insight, is that which causes "the renewal of becoming".

The Buddha's analysis of craving has come to be known in scripture as the Four Noble Truths. They form an acute summary of pain, the product of craving. First comes the definition of what is painful: birth, age, sickness, sorrow, despair, ugliness and so on. Secondly comes the definition of the cause of pain, which is craving. Thirdly comes the definition of how pain is to be overcome, which is by non-attachment. Fourthly comes the definition of the doctrine whereby non-attachment may be attained, which is the Eightfold Path.

Beginning with the five ascetics or *Bhikkus*, who became the first genuine Buddhist monks, the Buddha proceeded to make converts by the hundred, by the thousand, and in due course by the million. Accredited missionaries were sent throughout Oudh, Bihar, and Bengal, but in effect every monk with his begging-bowl was a missionary, a witness to enlightenment. "Go your rounds," was the Buddha's daily order to his monks, "for the salvation of many, for the happiness of many, with compassion for all, for the good of gods and men." Although the Buddha both preached and practised the virtues of gentleness, humility, self-discipline, and forbearance, it will not do to imagine him as lacking in energy, fire, or even passion. Some of the Buddha's recorded sermons are instinct with the kind of gentleness and sweetness that we associate, not always accurately, with St. Francis of Assisi. Others, particularly the famous Fire Sermon or the "Sermon on the Lessons to be drawn from Burning", one of the greatest of his utterances, exhibit the kind of passion that we find in the major Hebrew prophets, besides being conveyed in language that poets have not always sustained at such a pitch of intensity. The Fire Sermon ought not to be quoted in excerpts; it forms one long passage of incandescent expression. Never before, and in no other part of the world except perhaps Babylon among the captive Jews—for Buddha may have been a contemporary of the second Isaiah—had human nature been, as it were, branded with such eloquence:

> "All things, O priests, are on fire. Forms are on fire. Eye-consciousness is on fire. Impressions received by the eye are on fire. And whatever sensation, pleasant or unpleasant or indifferent, originates in dependence on impressions received by

the fire, that also is on fire. And with what are these on fire?

With the fire of passion, say I, with the fire of hatred, with the fire of infatuation. With birth, old age, death, sorrow, lamentation, misery, grief, and despair are they on fire.

The ear is on fire. Sounds are on fire. . . . The nose is on fire. Odours are on fire. . . . The tongue is on fire. Tastes are on fire. . . . The body is on fire. Things tangible are on fire. . . . The mind is on fire. Ideas are on fire. . . . Mind consciousness is on fire. Impressions received by the mind are on fire. And whatever sensation, pleasant or unpleasant, or indifferent, originates in dependence on impressions received by the mind, that also is on fire. And with what are these on fire?

With the fire of passion, say I, with the fire of hatred, with the fire of infatuation. With birth, old age, death, sorrow, lamentation, misery, grief, and despair are they on fire.

Perceiving this, O priests, the learned and noble disciple conceives an aversion for the eye, conceives an aversion for forms, conceives an aversion for eye-consciousness, conceives an aversion for impressions received by the eye; and whatever sensation, pleasant or unpleasant, or indifferent, originates in dependence on impressions received by the eye, for that also he conceives an aversion. . . . And in conceiving this aversion, he becomes divested of passion, and by the absence of passion he becomes free, and when he is free, he becomes aware that he is free; and he knows that rebirth is exhausted, that he has lived the holy life, that he has done what it behoved him to do, and that he is no more for this world."

It may be wondered how a philosophy based almost wholly upon aversion for everything human and natural should have become the "view of life" of hundreds of millions of persons. Would not the logical conclusion of such repudiations of life be the self-starvation of the Jaina? Evidently not. Having deliberately experimented with such extreme asceticism, Buddha renounced it as a spiritual blind-alley. The professional fakir *tends* to be an exhibitionist. His rigours are displayed for all the world to see. The attitude to desire preached by the Buddha excludes such demonstrativeness. The struggle to overcome desire and craving is an inward thing. And whereas in the Buddha we find a rejection of the flesh, this rejection is not accompanied by the hysteria of much Western puritanism, which is simply evidence of covert attraction. To express unbounded loathing for the life of the senses is to add fuel to one of the "fires" which needs most urgently to be quenched, namely the fire of hatred.

It was not merely in the Fire Sermon that Buddha had recourse to the metaphor of fire. The image occurs again and again in his recorded sayings. We may recall that just before the Great Retirement, when he was awakening from the sleep into which the palace celebrations had plunged him, he experienced the feeling of one whose house was on fire. In other words, practical measures for salvation were, in his view, more important than enquiries into the origin of life, evil, god. Whenever the Buddha was asked questions about God, his responses were evasive, equivocal, and sometimes frankly unsatisfactory.[1] On one occasion, for instance, someone asked him, "Sir, is there a God?" To which he replied not with a statement but with the further question, "Did I say there is a God?" The questioner, confounded, rejoined with, "Then there is no God, Sir?" To which the Buddha quickly replied, "Did I say there is no God?" Such an evasive attitude, extraordinary in a religious leader, is comprehensible only if we bear in mind a remark that he was fond of making to his disciples, once more introducing the familiar image, "When a house is on fire, do you first go and trace the origin of the fire, or do you try to extinguish it?" "The Tathagata has no theories" sums up the mission of the Buddha very succinctly. He had only practice. In the great Buddhist epic poem called the *Dhammapada*, which some oriental scholars place higher than the *Bhagavad-Gita* itself, occur the words, "How is there laughter, how is there joy, as the world is always burning?"

Homecoming

To trace the events of the Buddha's life from the moment of his Enlightenment, which occurred about the age of thirty-five, to that of his death about forty-five years later, is rendered difficult by reason of the variety of legends that has accumulated around his name. Of the great events of his life to which we can attach credence, his return to his home country and his family is perhaps the most dramatic. Whatever intelligence of his acts and conduct had reached the remote Himalayan Kingdom, the old king and the still young wife were totally unprepared for the sight which finally greeted them, though they had frequently sent messages to the Buddha begging him to return. Modestly robed in yellow, like a conventional ascetic, with shaven head and beardless face,[2] the prince who had exchanged an earthly for a heavenly kingdom entered the town of his birth in the manner his family least expected. The Jaina whom no woman could touch was not to be greeted by

[1] We shall see that Confucius responded in the same way.

[2] Cf. *The Light of Asia* (Edwin Arnold): "Three plain cloths, yellow, of stitched stuff, worn with shoulder bare, a girdle, almsbowl, strainer."

his own wife. And so the townsfolk were amazed to see the princess standing aside as her husband moved towards the Royal Palace from which he had departed with such stealth.

The Buddha's visit was a time of great missionary activity. But although Gotama had renounced all earthly ties, he was scruplous in paying respect to his family. He even made a special journey to the Lumbini Grove, where, to quote the *Buddha-Charita*, "he saw the holy fig-tree and stood by it remembering his birth, with a smile". This was the only occasion, it would seem, on which the subject of birth provoked in him something other than dejection. Having honoured the memory of his mother, he proceeded to receive into his Order a large number of his fellow-citizens, including members of his family, the chief being his wife, son, and brother. The brother, Nanda, was enticed into the Order by trickery, and forcibly shaved. The account of this press-gang operation is perhaps the only outright amusing episode in the scriptures of any faith. Thus Gotama's promise to return to his family was fulfilled, and the indignation of his wife gave way to lasting devotion. The Buddha never again returned home, though it is recorded that he undertook a spiritual journey to receive his father's dying breath, and on one occasion he spent three months in heaven instructing his mother in the Law.

Given his detestation of sex, the admission of women into his Order cannot have been made without considerable reflection. When he finally decided to permit women nuns, beginning with his aunt Maya-Prajapati, he is reported to have observed wryly that in so doing he was reducing by at least half the period during which his religion would exert influence in the world. Apparently he estimated this period at five hundred years: Buddhism has already flourished for four times as long. But although he warned his male followers to have as little as possible to do with women, he personally showed no reluctance to frequent their company. When, for example, the well-known courtezan Ambapali met him in her private mango grove at Vesali, whither he had apparently deliberately repaired, he greeted her with extreme politeness and at once proceeded to "instruct, arouse, incite, and gladden her with religious discourse". When, further, she invited him next day to a meal at her house, he accepted the invitation (by preserving the silence that gave consent) and arrived in company with his brethren, including his favourite Ananda,[1] whom he was specially to warn against womenkind. On this occasion he likewise took the opportunity of preaching at length to his hostess, following which the latter, like Mary Magdalene, hailed him as a divine messenger to

[1] Ananda was also a member of the Shakya clan, and a cousin of the Buddha.

humanity and made him a gift of land. It would seem that the Buddha wished to demonstrate, by a show of indifference, that he observed no distinction among humankind, whether of sex or of caste, the righteous or the sinful. Nevertheless he took care to enjoin his disciples, whose weaknesses he realized, not to become friends, companions, or intimates of sinners. Similarly, although he expected his monks "not to stop on their way to Nirvana", he knew as well as Zoroaster that the majority of mankind could be saved only by degrees. In the account of the Buddha's daily habits taken from the commentary by Buddhaghosha[1] on *Digha-Nikaya*, a collection of long Buddhist discourses, we read that "when he had finished his (morning) meal, the Blessed One, with due consideration for the different dispositions of their minds, would so teach them the doctrine that some would become established in the refuges, some in the five precepts, some would become converted, some would attain to the fruit of only one returning (to earth), or of never returning, while some would become established in the highest fruit, that of saintship, and would retire from the world". The truth is that in spite of the extreme rigour of his doctrine the Buddha, like Jesus, possessed an unusual insight into human frailty; and his compassion was equal to his understanding.

Approaching death

After the stay in Vesali, where his conduct was naturally considered by some to be an outrage, Gotama, now in the forty-fifth year of his Buddhahood, decided to spend the rainy season in the village of Beluva. Meanwhile, he had dismissed the greater number of his disciples. When the rains had set in, he suddenly fell ill. He was racked with pain, and seemed to be on the point of death. Throughout this ordeal, one thought obsessed him: he could not permit himself to die without taking leave of the members of his Order. He therefore decided to prolong his life for a brief period.

Mustering his will for an effort almost as great as that which had carried him, all those years ago, from humanity to Buddhahood, he "bent the sickness down again", and it temporarily retreated. The account of his subsequent conversation with Ananda is exceedingly moving. Ananda, who confessed that his own frame had wasted as soon as he learnt of his master's illness, rejoiced that it was still possible to receive a final benediction and farewell message. "What does the Order expect?" replied the Blessed One. "I have preached the truth without making any distinction between exoteric and esoteric doctrine: for in respect of truths, Ananda, the

[1] Lived 5th century A.D.

Tathagata[1] has no such thing as the closed fist of a teacher, who keeps some things back. . . . Now the Tathagata, Ananda, thinks not that it is he who should lead the Brotherhood, or that the Order is dependent upon him. Why then should he leave instructions in any matter concerning the Order? I too, O Ananda, am now grown old and full of years, my journey is drawing to its close, I have reached the sum of my days, I am turning eighty years of age; and just as the worn-out cask, Ananda, can be kept going only with the help of thongs, so methinks the body of the Tathagata can only be kept going by bandaging it up." He then enjoined Ananda to "remain strenuous, self-possessed and mindful, having overcome both the hankering and the dejection common in the world".

For a time the Buddha continued to lead his old mendicant life. One morning he invited Ananda to spend the day with him at the Chapola shrine. It was here that he received his last visit from Mara, the Evil One. Assuming a rôle superficially similar to that of Nicodemus, though animated by purely cynical motives, Mara hailed the approaching death of the Buddha as the final triumph of Good over Evil. The Blessed One, realizing the irony of Mara's invocation, answered him: "O Evil One! make thyself happy, the death of the Tathagata will take place before long. At the end of three months from this time the Tathagata will pass away." Having uttered these words, he decided to renounce that ingrained will to live upon which alone he had depended since the onset of his illness. As his hold upon life relaxed, the elements suffered a series of convulsions equal to that which had occurred at his conception. There were thunderstorms, earthquakes, and similar portents.

The last episode traditionally related of the Buddha is that concerning his visit to Chunda the smith, who incidentally and unwittingly was responsible for the master's death. It is a curious story. The Buddha decided to stay for a while at Chunda's mango grove, where his host invited him to a meal of sweet rice, cakes, and truffles. When the Blessed One was seated with his brethren, he directed Chunda to serve the sweet rice and cakes to the others, and to reserve the truffles for himself alone. He went further. He stipulated that whatever truffles were left over should be burned. "For I see no one," he explained, "on earth nor in Mara's realm, nor in Brahma's heaven, by whom, when he has eaten it, that food can be properly assimilated save by a Tathagata".

Within a short time of leaving Chunda's mango grove, the

[1] The title Tathagata literally means "he who neither comes from anywhere nor goes to anywhere".

already declining Buddha was once more taken ill, this time with an acute form of dysentery. He behaved as if this sudden malady was something for which he had been waiting. In his sufferings, however, he did not fail to take account of the feelings of his late host. Realizing that Chunda would be filled with horror and self-reproach at having been the indirect cause of the Blessed One's distress, he specially instructed Ananda to comfort and reassure him. To have provided the food whereby the Buddha should "pass away by that utter passing away in which nothing whatever remains behind" amounted, he explained, to a kind of merit. Undertaken in good faith and as a token of respect, Chunda's act would earn for its perpetrator a remission of *Karma*, beginning with an extension of his life-span on earth and a substantial increase in fortune. So important an instrument of providence would be watched over by providence until the end of time. Thus was Chunda both comforted and rewarded.

At a spot called the Sala Grove of the Mallas, by the River Hiranyavati, the Buddha, now wasted with illness, decided to prepare for his last moments. It is said that the beautiful Sala trees, perceiving the recumbent body of the Blessed One, rained down their blossoms, while heavenly music was wafted earthwards, "out of reverence for the successor of the Buddhas of old". Perceiving this tribute on the part of nature, the Buddha turned to Ananda and said: "It is not thus, Ananda, that the Tathagata is rightly honoured. . . . But the brother and sister who continually fulfils all the greater and the lesser duties—it is he who rightly honours the Tathagata with the worthiest homage." He then proceeded to specify the places of pilgrimage, four in number, at which the pilgrims and disciples should be encouraged to assemble after death had deprived them of a living master. These were to be the place of Buddha's birth, the place at which he had attained to the vision of reality whereby his Buddhahood was confirmed, the place where he began to establish his heavenly Kingdom, and the spot at which he was at that moment lying down to die. These places have been held sacred until this day.

It was chiefly to his faithful friend and disciple Ananda, the St. John of Buddhism, that the Master confided his last thoughts, which have been recorded at length. If the Enlightened One did not bequeath any message longer than that which we have quoted, he left a series of miscellaneous instructions. It was on this occasion, for example, that he issued the warning to Ananda against women to which we have referred:

"How are we to conduct ourselves, Lord, with regard to womenkind?"

"As not seeing them, Ananda."

"But if we should see them, what are we to do?"

"No talking, Ananda."

"But if they should speak to us, Lord, what are we to do?"

"Keep wide awake, Ananda."[1]

In addition to this stern admonition, the Buddha gave certain instructions about the future administration of the Order from which we may observe the beginnings of inequality and privilege: features originally absent from the Buddhist Order, which represented not merely a form of opposition to the Brahman caste but a tacit protest against caste in general. Whereas during the Buddha's lifetime it had been the custom for the brethren to address one another as "Avus" or "Friend", the Master expressed a wish that such familiarity should thenceforth be abandoned, and that the elder brethren, while continuing to address their juniors in the old manner or by name, must themselves be greeted with the word "Sir" or even "Venerable Sir". On the other hand, the Buddha, who regarded his doctrine as likely to remain valid only until the arrival of another Buddha, in the true Jaina fashion, expressed a wish not to hamper his later disciples with rules and precepts likely to become out of date. Finally, he reaffirmed his faith in his disciples, whom he declared one and all—even the most backward—to have reached that stage of enlightenment at which rebirth into suffering was no longer necessary.

When he realized that his master was actually about to die, Ananda besought him to prolong his earthly existence for a while longer, and even, since it lay within his power, for as much as an eon. The Buddha reproached him almost sternly for expressing that which was contrary to the design of providence, and Ananda was finally persuaded to acquiesce in his master's bodily departure. "Have I not formerly declared to you," reasoned the Buddha, "that it is the very nature of all things, near and dear unto us, that we must divide ourselves from them, leave them, sever ourselves from them? How, then, Ananda, can this be possible—whereas anything, whatever born, brought into being and organized, contains within itself the inherent necessity of dissolution—how then can this be possible that such a being should not be dissolved?" So saying, he ordered Ananda to assemble all the brethren, to whom he delivered a brief address, his last important public utterance, in which he recapitulated the basic tenets of his doctrine, ending with words that have become famous: "All

[1] It is interesting to note that in Buddhist mythology the goddess of love or desire, Rati, is represented as the daughter of Mara himself.

component things must grow old. *Work out your salvation with diligence.*"[1]

Having finally severed communication with mankind, the Buddha sank into a condition of mystical possession, passing successively through the four states of *Jhanas* which culminate with the attainment of unitive vision. By entering these states, the soul gradually shed, as it were, its superficial forms of consciousness, and attained to the condition of "right rapture", the final stage of the famous Eightfold Path, the simultaneous possession of everything and of nothing, *Nirvana*. Thus the Bodhisattva, having excluded himself from heaven to save mankind from the tyranny of egoism and desire, signified the end of his mission by returning to the realm of *Brahman*. The final "life" which his *Karma* had reserved for him had taken its course.

In conformity with instructions given to Ananda, and as a token of the respect in which the people held him, the Buddha received a funeral worthy of the highest nobleman or ruler. His ashes (for his body was cremated) were divided among the members of his family and certain powerful men who had approved of his mission. An urn discovered at the end of the last century, and inscribed to the effect that it contained "the remains of the exalted Buddha of the Shakya clan", is considered to be that which was deposited by his family under a monument still standing.

The doctrine of Karma

At one time it was the fashion to cast doubt upon the existence of such great religious leaders as Zoroaster, Buddha, and Christ. No doubt history would be less perplexing if we could accept this view. But all the evidence suggests that such people really existed; and what is difficult to explain is not their historical authenticity but how their teaching, opposed as it is to certain fundamental instincts of mankind, should have obtained its prolonged hold upon the human mind.

The understanding of Gotama Buddha's thought is made difficult for the Western mind in two ways. Some of it is very nearly outside our comprehension, while that which is within the grasp of our intellects can still be misconceived. Whereas the Buddha distrusted "metaphysics" as much as did Socrates, and discouraged futile speculation about the origin of the world, he held very definite views about cosmology, or the way in which life in the universe manifested itself. This Buddhist theory of the cosmos differed little in essentials from that which has been entertained in India

[1] Cf. the words pronounced by the doctor-psychiatrist in T. S. Eliot's play *The Cocktail Party*, Act II.

from the earliest times: that is a point to which we have already drawn attention. Not once did the Buddha, or indeed any other known Jaina, refer to the origin or author of this extraordinary theory of conduct, one of the most comprehensive that has ever been formulated. He merely accepted it as a fact not to be disputed.[1]

There would seem to be no reason why reincarnation or transmigration should not commend itself as a belief to the Western mind. Among the unproved and unprovable theories of morality, it is not merely the most ingenious but the most logical. The "practical" Western man, with his strong sense of rewards and deserts, might have taken the idea to his heart more enthusiastically than the oriental, with his strong sense of fatality (a very different notion).[2] Why, except in very isolated cases,[3] has he never done so? The suggestion of the present writer is that the idea was never preached to him. In other words, it seems reasonable to believe that the doctrine of the transmigration of souls was conceived and preached in the Orient by a Jaina earlier than any of which we have record, perhaps earlier even than the "gods" themselves, for the latter, as the Buddha was careful to insist, were just as much subject to its law as men and animals.[4] Now a doctrine may derive a large part of its stimulus, and achieve much of its effect, from the fact that it runs directly counter to the temperamental instincts of the audience. The idea of fatality, which represents the furthest remove from a just and logical view of the universe, needs to be corrected by an opposite notion. The Jaina or *Nabi* gives the people what it lacks. Hence the Eastern faith which has achieved least success in the Orient is Christianity, with its indifference to the theory of transmigration. And its prodigious success in the West may be due to its emphasis upon aspects of conduct which needed, and still need, perpetual reaffirmation for a civilization ever prone to materialist excess.

If, in consenting to be born into the world, the Buddha was voluntarily deferring his personal salvation, this does not imply that he was a "perfect" man who, like Jesus Christ, abandoned heaven for the purpose of redeeming humanity. The Buddha had personally endured all the processes of transmigration. This had

[1] And not to be argued about either. Buddha listed it among four "unthinkables" (*Kammavipako* in Pali).

[2] At times the oriental fatalism overshadows the ethical aspect of *Karma*: cf. the *Vishnu Purana*: "Birth, education, conduct, character, virtue or connection avails not a man in this life. The effects of one's *Karma* and penance, done in a prior existence, fructify, like a tree at the opposite time, in the next." True: but the exertions in the "next" existence must presumably also fructify in their turn, or the burden of *Karma* would never be reduced.

[3] The idea appears, somewhat vaguely, in Plato.

[4] Shankara held a similar view. See p. 224.

taken some time. What made the Buddha "enlightened" above all previous prophets was that he could remember all the phases of life through which he had passed. All that the unenlightened mortal knew was that his present existence, whatever its nature, was the result of his own contrivance in the sum of his previous existences; but his conduct then and there might either redress a balance seriously upset, or else still further disturb it. However brief, a lifetime of effort or sloth might effect changes of the most remarkable kind. A good man might so successfully "work off" his *Karma* as to render further incarnation on earth unnecessary,[1] while a thoroughly bad man might be lucky to be allowed to remain within the confines of the natural world at all, but then only as some vile insect or reptile. For the wheel of existence might be eluded either by ascending to one of several different heavens, or by being consigned to one of the 136 hells of which later Buddhist theology speaks. Absolute good and absolute evil, both equally rare, would be rewarded by absolute salvation or damnation.

It is conventional to maintain that Buddhism is animated by an intense and ineradicable disgust for life. Certain statements of the Buddha, particularly in the Fire Sermon, might easily lend support to this view. As an aid to meditation, the Buddhist monks are instructed to keep before their minds such images as a skeleton, or a corpse in process of decomposition: attachment to bodily pleasures will thereby be reduced and finally repudiated. Nevertheless, the specific duties laid down for monks and mendicants were not necessarily obligatory for ordinary laymen. Certain Christian mystics, St. Catharine of Siena, for instance, were accustomed to engage in forms of "self-discipline" of which the bare description may induce nausea; for a very effective way of "divesting oneself of the love of created beings" (to quote the phrase of St. John of the Cross) is to concentrate upon those aspects which reveal life at its most unaesthetic and humiliating pitch. Yet Christianity has always prided itself upon its freedom from the scabrous and the morbid. Likewise, the most attractive side of Buddhism is perhaps its attitude to natural beauty. If the human body was revolting, nature as a whole was beautiful. Consequently the first Buddhist monasteries were built in places of idyllic loveliness—"not too far nor too near the town, remote from the tumult and the multitude, places of repose and favourable to solitary meditation". In such communities the brethren dwelt "in perfect joy, without enemies in an otherwise unfriendly world". "Gaiety is our nourishment," they declared.

To study Buddhism at all deeply is to become aware that what

[1]This was the avowed aim of the Yogi. See Chapter VI.

it repudiates is not "the body" (as is the case, for example, with Christian puritanism) but *individuality*, of which the body is an obvious symbol. Hence the attraction to be "alone with nature" was also that of being, in Shelley's phrase, "at one with nature". No longer was the individual lost and unattached. "In the verdant forest," says the monk, "in an airy cave among the mountains, I wish to bathe my body, and I wish to walk alone in the vast and lovely woods. When in the sky the storm clouds clash their cymbals, when torrents of rain fill the highways of the air, and the monk, in a mountain crevice, abandons himself to meditation, there is no greater joy. On the flower-covered river-bank he sits in ecstatic meditation: surely there is no greater joy than that."

Joy and ecstasy, far from being banished from the life of both monks and laymen, are regarded as the sign of an excellent spiritual disposition. Such a prevailing mood induced an attitude of gentleness towards all creatures. The Buddha's attack upon ritualism was the result of this attitude. Charity was superior to ritual sacrifice. "There is a form of sacrifice easier than that of milk, oil, and honey: it is charity. Instead of sacrificing animals, let them go free! Let them seek grass, water and fresh breezes." No wonder that the Buddhists were among the first to establish hospitals for animals. As the *Dhammapada* says, "If a man for a hundred years sacrifices month by month with a thousand, and if he but for one moment pay homage to a man whose soul is grounded in true knowledge, better is that homage than a sacrifice for a hundred years." Hence the double paradox of the teaching of Gotama. Life was both beautiful and ugly. Man must endeavour to root out of himself the desire for continued existence; but he might venerate to the point of sentimentality the life of natural things. He must endeavour to secure the cessation of birth; but at the same time he must connive at the continuance of rebirth until the *Karma* of humanity shall have been worked out. Life, however burdensome, must go on until it is purged of sin and egoism. The disposition of the monk must be a kind of stoic benevolence. According to the Master, if a monk is injured by his enemies, he should say to himself, "They are good, they are good, for at least they do not strike me." If he is then struck, he should say to himself, "They are good, they are good, for at least they are not killing me." If, finally, they set about killing him, he should say, "They are good, they are good, because all they are doing is to deliver me from this transitory life without imperilling my salvation."

Certain scholars have described the assumption that life is inherently evil as a later corruption of the Buddha's teaching.[1]

[1] Cf. M. Hiriyanna: *The Essentials of Indian Philosophy*, p. 75.

Save for certain of the images employed, the teaching of the Buddha does not suggest a nature morbidly obsessed with the fouller aspects of physical existence. Whatever the Buddha's personal temperament, he was as far removed from the hysterical and the neurotic as Mahavira may, from what we gather, have been the reverse. Moreover, a philosophy cannot be dismissed as wholly negative and despairing which offers, even though fleetingly and at a stupendous price, some modicum of hope: and the Buddha offered *Arahatship* here and now to those prepared to quench the fire of desire and passion in their hearts.

The two "Vehicles": Ashoka

With the growth of a Buddhist *system*, and with the development of a church from a group of monks which was never intended to form a priesthood, the gentle and wise notions of the Buddha became hardened into precepts, until in due course the simple doctrine developed a rift which, far from the land in which the Buddha first preached, has persisted until this day. This rift was between so-called Hinayana Buddhism and Mahayana Buddhism, or the "Little Vehicle" and the "Great Vehicle", terms which do not in themselves prove very enlightening. Which of these two forms of Buddhism comes nearest to that preached by the Enlightened One is difficult to say at such great distance in time; but they differ from each other as profoundly as both differ from a further variation known as Zen Buddhism, which flourished chiefly in Japan. The history of these various schools is very instructive, but, like all histories of denominational strife, it can be depressing.

Buddhism had no Judas; but in the disciple Subhadda it had its doubting Thomas. On receiving news of the Blessed One's death, he is supposed to have remarked, "Now we shall be able to do whatever we like; and what we do not like, that we shall not have to do." This is a good summary of what happened. Even before the schism of the Little and Great Vehicle effected a broad geographical division of Buddhism, no less than eighteen different sects appeared. The process of disintegration, inevitable to some extent in every faith, might have ended in utter chaos but for the conversion to the Buddhist faith of one of the most remarkable rulers in ancient history, Ashokavardhana or Ashoka. It seems that no religion can survive without its imperial champion; Ashoka, who began to rule the whole of India (except the very south) in 273 B.C., was to Buddha what Constantine was to Christianity. Unless our conjectures are wholly mistaken, Ashoka represents one of the few rulers in history for whom absolute power did not spell absolute corruption. Beginning as a monarch of conventional ruthlessness, he seems to have undergone in middle age an experience of revulsion from the life of alternate pageantry and slaughter which, for purposes of prestige, he was obliged to follow. Some say that this was due to the heroism of a Buddhist monk whom he had cast into his prison-inferno; others that it followed the news of one of his more sanguinary victories, that over the Kalinga, in which several hundred thousand persons were killed, maimed, or rendered homeless. All we know is that he suddenly decided to become a Buddhist lay-brother or *upasaka*, and that the rest of his life (he may later have become a monk) was devoted to governing his people according to Buddhist principles.

How far Ashoka was successful in turning Buddhism into a state religion, we cannot tell: he certainly went to great lengths to inculcate his people with moral teaching. Our modern efforts in political propaganda neither match those employed by Ashoka nor are likely to survive for so long. At carefully selected points throughout his kingdom he set up huge stone pillars upon which were carved, usually in the dialect of the region, the essentials of the Buddhist ethic. Similar inscriptions were cut upon numerous rock faces. Both the rock inscriptions and a number of the pillars may still be seen. As might be expected, these writings deal not so much with abstract theological matters (curiously enough they do not once refer to the Buddha by name) as with civic or social morality. In a society threatend with the danger of being split into irreconcilable sects, they make an earnest appeal for religious toleration. The Rock Edict No. 12, for instance, contains the interesting passage: "A man must not do reverence to his own sect, or disparage that of another, without reason. Depreciation should be for specific reasons only, because the sects of other people all deserve reverence for some reason or another. By thus acting a man exalts his own sect, and at the same time does service to the sects of other people. By acting contrariwise a man hurts his own sect, and does disservice to the sects of other people. . . . Concord is meritorious." That is the statement of a man who, while understanding the violence of religious passions too well to engage in persecution, yet realizes the heavy responsibilities of permitting religious freedom.

A slightly sententious edict such as the above might suggest that Ashoka, though tolerant of religion, lacked a personal faith. The presumption is probably false. Like Ikhnaton, Ashoka seems to have been a pious and sincere convert. As an administrator, he was a great deal more capable than the idealistic worshipper of Aton. He established monastries by the thousand, and started veterinary hospitals. He held a gigantic Buddhist Congress and reformed the Church. And having thoroughly evangelized his own country from end to end, he embarked upon the organization of foreign missions. Ashoka's monks travelled over almost the entire known world, ranging as far as Greece in the west and, shortly after his death, carrying the gospel of enlightenment to Tibet, China, and Japan, where it later took permanent root.

The public inscriptions of Ashoka were not merely intended as exhortations to virtue; they often consisted of reports upon the results so far achieved. Even allowing for official exaggeration, these results seem to have been remarkable. Not merely had the officials acted with forbearance, but the people had shown qualities of virtue not to be left unacknowledged. Rock Edict No. 5 must have been cut at a moment of singular calm and prosperity: "Now by reason of the practice of piety by his sacred and gracious Majesty the King, the reverberation of the war-drums has become the reverberation of the Law. . . . As for many years before has not happened, now . . . there is increased abstention from the sacrificial slaughter of living creatures, abstention from the killing of animal beings, seemly behaviour to relatives, seemly behaviour to Brahmans, hearkening to father and mother, hearkening to elders." In short, there was something approaching public order and decency.

The final years of Ashoka's reign (which lasted forty years) are as obscure and confused as those of Ikhnaton. Failure and back-sliding there must have been at all times, and possibly Ashoka insisted too much upon outward conformity, thus confusing "seemly behaviour" with inner moral rectitude. Moreover, the maintenance of public virtue at a level considerably higher than that prevailing in any ordinary society must have required a great deal of exasperating inspection and vigilance; and whatever the humbler part of the community might have been prepared to endure, there were powerful influences working against the king's regulated virtue. Chief of these influences was that of the Brahmans, who, like the priests of Amon, awaited an opportunity to reassert their power, and incidentally to resume such forbidden customs as the sacrificing of animals. In the end, Ashoka was apparently deposed and succeeded by his grandson, though it may be that he withdrew from public life and, like the Emperor Charles V, devoted his last years to religious practices.

The apotheosis of The Buddha

Even though his system was abandoned, the Buddhist religion, somewhat modified, continued to win adherents at a rate unparalleled and no doubt on a scale greater than its originator anticipated. For just as there are two "legendary" Buddhas, the young and brilliant prince and the humble apostle of gentleness and forbearance, so there were two conflicting Buddhist ideals, that of converting the whole world to *Arahatship*, and that of founding a gospel sufficiently durable, not to say flexible, to serve humanity until the arrival of the next Buddha. That Gotama seems to have regarded the caste system as a permanent feature of society, even though he may personally have flouted its conventions, is suggested by the fact that this next Buddha was to be of the Brahman class. To this point we shall return. In course of time the division between Mahayana Buddhism and Hinayana Buddhism assumed a territorial character. Hinayana, a creed which sought to preserve the simplicity of the Buddha's teaching, flourished for some time in the south of India, including Ceylon, whereas the Mahayana, a more sophisticated creed, took hold in the north, spreading thence across China, Tibet, and Mongolia to Japan.[1] As the simpler faith, Hinayana revered the Buddha as a great and even divine teacher; and the monastic communities continued to be organized on the lines indicated by the Master. Thus even today, in Ceylon, the monasteries probably preserve better than anywhere else the characteristics of the original Buddhist communities.[2] The Mahayana creed or creeds, on the other hand, exalted the Buddha to such a degree that he came at length to be regarded as a God: with the result that the atheist prophet was in due course responsible for an elaborate system of theology and metaphysics. At a grand ecclesiastical council convened by the great Kushan ruler Kanishka (*c.* A.D. 120), who ruled an immense Indian and Asiatic Empire from his capital at Kabul, the doctrine of Mahayana was established with minute elaboration and scriptural wealth. Among the achievements of the delegates was the composition of three hundred thousand *Sutras* or theological essays, bearing upon almost every conceivable problem with which the faithful were likely to be confronted. Buddhism now formed the faith of a powerful established Church.

Was the "Great Vehicle" constructed merely as a useful engine of government? There will always be historians for whom the *development* or modification of a faith represents a departure from original innocence and truth, engineered as a rule for political purposes, or caused by the periodical disposition of human nature to flag and seek repose in dogma. A more profound scrutiny, however, while admitting degeneracy, will also recognize a certain advance, and sees nothing inherently absurd in the two processes

[1] The division is rough. Mahayana took hold likewise in Korea and also Hawaii.
[2] Cf. the article on Buddhism by de la Vallée Poussin in *The Legacy of India* (1938).

occurring simultaneously. Coupled with the growth of ritualism, relic-worship, and an immensely complicated theology, went a more liberal and refined moral outlook. Instead of propagating the doctrine that none but the saint or *Arahat* could be saved, Mahayana Buddhism opened the way of salvation to all mankind. Furthermore, it conceived this way of salvation in a much less abstruse and negative manner than had hitherto been entertained. *Nirvana* ceased to mean (if it ever did mean) absolute *extinction*, and became an abode of blessedness and peace beyond the reach of the transmigratory process. This development, though accompanied by much superstitious or *tantric* (magical) ceremonial, bears a remarkable resemblance to that which took place in Egypt after the revolution of Ikhnaton and simultaneously with the compilation of *The Book of the Dead*. Perhaps the most interesting development of Mahayana, however, is the doctrine of Bodhisattvas: that is to say, Buddhas who abstain from entry into *Nirvana* in order to work for the promotion of universal deliverance. The veneration of these future Buddhas tends sometimes to obscure the revered name of the "historical" Buddha. Instead of concentrating upon the attainment of *Nirvana*, the faithful tended to aspire towards one of two conditions: either that of rebirth during the lifetime of one of the Bodhisattvas, or, more ambitious still, that of Buddhahood itself. As to the best means of achieving the latter end, theologians disagreed violently. Meanwhile it was natural that the devotee should seek to invoke the aid of saints, gods, and all the Buddhas who had ever existed; and hence the simple notions of Gotama were in due time swamped by an inrush of dogma and myth. Osiris and the *fravashis* cannot long remain in the background.

The diffusion of Buddhism

One of the most extraordinary phenomena in history is the fact that several of the world's great religions—and there are usually agreed to be eleven of them—have flourished least readily in the place of their origin. This is particularly true of the Buddhist faith. Today, the number of professing Buddhists in India is negligible.[1] Why did so powerful a religion fail to take permanent root in the land that originally embraced it with such ardour? The answer lies in a fact often ignored or underestimated. Buddhism did not drive out the religion that preceded it. By its very looseness and tolerance, the Hindu faith survived and finally enveloped the younger and more exacting doctrine. For in so far as Buddhism accumulated superstitions and developed an intelligible if abstruse

[1] About three million.

theology, so it approximated to the condition of a popular faith such as Hinduism, in spite of its intellectual appanage, had always remained: until finally the Buddha himself came to be included among the gods of the Hindu pantheon. Secondly, owing to the Buddha's distrust of sacrifice, ritual, and ceremony, the *Sangha* or Buddhist brotherhood undertook few, if any, of the duties naturally incumbent upon priests: notably the performance of ceremonies connected with birth, marriage, and death, and the fulfilment of numerous other religious and civic functions. These offices continued to be performed as a matter of course by the Brahmans. Without this caste of respected if sometimes corrupt persons, social life in Hindustan would have lost its continuity. Although the Buddha had tacitly opposed the Brahmans, he seems not merely to have acquiesced in their priestly status, but assumed it to be a permanent feature of social life. The Buddha remained indifferent rather than hostile to the caste structure of society.

Although Brahmanism exerted so powerful an influence upon Indian society, the *Sangha* enjoyed a period of immense prestige. Indeed, there came a time when its attraction exerted such influence upon the young men of the Magadha (north-east India) that society seemed likely to perish from an excess of celibacy. Another debilitating factor was the strict pacifism of the Buddhist doctrine: for while a display of force may not necessarily destroy non-violent beliefs, it can often exert an influence upon where they shall be preached. Thus the expulsion of Buddhism from India was brought about by the arrival of a people inspired by a faith of militant fervour, the Moslems. And Islam has retained a firm foothold in India to this day. Even so, it has succeeded no better than Buddhism in ousting that extraordinary conglomeration of exalted metaphysical beliefs, myths, superstitions, and apparent obscenities, which make up the historical Hindu faith.

A history of Buddhism from its extinction in India until the present day may strike the Western reader as a prolix and bewildering process in which the pure faith of the Buddha almost ceases to be recognizable. Certainly the Buddhism of Asia, including Japan, is a faith that exhibits a great deal of internal variation. Surveying the history of Christianity in the West, an Eastern scholar would no doubt experience a similar impression of violent conflict, glaring disparity of profession and practice, and rank superstition. The purest Buddhism is perhaps that to be found in Burma, the least pure in Japan; but the test of a faith is finally in the lives of individuals. The literature of Zen Buddhism contains some pieces of great beauty and spiritual insight:

Let others speak ill of me, I acquire the chance of gaining merit,
For they are really my good friends;
When I cherish, being vituperated, neither enmity nor favouritism,
There grows within me the power of love and humility which is born of the unborn.

(From Yoka Daishi's *Song of Enlightenment.*)

Perhaps the most interesting form of later Buddhism, however, is that which began to flourish in Tibet from the 7th century A.D. The conqueror Strong-tsan Gampo (629–50), having become master of this country of difficult access, set up his capital at Lhasa and, with rare wisdom, began to Buddhize his people with the help of missionaries specially summoned from India, such as the saintly Padma Sambhava. The faith quickly took root.[1] Two powerful authorities, the Dalai Lama ("The all-embracing priest") and the Tashi Lama, wielded theocratic rule over the country. Even today the successor of the first is considered to be the incarnation of a Bodhisattva, while the second is believed to be the *avatar* of a Buddha. The Lama theology is expounded in a voluminous series of scriptures. The faithful are believed to acquire merit by the strict performance of ritual, including the use of the prayer-wheel and the so-called "trees of the law", long beflagged poles. In spite of this *tantric* aspect, however, the Lama wisdom contains teaching that calls to mind the wisdom of China or the *Book of Proverbs*.

A foolish man proclaimeth his qualifications,
A wise man keepeth them secret within himself.
A straw floateth on the surface of water,
But a precious gem placed upon it sinketh.

or more loftily:

The path is one for all,
The means to reach the goal must vary with the pilgrims.
Thou shalt not let thy senses make a playground of thy mind,
Hast thou attuned thy being to humanity's great pain, O candidate for light?
For know, that the Eternal knows no change.

As we write, the country remarkable for having preserved intact its social and religious hierarchy over a period of thirteen centuries lies open to foreign influence and to an alien doctrine, with consequences that we in the West are unable for the present to foresee.

[1] It may have begun to penetrate Tibet much earlier.

CHAPTER VI

THE HINDU SYSTEMS

Kapila

IN expounding the thought of India, even in the simple manner here adopted, we run the risk of both misrepresentation and omission, or worst of all, dilution. The monotonous abstractions of the *Upanishads* are with difficulty imagined as having moved men and women—whole multitudes of them—to devotional ecstasy, still less to the extremes of asceticism. But we know that they did. A bare account of the life of Mahavira, with its succession of macerations, does little to convey the fire and passion of the man, his frightful yet inspiring presence. Even the story of Shakyamuni,[1] the Buddha, embellished as it has been with legend and parable and augmented by accounts of his five hundred and fifty previous existences, fails to come alive unless we picture a man of infinite pity and gentleness, a wanderer, a lover of cave and ravine as well as of bathing-Ghat and the shaded grove, a solitary and yet a good companion, a preacher of uncompromising sternness and yet a man of wit and even humour. To understand Hinduism as a living faith we need to read the great epics such as the *Mahabharata* and the *Ramayana*. To enter into the spirit of the Buddhist gospel we must go to the *Dhammapada*.

When we approach the Hindu "systems" proper, the task of infusing life and spirit into abstract philosophical statements becomes one of extreme difficulty. These systems are among the most complex thought-structures that have been invented. In Europe we have become unaccustomed to philosophical systems. To us, philosophy tends to be an abstruse game, a debate about definitions, words set to chase words. The faith or system of belief we live by —and we must live by something—is almost totally unrelated to the contents of philosophical text-books. The earliest philosophers appreciated the need of system; a philosophy that failed to embrace experience as a whole was a philosophy that had failed to complete its work. Obsessed with trifles, we may well arrive at a state of mind in which the notion of the unity of experience has been completely abandoned: a sensation experienced by anyone who listens to papers read before certain select philosophical assemblies.

What was the oldest of Indian philosophical systems? It is probably that which was known as Sankhya, of which the author

[1] One of the Buddha's many titles, derived from the name of his clan.

was Kapila, a sage who may have lived as early as the 6th century B.C.

It is no small merit for a man to sit down and endeavour to expound the whole meaning of life to his contemporaries and for posterity: and if, as we suspect, Kapila's work consisted largely in the codification of previous ideas, he does not for that reason become less remarkable a thinker. The principle from which Kapila starts is one with which our study of the *Upanishads* has made us tolerably familiar. Experience itself is not merely evil, but always painful. The aim of existence, therefore, is not "fullness of life" or the "enrichment of experience", as almost all Western philosophers (save Schopenhauer) implicitly believe, but the voiding of the mind of its entire contents, followed automatically by the collapse and dismemberment of the mind-structure itself. Experience is codified, labelled, and measured as a necessary prelude to its dismantling.

Kapila's analysis of experience is extremely thorough. He finds reason to sort reality into twenty-five categories. Hence one of the possible meanings of *Sankhya*, namely the "science of numbers". He begins rather like Spinoza by positing the existence of a general Substance called *Prakriti*. From this basic substance are derived three "realities", or agents of reality, called *gunas*. The first achievement of these *gunas* (which act somewhat like catalysts in chemical reaction) is to create the intellect or, since the appropriate word is *Buddhi*, the enlightening power or perceptive faculty. The next stage in this process, which is an evolutionary one, consists in the articulation, again by means of the seminal *gunas*, of the faculty of perception into the five senses. These senses proceed to create the physical organ with which they are associated: sight created the eye, hearing the ear, sexual desire the generative organs. This may well seem a reversal of the proper order of things, though Schopenhauer consciously and some of our modern evolutionists have followed Kapila. Finally, the *gunas*, operating upon the raw material of *Prakriti*, produce the constituents of the so-called "external world": ether, water, earth, fire, etc. These are the result of what is called "secondary evolution".

Set over against this basic substance *Prakriti*, but not intervening in its individual activities, is its complete opposite: Spirit or *Purusha*. Whereas *Prakriti* is passive (though not static), *Purusha*, being spirit, is activating, though not exactly dynamic. Whatever is active in the world is spirit ("The spirit of God moved upon the face of the waters"): a "man of spirit" is a man who does things. What *Purusha* does is to exercise a "lure" (to employ the term of the modern English philosopher Whitehead) over *Prakriti*, so that the creative *gunas* are set in motion. As the Sankhya commentator of the

2nd century A.D., Ishvara Krishna, remarked, "*Purusha's* purpose is the sole cause of *Prakriti's* evolution." In other words, *Purusha* is the sun which, directing its rays upon the rich humus of *Prakriti*, stimulates life and growth. Under the influence of this distant but vivifying power the "things" in the universe came into being: a *nisus* or urge impels them to do so. Such a process might at first sight be thought to resemble that occasioned by Aristotle's Unmover Mover: but *Purusha*, in operating upon *Prakriti*,[1] is in fact working out its own purpose. "The organ of sight comes into existence because it is necessary if *Purusha* is to see."[2]

At first glance this account of the origin of life and mind may seem absurdly fanciful. Taken at its face value, what does it amount to but idle juggling with abstractions? Admittedly, philosophies have been criticized for slighter faults: but when a system of thought has survived for twenty or so centuries, we cannot lightly dismiss it. Errors in practical everyday life may be brushed aside; in philosophy they must be accounted for. Error in philosophy is another word for opportunity; for every form of belief, however removed in spirit from that to which we are accustomed, represents a challenge. The Sankhya system, at least in its general outline, bears a resemblance to certain modern philosophies of "emergent evolution", such as those expounded by A. N. Whitehead and S. Alexander: so much so that it is best described in terms employed by these thinkers. Whereas the philosophy of emergent evolution is usually shot through with optimism, however, the Sankhya system is a structure erected over a pit of nihilistic acedia. For instead of the evolution of matter and life being regarded as something good and wonderful, it is regarded by Kapila as the result of a gigantic cosmic error.

To expound the nature of this error, this evolutionary mistake, is by no means easy.[3] The argument borders upon the abstruse—a realm upon which no philosopher ever ventured who returned of sound mind. Instead of parading the sort of abstract argument which some Indian philosophers enjoy, we should bear in mind certain basic principles common to all Vedic or Vedantic philosophy. One of these principles is the evil of individuality. Individuality is an obstacle to enlightenment. Now the work of the *gunas* is precisely to individualize, or egotize: therefore one of the commonest illusions from which mankind suffers is to identify the work of the *gunas* with the goal of *Purusha*. It is like mistaking physical growth —obviously not a bad thing in itself—with the true and complete

[1] It is not, however, an "agent" in the crude sense.
[2] Hiriyanna: *Essentials of Indian Philosophy* (1949), p. 119.
[3] Even Indian philosophers admit this. See *op. cit.*, p. 116.

end of man, which is presumably a spiritual fruition: or perhaps to do something even more common, to confuse the beauty of an experience of physical (say sexual) origin with certain higher experiences, of which the former can at best provide an intimation. In short, the beginning of wisdom is to escape from individuality, because to do so is to escape from illusion. "Liberation obtained through knowledge of the twenty-five realities (categories)," Kapila is reputed to have declared, "teaches the one only knowledge, that neither I am, nor anything is mine, nor do I exist." Such liberation involves an immediate perception of the fundamental difference between *Prakriti* and *Purusha*. When we have attained to the highest experiences of which the mind is capable we find mere physical enjoyments paltry by comparison. Unlike certain forms of Buddhism, the Sankhya system does not necessarily condemn bodily pleasures as evil. The tendency of Hinduism, especially in its later development, is to assert the contrary: hence the preponderance of ritual and conduct which, as Gandhi once remarked, became "obscene" only when the Western conquerors arrived to pronounce it so. Possibly the Orient was wiser to permit the open parade of such tendencies within the sphere of religious ritual than their covert parade through the dream-world, as in our Western consciousness. The worship of Shiva, with its undisguised emphasis upon the generative organs of both sexes, the *linga* and *yoni*, does not strike the Hindu, however young and innocent, as obscene: "obscenity" might rather be attributed to the tendency found almost universally in the Occident, namely to associate sexual operation with other purely automatic activities.

Patanjali and Yoga

The system of Kapila has been described by a great orientalist, Professor Garbe, as exhibiting for the first time "the complete independence and freedom of the human mind, its full confidence in its own powers". We now pass from an elaborate philosophical system to something to which we should perhaps give the name of a philosophical technique. For everyone who has heard of the Sankhya system there are a hundred—perhaps a thousand—who have heard of the system of Yoga. Of all the products of oriental thought, Yoga has perhaps exerted the greatest fascination over the Western mind. To account for this fascination is not difficult. The "mysterious East"—or what Disraeli, in the person of Sidonia in *Tancred*, called "the great Asian mystery"—seems to find its embodiment in the Yogi. Even allowing for differences of appearance and practice, such holy men represent the farthest remove from what to Western eyes is a useful or decent member of society.

In the first place the Yogi does no work: that is to say, his intense exertions are devoted to nothing of apparent social utility. In the second place, he possesses, or claims to possess, powers beyond normal human attainment: a fact calculated to rouse immediate interest in a European and even more perhaps in an American. Dissatisfied with traditional religion and finding no exhilaration in the absence of faith (which was at one time supposed to be the condition most to be envied), many a lonely Western man or woman has sought in some oriental discipline the way to spiritual repose.

The principles of Yoga are deceptively simple. Their practice, particularly by anyone with a living to earn, is extremely difficult and inconvenient. Just as the appreciation of education is itself the consequence of education,[1] so "the only way to find Yoga is through Yoga". In his little book *A Confession*, Tolstoy records how, once the unsatisfactoriness of his unregenerate life became clear to him, he believed himself capable forthwith of embarking upon a career of the highest sanctity. Experience did not bear out this confidence. Similarly, the student of a new faith feels as if the bare assent to its principles, the mere expression of approval, will ensure his being at once admitted to its most profound secrets. What we find in reality is something rather less edifying. There is an initial enthusiasm, sometimes overwhelming and always infectious. In the absence of immediate and visible results, the novelty wears off. Finally, what was initiated with enthusiasm is abandoned with scarcely a regret. The seeker after faith may then turn, with the least show of embarrassment, to one of the many other systems of belief for which his suffrage is invited: until it will become clear to others, though rarely to himself, that what he desires is not so much to live steadily and earnestly by a faith as to enjoy the intoxication of surrendering to one faith after another, as to so many spiritual mistresses.

Detailed descriptions of Yoga exercises or an account of the habits of fakirs—a word used chiefly by Moslems to denote a man dedicated to poverty—may excite curiosity, but it will not necessarily promote understanding. If a half-naked or wholly naked Hindu squats down on the ground and directs his gaze at the tip of his nose or at his navel; or if he persists in holding his arm in the air until, deprived of circulation, it begins to wither and atrophy; or if, preferring not to remain seated, he adopts a mode of progress that consists of rolling himself in the direction of some shrine or holy place; or if, the better to demonstrate his indifference to material wants, he starves himself to within an ace of death or nearly buries himself alive—or actually does so—we tend to dismiss these acts

[1] Lecky.

as mere wanton aberrations, the product of ascetic high spirits. Such a judgment is superficial. The practice of Yoga is not for everybody, but nor is the exercise of supreme command in the army, or that of premiership or the pursuit of scientific research. Yet just as every society must have a few men prepared to work longer and harder than their fellows, otherwise certain urgent and necessary tasks would never be accomplished, so every religion must have its extremists—its prophets, saints, and martyrs—without whom certain urgent spiritual tasks would remain unfulfilled. The Yogi is simply a man who takes the Hindu philosophy to its logical conclusion. That such a man should be called an extremist, as well he may be, serves to show with what half measures most people practise their professed religion.

What are the origins of Yoga? Undoubtedly they are of great antiquity. It is tempting, especially in the absence of definite proof, to compare these gymnosophists, these athletes of the soul, with the extraordinary figures in primitive society called *shaman*. The *shaman* is usually a recluse to whom strange powers are attributed. His withdrawal from society is both voluntary and lifelong. His "social function" is not necessarily to prophesy or even to dispense advice: only modern societies require a man that he shall give, rather than simply be, something. The *shaman*, so far as we can judge, is permitted to engage in meditation because the community believes such activities to be useful in themselves. In northern Nigeria, for instance, a member of the Abuan tribe, questioned by an anthropologist about the social function of a figure called the Ak-Abuan, replied that such a man existed "to be holy on our behalf, keeping all the laws that ordinary men have no time to remember because of their regular work". If the Indian Yogi is not identical with the primitive *shaman* in all respects, he at least fulfils certain of the religious functions of that figure.

The practice of Yoga meditation was unquestionably familiar to the men who composed the *Vedas*. To the author of the *Upanishads* it is a recognized technique for arriving at knowledge of *Brahman*, while in the *Gita* Krishna prescribes its rules to the bewildered and distressed Arjuna. When, sometime between 300 and 150 B.C., the sage Patanjali composed the *Yoga Sutras*, he was probably engaged in the codification of many ancient traditions. Men who devote a lifetime to the practice of ascetic meditation must evolve a great variety of techniques; but the comparative simplicity of Patanjali's rules must not blind us to the elaborate metaphysics upon which they are based. The practice, however scrupulous, of such rules of posture, breathing, etc., by the enthusiastic Westerner can scarcely do harm; but abstract gymnastics are no substitute for the arduous consecration of a lifetime to reflection, *askesis*, and worship. By learning to sit or breath properly, the Westerner thinks that he may inevitably acquire better health or poise; whereas to the genuine practitioner of Yoga, such ambition must appear paltry. Finally, "Yoga powers are not obtained by wearing the dress of a Yogi, or by talking about them, but untiring practice is the secret of success" (Patanjali).

To put the matter briefly, Yoga is a system for freeing the mind from attachment to the senses. Once freed, the mind does not wander aimlessly about in a world superior to nature; it actually becomes that which it is seeking. Now the quest of the soul or the *Atman* is for *Brahman*. Therefore the aim of Yoga is to effect a fusion of *Atman* with *Brahman*. Having passed through the successive states of Yoga discipline, the Yogi, though physically unchanged (or at least still present), is psychically transmogrified. Occasionally, it is claimed, he can be physically modified too. The Yogi can render himself invisible, engage in feats of levitation, enter another body, and remain buried in the ground for days at a time.

The Brahmans have always distrusted Yoga. Similarly, the priests of Christianity take care not to encourage mysticism, save in the case of those for whom it is evidently a vocation. Although the number of practitioners of Yoga is today between two and three million, we cannot suppose that more than a few of these adepts have consistently reached the final state of union or *Samadhi*. Not merely is such a state difficult to reach in itself; the Yoga ascetic ought not be content with its momentary or sporadic attainment. For what he is seeking to do is nothing less than to remove, in the space of one lifetime, the whole burden of *Karma* inherited from his previous existences. That which the ordinary man hopes, all being well, to eliminate in the course of a series of existences, the Yoga seeks to liquidate (if the word may be employed) in the space of one.[1]

What are the stages of attainment of *Samadhi*, or complete absorption? They are eight in number. These stages form the means whereby the five so-called "hindrances", or obstructions to detachment, may be eliminated: that is to say, Ignorance (*Avidya*), the notion of personality (i.e. that man is a self-contained individual), desire, hatred, and attachment to the things of the senses. The stages are as follows. First comes *Yama*, perhaps the most difficult stage of all and therefore that at which many an enthusiast

[1] His exertions need not be directed exclusively to selfish ends. According to the Chinese treatise *I-Ching* (see Chapter VII), "if you only meditate (according to the prescribed rules) for a $\frac{1}{4}$ hour, you set ten thousand aeons and a thousand births at rest".

turns back; it involves the extinction of desire and egotism and their replacement by charity and unselfishness. Secondly comes *Niyama*, the stage at which certain rules of conduct must be adopted, such as the maintenance of cleanliness, the pursuit of devotional studies, and the fulfilment of certain rituals of purification. Thirdly comes the stage to which greatest attention has been paid, namely *Asana*, or the attainment of correct posture. Just as the first stage of *Yama* involved the stilling of all desire, so the third stage involves the reduction to a minimum of all bodily movement. How is this to be done? To arrive at a satisfactory position, a great deal of experimentation must have taken place. The usual posture of the concentrating Yoga is familiar to most people from pictures. Resting his right foot upon his left thigh and his left foot upon his right thigh, the adept crosses his hands so as to be able to hold his two big toes, and, thus co-ordinated, lowers his head with the object of gazing either at his navel or at the tip of his nose.[1]

This is the kind of posture to which the Western body, unless taken in hand early, is ill-adapted, which probably accounts for its fascination: our office-existence is "sedentary" only in a very artificial sense, and our bodies suffer for it. Alarmed at his slouching laziness, the Westerner may see in a strenuous course of gymnosophy a means of counteracting the harm done by his daily routine. This is to mistake the nature and purpose of *Asana*. The *Yoga Sutras* make it clear both that "the posture assumed must be steady and easy", and that such steadiness and ease of posture is to be achieved through "persistent slight effort". It is not the purpose of this book to recommend the adoption of the belief and practice of any system here described: possibly it should be the author's duty to issue a warning against such conduct, which may end in disappointment and even disgust. In the case of those wishing to pursue such matters seriously, however, what is to be avoided above all is the furious enthusiasm of the novice.

Asana is not an end in itself; it is a means to the next stage, which is called *Pranayama*, the "right control of the life-force" or breathing. By regulating the breath, the Yogi hopes to arrive at two conditions: that in which he concentrates upon the process of breathing alone, and that in which, after due practice, he all but ceases to breath at all. The first condition, by evacuating the mind of all outer impressions, enables him to attain to complete spiritual repose: this is a necessary prelude to the flooding-in of divine light. The second condition enables him, if necessary, to undergo feats of endurance, such as those of which we have spoken.

[1] According to Swatmaram Swami, this posture is called "the Lotus seat" and destroys all diseases.

Having contemplated the foregoing stages of discipline, the amateur of Yoga may find it difficult to imagine through what further rigours he must brace himself to pass. But there are still four stages to come. *Pratyahara*, or abstraction, which means the mind's complete withdrawal from the world of sense, is followed by *Dharana*. Here an attempt is made to bring the mind to think only of one thing, or in effect to think of nothing specific at all. We have now reached a level at which it is difficult, without employing metaphors, to give an account of what is happening. Fortunately, Indian thinkers are equally aware of this difficulty. Having invited us to consider a mental state at which there is only one thing to think about, they are now obliged to give us some idea of what this is. At this point the teacher invokes the sacred syllable *OM*.

The reader will recall our references to *OM* in connection with the *Upanishads*. To provide the mind with subject-matter for meditation, the Yogi is recommended to repeat this sacred syllable, which thus generates a subject-matter otherwise inexpressible. "Through the sound of the word and through reflection upon its meaning," says Patanjali, "the way is found. From this comes the realization of the Self (or Soul, *Atman*), and the removal of all obstacles."[1]

No doubt the repeated invocation of the word *OM* induces a condition almost of hypnosis. Now the final stage of Yoga supervenes logically upon that which preceded it: for *Samadhi*, the eighth rung of this spiritual ladder, takes the form of a deep and complete trance. If we are to believe the experts, the trance state of *Samadhi* is a sign of the complete identification of soul with reality, *Atman* with *Brahman*. The soul in its individuality no longer exists: "like camphor in the flame and like salt with the water of the ocean," it has merged with the ocean of Being. The Yoga philosophers delight to represent this ineffable state by such metaphors. "The Yogi in highest meditation," says Swatmaram Swami, "is void within and without like a pot in the world-space. He is also like a pot in the ocean, void within and without." Naturally, to one in such a condition, nothing evil can happen. "A Yogi in *Samadhi* is invulnerable to all weapons; all the world cannot overpower him, and he is beyond the powers of incantations and magical diagrams."

Of mysticism Bossuet observed that the genuine article was so rare a thing, and false mysticism so common, that the whole subject

[1] The repetition of the sacred syllable has sometimes been recommended on purely psychological grounds. The Rajah of Aundh, author of an instructive manual of physical exercises, suggests that certain bodily movements should be accompanied by the pronunciation of various Indian vocables, of which *OM* is the most important. At least this reveals the connection of the syllable with regulated breathing, which no one denies to be of therapeutic value.

were best left alone by the laity. That is the view of an official. The official attitude, whether in religion or politics, was defined by Burke as the knowledge of "how much evil to tolerate". The historian of philosophy is not concerned to keep the peace; he is concerned to understand, first, how men come to think as they do, and, secondly, whether what they think is reasonable and consistent. Mysticism is a fact. The endeavour to suppress it has on the whole failed. If on occasion its practice has given rise to serious abuses, this may be the least cogent reason for dismissing it as fraudulent. No one is likely to question the value of liberty on the basis of Madame Roland's remark as to the number of crimes, including her own execution, committed in its name. And the same may be said of the celebrated remark of Lucretius on the evils of religion. A system such as Yoga may prove a fearful weapon in the hands of those who, misusing its discipline, claim to exercise powers purporting to be divine; but unless such a claim is sometimes made, even by the unscrupulous, Yoga is not worth the serious consideration that students of religion and psychology have agreed to give it. Without some rudiments of organization, it is difficult to imagine any religion surviving much beyond its founder's lifetime; but that same religion, contained within the ritual of a church, is faced with a more serious problem of survival if it cannot, every few generations, issue forth in some refreshing novelty, embarrassing no doubt to its official custodians but revealing to a profounder gaze something essential to its health. Mysticism interrupts religion for the purpose of asserting its continuity.

In studying Yoga it is tempting to raise the question of the relation of magic to religion. There have been times when the two were regarded as the same thing, as perhaps in Sumeria. There have been other times when the two were regarded as opposite things, as often in our own civilization. Leaving aside the trick-magic of our entertainers, it is possible to see in magic a necessary ally of religion. We tend to concentrate less upon the end of magic than upon the means. The end is to heighten our emotional life, to raise it to that level of concentration and impetus from which, and from which only, a leap into another dimension may be made. To deny the possibility of such another dimension in the name of rationalism or "free thought" is to take a very narrow view of the capacities of reason, and to fail to explain how thought, thus circumscribed, can be free.

Shankara and Vedanta

In outlining the principal Hindu systems we have introduced the minimum of philosophical terms. A technical history of Indian philosophy would need, in speaking of Yoga, to go into detail concerning the pacification of the *chitta* or mind stuff, the control of the *vrittis*, which produce false versions of reality, the detailed action of the *gunas*, and so forth. The mere parade of such terms cannot but bewilder the laymen, as well as exasperate, by their random introduction, the expert. All we can do is to emphasize, without elaborating, the complex theoretical foundation of this famous system. We ought likewise to cite the attempts of modern psychologists, above all C. G. Jung, to relate some of their own theories to those of Eastern philosophers: for it is with the same reality that philosophers of every age have to do. An argument raised by one philosopher may be resumed in earnest many centuries later, as happened with Parmenides and Bergson, with Shankara and Kant, and possibly with many others of whom no record has been preserved: we have repeatedly drawn attention to the fact that the earliest extant philosophical documents must presuppose many centuries of speculation. Nevertheless, jargon has always been the enemy of clear thinking. From time to time the Indian systems have been denounced for their abstraction, their abstruseness, and occasionally their impiety. The system (if such it can be called) of *Purva Mimansa* represented a protest against the impressive but covertly atheistic systems such as the *Sankhya*. The originators of such systems were careful to pay lip-service to the *Vedas*; but, having done so, they proceeded to indulge in speculations that have nothing to do with those inspired documents. Jaimini,[1] the founder of *Purva Mimansa*, was what we should today call a fundamentalist. He urges his countrymen to return to the word of God, to recognize the finitude of their intellects, and to practise charity instead of parotting abstractions. Apart from duly recording his protest, however, there is little about his work upon which we need linger.

With Shankara we have to do with a philosopher of very different calibre: in fact we have to do with one of the greatest of all philosophers, whose work ought to be better known in the Occident than it is. Shankara's thought not merely effected a revolution in the Orient—for it was one of the causes of the disappearance of Buddhism from India; it assumed a direction (as we have hinted) almost identical with that later pursued by the German philosopher Immanuel Kant. The resemblance is so close as to invite speculation as to whether Kant could possibly have been acquainted with the work of Shankara. Not a shred of evidence has been produced suggesting even indirect influence: indeed, the debt, if genuine, would have been too great not to receive acknowledgment upon

[1] 4th century B.C.

practically every page. We have to be content with the view, hardly less remarkable, that two major thinkers separated by a thousand years offered similar interpretations of reality. On reflection, what is strange is not so much that this should have happened once or twice in history, as that it should not have happened more often. If reality *is* of a certain nature, it is curious that men dedicated to its study should not have been more frequently disposed to agreement.

The system expounded by Shankara is traditionally known as Vedanta. Strictly speaking, Vedanta means the conclusion or completion of the *Vedas*. Now the conclusion of the *Vedas*, as we have seen, is the *Upanishads*. What the *Upanishads* teach is the identification of *Atman* with *Brahman*: this teaching is not so much analysed or explained as dogmatically asserted. When you are obliged to defend your dogmas, either against criticism or against other dogmas, you must provide them with a rational basis. The philosophy of Vedanta is that by which the *Upanishad* dogmas are supported by argument, demonstration, and proof. And just as St. Thomas Aquinas was there to sustain Christian dogma by rational argument, so Shankara was there to perform the same service for Hindu dogma.

Shankara, or Sankaracharya,[1] lived from A.D. 788–820. These dates are striking in two ways. First of all they show that the great system-maker of India lived for only thirty-two years. Secondly they reveal that Shankara lived a thousand years, and perhaps more, after the composition of the *Upanishads*. The shortness of Shankara's life derives its significance from the magnitude of his achievement. As to his separation in time from the sages whose ideas he systematized, this is hardly more remarkable than Aquinas's systematization in the 13th century of Christian thought originating in the 2nd or 3rd centuries. And just as Aquinas had the Christian Fathers and Augustine behind him, so Shankara was preceded by such men as Badarayana (2nd century B.C.), author of the *Brahma Sutra* (a composition of 550 aphorisms or apophthegms), Gaudapada (7th century A.D.), and finally Govinda, who transmitted the doctrine of *Brahman* to Shankara himself.

Still to dwell for a moment upon resemblances, Shankara reminds us of Aquinas not merely in his place in history and his attempt at synthesis, but in the holiness of his life. Born in Malabar, he was a member of the caste of Nambudri Brahmans, who combined the twin ideals of the saint and the *savant*. Shankara appears early to have felt the call of renunciation and asceticism. He became a hermit-saint or *samyosi* at an age when other young men, far from rejecting the world, are busy tasting its pleasures. Nor did Shankara engage in ascetic practices merely according to the routine laid

[1] "Acharya" means a spiritual teacher.

down for hermits: it is recorded that he achieved as a matter of common experience the condition of *Samadhi*. Consequently, his lifelong opposition to both the *Sankhya* system of Kapila and the equally atheist ideas of the Buddha was dictated by reasons as much emotional as intellectual. A philosopher who regularly achieves union with the divine, or at least who thinks he does, is not likely to be content with the verbal carping and logical aridities of so much theological discussion; he will organize his thought upon a majestic basis, and recommend it the more effectively by living it.

It is sometimes maintained that the best debaters are those who do not believe in what they advocate. Such a view depends for its plausibility upon the level at which the debate is conducted. Those who believe strongly, passionately, are admittedly not always in the best condition to defend their arguments. Aware of their inward certitude, they see no reason to engage in elaborate disputation. The capacity to believe has been described, with justice, as a kind of genius. Such genius, united to unusual intellectual vigour, produces the great philosophical leaders of the world. Most generalizations about human nature have a superficial ring because they are based upon inspection of those who are "above the mob but lower than the man of genius". To suggest that Augustine, Aquinas, or Shankara would have been superior dialecticians had they been less convinced of their ideas is at once to make nonsense of belief and to degrade human intelligence.

Summoned by the Pope from a life of solitude and devotion, Aquinas arrived in Paris for the purpose of defending orthodoxy. In spite of his obvious preference for a hermit life, Shankara was obliged, while still a youth, to undertake a similar mission. The centre of debate was the holy city of Benares. Acting as a kind of representative of south India, Shankara proved himself a redoubtable champion of Brahmanism. Very soon his services were required at other centres. He attacked and demolished heresy wherever it might be found. Nor was the demolition merely rhetorical and dogmatic; it was characterized by subtle argument and reasoned apologetic.

We should give a great deal to possess a *procès-verbal* of some of the encounters in which Shankara distinguished himself. The writings attributed to him are voluminous: like the great *Summae* of Aquinas, and like *The Critique of Pure Reason* of Kant, they are confessedly not easy reading. We must remember that they represent no more than a skeleton or—if it is preferred—a blueprint of Shankara's thought. It is unreasonable to expect that profound philosophical works should, to use the favourite criterion of interest, "read like a novel", which may imply that they will as soon be forgotten. The greatest essays in philosophical enquiry are merely notes or memoranda, the basis of an actual or imaginary exchange of views. Only civilizations organized differently from our own, such as the City States of ancient Greece, have provided leisure enough for philosophers to record their thought in the way best suited to it, namely in the form of dialogue.[1] And what was thus recorded was not strictly thought but thinking.

While at Benares, Shankara wrote his famous commentaries on both the *Upanishads* and the *Bhagavad-Gita*. Synthesizing all that Badarayana, Gaudapada, and Govinda had maintained, these learned and elaborate works did more than anything to re-establish in India the intellectual ascendancy of Brahmanism. Shankara's approach to the Scriptures was fully as orthodox as that of Aquinas: he is not attempting anything in the nature of "higher" criticism, which depends paradoxically upon an initial belittlement of the subject to be criticized. The task to which he devoted himself was that of finding a basis in reason for that which was given in revelation: an aim that appears impious only to those who fail to see in human reason a secondary channel of revelation.

The word secondary is important. Admittedly reason cannot take us all the way. It is an instrument which, though of great utility, may be used to further any cause whatever; it is not loaded in any particular direction. We need another and even higher faculty, a kind of intuition, whereby to discriminate between truth and error. This higher faculty is acquired through the cultivation of detachment, the withdrawal from the life of sense, and, if possible, a total absorption in *Brahman*. In short, the philosopher must be not simply a man given to reflection, still less a man endowed with keen wit and capacity for argument; he must be both pure in heart and a lover of wisdom. In the appointment of our own teachers of philosophy, such characteristics are not normally insisted upon.

Having made clear in what respect philosophy differs from other intellectual disciplines, Shankara proceeds to expound his system. The reader may conclude, from what has been said, that the argument is conducted upon a somewhat rarefied level. If we are to accept the view that none but the saint can be a true philosopher, and if philosophical knowledge is in effect the same as *moksha*—a kind of ignorance (or bliss) due to liberation from all other forms of ignorance—then philosophical enquiry is evidently beyond the reach of ordinary men. But no: Shankara is prepared, as we shall see, to begin at the beginning. He starts by asking the simplest, if most fundamental, questions. Having dwelt upon the majesty of

[1] Aristotle may be cited as an exception, but Aristotle wrote a number of dialogues, all of which have been lost.

knowledge at its supreme point, he turns aside to consider how knowledge, of whatever kind, is possible at all. Both his formulation of the question and the answer he gives to it put us immediately in mind of Kant.

According to Shankara, our knowledge of the external world is sense-bound: that is to say, our senses, in endeavouring to contact "reality", inevitably adapt that reality to their own uses. The world that we see, hear, and feel is a world that appears to be extended and in movement, a world of changing phenomena. This phenomenal world is not merely the world that our senses apprehend; it assumes this phenomenal form precisely because our senses apprehend it. Extension and temporality are, in the Kantian phrase, "forms of our sensibility". In brief, the world accessible to our senses is in great part the world that our senses have constructed. In the external world we perceive that which we have contributed.

The external world, then, is a world of *Maya*. Now we have met the term *Maya* already. To render it satisfactorily in Western philosophical terminology is extremely difficult. If we here translate it as "illusion", we shall be committing a serious error: for Shankara does not for one moment suggest that the world apprehensible by our senses is a world that is not, as it were, "there". A similar misunderstanding is frequently met in discussion of the theory of knowledge advanced, though in different terms, by Bishop Berkeley. *Maya* is perhaps better translated as "delusion" rather than "illusion". On this assumption a world of *Maya* is a world pretending to be that which it is not. It is a world of half-lights and half-truths, of inexactitude and imprecision, of promise without fulfilment. Is there anything particularly startling or unfamiliar about such a world? Not at all: it is the world, surely, with which we are familiar in everyday life.

To introduce a further comparison, the world of *Maya* is much the same as the shadowy, phenomenal world described by Plato. Although only the eternal Forms are real, Plato's world of appearance is still very much "there". The late R. G. Collingwood used to explain the distinction very aptly. If Plato's world of appearance is a "pack of lies", he pointed out, they are nevertheless lies that are "really told". *Maya* exists. We live in *Maya*. Ignorance, *Avidya*, sees no more in experience that this realm of *Maya*. Just as Plato asserted the existence of a world of Forms behind appearance, so Shankara maintained the existence behind and beyond *Maya* of a world of timeless Being.

How do we know that such a suprasensible realm exists? Indeed, what right have we to assume its existence? Certain philosophers, namely the so-called empiricists, declare that we have no right at all. All knowledge, they hold, is obtained through the senses. Now clearly the senses yield no knowledge of the realm of which Shankara speaks: how could they, seeing that such a realm is by definition above and beyond the sensuous plane? Nevertheless, as Kant argued, the world of phenomena logically implied another world, the noumenal world, the region of the Thing-in-itself. Appearance presupposes Reality. Such a world, therefore, necessarily exists. What remains to be determined is, first, what is its nature, and, secondly, how do we make contact with it?

Students of *The Critique of Pure Reason* will recall the ingenious answers given to these questions by Kant. The noumenal realm, he maintained, is a realm of Being rather than beings, because it is the nature of our senses to regard the world as a multiplicity: that is to say, the senses are so constituted as to perceive the world as a number of separate *things*. For practical purposes this mode of apprehension is both necessary and desirable. Not merely do our bodies form part of the sensuous or material world, but our perceptive faculty is composed of at least five separate "senses". A condition of "sensing" anything is that it shall be sensed as one thing among others, and simultaneously as a unity composed of "parts". It follows that the reality behind and inaccessible to the senses will be not *Many* but *One*: a Thing-in-itself.

So much for the nature of the realm of Being. Now for the means whereby such a realm may be contacted. Again, Kant's answer will form a useful prelude to that advanced by Shankara. Let us refrain for a moment from speaking of material things, and observe the nature of personalities or selves. When we consider mankind we regard it inevitably as composed of a great number of different individuals. I am aware of myself as a distinct personality, and I assume everyone else to regard himself in the same manner. Such an impression, says Kant, is the result of our belonging in part, at least, to the world of phenomena. But there is more to us than that. My real self, or, as Kant calls it, my moral self, belongs to a different order. In exercising my moral will, I as it were pierce the world of phenomena, and make direct contact with the noumenal world of the Thing-in-itself. Indeed, my real Self and the Thing-in-itself are, in some mysterious way, the same thing; to know the one is to know the other. This is the answer to the second problem. We make contact with the realm of Being only when, disregarding the accidents of "character" and "personality", we attain to genuine Selfhood. To act thus morally is to act freely, and freedom is the shedding of the bonds of the senses. We might add, what has often been denied by the practitioners of that science, that the study of "character" and "personality" is the proper domain of psychology, since "character" and "personality" belong to the phenomenal realm: whereas the moral self is the domain of philosophy proper.

Now let us compare the Kantian view with that of Shankara. According to the latter, the self in the sense of the ego belongs to the world of phenomena or *Maya*. We are under the impression, for instance, that our individuality, our passions, our opinions, are real things, capable of subsisting by themselves. Such an impression, however, is mistaken. The *Upanishads* teach that our real self is not the ego but the *Atman*, the reality lying behind appearances, the divine spark, the light that lighteth every man that cometh into the world. And knowledge of Reality, of eternal Being, is acquired, as we know, by realizing the identity of *Atman* with *Brahman*. In other words, we make contact with Reality by means of the true or moral self. Science, in the sense of the technique for analysis and measurement, is concerned solely with phenomena.

To hazard reasons why Shankara and Kant should have evolved a similar idealist theory of knowledge is, as we have said, tempting: but such a study hardly comes within the scope of the present work. Nor do we wish to enter into comparisons regarding the superiority in detail of the one philosophy over the other. The present account affords little idea of the ingenuity with which in both cases the argument is pursued. Nevertheless, to give the Western reader some notion of what is being discussed, we must emphasize that the subtleties of Kant, though difficult to underestimate, appear simple in comparison with those of Shankara. And although subtlety does not necessarily imply profundity, it must equally be admitted that Shankara is by far the more profound philosopher. Indeed, his profundity is to some extent the result of the extraordinary range of his thought, just as Kant's attainment just short of sublimity is the result of the voluntary limitation of his subject. The concepts which Kant expressly excluded from philosophical treatment were those of God, Freedom, and Immortality. In so doing he excluded almost everything that an Indian philosopher will think worthy of serious discussion.

Having given us an extremely ingenious theory of knowledge, Shankara naturally feels under the obligation to discuss the nature of God. In the case of so thorough a devotee of *Brahman*, it may appear surprising that he should have asserted the existence of two gods, *Ishvara* as well as *Brahman*. If, however, we examine why he did so, we shall see that he still remains a complete and absolute monotheist. The god *Ishvara* represents the god of what we are accustomed to call Natural Religion. As there is no such thing as a world without a god, the god of the world of phenomena is *Ishvara*. *Ishvara* is, in fact, the creator, the author of phenomena. And since the world of phenomena is a world of multiplicity, the supremacy of *Ishvara* is fully compatible with the existence of other, if lesser, deities. In short, the polytheism of the people to which Shankara was wise enough to defer is both the consequence and the correlative of the "deism" of scientists and intellectuals.

It follows that God as both person and creator is a feature of the realm of *Maya*. But *Ishvara* is also something more: He is the purveyor of rewards and punishments, and therefore the arbiter of *Karma*. Is, then, the whole process of *Karma*, the fundamental tenet of the Hindu faith, illusory? Again, we must remind ourselves, not illusory, but simply a process pertaining to a level of experience short of the highest. In a sense *Karma* must belong to *Maya*, because the successive rebirths of the soul take place inevitably in the natural world. To escape from *Karma* is the same as to escape from *Maya*. Such escape involves at once release from the authority of *Ishvara* and absorption in *Brahman*.

If rewards and punishments are features of the world of *Maya*, so are the good and bad actions which elicit them. Those who think to obtain absorption in *Brahman* merely by doing good works, by behaving decently or inoffensively, and by keeping the laws, are under a serious misapprehension. Admittedly good conduct is at all times to be encouraged, because, in so acting, the chain of rebirth may be shortened. The people must be taught "morals". But social conformity is not the same as holiness. To the sage it appears immediately evident that the individual self which performs good or evil actions, and to which the law of *Karma* applies, enjoys no real or ultimate separateness at all. And to achieve this realization is to be delivered for ever from the bondage of reincarnation. Even among sages, however, such a degree of holiness is rarely to be attained.

Life as we commonly know it, then, is lived on the plane of *Maya*. And if life, then death. And if pleasure, then suffering. These are phenomena, without true substance. One of the most remarkable passages of Kant is that in which, almost in the manner of an oriental thinker, he suddenly rises to a theme all too frequently obscured by the thickets of his concentrated argument:

"It is difficult to suppose that a creature whose life has its first beginning in circumstances so trivial and so entirely independent of our own choice, should have an existence that extends to all eternity. As regards the continuance here on earth of the species as a whole, this difficulty is negligible, since accident in the individual case is still subject to a general law, but as regards each individual it certainly seems highly questionable to expect so potent an effect from causes so insignificant. But to meet these objections we can propound a transcendental hypothesis, namely that all life is strictly speaking intelligible only, is not subject to changes of time, and neither begins in birth nor ends in death; that this life is an appearance only; that is, a sensible representation of the purely spiritual life, and the whole sensible world is a mere picture which in our present mode of knowledge hovers before us, and like a dream has in itself no objective reality; that if we could intuit ourselves and things as they are, we should see ourselves in a world of spiritual beings, our sole and true community, which has not begun through birth and will not cease through bodily death—both birth and death being mere appearances."

This passage is entirely in the spirit of the philosophy of Shankara. We may cite passage after passage from the latter in the same vein. The *Atma Bodha*, or "Knowledge of Spirit", sums up Vedanta as follows:

"The spirit is smothered, as it were, by ignorance, but as soon as ignorance is destroyed, spirit shines forth, like the sun when released from clouds. After the soul, afflicted by ignorance, has been purified by knowledge, knowledge disappears, as the seed or berry of the *Kataka* after it has purified water.

"Like an image in a dream, the world is troubled by love, hatred and other poisons. So long as the dream lasts, the image appears to be real; but on awakening it vanishes.

"The world appears real, as an oyster-shell appears to be silver; but only so long as the *Brahman* remains unknown, he who is above all and indivisible. That Being, true, intelligent, comprehends within itself every variety of being, penetrating and permeating all as a thread which strings together beads.

"In consequence of possessing diverse attributes, the supreme existence appears manifold, but when the attributes are annihilated, unity is restored. In consequence of these diverse attributes a variety of names and conditions are supposed proper to spirit, just as a variety of tastes and colours are attributed to water.

"The body, formed by the union of five elements produced by the effect of action, is considered to be the seat of pleasure and pain. . . . All that belongs to the body (must be considered) as the product of ignorance. It is visible; it is perishable as bubbles of air (on the surface of water); but that which has not these signs must be recognized as pure spirit, which says of itself, I am *Brahman*. Because I am distinct from body, I experience neither birth, old age, decrepitude, nor extinction, and detached from organs of sense, I have no longer any connection with their objects."

To the Western reader passages such as the above may appear impressive and even moving. But do not they represent a kind of poetry, a mystical lyricism? How, it may be asked, do we *know* all this? Why should not the *Nastiks* and the *Charvakas* have been right to deny *Brahman*, and indeed all forms of suprasensible experience? As to the first question, it is impossible to deny that much of Shankara—and not Shankara only—can be read as poetry: that is to say, it can be appreciated for its emotional rather than for its intellectual appeal. But then, in addition to being a philosopher, Shankara was a poet, and a very accomplished one. Aquinas, it will be remembered, was also a poet. A further point to bear in mind is the following. Classical Indian philosophy remains indifferent to the distinction between poetry and prose: the fact that we tend to stress this distinction may indicate too hard and fast a separation between our intellectual and emotional life. The *Vedas* are not merely inspired philosophy, but inspired poetry: the same is true of many of the *Upanishads*. Hindu thought reserves its prose for such documents as the *Ordinances of Manu*, with its laws and regulations mostly concerning morals and hygiene—the Hindu equivalent of the *Book of Leviticus*. As to the second question, Shankara, though as convinced as Aquinas of the truth of revelation, is prepared to argue at great length concerning the existence of *Brahman*. To Shankara it is not so much *Brahman*'s existence that presents difficulty; what is far more difficult to imagine is how, in the absence of *Brahman*, anything else can be said to enjoy existence. If *anything* exists, then God must. In other words, you have to account for existence itself; and the consciousness of imperfection, vanity, futility, illusion, implies the capacity to apprehend, though not necessarily to enjoy, perfection. The "problem of evil" may be difficult to solve on a spiritual view of the world. On a materialistic view it admits of no solution whatever; it has to be explained away in terms of "environment", upbringing, etc.

According to the limited information we possess, Shankara ended his days in a monastery on the foothills of the Himalayas. His incessant labours in the service of the orthodox Hindu faith had rendered him not an old man before his time—because he seems always to have been adult—but a man for whom half a lifetime had consumed the energies normally expended in half a dozen. Ten religious orders quickly sprang up, dedicated to the propagation of his ideas. And these ideas, studied and taught all over India from the 9th century to the present day, have ensured the survival of the Brahmanical tradition in a manner that, given the strength of the forces opposing it, is truly remarkable. But those who despise metaphysics, like those who ignore it, must be prepared for it to outlive them.

A history of Indian thought would need to dwell upon the various attempts to synthesize and introduce harmony into so many conflicting traditions. To undertake this task, which is outside our scope, would require in itself a volume much larger than the present. In conclusion, however, we ought not to leave the impression that Vedanta, the completion of the *Vedic* tradition, has failed to undergo development since the time of Shankara. Nor must we dismiss as without significance the long line of saints and sages who, down to our own time, have kept the pure Vedanta tradition alive: for we are too apt to regard the oriental tradition as having become bogged in a slough of fanaticism and corruption, paying "divine honours to the maniac and the fool".[1] From time to time powerful rulers such as Akbar (1556–1605) have attempted to impose a synthetic state religion on the people. Other reformers, such as Kebir (1440–1518), founder of the very interesting religion of the Sikhs, have attacked and thrown back the tendency towards polytheism which is never likely to be wholly eradicated. In the last century several men of powerful personality, such as Ram Mohan Ray, have felt the need to unite Vedanta with what they considered best in both Christianity and Islam. Perhaps the most attractive of these sages was Sri Ramakrishna (1836–86), who, having made a close study of both Christianity and Islam, finally returned to Hinduism, and whose disciples, Brahmananda and Vivekananda, have exerted almost as much influence abroad as in India herself. In these men we see the Vedanta faith at its noblest pitch: for they combined great intellectual force with personal humility. And we may perhaps see in Ramakrishna's lifelong devotion to Kali, the Mother goddess of the universe, a link with that form of worship which may have antedated the Aryan invasion of India, and which represents, however vaguely, a natural acceptance by man of life in all its aspects, the pain and destruction (for Kali, besides being Creator, was also Destroyer) as well as the rapture and fruition.[2]

There are only two ways in which man's part in the universe may be regarded: either he is a mischievous and predatory animal who must live by exploiting the natural world, or he is a creature to whom the universe, in spite of its immensity, is in some sense intended to be his home. Whatever he undertakes, he is implicitly adopting one or other of these attitudes. In the Western World it has usually been left to the poets and mystics to reveal the true path, while the philosophers have too often confined their attention to debating

[1] Disraeli: *Contarini Fleming*, Chapter I.

[2] Kali was the wife of Shiva, the Destroyer, who, according to Sir John Marshall, was worshipped in Mohenjo-daro. Shivaism may therefore be "the most ancient living faith in the world". Shiva is thus the Osiris of Hinduism, opposed to Vishnu, the Preserver.

whether or not there are such things as chairs or tables. Only rarely do we find a thinker to whom it is obvious that, as a prelude to the "divine connection", there must first be a "natural connection"—a truth which is beginning to be appreciated in the sphere of agriculture, where failure to realize that nature is something *alive* has brought us to the brink of disaster, and which we dimly perceive, though more often misconceive, in relation to such a process as sexual love. The words of Marcus Aurelius, so often dismissed as a vague pantheism, are consistent with this view: "Everything harmonizes with me that is harmonious with thee, O Universe. Nothing for me is too early or too late, which is in due time for thee. Everything is fruit to me which thy seasons bring, O Nature: from thee are all things, in thee are all things, to thee all things return."

CHAPTER VII

THE CHINESE SAGES

A peasant civilization

"MEN always have the greatest respect," said Thucydides, "for that which is farthest off." He might have added—because it is still more true—"and fear", which is an element in respect. For many centuries the European attitude to China illustrated that maxim, as well as its corollary. Save for the visit of an occasional explorer and several missionaries (the earliest being the Nestorian Christians), European contact with China is of comparatively recent origin. Already in the 17th century, however, the intellectual world of Europe was evincing great interest in Chinese culture. How little it understood that culture may be surmised from the fact that we, with our much closer contact, still understand very little of it. To speak of contact between one country and another, even countries as near as England and France, is to refer perhaps to continuous contact only at the most superficial level—say the diplomatic level—supplemented by miscellaneous "contacts" by individuals, business firms, or, at times of emergency, armed forces: which latter is by hypothesis the least typical of all. The first translations of Chinese classical literature, even more perhaps than those of India, exerted a profound influence upon the European mind, particularly the French mind of the 18th century. In his brilliant but forgotten study *The Illusions of Progress*, Georges Sorel shows how the French Physiocrats regarded ancient China as a kind of idyllic commonwealth, governed by a Natural Law of right and justice, and providing the model from which "decadent Europe" might learn salutary lessons. This impression, while not without an element of truth, was the result of generalization from a few instances. The "wisdom" of Confucius, for instance, is extremely refreshing and stimulating to the European mind. When it first became accessible it appeared to open up a new world of balance, maturity, and common-sense. It was the kind of message for which Europeans, weary of fanaticism and the wars resulting therefrom, had been waiting. That it should appeal to the French in particular was natural: a balanced, humanist culture was and still is the French ideal of life.

The fact remains that if Confucius had been "typical" of the Chinese culture of his day, his career would have been very different from what we know it to have been. The apostle of balance and the middle way led a life of much greater struggle than the Buddha, whose ideals were far more difficult to attain. Inviting men to renounce the world, the Buddha moved from place to place at leisure and amid adulation; for men respond more readily to the call of the impossible than of the possible. Save for brief intervals of power and influence, Confucius not merely experienced the bitterness of long exile but died, as we shall see, a disappointed man. In due course he was worshipped. This alone was proof enough of his distinctness from ordinary men, for the day of the apotheosis of the Common Man was far distant. Of the Master one of his disciples said: "He is the sun, the moon, which there is no way of climbing over, and though a man desire to cut himself off from them, what harm does he do to the sun and moon? . . . The impossibility of equalling our Master is like the impossibility of scaling a ladder and ascending to the skies." The wisdom of China, like that of any other country, represents the best that country could do in the person of a few sages. Nor would these sages have taught as they did if the lives of their fellow-citizens had not fallen far short of virtue.

Knowledge, even more than love, is reputed to cast out fear: a generalization which is not perhaps so true in fact as it is supposed to be in theory. Certainly the distrust of "orientals" is less prevalent than it was, perhaps as a result of closer contact. It is difficult, on the other hand, to say whether the traditional oriental "contempt" for westerners, as being materialistic upstarts, has diminished, or has had any reason to do so. We must make due allowance for the fact that for centuries and indeed millennia the oriental and the occidental world grew up in complete isolation. The mind is the last thing about a person that one comes to know. The "mind" of another culture, to use a vague term for an exceedingly vague relationship, cannot be known at all until it has become so penetrated by outside influences that it has changed its character. Much insight can be obtained from the study of past literature, so long as such researches are pursued by men of imagination and sympathy (one of the misfortunes of civilized existence is that research is left to scholars, who, because of the time needed to learn the technique of their job, tend often to lose contact with normal life); and among such literature, works of philosophy or wisdom are of particular value as being the quintessence of that which many have vaguely felt but lacked ability to express.

Until the 19th century the Far East consisted of a gigantic peasant civilization. A peasantry is by nature conservative. You cannot change it; you can only break it up. The peasantry of China and Japan was broken up, or partially broken up, from outside. Europe discovered China and Japan and not *vice versa*; and having discovered these countries, Europe began to "civilize" them, largely by force. The second dissolvent of a peasantry is a sudden rise in the standard of living: for what holds a peasantry together, and in particular what holds it down, is not government or police or excessive taxation, but natural adversity. The "natural wisdom" attributed to so many peasants is due, as Tolstoy realized when he set out to enquire into the docility of the peasant mentality, to a realization that his situation, never much above subsistence level, is grounded in the nature of things. And until recently, until about a century ago, the nature of things was that most people in the world were obliged to endure a life of hard work with little return, punctuated by private misfortunes for which small provision could usually be made, and often reduced to a level of untold misery as a result of pestilence or war.

Apart from the physical circumstances of his existence, however, it would be a mistake to assume that the life of a Chinese peasant, even in the most arid districts, was necessarily brutish. Brutish is a relative term. The life of Squire Western in *Tom Jones* was probably a great deal more brutish than that of many of the servants on his estate. If brutish signifies a mixture of brutality and irresponsibility, then the life of the average Chinese peasant was certainly less brutish than that of many an overlord and many an emperor. A tradition of family solidarity and of filial piety had existed from (the *cliché* is apt) time immemorial. The Western World has known nothing like it. The family formed a miniature state of which the father was the ruler. Likewise the family formed an economic unit, every member contributing to the common welfare and having his particular function to fulfil—not least the old, for whom modern European civilization has found decreasing use. Finally, the family formed its own church, because reverence for ancestors was a cult stronger than devotion to any supernatural being. If we think of religion in the sense given to it in India, then China appears to have no religion at all: but if we define the religious instinct as that which prevails over such powerful instincts as that of sex and survival, then the Chinese can certainly be counted as profoundly religious. The bodies of ancestors, for instance, were buried in the plot of land belonging to the family. This plot was always small, but the ancestors were allotted the richest part of it as a matter of course.

The idea of "The Way": Lao-Tze

Sages such as Lao-Tze and Confucius are often regarded as having taught the people a new way of life. That is not how they conceived of their own mission. Their task—the task of the "prophet", as we have come to understand it throughout this book —was to lead men back to the ancient wisdom. Confucius in

W. F. Mansell

LAO-TZE AND HIS DISCIPLES

Chinese painting (16th century)

particular did not claim any originality for his ideas. He merely regretted that, owing to neglect and ignorance, many of the old rituals had fallen into desuetude, with the consequent loss of the truths they had symbolized. He regarded himself as essentially a "transmitter". Like Lao-Tze, the older of the two, he set out to show men the road to virtue and contentment. This road was very properly called the Way, the *Tao*. As to how this Way might be found, however, Lao-Tze and Confucius differed markedly one from the other.

To translate *Tao* as "Way" is reasonable so long as we do not identify it with a technique, a recipe for happiness, which is only a small part of its meaning. It means also the principle of the universe, that which maintains it and gives it motion and order. Just as the stars have fixed courses, so there is a course for man, a means whereby he may link his being with reality: a reality from which he has somehow become alienated. As *Tao* is the origin of all meaning in the universe, it is also responsible for all created things. But things have to be engendered, and creation is in fact brought about by two principles, called *yin* and *yang*. *Yin* literally means "shadow". It is represented pictographically by the north side of a mountain and the south side of a river, since in daytime the south of the river is shrouded in darkness. *Yang*, on the other hand, means "light", and is represented in an opposite fashion. *Yang* is active, *yin* passive, the one male and the other female. But *yin* and *yang* do not form a dualism which splits the world in two. These principles characterize only the phenomenal world. At the core of reality is *Tao*, unity.

The first elaboration of these ideas of *yin* and *yang* was made, so far as we know, in a book of which the title is as obscure as its contents. It was called the *I-Ching*, or *Book of Changes*. Those who declare the Chinese mind to be incapable of metaphysical speculation omit to account for the immense prestige enjoyed by this book. Even Confucius, who otherwise took little interest in metaphysics, edited it and added his own notes. In due course this manual, with its list of sixty-four *hsiangs* or "ideas" which in combination make up reality, became a source of trivial magic and divination. This was a further sign of its traditionally sacred character, because only books believed to contain genuine spiritual content are likely to be put to such use or abuse.[1] We have used the word "trivial" deliberately: for if the original purpose of the *I-Ching* was astrological, as seems certain, this does not detract from its basic profundity. A great modern psychologist, C. G. Jung, has declared the *I-Ching* to embody the essence of Chinese culture. For what the modern rationalist dismisses—without understanding it—as astro-

[1] Cf. the *Sortes Virgilianae* of the Middle Ages.

logical, and what modern science regards as sheer superstition, Jung sees as a form of knowledge older by thousands of years than our cause-and-effect technique which, with its dwarfing effect, we call science. To Jung, the *I-Ching* forms a treatise on what may be termed, in the words of modern psychology, "psychic parallelisms", united by the principle of "synchronism", or relative simultaneity: for the fundamental truth of astrology, or "the summation of all the psychological knowledge of antiquity", is not so much that man's destiny is controlled by the stars as that "whatever is born or done this moment of time has the qualities of this moment of time".[1] We do not know with any exactitude how old a book the *I-Ching* may be; but we know that it was handed down from generation to generation as embodying precious wisdom. Such fate does not befall a mere compendium of abracadabra.

The first philosopher to be associated with the elaboration of the doctrine of *Tao* was Lao-Tze. He is the reputed author of a book called the *Tao-Te-Ching*, which means "The Book of the Way and of Virtue". Lao-Tze is an obscure figure. Indeed, there is some doubt as to whether he existed at all. His very name may suggest a legendary personage, for it means simply "The Old Master": but apparently he had another name, Li, which means a plum. On the other hand Confucius is said to have met him, and he is mentioned by several other philosophers. When historians dismiss a man as being legendary without producing any other evidence about him, all they usually mean is that they have not yet discovered another set of legends. At any rate, Lao-Tze is supposed to have been born in 604 B.C. in Honan province in Central China. Although brought up in a poor home, he rose to become curator of the Royal Library at Chou and lived to an advanced age. His reputation for wisdom was great, but he evidently failed to exert any marked influence outside a small circle. Towards the end of his life, believing that his native state was doomed to anarchy, he made up his mind to leave it. At the frontier, the customs official, recognizing the venerable sage, gave him permission to depart with all his goods on condition that he left one thing behind for the benefit of his country: namely his wisdom. Lao-Tze, to whom it had never hitherto occurred to write down his thoughts, consented. Setting to work at once, he condensed all his ideas into five thousand words, which must be a record in the annals of philosophy. Thus the *Tao-Te-Ching* came to be written. What happened to Lao-Tze after that not even legend says anything except to record the date of his death, which is put at 517 B.C.

[1] *The Secret of the Golden Flower:* translated and explained by Richard Wilhelm, with a European commentary by C. G. Jung (Kegan Paul, 1945).

The philosophy of the *Tao-Te-Ching* is perhaps one of the most revolutionary that has ever been formulated. Interpreted literally, or as literally as we are able to understand it, it represents an attack upon everything that has gone to make up what is called civilization. Lao-Tze tells us to "let things alone". He tells governments in particular to let things alone: in short he sees nothing but evil in the idea of government. Unlike almost all other philosophers, he does not extol knowledge, nor does he identify it, as Socrates did a little later, with virtue. On the contrary he extols ignorance, which he identifies quite categorically with bliss. Again, the true sage refuses to argue. By following the *Tao*, he sets an example of simplicity and contentment which, being naturally infectious, produces a tranquillizing effect upon his fellows. "The sage," says Lao-Tze, "carries on his business without action, and gives his teaching without words." All the normal recipes for bringing into being a just society are dismissed by this philosopher as futile, even dangerous. We must refrain, because it is most dangerous of all, from inculcating righteousness itself, since all attempts to introduce goodness through legislation will produce the opposite of that which is intended. "Do away with learning, and grief will not be known. Do away with sages and eject wisdom, and the people will be benefitted a hundred times. Do away with benevolence and eject righteousness and the people will return to filial duty and parental love. Do away with artifice and eject gains, and there will be no robbers and thieves. . . . Appear in plainness and hold to simplicity." That is the substance of his message.

Just as Lao-Tze tells his fellow-men to "let things alone", so he tells them to stay where they are. "Without going out of the door, one can know the whole world. Without peeping out of the window, one can see the *Tao* of heaven. The further one travels, the less one knows. Therefore the sages know everything without travelling. He names everything without seeing it. He accomplishes everything without doing it." The ideal society, therefore, is "a small state with few people". These few must be content with what they have. And they will be content with what they have if they do not seek to enlarge their horizon. "Though the neighbouring states are within sight, and their cocks' crowing and dogs' barking within hearing, the people (of that small state) will not go near them all their lives." No doubt this was strange doctrine to issue from one who, while committing it to paper (or split bamboo, as in fact was the procedure at the time), was in the very act of leaving his own country; but his point of view is interesting as being a solution which human beings, never having tried, can hardly condemn out of hand. Perhaps Lao-Tze's ideas on the art of government can best be summed up in a phrase typical in both expression and thought of all Chinese wisdom, "Govern a state as you would cook a small fish: do it gently."

Such teaching, expressed with remarkable compression and sharpness, has found an echo in every age, almost in every generation. There is no evidence that Jean-Jacques Rousseau knew the works of Lao-Tze; but his early ideas on society and government are very similar, with nature taking the place of *Tao*. The problem raised by such an ideal vision of existence is, needless to say, a practical one: what happens to the little state when, as must occur sooner or later, it meets with outside attack or interference? Lao-Tze was sage enough to have anticipated this difficulty. He also anticipated, alone of the thinkers of antiquity, the words of Christ. "Recompense injury with kindness. To those who are good I am good, and to those who are not good I am also good; thus all get to be good. To those who are sincere I am sincere, and to those who are not sincere I am also sincere; and thus all get to be sincere. . . . The softest thing in the world dashes against and overcomes the hardest. . . . There is nothing in the world softer or weaker than water, and yet for attacking things that are firm and strong there is nothing that can take precedence of it." And he adds, with justice: "This all the world knows but does not practice. . . . These are the words of truth, though they seem paradoxical."

Why does Lao-Tze place such emphasis upon passivity, even going so far as to enunciate the further paradox, stated in slightly different terms by Krishna, that we should "act inaction"?[1] It is not that he values paradox for its own sake, as we suspect certain of the Indian sages to have done. His doctrine of passivity follows logically from his conception of the nature of *Tao*. *Tao*, as we have seen, is a conception very similar to the Egyptian *Maat* and the Greek *Logos*. It animates, it pervades reality: it also generates and becomes incarnate. Indeed, Chinese translations of the opening of the Fourth Gospel run, "In the beginning was the *Tao*, and the *Tao* was with God and the *Tao* was God." And just as at some point the "Word is made flesh", so the "light that lighteth every man" comes to recognize its kinship with the divine power. To translate this process in terms of Indian thought, *Atman* becomes *Brahman*. The Taoist philosopher conceives of a similar identification. The world is in a condition of misery, or rather man is not at home in his world, because he has failed to identify his *Tao* with that of the universe. The two are at loggerheads. Let him eschew learning, convention, even civilization, and harmony will be restored. The *Tao* in his innermost self will turn out to be the *Tao* that "existed before heaven

[1] The term for this celebrated concept of "inaction" is *Wu Wei*.

and earth, motionless and fathomless, standing alone and never changing, the Mother of the Universe".

Kung-fu-tze: birth and upbringing

No two philosophers were more unlike each other in personality than Lao-Tze and Confucius. Given this difference in outlook, their influence was bound to be unequal. Taoism is still a living faith: the latest estimate is that forty-three million Taoists still live in China. This is a large number; but it is probably as little indicative of the intensity of the faith as to say that a similar number of people in France is Catholic. Moreover, it must be borne in mind, when speaking of China, that adherence to one form of belief does not exclude sympathy with another or several others. An educated Chinese, just because he is educated, is willing to accord respect to any congenial faith; what he holds in abhorrence is fanaticism and bigotry. Possibly the real religion of China, at its most intellectual level, is that of toleration. At the same time we must not imagine that willingness and ability to tolerate other beliefs is necessarily instinctive with the Chinese people (who are in any case too numerous to be summed up by a generalization of this kind): such an attitude is the product of long and deep-rooted tradition. And the founder of this tradition—one of the great traditions of humanity—is Confucius.

The name Confucius is the best that Europe, with its Latin culture, could make of the words *Kung-fu-tze*, which means literally "Kung, the Master". His real name was Kung-Chiu. Like the other great spiritual leaders of mankind, Confucius was credited with a miraculous birth, accompanied by celestial wonders. He was the illegitimate son of a father already well advanced in years. Born in 551 B.C. in the kingdom of Lu, now Shantung, he was described, presumably metaphorically, as having the lips of an ox and a mouth like the sea. More plausibly, he had an immense forehead: hence the name Chiu. As with Buddha, a jet of water sprang up to wash the new-born baby, who was delivered in a cave to which his mother had been directed by an annunciatory spirit. The boy's upbringing was hard. After his father's death he was obliged to support his mother by doing odd jobs after school hours. No doubt he was always old for his years: we can imagine the boyhood of almost all the great philosophers save Confucius—that immense forehead must have lent him premature adulthood. Even so, he was by no means a solitary or a book-worm. Sport he loved, particularly archery and fishing; and he was from earliest youth a passionate devotee of music, though his tastes—here as elsewhere—were conservative. He married at the age of nineteen. We do not know much about his married life. The lady, we gather, came from Sung, a neighbouring state. Some records suggest that the couple were divorced after four years; others that the parting came at the time of Confucius' exile, which was twenty years later. The sketchiness of the information at our disposal suggests that the marriage bond, having been entered into for conventional reasons, was preserved for as long as convention dictated. A son was born of the marriage, Kung Li, or, as he is called in *The Analects*, Po Yü. We know that Po Yü became a disciple of his father, but, strange to say, the two do not seem to have been united by any stronger sympathy. The disciple whom Confucius loved—the St. John or the Ananda of Confucianism—was Yen Hui, whose life was a model of what the true sage should be.

Confucius entered upon his mission as a teacher or sage earlier in life than most spiritual leaders of mankind. By the age of twenty-two he was already well known both for his wisdom and for his upright life. Moreover, he had a marked gift of eloquence. Encouraged by a few enthusiastic associates, he decided to set up a school. What this amounted to was that his house was thrown open to anyone seeking instruction: fees were exacted according to the pupil's capacity to pay. Not that Confucius set out to purvey a kind of abstract wisdom. He undertook to teach definite "subjects", above all history, poetry, and the principles of what he called decorum. Believing that society was suffering from neglect of the traditional wisdom, Confucius took great pains to instil into his disciples the meaning of the ancient rites and ceremonial Odes, to say nothing of such repositories of truth as the *Book of Changes*. Above all, he had a great belief in the efficacy of music as giving a last polish to a man's character; but he would have nothing to do with modern music—"the songs of Cheng"—which produced the opposite effect. Confucius's attitude to music was somewhat similar to that of Schopenhauer: he believed that it not merely typified the harmony of the universe but symbolized the concord which, given enlightened rulers, might prevail in the state. How he would have been perplexed by our modern educational curricula, where music is so often treated as an "extra" or at best an added accomplishment. The neglect of the "philosophy" of music may be the clearest sign of man's feeling of isolation in the universe.

Growing fame

As the number of his pupils grew, Confucius began to be a power in the land, because many of these young men soon obtained responsible positions. In 518 B.C. the minister of Lu expressed the wish on his deathbed that his son should be entered at Confucius's school. From that moment Confucius became the equal, as well as the instructor, of princes. Hitherto he had been content to remain at his little academy, a conscientious pedagogue; now he felt the desire, and likewise received official encouragement, to travel. His first important excursion was to the capital of the province, Lo-yang, now in Honan. What he saw in this busy place fascinated him, especially the ancient court rituals and the ceremonies in the magnificent temples.

At Lo-yang, too, was another source of attraction for Confucius. Lao-Tze was there, then a man of eighty-seven. Less than half his age, Confucius, though duly respectful, seems have made less impression upon Lao-Tze than upon most other people. In reply to some recondite questions about past history and ancient men of wisdom, the old man expressed himself both forcibly and frankly. "Those about whom you enquire," he said, "have mouldered with their bones into dust. When the hour of the great man has struck he rises to leadership; but before his time has come he is hampered in all that he attempts. I have heard that the successful merchant carefully conceals his wealth, and acts as though he had nothing—that the great man, though abounding in achievements, is simple in his manners and appearance. Get rid of your pride and your many ambitions, your affectation and your extravagant aims. Your character gains nothing from all these. This is my advice to you."

It appears that Confucius took these words seriously to heart, for when he returned to his school he conveyed his impression of the old exile in the following vivid phrases: "I know how birds can fly, fishes swim, and animals run. But the runner can be snared, the swimmer hooked, and the flier shot by the arrow. But there is the dragon—I cannot tell how he mounts on the wind through the clouds, and rises to heaven. Today I have seen Lao-Tze, and can compare him only to the dragon." Such was the tribute of the philosopher of humanism to the apostle of mystic naturalism: a tribute best described as that of respectful incomprehension.

If Confucius showed no personal disposition to mystical thought, he was aware of the fascination that such thought exerted over the mass of mankind. It was not that he denied the existence of a transcendental world of spirit; it was rather that he gave priority to considerations of human government and welfare. As in his teaching, so in his private speculations, he adopted the method of rational and logical enquiry. The cultivation of trance-states according to Yoga principles was something to which, after some early experiments, he refused ever after to apply himself. "I have spent the whole day without food and the whole night without sleep in order to meditate. It was of no use. It is better to learn." Again and again, when questioned about matters beyond immediate human experience, Confucius answered in terms more downright than the Buddha himself, though from very different motives. When his disciple Tzu-Lu asked him to discourse on man's duty to the spirits of the departed, he replied, "While still unable to do your duty to the living, how can you do your duty to the dead?" And on another occasion, when asked about the nature of death itself, he answered, perhaps begging the question slightly, "Not understanding life, how can you presume to understand death?" Frequently his disciples came under the criticisms and even the jeers of ascetic practitioners of the simple and reclusive life: for hitherto the true sage had been regarded as one who, the better to concentrate his thoughts, renounced all contact with the world. To such gibes Confucius always had a telling reply: "I cannot herd with birds and beasts, and if I may not associate with mankind, with whom am I to associate? If right rule prevailed in the world, I should not be taking part in reforming it."

In 517 B.C. a crisis occurred in the province of Lu. The duke, who had been oppressed by some powerful chieftains, endeavoured to reassert his authority. The *coup* failed. Confucius, thereby compromised, followed his master into exile. As they were making their way to the neighbouring province of T'si, the sage and his disciples came across an old woman weeping at a graveside. They asked her what had happened. She replied that at that same spot a triple tragedy had occurred: her father-in-law, her husband, and finally her son had all been killed by tigers. Having tried to console her, Confucius enquired why her family had nevertheless decided to settle in such a dangerous part of the country. "There is no oppressive government here," she answered. Turning to his pupils, Confucius remarked: "Take note of this. Oppressive government is fiercer than a tiger."

On arrival at T'si, the duke at once received Confucius in audience. The sage's observations on the art of government pleased him, and he considered appointing Confucius to high office. Opposition came from the other ministers. They ridiculed the little band of scholars as impractical pedants. As for Confucius himself, they regarded him as nothing but an eccentric busybody, obsessed with the niceties of etiquette. "It would take generations," they said, "to exhaust all that he knows about the ceremonies of going up and going down." Confucius stayed on for several years, but without obtaining even minor government employment. Finally, on learning that the situation in Lu was somewhat improved, he returned home.

Picture Post Library

CONFUCIUS

From an old print

The sage in office: exile

His patience was now rewarded. The new duke, Ting by name, decided to try the experiment of entrusting affairs of state to someone without overt political ambition. The man who had observed that "I am not concerned that I have no place: I am concerned how I may fit myself for one," was the obvious choice. In 501, Confucius became chief magistrate or governor of the city of Chung-tu. He forthwith set to work. In a very short time, we are told, an amazing social transformation occurred. The standard of morality reached a height never before attained; the Golden Age seemed to have returned. Public honesty was such that valuable objects dropped in the street were either left or returned to their owners: the people became astonished at their own virtue. Finding the burden of government considerably lightened, the duke promoted Confucius to the office of Minister of Public Works. The new minister, determined to be practical, introduced measures for surveying the land and improving agriculture. As a result, prosperity rapidly followed upon exemplary conduct. The duke, no less delighted than his subjects, saddled Confucius with further responsibilities. Having been advanced to the office of Minister of Justice and finally to that of Prime Minister, Confucius soon wielded an authority second in name, and far superior in practice, to that of Ting himself. At this point the Chinese records grow lyrical. "Dishonesty and dissoluteness," we read, "were ashamed and hid their heads. Loyalty and good faith became the characteristics of the men, and chastity and docility those of the women. Strangers came in crowds from other states. Confucius became the idol of the people." An exaggeration, no doubt: but we have the commemorative pillars of Ashoka to prove that, given a ruler of powerful personality, such changes are not impossible. What is impossible, given human nature, is that they should endure.

Nor did they—though Confucius can hardly be held to blame. The disruptive element came not from within but from outside. The rulers of states bordering upon Lu began to grow seriously alarmed. Confucius's achievement, which was even celebrated in poetry, might cause oppressed peoples elsewhere to insist upon the display of similar conduct on the part of their rulers. These despots were convinced neither of the benefits of public righteousness nor of the sincerity of its exponents in Lu. Feeling it incumbent upon him to do something drastic before the contagion of honesty spread, the Minister of T'si devised a scheme for setting Confucius and his master one against the other. One day the Duke of Lu received a sumptuous present. It consisted of eighty beautiful singing girls or courtezans, and one hundred and twenty horses. On learning the nature of this gift, Confucius ordered that the entire party should be lodged outside the capital. Unfortunately, one of the duke's officials, who slipped out to inspect them, returned with a glowing account of what he had seen. In spite of Confucius's protestations, the duke yielded to temptation, and the girls were taken into the royal harem. Festivities of a kind long abandoned ensued. Public business, including the ritual sacrifices, was interrupted. Ignored and humiliated, Confucius found he could do nothing. He chose the most dignified way of showing his disgust, which was to embark once more upon the life of an exile. His comment on this fiasco was apt. "I have never met," he said, "one who loves virtue as he loves beauty."

His wanderings lasted for no less than thirteen years. First of all he decided to pay a visit to the state of Wei, where he felt he could at least count upon the hospitality of his brother-in-law. The duke, Ling by name, welcomed him at first with great respect. Confucius was not merely fêted as Plato was fêted by the younger Dionysius of Syracuse, but he was offered a substantial pension in kind. In spite of this, he was to suffer the same disillusionment as Plato himself. On acquaintance, Ling proved to be more of a blackguard than Ting. Again Confucius decided to leave, but he met with such perils on the road that he was obliged to return, though with reluctance, to Wei. Evidently the court were in no mood to welcome him back, for the wife of the duke, Wan-Tzu, a lady of wanton character, had always strongly objected to him. There was once a statue in Paris of King Louis XV on horseback, surrounded by figures of the four Virtues. The popular saying was, "*Les Vertus sont à pied, le Vice est à cheval.*" When Confucius drove in his carriage behind Wan-Tzu, the public comment was similar: "Lust in front, virtue behind." As soon as he could manage it, Confucius took his leave once more.

In company with the faithful disciple Tze-Kung, the now aging philosopher experienced the most severe of all his trials. Having incurred ridicule both from men of the world and from those who posed as being other-worldly, he found himself tempted to regard all men as potential enemies. From the highest office he had sunk to the condition of an outlaw, the butt of ridicule, the target of abuse, and on at least one occasion the object of violence; for the brother of one of his disciples nearly succeeded in killing the little party outright by pulling down a tree in their path. Although no one was hurt, the act was sufficient to scatter the alarmed disciples; for some time Confucius wandered about alone. When Tze-Kung enquired of some peasants whether they had seen the Master, the reply was that an old man "disconsolate as a stray dog" had been observed in the neighbourhood. On being later informed of this description, Confucius laughed heartily. "Well put," he said. All his life Confucius seems to have retained a wry sense of humour.

With so many disappointments and rebuffs it is a wonder that Confucius did not despair of ever making himself permanently useful to his fellows. But he never lost hope. "If there were any princes who would employ me," he once declared, "in the course of twelve months I should have done something considerable. In three years the government would be perfected." He was always willing to put his services at the disposal of anyone who required them, but he refused to accept offers that might involve a compromise with his principles. Thus although Duke Ling of Wei several times invited him to return, Confucius accepted no place of distinction at his court: absolute control or exile were the two poles between which his public career continued to move. We cannot blame his disciples for occasionally losing confidence in their Master, especially under the taunts or chidings of the hermits and ascetics whom they so frequently met in the course of their peregrinations. "Rather than follow one who withdraws from this state and that state," said one aged hermit to Tzu-Lu, "had you not better follow those who withdraw from the world altogether?" It seemed plausible advice, but to Confucius despair of mankind was still the greatest of sins. Nor did he feel that his wandering life was altogether useless. The world now knew him as a sage of remarkable character and determination, whom governments could exile but not silence, and whose rejection by princes was a signal reproach to the waywardness of mankind. Unknown to the countrymen of Confucius, a figure of comparable wisdom was receiving even worse treatment in the City-State of Athens. Except for a brief period, Socrates never enjoyed public office; but at his trial he claimed the right, as a man of wisdom and public spirit, to be supported at the public expense. They gave him a month in gaol as an example, and then, for economy's sake, poisoned him.

Recognition and retirement

In spite of its reputation for savagery, the Orient has tended to be less violent with its saints and sages than the Occident, which possesses a somewhat black record in that respect. The most power-crazed of oriental despots have stayed their hand when confronted with the *Nabi*. Croesus spared few of his rivals, but he spared Solon, and Nebuchadnezzar spared Jeremiah; whereas Socrates was done to death by the people to whom the Western World owes its highest ideals of culture, and Christ was crucified by the people to whom we owe our highest conceptions of law. Several local tyrants of China regarded Confucius as a menace to their authority or an obstacle to their enjoyment of the spoils of oppression; but no ruler dared to put him under arrest and cut off his head, though jealous ministers often contrived to expose him to ridicule. In the end, however, Confucius received a measure of recognition the more touching in that it was extended from his home-state, that of Lu. Duke Ting had long been dead of dancing-girls and other luxuries, and the throne was occupied by Duke Gae. The latter sent the sixty-nine-year-old philosopher some presents and an invitation to return home. Confucius was overjoyed. In accepting the invitation, however, he made it clear that the days of his power were over. He would advise, he would study, he would rest. Those who wished to listen to him could do so. He was a tired but also a resigned man.

He enjoyed five years of honourable and studious life at Lu before he died. The ministers consulted him but did not seek to disturb his repose. He was now able to undertake a work that he had so long deferred as almost to have lost hope of accomplishing, namely the editing of the famous "Classics". He also devoted his time to writing a history of his people, to reclassifying the traditional Odes, and to rearranging the ceremonial music.

One morning the old man, now seventy-three, was observed to rise from his couch with more than usual difficulty, and to shuffle out of doors singing a sad song. The words were those of an Ode for which he had always shown particular affection, but on this occasion the disciples detected an ominous meaning in them:

"The great mountain must crumble,
The strong beam must break,
And the wise man wither away like a plant."

He then gave some directions as to how his body should be buried, being careful to specify the rites that were to accompany his funeral. That his mind should have dwelt upon the niceties of ceremonial was characteristic; but his last words to his disciples were to do with his mission, and might well have been spoken by the prophetic "transmitters" of every age: "No intelligent monarch arises: there is not one in the empire that will make me his Master. My time has come to die." He returned to his couch, lay there for a week, and, without uttering another word, died. The disciples buried him with meticulous attention to his directions, and, by building little shacks by his tomb, prepared to mourn over his remains for several years. It is said that Tze-Kung, his most devoted follower, remained at the spot for as long as six years. The descendants of Confucius were in due course elevated to the rank of dukes, and the family flourishes in China to this day.

We may learn a good deal about Confucius, the man, from his recorded sayings or *Analects*. These sayings are terse, mordant, sometimes a trifle sarcastic, never sentimental. That he showed great pity for human suffering we know; but he liked best to express his sentiments in action. When one of his friends had sustained a personal loss, he ordered one of the horses of his carriage to be loosed and presented to the mourning family. "I dislike the thought," he explained, "of my tears not being followed by practical sympathy." That was his habitual attitude. From the various descriptions we have of him, and also from the majestic image at the temple erected at his birthplace, we may assume that he was both physically and mentally tough. Indeed, no man of poor physique or weak will could have survived the ordeal of his various terms of exile. It is a curious turn of fate that the philosopher most attached to ideas of decorum, good form, and social grace, should have been obliged to spend so much of his life in the wilderness, deprived of civilizing influences, condemned to be a displaced person, and begging in vain to be employed to some purpose. Equally ironical, perhaps, was the fact that Lao-Tze, who reputedly despised urban life, should have been living, when encountered by Confucius, in one of the biggest towns in China. Confucius has been accused, against the testimony of his close friends, of overweening egoism. He certainly made some statements which, if not exactly egoistic, do not err on the side of modesty. "In a hamlet of ten families," he said on one occasion, "there may be found one honourable and sincere as I am, but not so fond of learning." More celebrated is his remark: "At fifteen I set my mind upon wisdom. At thirty I stood firm. At forty my ear was still docile. At seventy I could follow the desires of my heart without transgressing the right." We can only affirm that if a man has really attained to such a pitch of perfection, he is entitled to say so. There are today about 550 millions who believe him to have been justified.

The "Classics"

The canonical books of the Confucian faith—for so we may legitimately call it—are known as the Nine Classics. Five of them, called the Five *Ching*, were probably the work of his own hand, either in an author's or in an editorial capacity. They consist of the *Li-Chi* or *Book of Rights*, a repository of rules of propriety, designed to inculcate spiritual as well as physical deportment. The second was a commentary on the remarkable book to which we have already referred, namely the *I-Ching* or *Book of Changes*. The third was the *Shi-Ching* or *Book of Odes*, another piece of editorial work: these poems, though beautiful in themselves, were of obvious didactic purpose. The fourth and fifth, the *Ch'un Ch'iu* or *Spring and Autumn Annals* and the *Shu-Ching* or *Book of History*, treated the past of the province of Lu and of the Chinese Empire as an inspiring record of heroism and order, thus bringing it into contrast with the prevailing anarchy. So much for the direct work of Confucius. The remaining four Classics are compositions which, though inspired by the Master, were written, so far as we know, by his disciples. Most famous of all are the *Analects* (or "fragments") to which we have referred. These sayings, bearing the stamp of a single personality, are probably as accurate a record of what the Master said as the notes of Boswell. The next *Shu*, or Book, is that entitled the *Ta-Hsueh* or *The Great Learning*, which many scholars regard as the clearest summary of the Confucian creed: parts of it, indeed, may be by Confucius himself. The grandson of the sage, Kung Chi, is considered to be the author of the Third *Shu*, the *Chung Yung* or *Doctrine of the Steadfast Mean*. The last is the *Book of Mencius*, named after Confucius's great disciple.

In *The Great Learning*, the Confucian ethic is pared down to its bare essentials. There is probably more concentrated wisdom, more solid truth, in this remarkable work than in any other philosophical treatise, even though it may be wisdom of a worldly kind: Lao-Tze would have dismissed it as folly, the more so in view of its presumptuous title. "Things have their root and their branches," says the treatise, "affairs have their end and their beginning. To know what is first and what is last will lead one near to what is taught in The Great Learning." We are then told how the Ancients set about ordering their kingdoms according to virtue. In order to achieve public tranquillity, they discovered that they must first set a good example in their family life, which in turn led them to a kind of inquisition into their own souls, culminating in the realization that they must "extend to the utmost their knowledge", until it penetrated to the heart of "reality" or the "nature of things". In other words, good government is not to be attained by the imposition of external regulations: on the contrary, it is to be attained only by each individual, the governor as well as the governed, engaging in self-cultivation according to the natural law of life. A vague aspiration, some will say: for what is this natural law of life? That is a question to which Confucius was more reluctant to give an answer than Lao-Tze, who said that the law was *Tao*, or than Hsun-Tze, who said that no such law existed. But Confucius, when pressed to give an answer to this problem, left no doubt in anyone's mind that, like his great predecessors, he was an apostle of the divine connection. "I seek *unity*, all pervading," he once remarked *apropos* of nothing, but in reality of everything. The reality of which he spoke was not the less real for being inaccessible to the majority of mankind. We must remember that, according to his own admission, he was fifty years old before he understood "the laws of heaven".

To open a modern text-book of ethics (which surely no one would willingly do unless obliged to pass an examination) is to find oneself in a world totally different from that inhabited by the great sages. In the first place, most text-books of this kind are occupied exclusively with enquiry into the meaning of terms, such as Right, Good, Duty, etc.: feigning a kind of academic unawareness of what these notions can really convey, and frequently arriving at the conclusion that they do convey nothing at all. The conception of human conduct as somehow related to the world in which man lives, virtuous action being that which is in harmony with some divine purpose, has become so thoroughly alien to the Western academic mind as almost to seem preposterous. Yet such is the message, albeit sometimes difficult to decipher, of all the spiritual leaders of mankind: nor would it appear that past civilizations would have accorded a man this status unless he had made good his claim to provide such enlightenment. The last great moralist after Spinoza to preach a kind of universalism in ethics was Kant; but Kant's statement that we must "act so that the maxim of our conduct shall become a universal law" is a pale abstract regulation, promulgated without reference to the purpose of nature and of a world superior to nature.[1] Confucius made a remark very similar to that of Kant. "The Higher Man," he said, "behaves so as to make his conduct in all generations a universal law"; but he uttered this maxim against the background of the traditional wisdom that he did so much to keep alive. It was not for nothing that he should have spent the last years of his life studying the most ancient piece of Chinese metaphysical thinking, the *Book of Changes*. The *I-Ching*, as we have seen, is a treatise on "the laws of heaven"; and if these laws, as thus interpreted, appear obscure, nobody before or since has pretended them to be otherwise. What is important is the recognition of their ceaseless, if imperceptible, operation. As we read in the *Doctrine of the Steadfast Mean*,[2] "what heaven has conferred is called The Nature. An accordance with this Nature is called The Path of Duty". The point is hammered home until it takes on the aspect of a platitude; but in fact it is a truth that counts above all

[1] The reader may wish slightly to qualify this remark in the light of our reference to Kant in the section on Shankara, Chapter VI.

[2] Rendered incisively by Ezra Pound as "The Doctrine of the Unwobbling Pivot".

others. "Unroll it, and it fills the universe; roll it up, and it retires and lies hid in mysteriousness." A platitude is a truth that mankind has been content thus to roll up and hide away. A platitude is the product of a conspiracy between human inertia and verbalism.

Compromise and the Mean

Like the Buddha, whose faith has proved the most powerful competitor to the doctrine of decorum and the Mean, Confucius was aware even to the point of over-simplification of the necessity of compromise. To the common people he preached a doctrine that might be understood without recourse to philosophical subtleties. He made allowance for the incapacity of most men to apprehend truths outside their immediate experience. "To give oneself earnestly to the duties of men, and, while respecting spiritual beings, to keep aloof from them—that is wisdom." It is, indeed, if you have in mind the bulk of humanity. With the same object of keeping within the normal range of experience, Confucius laid emphasis upon the virtue of family solidarity and in particular of filial piety. In the family he saw the natural unit of both order and continuity. It is here that virtue becomes concrete, duty a reality. The abstract theorist may reduce ethics to a few rules of expediency: common humanity will continue to respect the teachings of the sages, even if more in the breach than the observance. The Confucian teaching has entered so deeply into the Chinese mentality that all other doctrines have been obliged, by a kind of irony, to compromise with it. When historians and publicists speak of the futility of trying to conquer or subdue the Chinese people, they sometimes appear to have in mind the sheer vastness of the country. Strategists, speaking knowingly of "long lines of communication", think they have thus settled the matter. But the difficulty of "conquering" a people such as the Chinese (if the notion of conquest still retains any meaning) is the difficulty of breaking the power of a deeply-instilled and almost unconscious ethic. The "long lines of communication" which play a vital part in such a process are the channels whereby a realist doctrine of social responsibility has been handed down for two and a half millennia. Break that, and you will have achieved a victory without parallel in history. But we have yet to see whether, at the moment that your "pacification" or your "communization" seems complete, it has not broken you.

After the death of Confucius, his teaching achieved a success far beyond the modest expectations of its founder: how great a success the violence of certain opposition movements can best testify. As the doctrines of the Mean, the Golden Rule ("do unto others as you would have them do to you"), and the ideal of Filial Piety seeped

Picture Post Library

MENCIUS

From a Chinese portrait

into the public consciousness, so a new aristocracy of Confucian scholars was gradually formed. Nor were these scholars necessarily men of retiring or hermit-like disposition: the ideal of the philosopher king, or rather the ministerial sage, was always before them. Likewise, the Master's example in founding a school was followed by men of public spirit all over the country. Such schools, though often reducing the living teaching to absurdly formal patterns, preserved art and learning and therefore civilization through many centuries of disorder and indifference. For civilization, never at any time in great public demand, is obliged at different epochs to be content with teaching itself to itself, just as the exiled Confucius kept up his spirits by rehearsing the Odes for his own amusement, and playing his lute. While a number of rulers adopted a nominal Confucian doctrine as the official creed of their state, others, following the susceptible Duke Ting, burked at the obligation to set a shining moral example to their subjects. They were content to proclaim rigorous laws and see to their enforcement upon others. The Emperor Shih Huang-ti (221–211 B.C.), wishing to demonstrate that history began with himself and resenting the influence of Confucius's doctrines (as well as all others), ordered a gigantic "Burning of the Books". The act was largely symbolic: as an attempt to destroy learning it was futile. Many scholars had the Confucian scriptures by heart. Others, at great personal risk, hid the split-bamboo packets against a more enlightened reign. Having ruled for a brief period, Shih Huang-ti was fortunately succeeded by just the monarch for whom the scholars had been waiting. Wu Ti, by way of reaction, proclaimed the Confucian doctrine the official religion of the state in 136 B.C. The Master was in effect elevated to the status of a divinity.

In due course Confucianism began to spread to other countries. Taoism and later on Buddhism exerted a profound influence on the Chinese mind; but whereas Buddhism had been driven from India by a more belligerent doctrine, its diffusion throughout China did not weaken to the same extent the hold of Confucianism, which proved too "natural" and congenial a philosophy to be eliminated, and which will perhaps outlast every creed that seeks to take root in the minds of that most ethical, because Confucian, of people.

Wisdom genuine and counterfeit

A concentrated study of Indian and Chinese philosophy, viewed out of its historical context, may lead one to suppose that Hindustan and the Middle Kingdom[1] were crowded with little princelings

[1] I.e. *Chung-Kuo*. China is sometimes called also *Chung-hwa-kuo*—"Middle Flowery Kingdom".

round whom philosophers buzzed like gadflies, seeking to influence affairs of state, proffering gratuitous advice, and losing no opportunity for admonition. The impression needs to be corrected by reflecting upon the size of the country, the absence of communications and the comparatively small areas over which effective government could be exercised. Granted such conditions, however, we cannot help being once more struck by the fact that, in contrast to our own times, the five centuries preceding the birth of Christ saw the rise of more world philosophies than all the years that have followed. In a recent book, Professor Karl Jaspers has endeavoured to show that the contemporaneity, to employ the term somewhat loosely, of such men as Buddha, Confucius, Lao-Tze, Zoroaster, and the second Isaiah, indicates a common and related movement of thought throughout the oriental world. If so, such a movement has never been repeated; nor is it ever likely to be explained. There is one possibility, on the other hand, which the study of pre-history has rendered more plausible than it would have been considered a century ago: namely that the ancient world was perhaps less isolated than we sometimes suppose. Travel may have been difficult, hazardous, and above all slow; but immense distances were covered by both individuals and groups. The slowness may have been an asset; modern travel is too quick. Moreover, a long journey was something to be accomplished in stages; it amounted to taking up an abode at a series of points along a line not always predetermined. It consisted not so much of leaving your home as of moving it, or at least of establishing new ones. Nor were these interim dwellings necessarily as provisional as the camps of a tribe of nomads. Many of the castles built throughout the Middle East by the Crusaders, to take a later example from European history, are good for another thousand years if we discount the possibility of deliberate demolition. The "conquest of distance"—a victory not two centuries old—may have exerted from a psychological point of view much less influence upon bringing the right man and the right ideas together than the pioneers of locomotion and flight, and apostles of Free Trade such as Cobden, hoped. What distance has conquered is not ignorance but mature reflection, just as the invention of the typewriter has meant that we now write half a dozen letters instead of one. In short, pre-industrial travel may have been as effective a transmitter in space as the oral tradition was an effective preserver in time.

It follows that if the influence of individual philosophers has on occasion been exaggerated, we must not fall into the opposite error of underestimating such influence. We know that in India and China philosophy was respectable and respected, because it paid men to pretend to philosophical ability even when they did not possess it, except in a very debased form. Although modern rulers, especially in times of war, may sometimes consult psychologists, no Western ruler has ever been known to put himself under the tutelage of a major philosopher. The modern passion for administration, which produces committees of advisers on technical questions, has completely obscured the more fundamental problem of what is good government. In the centuries following the death of Confucius, Chinese society was much influenced by men resembling in their methods the Greek Sophists; the so-called Dialecticians and Logicians (*Pien Che* and *Ming Chia*, as their schools were respectively called). These men were not necessarily all charlatans, any more than our modern advertisers are all liars; but having set themselves up as purveyors of wisdom and experts in controversy they were obliged to lay claim to an omniscience which, had they been genuine spiritual leaders, they would have been the first to disown. Once you turn philosophy into a business, your aim ceases to be the pursuit of truth or the achievement of wisdom and becomes rather the maintenance of solvency. Such commercial philosophy provides convincing evidence of the prestige in which sagacity was held: the Western World tends to accord a similar pre-eminence to prosperity, in spite of the mild protest of the Churches.

Among the sages that gravitated towards the city of Lo-Yang were some who more nearly conformed to the traditional idea of the sage. There were men such as Mo Ti (*c.* 450 B.C.) who, in addition to being a logician, preached a gospel of universal brotherhood based upon the contention that men are by nature good: his books, considered subversive of good government and authority, were burnt together with the works of Confucius by the Emperor Shih Huang-ti. There was Yang Chu (*c.* 390 B.C.) an opponent of both Confucius and Mo Ti, who believed that since life was inherently evil and pointless we should endeavour to extract from experience as much pleasure as possible, without regard to the feelings of others. His argument, stated more incisively than it has ever been since, was that the "good name" of which the moralists speak is a figment. To whom is it good? For whom is it left behind? A man may toil and sacrifice, engage in fasts and prayer, perform innumerable good works. So far so good. When he dies he may be revered as a saint. Men may even begin to worship him. But of what use to *him* is all this posthumous adulation? He is not there to enjoy it. "Such fame," says Yang Chu, "is what no one who cares for what is real would choose. Celebrate him—he does not know it. Reward him—he does not know it. His fame is no more to him than to the trunk of a tree, or a clod of earth." On the other hand there may be men who, having the power and the means, live a life of unbridled self-indulgence. After their death their names are held in execration. They become models or epitomes of tyranny, rapaciousness, and lust. But what effect can such evil reputation have upon them? None at all. "Reproach them—they do not know it. Their ill-fame is no more to them than to the trunk of a tree or a clod of earth." In short, since good and evil reputation are equally meaningless, there is no point in concerning oneself with moral virtue in life. The only reality is the fulfilment of desire, here and now, and for oneself alone.

Mencius

To sages with a deeper sense of moral responsibility, such a gospel represented a serious danger to society. Like the idealism of Mo Ti, it could not be put into practice without bringing about anarchy. It is the ethical doctrine of the solipsist. Mencius, the great disciple of Confucius, regarded his life's work as an attempt to combat the two gospels, between which he saw little to choose: "The words of Yang Chu and Mo Ti fill the world. If you listen to people's discourses about it, you will find that they have adopted the views of the one or the other. Now Yang's principle is 'Each for himself'—which does not acknowledge the claims of the sovereign. Mo's principle is 'to love all equally'—which does not acknowledge the peculiar affection due to a father. To acknowledge neither king nor father is to be in the state of a beast. If their principles are not stopped and the principles of Confucius set forth, their perverse speaking will delude the people, and stop up the path of benevolence and righteousness. . . . I am alarmed by these things and address myself to the defence of the doctrines of the former sages and to oppose Yang and Mo."

The above passage reveals one of the outstanding qualities of Mencius; his sanity or, what comes to the same thing, his pursuit of the Golden Mean. We observe also another quality, humility: for Mencius claimed no particular originality for what he taught. All his life he sought to further the doctrines of Confucius, whom he regarded as the greatest teacher the world had known. He was of distinguished birth. By name Mang Ho, the imperial government later caused him to be known as Mang-tze, which means Mang, the Master. Having converted *Kung-fu-Tze* into Confucius, the Western doctors latinized *Mang-Tze* into Mencius. He was born in 372 B.C., about a century after Confucius's death.

The formative influence in Mencius's life was his mother, whose husband had died when the boy was very young. She represents in Chinese tradition the model of motherhood, and her son the model of filial piety. Many stories are told of her devotion and care for her son's welfare. On one occasion, grieved to see him idle, she deliberately severed the thread of her shuttle as he watched her at work. He enquired the reason for this unexpected act. She explained that it represented his own failure to concentrate on his studies, so that his life consisted of unco-ordinated bits and pieces. The lesson proved effective. Mencius became a conscientious student, and in due course followed in his Master's footsteps by starting a school of his own.

The authorities from whom he profited most were themselves pupils of Confucius's grandson. Mencius forthwith determined not merely to live according to the wisdom of the Master but to follow a similar career. He lived to a great age, dying at eighty-four, and spent his active years at the courts of princes, sometimes holding office and sometimes merely seeking to influence those who did so. We gather that he met with many disappointments, though not more than Confucius himself or than his own contemporary, Plato. In old age he decided to set down the results of his reflections, and these form the fourth Confucian "Classic", which, as we saw, is named after him.

At first sight the fundamental principle of Mencius's philosophy bears a strong resemblance to that of Mo Ti, for Mencius believed that human nature is at heart good. But he did not subscribe to the naive view that men, left to themselves, will automatically do what is right. What he maintained was that they have the capacity, well within their reach, to exercise benevolence and to train themselves to make the correct responses. "Speaking realistically," he wrote, "it is possible for men to be good, and that is what I mean when I say that man's nature is good. If they become evil, it is not the fault of their natural powers. Thus all men have a sense of compassion, also a sense of shame over wickedness, a sense of reverence, and a sense of truth and error. The sense of compassion is equivalent to individual morality, the sense of shame to public morality, the sense of reverence to ritual propriety, and the sense of right and wrong equals wisdom." He refers to these faculties as the "four tender shoots" of human nature. The expression is apt. Man is inherently endowed with these good impulses; but they are sensitive growths which must be tended and cared for. Rough handling and an unfavourable environment will deform and even destroy them.

Because he believed that human beings were capable of organizing the good life in society, Mencius did not hesitate to advocate the overthrow of princes whose rule was inherently oppressive. "The people," he declared, "are the most important element in a nation: the sovereign is the lightest." A man needed to have courage to make such statements in public, and Mencius was supremely courageous. He argued the matter with kings. "Suppose that the chief criminal judge could not regulate the officers under him, how would you deal with him?" The king said, "Dismiss him." Mencius again said, "If within the four borders of your kingdom there is not good government, what is to be done?" The king looked to the right and left and spoke of other matters. The second principle to which Mencius gave emphasis was that of filial piety, the bulwark of the Confucian tradition, which was to bind Chinese society together for more than two thousand years. "The desire of the child," said Mencius, "is towards his father and mother. When he becomes conscious of the attractions of beauty, his desire is towards young and beautiful women. When he comes to have a wife and children, his desire is towards them. When he obtains office, his desire is towards his sovereign. . . . *But the man of great filial piety to the end of his life has his desire towards his parent.*"

Confucius and Mencius exerted permanent influence over Chinese civilization because their doctrine, for all its prudence, was essentially one of hope, based upon faith in human nature. Such faith can easily be belittled and made subject to ridicule: for human nature can always be invoked in discredit of itself. The most powerful criticism of Mencius's doctrine was that levelled against it by a contemporary called Hsun-Tze, who is thought to have died about 235 B.C. According to this philosopher, human nature was thoroughly evil. While Mencius had pointed to the "four tender shoots" of human nature, Hsun-Tze pointed to as many thorns. Above all he drew attention to the fact, difficult enough to confute, that human beings were animated by an ineradicable acquisitiveness, a desire for power and gain. Against such an instinct, what availed benevolence and kindness? "There belongs (to human nature)," he said, "even at birth, the love of gain; and as actions are in accordance with this, contentions and robberies grow up, and self-denying and yielding to others are not to be found. There belong to it envy and dislike; and as actions are in accordance with these, lewdness and disorder spring up, and righteousness and propriety, with their various orderly displays, are not to be found. It thus appears that to follow man's nature and yield obedience to its feelings will assuredly conduct to contentions and robberies, to the violation of duties belonging to every one's lot, and the confounding of all distinctions, till the issue be a state of savagery."

What was Hsun-Tze's remedy for this state of affairs? He had none. He had merely a palliative. The acquisitive desires could never be rooted out. They might simply be kept within bounds. Institutions were necessary. "The sage kings of antiquity, understanding that the nature of man was thus evil, set up the principles of righteousness and propriety, and framed laws and regulations to straighten and ornament the feelings of that nature and correct them." The European thinker who most resembles Hsun-Tze is undoubtedly Thomas Hobbes, who held a similar view of human nature and prescribed the same kind of remedies for its shortcomings.

Chuang-Tze

We have no evidence to suggest that Hsun-Tze ever met the great Taoist philosopher Chuang-Tze, but the two were contemporaries, and they frequented the same courtly circles. We should certainly have heard of any such meeting, because it would have resulted in a disputation far more heated, we may suppose, than that in which Confucius and Lao-Tze engaged. Chuang-Tze has been called the St. Paul of the Taoist faith, and the description is just. His work is a restatement of the doctrine of Inaction in terms at once profound and elegant, for Chuang-Tze was a master of language and gifted with a poetic imagination. He was born in the province of Sung in the 3rd century B.C. Although several times offered important positions, he preferred to live a life of quiet teaching and meditation. To the emissaries sent by the Duke of Wei, who offered him the post of Prime Minister, he replied in terms which ensured that the invitation would not be repeated: "Go away quickly, and do not soil me with your presence. I would rather amuse and enjoy myself in a filthy ditch than be subject to the rules and restrictions in the court of a sovereign." It is reported that he did not trouble even to turn round from his fishing when the king of Khu sent two officials offering him supreme control of all his territories. In comparison, Confucius appears like an ambitious place-seeker.

Chuang-Tze attacked the idea of government even more vehemently than his master Lao-Tze himself. "There has been such a thing as letting mankind alone," he said; "there has never been such a thing as governing mankind." He quotes the answer of Lao-Tze to one of his disciples who enquired how, on such a theory, men were to be kept in order. "Be careful not to interfere with the natural goodness of the heart of men. Man's heart may be forced down or stirred up. In each case the issue is fatal. By gentleness the hardest heart may be softened. But try to cut and polish it—'twill glow like fire or freeze like ice. In the twinkling of an eye it will pass beyond the limits of the Four Seas. In repose, profoundly still; in motion, far away in the sky. No bolt can bar, no bond can bind—such is the human heart." An absolute quietism is recommended: "Cherish that which is within you, and shut off that which is without: for much knowledge is a curse." Consequently, all the conventional values are seen to be snares and delusions. "Appeal to arms is the lowest form of virtue. Rewards and punishments are the lowest form of education. Ceremonies and laws are the lowest form of government. Music and fine clothes are the lowest form of happiness. Weeping and mourning are the lowest form of grief." The true sage, on the other hand, "places himself outside the universe, beyond all creation, where his soul is free from care. Apprehending *Tao*, he is in accord with virtue. He leaves charity and duty to one's neighbour alone. He treats ceremonies and music as adventitious. And so the mind of the perfect man is at peace." Is such a condition the same as that which men call happiness? Yes, answers Chuang-Tze; but there is a counterfeit happiness of which we should beware. "I make true pleasure," he says, "to consist in inaction, which the world regards as great pain. Thus it has been said: 'Perfect happiness is the absence of happiness: perfect renown is the absence of renown.' Now in this sublunary world of ours it is impossible to assign positive and negative absolutely. Nevertheless, in inaction they can be so assigned. Perfect happiness and preservation of life are to be sought for only in inaction." And the argument culminates in a passage of great beauty. "Let us consider. Heaven does nothing, yet it is clear. Earth does nothing, yet it enjoys repose. From the inaction of these two proceed all the modification of things. How vast, how infinite, how vast, yet without form! The endless variety of things around us all spring from inaction. Therefore it has been said, 'Heaven and earth do nothing, yet there is nothing which they do not accomplish.' But among men, who can attain to inaction?"

We find in the work of Chuang-Tze a strong vein of mysticism. To some extent this is reminiscent of Buddhist thought; and perhaps the originality and fascination of Chuang-Tze resides in this blend of fancy and commonsense. "Those who dream of the banquet, wake to lamentation and sorrow. Those who dream of lamentation and sorrow, wake to join the hunt. While they dream they do not know that they dream. Some will even interpret the very dream that they are dreaming; and only when they are awake do they know it was a dream. By and by comes the Great Awakening, and then we find out that this life is really a great dream. Fools think that they are awake now." The passage ends with an image that blurs the distinction between reality and illusion. "Once upon a time I, Chuang-Tze, dreamt I was a butterfly, fluttering hither and thither, to all intents and purposes a butterfly. I was conscious only of following my fancies as a butterfly, and was unconscious of my individuality as a man. Suddenly I awaked, and there I lay, myself again. Now I do not know whether I was then a man dreaming I was a butterfly, or whether I am now a butterfly dreaming I am a man."

Yet we must not suppose Chuang-Tze to have been lacking in shrewdness or even humour. Interspersed with the lyrical passages on the nature of *Tao* there is much brute commonsense—a toughness that is Confucian or, more accurately, that is inherently Chinese: witness the reply of Chuang-Tze to his disciples when they expressed the wish to give him an elaborate funeral. "We fear," they had said, "lest the carrion kite should eat the body of our Master." "Above ground," said the dying man, "I shall be food for kites; below I shall be food for mole-crickets and ants. Why rot one to feed the other?" But what better summary of Chinese wisdom can be found than the words quoted by Chuang-Tze of his Master, "The art of preserving life consists in being able to keep all in One, to lose nothing, to estimate good and evil without divination, to know when to stop, and how much is enough, to leave others alone and attend to oneself, to be without cares and without knowledge—to be in fact as a child." All the profound philosophies of the world boil down in the end to something like that, in violent contrast to the conclusions of the pseudo-philosophies. And Lao-Tze is reported to have gone on to elaborate what he meant by living as a child, arriving at the summit of Chinese wisdom: "A child acts without knowing what it does; moves without knowing whither. Its body is like a dry branch; its heart like dead ashes. Thus good and evil fortune find no lodgement therein; and there where good and evil fortunes are not, how can the troubles of mortality be? Those whose hearts are in a state of repose give forth a divine radiance, by the light of which they see themselves as they are. And only by cultivating such repose can man attain to the constant. Those who are sought after by men are assisted by God. Those who are sought after by men are the people of God. Those who are assisted by God are His chosen children.

"To study this is to study what cannot be learnt. To practise this is to practise what can never be accomplished. To discuss this is to discuss what can never be proved. Let knowledge stop at the unknowable. That is perfection."

CHAPTER VIII

MOHAMMED

The Uniqueness of Islam

MAN'S Faith in God or the gods is the one factor in human history about which it is dangerous to make prophesies. There have been periods—of which the present may be one—in which Christianity as an influence upon social life has suffered such spectacular decline that recovery seemed impossible. Whether Pope Leo X actually committed himself to the statement that "the myth of Christ hath brought much gain" is doubtful. Sufficient evidence of the infidelity of the age lies in the fact that such a remark could be attributed, without a sense of outrage, to the vicegerent of God and successor of St. Peter. Similarly, there have been periods—of which the present may equally be one—in which the Islamic faith seems to have run into the sand from which, at an unexpected moment, it originally issued. Are we therefore to look upon the religion of the Prophet as moribund? We should be as foolish to do so as to attempt to speculate upon the circumstances of its revival.

In many ways the faith of Islam is unique. It is unique not in the sense that it owes little to any other faith—for the reverse is true. It is unique in the same sense that it is the one post-Christian faith to have achieved and for centuries maintained world influence, while remaining alive and fertile in the land of its origin. The centre of gravity of almost every other faith has shifted, sometimes by many thousands of miles. The path to Rome, for example, is more frequently traversed by Catholics than the path to Jerusalem, which is crowded with the returning exiles of an earlier faith. But the pilgrimage to Mecca is still incumbent upon all true Moslems who can afford the journey, just as the ceremonial language of Moslems of every nation is still Arabic, whether the faithful can understand it or not.[1]

A further curiosity about the Islamic faith, or more strictly about its founder, is that it appears to have had no distinct precursors. Christianity is remarkable for the prophetic succession of which it forms, to the devout, the culmination or fulfilment. The Buddha was the Buddha of Buddhas, but not necessarily the last of his kind. The basic beliefs of Hinduism seem to be as old as the human race. Confucius was one, if the greatest, of a long line of

[1] This applies to the "set prayers". An exception is Turkey, where Islam was "disestablished" in 1928.

Chinese sages. But Mohammed begins with himself. He had neither an Isaiah nor even a John the Baptist. Nor, apart from the Khalifs, had he any successors. Of all the great apostles of the divine connection he was the one whose great influence upon history might least have been anticipated.

Such emphasis upon Mohammed's unique historical mission has received a sharp challenge in certain quarters. What, it is asked, is so remarkable about the career of this leader of men? A close study of the society in which he lived reveals that his "religion"—if it was that, and not rather a political ruse—can be explained in very simple terms. It came at a time when its utility was most evident. It seems to have been devised to meet a particular set of conditions. In short, it was a historical necessity. That is one reason for disposing of the view that its origin is in some way mysterious. The second reason, perhaps more plausible because more in harmony with modern trends of thought, is psychological. The "appeal" of Islam to a desert community is obvious. The conditions of the desert, we are often told, conduce to unity of thought, to concentration upon essentials, and therefore to an inclination towards monotheism.

Do they indeed? If so, the theory raises some curious reflections. Even allowing for a period in which the process of soil desiccation and erosion was much less advanced, the desert is a great deal older than Islam. It may be as old as the human race, which, however ancient as a species, has probably enjoyed about a million years of sub-civilization, and not less than ten thousand years of culture.[1] But the desert, it appears, had to wait until the 7th century A.D. before it "generated" the monotheism that is appropriate to it. Such arguments, as we have already seen, explain nothing. To those who know it, the desert is a crowded, oppressive place. The terrors of loneliness are more likely to be experienced in the heart of a great metropolis.

The remarkable unification of the Arabian tribes for which Mohammed was responsible might suggest that in his day, or during his youth, Arabian society was particularly disunited. We must not forget, however, that even today Arabia is a country with few stable centres and a largely fluid population. In this respect it preserves, as few other countries have done, the conditions in which all human societies have existed for much the greater part of history. Only with the Industrial Revolution in the West, and then chiefly in England, has the average man ceased to be a countryman and become a townsman: we fail to appreciate how short a time he has had to become adjusted to urban conditions.

[1] Or much more, if we take into account the twenty-five-century-old art of Lascaux in the Dordogne.

The earliest stable society in Arabia was that which existed at Saba in the modern Yemen. Even today the strong and stately castles of that epoch—gigantic window-pocked tenements of baked mud—remain standing. Like Ur, Saba was a town of which the titular governor was a god. The ruler held office nominally at the god's sufferance, though he (or she) sometimes chose to become identified with him. Not merely was the constitution of Sabaean society matriarchal, but some of its queens, such as Balkis, attained great reputation for wisdom and beauty. In contrast, the Bedouin tribes were, and still remain, rigidly patriarchal. From Saba, an important caravan centre, the tribes set out upon trading journeys to such cities as Petra, now in Jordan, and Palmyra in Syria, which served as links between the Roman Empire and the Sassanian Empire of Persia. So wealthy a city was Saba, in fact, that the Persians considered it worth capturing in A.D. 570. Along the trade-route to the north lay another flourishing city, Mecca, which had been dominated during the 4th century by a powerful tribe called the Quarash.

Mecca was not simply a commercial centre for the trading of spices, silk, ivory, and precious stones. Like Saba, it was a temple city, of which the tutelary god was named Horbal. The shrine of this god took the form of a sanctuary containing a large black stone or cube, which was known as the Kaaba. In this temple, of which the Quarash were guardians, stood many hundreds of images. These were the gods, or their replicas, of the numerous tribes which visited the town, and their material presence enabled the traveller to worship conveniently his own particular deity. A nearby mountain, Arafat, was the centre of an annual pilgrimage as well as a sacred fair of great antiquity. The attraction of the Kaaba itself was that it was supposed to have come down from heaven at the time of Abraham. If, as many suppose, it is a meteorite, this tradition may have some foundation in fact. As for the association with Abraham, the interest of this will in due course appear.

The youth of Mohammed

Mohammed was born in Mecca about the year A.D. 570. His family, though belonging to the Quarash tribe, was poor, and he appears to have spent a lonely boyhood. Both his father and mother died before he was six years old, and he was entrusted to the care first of his grandfather and then of his uncle. In early youth he became a camel driver, and soon began to accompany his uncle on trading journeys, particularly to Syria. Realizing the boy's latent business abilities, his uncle sought to further his interests by obtain-for him employment in the service of a rich widow and business woman called Kadijah. This was the foundation of his fortunes. As his new work brought him into contact with merchants of many different nations, Mohammed was not slow to realize the backward state of his own country compared with the powerful empires ruled from Byzantium and Persia. No doubt he was impressed initially by the fact that order and stability promoted wealth; but, being of a reflective turn of mind, he was equally struck by the contrast between the religious beliefs of some of these foreign communities and the crude polytheism of his own countrymen. For just as he began to acquire knowledge of the great world empires, so he came to learn of the so-called world religions: it is certain that he mixed freely with Zoroastrians, Christians, and Jews. He may indeed have been attracted to one or other of these sects without penetrating very deeply into its tenets: or he may have been principally attracted by what was common to all three faiths, namely their grasp of certain basic spiritual facts, such as the struggle between good and evil forces, represented by Ahura Mazda and Ahriman, Jehovah and Lucifer, Christ and Satan. There were strong Jewish communities in southern Arabia and at Medina, while Christian ideas, especially in their monophysite form, had begun to penetrate Arabia in the 5th century. Mohammed describes both Jews and Christians as the "people of the Book", but it is unlikely that he knew the Bible at first hand. There is reason to think that the same is true of some of his Christian contemporaries.

It is tempting, and indeed legitimate, to draw a comparison between Mohammed and Abraham. Both were inhabitants of a temple city, a civic theocracy. Both were early engaged in the kind of trade that enabled them to acquire both considerable experience of the outer world and marked independence of mind. Both were obliged, at a critical moment of their lives, to quit the city of their birth and to seek their fortunes elsewhere. Both felt the necessity, once this uprooting had taken place, of dissociating themselves from their formal convictions and following a different faith. Finally, each believed himself to be the vehicle of a special revelation from heaven. Now the faith in question was not necessarily a new faith. It was an old faith. The faith of Abraham was faith in the god of his fathers. The faith of Mohammed was the faith of Father Abraham.

Mohammed's youth and early manhood were overtly occupied with business. So assiduously did he serve his mistress that in due course she agreed, though fifteen years his senior, to become his wife. The marriage proved a success. Mohammed, now a rich man, established a large family. His worldly ambitions were satisfied. To the men of his race and community he represented the kind of being to whom the gods had been unusually bountiful: for those whom such gods loved enjoyed prosperity and died full of years. What other evidence could be found of divine favour?

The voice in the desert

In spite of the sudden revolution in Mohammed's conduct and beliefs about the age of forty, we need not necessarily assume that the "revelation", when it came, was altogether unexpected. The theory of the "sudden conversion", which has been exploited by certain revivalist sects, is not merely discounted by modern psychologists but regarded with suspicion by most spiritual directors: for that which arrives so suddenly can as suddenly depart, leaving the mind little changed for this momentary diversion. We may surmise that such fundamental spiritual changes begin at a level far below that of conscious reflection, for the compost of the psyche best generates its heat when left undisturbed. Consequently, a life of routine, particularly business routine, is in some ways more favourable to the regeneration of personality than occupations of a more reflective character; the depths of the mind are rarely invoked. Nevertheless, however long Mohammed remained unconscious of these hidden forces, there came a time when the inner turmoil issued in an outer restlessness. Feeling an imperative need for periods of solitude and retirement, he remained alone for days at a time in the desert or in some remote cave. In due course he began to see visions and to hear voices, or rather one particular voice: for, like the daemon of Socrates, the voice that addressed him was invariably the same, the words falling into a rhythm that grew more and more compulsive. Between periods of great exaltation of spirits, he would fall into a dejection no less extreme.

At length Mohammed became convinced that the bearer of the messages was the Archangel Gabriel himself, and that the messages came from God. Such communications were made, he knew, only to one whom God has chosen to be his *Nabi*, his Prophet, whose task was to lead men back to a faith from which they had strayed. The feeling assumed the character of a burning conviction when one day he heard the voice of God say plainly: "Thou art the man. Thou art God's new prophet to convert the people of Arabia."

Did Mohammed really hear those words, did he imagine them, or did he fabricate the whole story of his divine revelation? These questions will always be asked, though, being unanswerable, they are idle enquiries. To those who regard Mohammed (or Buddha, Christ, or Joan of Arc for that matter) as having been at best the victim of an illusion, the difficulty is to give a coherent account of the later course of history. For, within a century of the supposed revelation, an Islamic empire had been established which not merely threatened with destruction all the empires of the world, but continued for centuries to exert pressure upon Christian Europe from at least three fronts. At its height this empire stretched from India to the neighbourhood of Poitiers. By belittling the cause, rationalism renders itself correspondingly less able to explain the effect. It may finally be more reasonable, if less rationalistic, to admit the possibility of supernatural intervention than to pile upon naturalism a load greater than it can bear.

The fact that his mission as Prophet was announced to him by the Archangel Gabriel disposes of the view that Mohammed was commissioned to preach to mankind a new faith. While interested in the beliefs of the Jews and Christians, he regarded these beliefs as themselves deformations of the pure monotheism preached by the Father of Semitic religion, Abraham. If the Koran bears evidence that Mohammed misunderstood Christianity, it is at least as reasonable to suppose that the Christians whom he met were responsible for this misapprehension as that he was obstinately stupid. He believed that his mission was similar to that of the great Prophets who had succeeded Abraham: above all, Moses and Jesus. For a time, it seems, he imagined that "the people of the Book" could be brought to a truer understanding of their own fundamental beliefs, thereby enabling his people to unite with others in worship of the true God. Only with the passage of years did he come to the view that it was his duty to give to his people a new Book.

First converts

It was to Kadijah that he first confided the substance of the revelations he had received. Filled with awe and enthusiasm, she forthwith became her husband's first convert and disciple. Other members of his family followed her example, above all his uncle's son Ali. His guardian, being essentially worldly in outlook, was less certain. An early convert outside the family circle was Abu Bekr, a man who exerted great influence in the Quarash tribe and who later came to succeed the Prophet himself. Even so, the faith made little headway at first among the bulk of the people of Mecca. Indeed, it met with considerable opposition, especially from Mohammed's fellow merchants. Since the temple city drew much of its revenue from religious dues and offerings, the attack on idols was thought likely to have an adverse effect on trade. There were others, less materialist-minded, who, learning of Mohammed's mystical transports, denounced him at best as a harmless poet and at worst as a false prophet. Among the tribes themselves, whose lives were largely taken up with vendettas and pillage, the doctrine, though simple and severe, made no immediate appeal. Bearing in mind the statements made concerning the aptitude of the desert-bound Bedouin for monotheism, we may recall with interest Mohammed's own opinion on this subject: "The Arabs of the desert are most stout in unbelief and dissimulation, and it is not likely that they should be aware of the laws which God has sent down to his apostle" (Koran, *sura* IX). Mohammed, like Abraham, was at heart essentially a townsman.

Some idea of the slowness with which the faith made headway may be judged from the fact that during the next four years Mohammed made only forty converts. The mission of Christ, it may be remembered, was completed in three years. As men doubted Mohammed and his claims, so on occasion he doubted himself. He even abandoned Mecca, retiring for several years to a safe place in the country of his uncle's choosing; for the latter, though sceptical, stood by him in all his trials. His return, though indicating the passing of public displeasure, was followed by private misfortune. Both Kadijah and his uncle died. He suffered money troubles. It seemed as if the visions and the voice had altogether misled him.

Twelve years from the time of the first revelation, however, a significant event occurred. A group of pilgrims reached Mecca from the town of Yathreb, which was situated about two hundred and fifty miles to the north. They sought out Mohammed, whose fame had spread as far as the rival city, and pledged themselves to accept his doctrine, agreeing to renounce idolatry, fornication, the exposure of children at birth (a custom among those unable to afford their upkeep), and other pagan habits. This mission, numerically so insignificant, was followed by others. The men of Yathreb were eager both to learn and to spread the gospel among their fellows. Such enthusiasm was something to which Mohammed had not been accustomed. It dawned upon him that he might do well, if only as a temporary expedient, to leave Mecca and to establish his headquarters at Yathreb.

This decision and its accomplishment, undertaken in conditions of the greatest secrecy, marked the beginning of an era in the history of Islam. Mohammed's flight to Yathreb in the summer of 622 is known as the *Hegira* (or Flight), and from it Moslem chronology begins. Yathreb was thereafter known as Medinat al Nabi, the City of the Prophet, or simply Medina, the City.

The great welcome given to Mohammed in Medina was due to two causes. His teaching found eager disciples there, certainly: the celebrated saying of Christ concerning the honour denied to prophets in their own country applied equally to his great rival of the Christian era. But the men of Medina not merely agreed to provide asylum to Mohammed; they hoped to profit from his

Picture Post Library

MOHAMMED

From an old print

presence. They had cause to hate the people of Mecca, whose prosperity was purchased to a great extent at their expense; for they resented above all the fact that caravans passing across Arabia made their chief halting-place at the sanctuary of the Kaaba rather than at the equally fertile Medina. On more than one occasion these animosities had boiled over into open warfare. It is difficult to effect a serious aggression, however, without the aid of some exalted war-cry. No one engages in immorality without thinking up some moral reason for so doing. Inflamed by Mohammed's summons to wreak God's vengeance on those who had rejected His Prophet, the people of Medina launched a crusade against Mecca and inflicted a series of defeats upon its defenders, though the town was not finally taken until later. The immediate task was to assume control over the surrounding country and its unruly tribes.

When Mohammed first arrived at Medina, he had expected to receive a particularly warm welcome from the Jews. Here he gravely miscalculated. The people who looked to Abraham as their father refused to take seriously the man who believed himself summoned by God to lead men back to the Patriarchal faith. Far from regarding him as the Saviour whom they awaited, they treated him as merely the latest of the false prophets. While Mohammed accused them of having departed from the faith of Abraham, the Jews accused Mohammed of attempting to manipulate that faith for his own uses. That the two doctrines had much in common was precisely the trouble, for the followers of two creeds dissimilar in certain particulars are more prone to enmity than those of widely-divergent doctrine.

The return to Mecca

In the end, Mohammed felt obliged to break with the Jews altogether. At one time he had ordained that his followers, when praying, should turn towards Jerusalem, the Holy City of the Jews. Now he decided that the faithful, a growing body, should turn towards the Holy City of the Arabs, which was Mecca. A radical change in his outlook occurred. In his youth it had seemed to him, an inquisitive but ignorant Arab, that enlightenment, learning, and civilization must all come from beyond the borders of Arabia. He betrayed the exaggerated respect of unsophisticated people for those of superior education and training. He nourished the idea of civilizing Arabia from without. Not only did he become increasingly dissatisfied with the "civilization" that he hoped to import (for he may have realized that by the time such a thing reached the cities of Arabia it had become considerably debased), but he grew to appreciate the true significance of Gabriel's message, and above all the manner of its delivery. The revelation had been made in the desert. It had been addressed to him as an Arab. It owed nothing to either Persia or Byzantium or Jerusalem. The enlightenment it provided was of a kind to which nothing in these civilized centres could show any parallel. Instead of civilizing Arabia from without, Mohammed now addressed himself to the high mission of enlightening the world from within. He might rule at Medina for some time—in fact he stayed there for as long as ten years; but his true task was to return in triumph to Mecca and so reconsecrate that city in the name of the one God.[1]

The God was Allah, and so the word God is still translated. But there was a special reason why Mohammed should have employed this word. The Quarash tribe had two special deities, one male and the other female, Allah and Al-lat. By calling the God of Abraham Allah, Mohammed was not merely preserving a name with which his people, and above all the people of Mecca, were familiar; he was in effect identifying the "new" God with the traditional God of his own family. Such an identification was no more abitrary in his case than it was in the case of Abraham. One of the most remarkable differences in outlook between the Western World and almost all ancient civilizations is that modern man, in seeking spiritual guidance, tends to look to the future. Salvation, even on the plane of pure materialism, is thought to be achieved by following a path leading towards some distant but theoretically accessible goal. Hence Science, or rather the impulse behind scientific enquiry, comes to be regarded as almost a sacred process, since the pursuit of such enquiry (to which nothing seems impossible; another "divine" characteristic) promises to remove all obstacles to happiness, even though final salvation may be reserved for a generation so far distant as hardly to interest us. The objection to such an outlook is that in freeing us from slavery to the past it delivers us over to another form of bondage, namely slavery to the future. Archaic man, who was more conscious of the need for guidance than we, first looked to the past.[2] Differing from us again in the strength of his group-loyalties, he would fall back in times of crisis upon tribal or family

[1] In order to break the tribal power, Mohammed introduced the custom of uniting pairs of men together in brotherhood, one being from Mecca and the other from Medina. The aim, soon to be established, was to found a Moslem brotherhood superseding ties of race.

[2] It may be suggested that the whole mission of the Hebrew Prophets contradicts this; but their mission was only indirectly with the future. "The connection of the *Nabi* with the future is not that of one who predicts. To be a *Nabi* means to set the audience, to whom the words are addressed, before the choice and decision, directly or indirectly. The future is not something already fixed in the present hour, it is dependent upon the real decision, that is to say the decision in which man takes part in this hour."—Martin Buber: *The Prophetic Faith* (New York, 1949, p. 2).

deities, whose worth had been put to the trial on occasions within every man's memory and with whom the ancestors were closely identified. Thus it is too simple an explanation to suggest that Mohammed called his God Allah so that the ignorant Bedouin, familiar with that pagan deity, should find the transition from one faith to the other easy. Mohammed wished to preserve continuity in his own spiritual development: another instance of the tendency of the great world faiths to avoid wholesale repudiation.

The final conquest of Mecca was achieved by a combination of violence and trickery. Mohammed did not hesitate to attack the Meccan caravans during the months of pilgrimage, though such action was regarded as sacrilege. That he dared thus to violate the truce of God, while shocking the few, served to increase his reputation among a people to whom power and success have always been objects of reverence.[1] Finally, at a great battle fought at Badr, the power of Mecca was finally shaken, but it was six years before Mohammed was master of the two great cities of Arabia. Having removed the idols from the sanctuary of the Kaaba, he proclaimed himself civil and religious governor of the city, being at once priest, king, law-giver, and judge. Thenceforth the faith prospered as almost no faith had done before; for the spiritual energy released in that small Arabian city did not spend itself in the West until the armies of Islam were turned back by Charles Martel at Tour in 732. Had the decision been otherwise, it is possible that the whole of the Occident, including the American continent, would today form part of a gigantic Islamic empire, and that the writer and readers of this book would be Moslems.

The rapidity with which tribe after tribe was enlisted in his service encouraged Mohammed in the hope that his authority might one day extend beyond the borders of Arabia, and that the rulers of much more powerful nations might come to accept Islam. He was therefore emboldened to address letters to both the Emperor at Constantinople and to the King of Persia inviting them to adopt the Islamic faith. The latter, not being accustomed to receive appeals of this kind, reacted in a most hostile manner. The emperor, who realized the wisdom of maintaining peace on his frontiers, responded more cordially. An appeal to the ruler in Egypt met with the most satisfactory response of all, part of it being made in kind: for Mohammed's envoy was sent back with two extremely attractive Egyptian women, whom the Prophet took into his harem.

[1] In *sura* 2 of the Koran, such conduct is excused as follows: "They will ask thee concerning war in the sacred month (i.e. Ramadan). Say: the act of fighting therein is a grave crime: but the act of turning others aside from the path of God and unbelief in him . . . is worse in the sight of God."

In the year 632, feeling that his end was approaching, Mohammed decided to lead in person a gigantic pilgrimage to Mecca. The number of the faithful on that occasion was about forty thousand, probably the largest concourse ever assembled in the presence of the leader of a world faith. Having conducted the ceremonial prayers, the Prophet, surveying the people from a high hill, declared that his work was at last accomplished. In words very similar to those spoken by the Buddha on his deathbed, he declared that every man's task was steadfastly to work out his own salvation, submitting only to the will of God. Not long after this ceremony he contracted a fever, possibly brought on by the effects of poison, and died.

The Koran

Although Mohammed could neither read nor write, he showed great respect for the written word, as is proved both by his interest in the Bible, and by his resolve to leave behind him a book of his own. The Koran (or *Qur'an*) is a collection of utterances, regulations, and legendary stories which Mohammed, claiming to be the mouthpiece of Allah, dictated over a period of more than twenty years. Recorded piecemeal on objects as various as stones and palm-leaves, the book was put together after the Prophet's death by Abu Bekr, who divided it none too skilfully into chapters or *suras*. To the orthodox Moslem it forms one prolonged inspired utterance, wherein provision is made for every contingency in life. That for which the Koran makes no provision is regarded as outside the experience of the devout. Thus the Koran (a word which means "that which is to be read") is a book which the Moslem must either accept as inspired or not accept at all; but if he does not accept it at all, he cannot be counted a Moslem. All Moslems are fundamentalists.

To the non-Moslem reader, the Koran is a puzzling and somewhat unsatisfactory book. Whereas the Bible, or substantial parts of it, can hold the interest for many chapters at a time, preserving in spite of apparent irrevelancies a recognizable theme, the Koran can be entered at any point: it represents a static collection of religious lore. It is likewise distinguished from the Bible in that the history of its chief personage, the Prophet himself, remains outside it. If you imagine the New Testament, for example, as containing only the sayings of Christ and not His acts, you would have a book very like the Koran. This deficiency was later repaired by the compilation of a book of almost equal interest, namely the *Sunna*, in which the life of Mohammed is fully recorded, though with exaggerations presumably intended to demonstrate his superiority to Christ. Mohammed is there portrayed as a wonder-worker of unexampled talent; and in order to show at least his equality with Christ, he is made to utter statements lifted from the New Testament. Furthermore, while the Koran is not devoid of sublimity,[1] and though Moslem scriptures contain passages of profound spiritual insight, especially in the works of the Sufi mystics and such poems as the Turkish *Mevludi Sherif*, the Koran can show nothing comparable to the Sermon on the Mount, the Fire Sermon, or certain passages in the *Bhagavad-Gita*. Perhaps the explanation lies in the difference between that which is *required* of a Moslem as compared with a Christian, a Buddhist, or a Hindu. Whereas the Moslem is called to be a good man, the others are "called to be saints". It may be argued, as Dostoevski suggested in the famous Grand Inquisitor passage in *The Brothers Karamazov*, that the Christian, and by implication the Buddhist and the follower of Krishna, are being called upon to reach a standard beyond human attainment. At any rate, we can hardly imagine the Grand Inquisitor objecting to Mohammed as he objected to Christ. We can see ourselves as attaining without undue effort the standard of righteousness set by the Prophet, though whether, with such a moderate aim in view, we should think it necessary to go to the trouble of embracing Islam is another matter.

To suggest that Mohammed enjoined upon his disciples a few ritual practices, and no more, would nevertheless be grossly inaccurate. Like Zoroaster, he laid great emphasis upon the "good disposition". In the first place, the disciple must pass in his lifetime one fundamental oral test. This is to declare, "There is no God but Allah and Mohammed is his Prophet." He must utter this statement with both understanding and conviction: a mere verbal repetition will not suffice. If the disciple makes this declaration with complete sincerity, he need do so only once, for he has thus enrolled himself irrevocably among the believers. The second condition is that he must be circumcised: Napoleon, as we saw in the first chapter, was put in a dilemma by this ordinance. Thirdly, the believer must pray five times a day at certain intervals: before dawn, at noon, in the afternoon, at sunset and at nightfall, adopting a series of deep obeisances[2] and facing in the direction of Mecca. Here again the mere performance of ritual is not sufficient. On that point the Koran is firm. "There is no piety in turning your faces towards the east or west, but he is pious who believes in God and the last day and the angels and the scriptures and the prophets; who for the love of God disburseth his wealth to his kindred, and to the orphans, and the

Particularly in its powerful language, charged with a poetry that only the Arabic scholar can appreciate.

[2] Hence the adoption of the fez. The Moslem cannot pray in a brimmed hat: hence the outcry against Kemal Atatürk's "Hat Law" in 1924.

needy and the wayfarer, and those who ask, and for ransoming; who observeth prayer, and payeth the legal arms, and who is one of those who is faithful to their engagements when they have engaged in them, and patient under ills and hardships and in time of trouble: these are they who are just, and these are they who fear God" (*sura* 2). In the same spirit the fast of Ramadan and, if feasible, the pilgrimage to Mecca, must be undertaken.

Mohammed and the Christians

Within two centuries of the Prophet's death the Moslem faith hardened into a rigid system. Although violent schisms occurred among the devout, the theology and law (*Shari'a*) of Islam have since remained unchanged. Whereas the Buddha regarded himself as merely one among a succession of Enlightened Ones, Mohammed was convinced of the finality of his mission. He claimed to be the "Seal of the Prophets", the last and greatest of a line which included Adam, Noah, Abraham, Moses, and Jesus. His "successor", therefore, was not another *Nabi* but simply the *Khalifat an-Nabi*, "successor to the Prophet". Consequently, much of the Bible scriptures are as sacred to the Moslem as to the Jew and the Christian. This applies above all to the Pentateuch (the first five books of the Bible), the Psalms of David, and even the Gospels.[1] It was not to Christ that Mohammed objected, but to Christians. Their theology, particularly as regards the Trinity, seemed to him to detract from the pure monotheism which he believed, with justice, to have been the faith of Abraham. We need not ridicule Mohammed for misunderstanding the Trinity. This "rude human soul", as Carlyle called him (and indeed the Prophet would have made a strange visitor at Cheyne Row), had as good an excuse for failing to grasp the idea of trinity-in-unity as those learned doctors of the Christian Church who had wrangled with one another at the Council of Chalcedon in 451.[2] In a sense Mohammed was simply a Christian heretic.[3] God, he maintained, "begetteth not nor is He begotten". To declare otherwise was to fall once more into polytheism. The Koran sums up the matter as follows: "They say moreover 'Become Jews or Christians, that ye may have the true guidance.' Say: Nay,

[1] Moslems accept the Virgin Birth and miracles of Jesus.

[2] "In the church of St. Euphemia at Chalcedon there were gathered all the forces that were henceforth to divide the Christian world. The rival forces of Egypt and the East shouted defiance and abuse at one another from either side of the nave, while the great officers of the Empire, seated in front of the chancel rails, with the Roman legates by their side, impassively dominated the turbulent assembly and guided it with inflexible persistence towards a final decision in accordance with the wishes of the Emperor and the Pope."—Christopher Dawson: *The Making of Europe*, Chapter VII, "The Awakening of the East".

[3] The description was first used by St. John of Damascus.

the religion of Abraham, the sound in faith, and not one of these who join gods with God is our religion." Those who "join gods with God" are the Christians.

So insistent was Mohammed upon his possession of the true faith that he imagines the covenant between God and Abraham to have presaged his own appearance as the final Prophet of God. There is an interesting passage in *sura* 2 of the Koran which makes this clear: "And when Abraham, with Ishmael, raised the foundations of the house, they said 'O our Lord! accept it from us: Thou of a truth art the hearer, the knower. O our Lord! make us thy Muslims (i.e. resigned to thee), and our posterity a Muslim people: and teach us our holy rites and be turned towards us. . . . O our Lord! and raise up among them an apostle from themselves who may rehearse thy signs unto them, and teach them "The Book", and wisdom, and purify them: of a truth thou art the Mighty and the Wise.' . . . And this to his children did Abraham enjoin, and Jacob also, saying 'O my children! truly God hath chosen a religion for you: so die not without having become Muslims.' "

The Khalifate and the sects

The development of a rift among the followers of Mohammed is remarkable not in itself but on account of its early emergence. The Sunnis are those who accept the spiritual authority of the first three Khalifs, or successors of Mohammed, namely Abu Bekr, Omar, and Othman.[1] To the Shiahs, on the other hand, these Khalifs are usurpers. Mohammed's true successor, they maintain, was the Prophet's cousin and son-in-law, Ali, son of Abu Talib and husband of Fatima. The Sunnis have always been the most numerous party, and their doctrine and ritual are preserved in the *Sunna*, from which they take their name. Nevertheless, the Shiah sect has likewise been powerful in many regions, and in modern Persia their beliefs are accepted as orthodox. As the simple doctrine of the Prophet underwent theological and juridical elaboration, various movements and sects arose dedicated to restore the ancient simplicity. Today the most important of these sects is that of the Wahabis, fanatical puritans, of whom King Ibn Saud is the chief representative. An offspring of Shiism is the Babi[2] sect, founded by Mirza Ali Mohammed (1820–50) and continued by a second "Messiah" called Mirza Huseyn Ali (1817–92), and his son Sir Abdul Baha (1844–1921). Baha'ism, as it is called, has converts not merely in Persia, but in India, China, Japan, and also America and England.

[1] All three, together with the fourth Ali, were members of the Quarash tribe, but only Ali was related to Mohammed.

[2] From the Arabic *bab* (door).

The rapid résumé of the last paragraph leaves out of account many features of modern Islam to which the student and the scholar would need to pay careful attention. A faith that can claim adherents in every part of the world, and that within the last few years has been largely responsible for the creation of a new nation, Pakistan,[1] can hardly be considered either as moribund or even in need of artificial respiration. Nevertheless, it remains paradoxical that while Zoroastrianism and Hinduism solicit no converts yet remain very much alive, Islam, one of the most proselytizing of faiths, shows signs, as we hinted, of losing ground among the Arab peoples themselves. After the abolition of the Khalifate in Turkey in 1928 no leader in the Middle East has felt himself sufficiently powerful to assume that ancient and responsible office. Nor does Islam, or even a modernized form of it, appear to make the smallest appeal to the younger generation of most countries of the Middle East. In Turkey, as the author has pointed out elsewhere,[2] the moral vacuum created by the disestablishment of Islam is causing no little concern to educationalists. For the younger generation has no *mystique* upon which to nourish itself except that of nationalism: a creed which, though it may enable the patriot to meet death, can do nothing to explain it. To pay successive visits to the Middle East countries today is to experience a sense of peculiar depression, as each frontier discloses a people claiming the same qualities of superiority, antiquity, and invincibility, and instilling these ideas, regardless of political realities, by every educational device into its children. It is to be hoped that Israel, with its concentrated talent and its experience of racial suffering, will not permit its free-thinking elements to effect that all-round secularization which, once hardened into dogma, may reintroduce religion in its worst form, that of destructive chauvinism.

The Sufis

When we speak of "The Prophets" we tend to think of a series of isolated figures whose message, though at first derided, won acceptance by a kind of imperious inner authority. We forget that among such people as the Jews the "prophet" was a figure only too familiar: indeed, he could often become a menace. In *Zechariah* xiii, for instance, we read: "And it shall come to pass that when any shall yet prophesy, then his father and his mother that begat him shall say unto him, Thou shalt not live: for thou speakest lies in the name of the Lord: and his father and his mother that begat him shall thrust him through when he prophesieth. And it shall come to pass in that

[1] Literally, "Land of the Pure", from the Urdu *pak*, meaning "pure" or "clean".
[2] Tomlin: *Life in Modern Turkey* (1946), p. 72.

day that the prophets shall be ashamed every one of his vision, when he hath prophesied; neither shall they wear a rough garment to deceive." Islam, like every other faith, has had its fill of false prophets; but there grew up a movement early in its history which, had it been suppressed (as for instance the Mu'tazilites were suppressed in the 9th century), might have deprived Islam of much of its later spiritual influence. This movement was associated with the Sufis, poets and mystics who were so-called because, like the men mentioned by Zechariah, they wore rough shirts of wool (*suf*). The Sufis were not isolated figures; they belonged, as their scattered successors still belong, to a closed brotherhood, membership of which necessitated a period of initiation, strict training, and participation in special services of meditation called *dhikrs*. Most Sufis, having reached a particular stage of training, joined one of the famous Dervish Orders: the Mevlevis or Whirling Dervishes, the Rufais or Howling Dervishes, and the Bektashis or People's Dervishes (who were primarily poets). The Sufis would probably have remained in a condition of spiritual outlawry, a potential danger to orthodoxy, but for the adoption of their faith by one of the greatest intellects of Islam, al-Ghazzali (died in 1111), who was professor of theology and canon law at the Nizamiya College at Baghdad, and whose conversion necessitated his resignation from that post.

While we may be tempted to see in Sufism traces of Buddhist and Vedantist thought, the influence of Christian mysticism is paramount. In his book called *The Precious Pearl*, al-Ghazzali imagines a group of poor people who were asked on the Day of Judgment why they had turned away from God. They answered that they had renounced their faith in consequence of their poverty. They were then asked, "Who is the poorest, you or Jesus?" "Without doubt Jesus," they replied. "That did not turn Him away," was the rejoinder, "from living according to the will of God Most High. . . . O reader, take Christ as your model, for it is said that He had no purse: for twenty years He wore the same shirt of wool (*suf*). . . ." In the work of al-Ghazzali, as in that of his successors such as Jalah ad-din ar-Rumi (*d.* 1273), Jesus is regarded as the "Seal of the Saints". In view of the bitter hostility between Moslems and Christians, and the use of the word "Giour" (pagan or unbeliever) as a term of abuse even by street urchins today, it is interesting to recall the passage from *sura* 5 of the Koran, "Verily, those who believe, and the Jews and the Sabaeans and the Christians—*whoever of them believeth in God and in the last day*, and doeth what is right, on them shall come no fear, nor shall they be put to grief": a statement as elevated in its way as Krishna's words in the *Bhagavad-Gita*.

CONCLUSION

The cult of the Unknowable

OUR journey, though somewhat rapid, has been a long one. Some readers will deplore the length of our pauses here and the brevity of our pauses there. Others will express regret and surprise that at certain stages of the journey we have made no pause at all. We could wish that time and space had permitted us to treat our subject in much greater detail: but just as we cannot always please other people, so we cannot always please ourselves.

Before closing, it will be useful to state, however tentatively, certain general conclusions: for the reader who has reached the present page will be aware of a thread of continuity running through the previous chapters. Three principal questions warrant our attention. In the first place, what are the basic differences between oriental and western thought? In the second place, what does the Western World owe to the thought of the East and *vice versa*? In the third place, to what extent is a *rapprochement* possible between the two worlds of thought, taking into account the great political and economic changes at present occurring in the Orient?

Twenty or thirty years ago such questions, particularly the last, might have seemed either trivial or irrelevant. The influence of "thought" tended to be belittled: men were supposed to be the product of their economic circumstances. We now realize that it matters a great deal what people think: which accounts for the trouble to which leaders of men go to mould public opinion. The violent penalties with which dictators visit the sin of "deviation", together with the daily evidence that such measures are by no means always effective, testify to a tough resilience, a spring of health in the human soul, a basic will to independent enquiry, which prevents mankind from descending to the level of mindless poltroons.

It is the fashion today to belittle the idea of Progress. "Progress," Wyndham Lewis has remarked in his *Time and Western Man*, "may even bring Progress to an end." If we accept a somewhat limited definition of progress, such a prophecy seems only too likely to be realized. In the course of two centuries the development of technical efficiency has wholly transformed a world that had remained stable for many thousands of years. We now live, as no other generation has lived, under the threat of sudden annihilation. If man is indeed the child of God, then God is in danger of assuming the rôle of a Frankenstein: a *dénouement* which it would be legitimate, if it were not presumably blasphemous, to describe as totally unforeseen. Compared with this present crisis in both human and cosmic affairs, all other crises in history assume an aspect of triviality. To commit oneself to such a statement is by no means to indulge in mere rhetoric. Man at last knows his fate, because he has at last learnt to know the consequences of his power.

Given this unique situation, two interesting facts emerge, both of which have a direct bearing upon our subject. In the first place, you have only to ask any individual man whether, in his opinion, the great technical advances of the last two centuries have served to increase human happiness (not the "sum of human happiness", because there is no such sum), and he will answer, unless he does not take the trouble to think, No. In the second place, you have only to ask him whether, in his opinion, the complete destruction of all human life would be such a deplorable thing, and he will likewise be tempted to answer (unless he thinks a little too carefully), No. In other words, it would seem to be the case that most men, reflecting on such matters cursorily, neither think very highly of human life nor consider that much can be done to improve it. Such pessimism is true of all save the young, who enjoy not so much life itself as the prospects that life seems to offer. And this may be the reason why our civilization, as shown above all in our modern educational systems, seems so intent upon perpetuating the conditions of youth and concealing by every device of propaganda the scandal of age: for this is its way of rendering life tolerable for a creature who, never particularly enthusiastic, now begins to show signs of regarding life with something approaching despair.

Whatever else may be said of history, it is full of the unexpected and the contingent. Prophecies of doom are heard in each generation. Evils come to pass, but not always the evils regarded as most imminent. To live under the threat of physical annihilation may not prove altogether unwholesome. Rapacity, cupidity, and complacency in all their forms are more likely to flourish at a time of increasing prosperity. Our age is one in which mankind, endowed with the means of self-destruction, may be prompted to enquire into the true value of that which he is about to throw away. This is particularly true of Western man, who, as we have often hinted, is by the circumstances of his material existence obliged to live at several removes from reality.

The social changes brought about by the Industrial Revolution in Europe impress us by their magnitude and their novelty. They should not blind us to the other changes that have taken place in Europe, as part of the normal rhythm of history. For Western civilization differs from any other in its dynamic character. This is the chief difference between Christian culture as fused with Greek and Roman ideals and any other culture. It has been the nature of Christian culture not so much to resist as to bring about social changes, even though many of these changes have been nominally "secular" in character. The great social movements of the 19th century, for example, were parasitic upon the Christian ideal which in many cases they repudiated. We may suggest that the eradication of Christianity, which is in some places a deliberate policy, will bring to an end such revolutionary social movements, contrary to the belief of many secular reformers: for the eradication of Christianity will deprive the Western World of an element of tension without which society is likely to sink into regimented uniformity. The Christian social ideal has always been dynamic because it has never become identified with, still less dominated by, a political regime. Church and State, sacred and secular: these polarities, instead of involving the betrayal of the Christian Gospel, have been the conditions of its social effectiveness. An apparent exception is the Byzantine Empire, with its rigid theocratic structure. But the Byzantine Empire was rightly called the Eastern Empire, and its constitution was largely oriental. For the norm of oriental civilization is that of a social heirarchy from which evolution is excluded.

The fact remains that all the great world faiths have come from the East, above all that of Christianity. Even when, as so often in America, a new religion is founded, the elements and usually the vocabulary of the faith are inevitably oriental: for the ordinary Western man feels, not perhaps without good reason, that the secrets of life, the arcana, are better known, if not always better practised, by the humblest oriental than by the most learned of western divines. Sometimes this respect for oriental wisdom assumes extravagant proportions. Thus Madame Blavatsky, a woman of remarkable personality, wrote such books as *The Secret Doctrine* (1888), and *Isis Unveiled*, in the course of which, having denounced the religion of the Western churches and in particular the Roman Church, she advocated the return to a more ancient and occult faith of oriental inspiration. To this faith she gave the name of the "secret doctrine". Now the trouble with the "secret doctrine" is that no one is able, unless prepared to undergo forms of initiation involving (in the end) considerable expense, to discover what it is. Every faith has its core of mystery, or it would cease to deserve the name of faith. But a faith of mere mystery is both a religious parody and a logical absurdity: for it attempts to throw light upon the mystery of existence simply by declaring it to be inherently inscrutable.

A missionary gospel such as Christianity, though beset with pagan adversaries, is threatened most seriously by faiths bearing a superficial resemblance to its own. This is what happened to the early Church. Whereas the barbarians came to heel, the great rival to the Christian creed was another creed of similar oriental origin. To call it a creed is perhaps to give it greater definition than it either deserves or ever possessed: for, in spite of important researches and recent discoveries, we still know very little about the vague cluster of beliefs called Gnosticism. The recent discovery north of Luxor in Egypt of forty-three sacred Gnostic books, which are at present undergoing study at the University of Louvain, will presumably afford us enlightenment upon many aspects of that form of belief: we must therefore beware at this stage of unsupported conjecture. At present, almost all we know of Gnosticism is derived from the tracts written by Christian Doctors and Fathers attacking it. And it is the extreme virulence of these attacks, for which there is hardly a parallel even in ecclesiastical history, that affords us an insight into the danger which they constituted, or were thought to constitute, for the Christian communities. There are two reasons why Gnosticism is of interest to us here. In the first place, it represents a system of belief which owes much to the great oriental religions of which we have written, so that it forms a kind of link between these faiths and Western Christianity. And in the second place, it represents a system of belief which, with due modifications, has flourished, however obscurely, in every age, including our own. Perhaps, indeed, Gnosticism is nothing but that universal abstract "religion" which public-spirited men in every generation, and also certain disillusioned rationalists, have been seeking as a means to the spiritual union of humanity. That would justify our having agreed, early in this book, to abandon so vague a word in treating the concrete faiths of the Orient.

Gnosticism is simply the religion of *Gnosis*, knowledge. Now what was the knowledge of which the Gnostics were in quest? It was suprasensible knowledge—that is to say, a knowledge of pure spirit. As far as we can see (though the belief assumed many forms), the Gnostics held the body to be evil, since it was immersed in a material world that was itself evil. Thus the way to salvation lay through *disincarnation*, an escape to the realm of spirit. Such an escape could be effected only by severe discipline and spiritual purgation; and as the technique of such discipline proved difficult, the seeker after salvation needed usually to be initiated into certain "mysteries". It is assumed that cults such as Orphism were training-schools for Gnostic disciples. Nevertheless, to sustain an interest and passion for pure spiritual apprehension is beyond the capacity of most men, and of no man for long at a time. While the mind is fixed upon an abstract One or All or *Brahman*, the passions, ignored and despised, muster for revolt. And as the mind in time tires from its labours, these grosser instincts may exact terrible reprisals. At its mildest, the cult degenerates into a trafficking with magic and sorcery (some of the newly-found Gnostic papyri provide evidence of this preoccupation): at its worst, the force of instinct transforms the faith from lofty spirituality into a witches' sabbath of depravity. Thus Gnosticism threw up, and continues to throw up, such heresies as that of Manichaeism, Catharism (at the beginning of the Middle Ages), Priscillianism (in Spain), the Albigensian heresy (in Provence), and that of the Bogamils (in Eastern Europe), as well as numerous other cults in Asia Minor and the Middle East. All these cults tended to be associated with gross practices consequent upon the desire, superficially logical in inspiration, to propitiate the forces of evil. The airborne devotee of the Absolute needs to return, even if only to refuel, to the world he shunned: and he need not wonder that the more frequent and prolonged his absences, the more this despised territory has become a prey to weeds, vermin, and decay.

It would be tempting, though hazardous, to see in Gnosticism a survival of that general movement of spiritual resurgence which is associated with the great names of Zoroaster, Buddha, Mahavira, Confucius, and Lao-Tze. That Gnosticism "came out of Asia" is certain. It bears distinct traces of Buddhist influence in its dismissal of material nature as "illusion"; of Persian influence in its conception of the struggle between Good and Evil as the opposition between light and darkness; of Egyptian influence (especially from the decadent period) in its truckling with magic, sorcery, and demonology.[1] Although on its most rarefied plane it is a faith likely to attract only the intellectual, we have reason to believe that it enjoyed considerable prestige among the common people. A vague cult of spirituality may attain its greatest reputation among the half-educated, especially the refined half-educated: witness the success of that modern diluted form of Gnosticism, Christian Science. A Gnosticism of a higher kind is that which Aldous Huxley and his colleagues are preaching with such eloquence from Los Angeles. Significantly enough, they regard their mission as that of introduc-

[1] Five of the Gnostic papyri referred to above are said to have been written by Hermes Trismegistus ("Thrice-Greatest Hermes"), the Greek version of the Egyptian Thoth. The syncretic writings of this author, presumably a priest or group of priests, were composed in the 3rd century A.D. Gnosticism was not merely syncretic (i.e. a reconciliation of many different tendencies), but apt to borrow terminology from the faiths it opposed, possibly for the purpose of "infiltration".

ing Vedanta to the Occident.[1] Equally significant is the fact that Huxley's standpoint, though sympathetic to the Christian mystics, is definitely hostile to the Christian Churches: a hostility that is reciprocated, especially by the Church of Rome.

The destruction of the Ego

In our account of the teaching of the Buddha we sought to show that the enlightenment to which Gotama claimed access appeared to illuminate a void. The unenlightened man, with his spiritual eyes closed, at least entertained visions, however illusory and deceptive. What benefit, then, followed upon forcibly opening the eyes of the spirit? What nourishment could be obtained by gazing fixedly at the "clear light of the void"? It is here that we come upon one of the chief enigmas of the great oriental faiths—an enigma that modern exponents of Vedanta are hard put to it to explain away. All the major world faiths preach the necessity of striving towards some form of spiritual reality, and this reality is usually identified with God. But Buddhism, like Jainism, has no God. And the ultimate reality of the Hindu systems is not God but *Brahman*, an impersonal reservoir of divinity. Consequently, the great oriental apostles of the divine connection find it difficult, when showing how the human soul may achieve blessedness, to avoid introducing at some point the notion of personality: for without personality it is impossible to account for that principle in the universe without which life and existence are rendered meaningless, namely love. Love must have an object: and that object, however infinite, must partake of the nature of the lover. To attempt to represent the object of love as being impersonal is, as we have seen, vain. And because the notion of love presupposes a relation, and since this relation presupposes reciprocity—a give and take, or rather a giving and a returning—the personality which loves and is loved presupposes a person or self that likewise is loved and loves. Consequently, the oriental faiths that deprive Divinity of personality are obliged, by an inevitable logic, to deprive the lover of his selfhood. In the course of our study we have seen this process repeatedly at work. In order to merge with *Brahman*, the individual ego is obliged to undergo complete self-immolation. The oriental distrust of individuality, in short, is the result of its obsession with a form of divine union which is equivalent, on the human side, to extinction.

What is love, it may nevertheless be asked, if it does not lead to self-effacing union? Are not the oriental sages preaching simply the highest and purest form of love, a passion (if that is not too gross a

[1] See *The Perennial Philosophy* by Aldous Huxley, and *Vedanta for the Western World*, edited by Christopher Isherwood.

word) from which all selfish elements are removed? Do not lovers, in spite of their humanity, experience the feeling, however fleetingly, of losing themselves in one another? The answer is yes; but we have only to reflect for a moment to realize that this is but half of the experience, not its totality. Genuine lovers not merely lose themselves in one another; they find themselves in one another. If not, their passion will end by destroying them. And that is the essence of passion in the physical sense: it is self-destroying. Each partner uses the other as an object upon which to "vent" itself. We all know that this extravagant lavishing of love, which may be found at a level far above mere lust, as in the relation between parents and children, ends by injuring the beloved object. The result is always sterility and destruction.

It is perhaps one of the greatest paradoxes of experience that the drama of love at its most elementary level—so elementary as almost to cease to deserve the name of love altogether—bears the strongest resemblance to the drama of love at its most intellectual level. This is the level to which the Gnostic, Buddhist, and Vedantic philosophies aspire. The exponents of these philosophies invite men to achieve an absorption in the divinity whereby the self is utterly destroyed or cancelled. Absorption and self-destruction involve each other. The process, being impersonal, is unilateral. The transformation in passion of the object into a "thing" is paralleled by the transformation in mysticism of the object into a "concept". The result is equally sterile. Just as blind passion involves stepping out of humanity at one end into brute animalism, so blind intellectualism involves stepping out of humanity at the other end into sterile spiritualism. This is the explanation of the fact that a cult of extreme mysticism may degenerate at any moment into its opposite: for the partition between the two spheres is very flimsy. An uncontrolled mysticism, from whatever point it starts, is always "orgiastic" or Dionysiac in the Nietzschean sense—a blind revel of soul or body. And the blind may work themselves into any state but that of vision.

Thus, as Max Scheler observed,[1] "the Buddha recommends the point of departure of love but not the end to which it leads; in other words it is only the self-detachment, the self-denial, which love implies, that he approves". One cannot help feeling that a realization of this inadequacy, both in Buddhism and in Vedanta itself, has prompted modern Indian sages such as Ramakrishna to lay such emphasis upon the fact that "knowledge and love of God are ultimately one and the same: there is no difference between pure knowledge and pure love". But there is. Knowledge or reason, as

[1] *Die Stellung des Menschen im Kosmos* (1928), chapter III.

we saw, is the apprehension of essences by means of concepts, and to such knowledge there is no return or requital. Love, on the other hand, implies the kind of relationship which Martin Buber has defined as that of "I and Thou" as opposed to "I and It". "When shall I be free?" asks Ramakrishna: "When the 'I' has vanished." But if the "I" has vanished altogether, how is the love-relationship possible, and what is meant by being free? There must be something for me to give, even if only to give up: and the paradox of love is that, in such giving up, the self increases in stature. Only the self that is incapable of such sacrifice remains sterile, a self-centred ego. On the plane of metaphysics, the Buddhist and Vedanta injunction to destroy the ego as a preliminary to merging with the Absolute is first to effect a cancellation, and then to propel a zero into infinity. We know that, according to Vedanta teaching, what is uncovered when the ego is cancelled is the *Atman*; and *Atman* is one with *Brahman*. But if there is no sacrifice, merely an annulment, there can be no merit; and if, from the side of divinity, there is no real intervention, there can be no Grace. Kapila, it will be remembered, contended that true knowledge reveals that "neither I am, nor anything is mine, nor do I exist". But we do exist; and the aim of philosophy is not so much to destroy existence as to render it significant.

We may now sum up our answers to the first two questions that we have set ourselves. The major difference between Eastern and Western thought, regarded very broadly, resides simply in that which happened to Eastern thought when, as a result of the Christian Revelation, a new spiritual principle entered the natural sphere for the purpose of transforming it. It is beyond the purpose of this book, which excludes apologetics, to ask why Christianity should have operated in this way; but it is worth pointing out both that no other oriental religion sought to fulfil such a purpose, and that the early apostles of Christianity, though men of different temperament and capacity, were perfectly clear in their own minds as to the novelty and originality of their faith. The Fourth Gospel, with its philosophical rendering of the Incarnation, is clearly directed at the Gnostic philosophies of "pure spirit" which were popular at the time.[1] In the *beginning*, says the writer (who may or may not have been John), was the Logos, and the Logos was with God and the Logos was God. In other words, prior to the Christian Revelation, the realm of spirit was at an infinite remove from that of matter. Religion might therefore assume two forms: either it was a yearning

[1] Dr. Dodd in his *About the Gospels* (C.U.P., 1950) says that the Fourth Gospel was written for those "who were moving away from the popular paganism and seeking a purer and more spiritual way of religion". One may assume that it was equally intended for those who, while attracted to philosophies of pure spirit, sought something more concrete.

of the soul for absorption in an inaccessible Godhead, or it became an undisguised nature-worship or pantheism. Such indeed were the forms religion took in the pre-Christian world. The coming of Christ, however, transformed the situation. For Christ's claim to be the Son of God represented, to the believer, the incarnation of the Logos, which thus became the Word-made-Flesh. Spirit had chosen to inhabit Matter. Time has been fertilized by eternity. Hence the historical process acquired a dynamism such as it had never before possessed. This is a matter not of imaginative projection, but of fact admitting proof. The social order of the Western World has displayed, as we have shown, a movement, a *Sturm und Drang*, if you wish, utterly foreign to anything in the Orient, until such time as the Orient became penetrated by Western ideas of nationalist idolatry. We may hope that the much-heralded "awakening of the East" will not prove to be an awakening from a private dream of bliss to somebody else's nightmare.

Reconciliation, true and false

The question to which we should finally address ourselves is concerned with the possibilities of a *rapprochement* between Eastern and Western thought. Before embarking upon this difficult if popular subject, it will be as well to make one point clear. No *rapprochement* that is deliberately contrived, or that becomes the subject of pious resolutions at some international conference, or that takes the form of a common denominator of ethical teaching, is likely to prove effective. To belittle the efforts of men of goodwill to introduce harmony among conflicting creeds, or to remove minor misunderstandings, would be churlish; but it remains open to doubt whether the desperate attempt to find a basis for agreement (which can usually be made to yield to verbal formulation of some kind) is as profitable as an open statement of differences. Men are perhaps too disposed to demonstrate how much they agree, or, as commonly in politico-ideological discussion, how each is a better champion of a particular ideal (such as Democracy) than the other. In working together, *unanimity* is much less necessary, and indeed much less common, than is usually supposed. This is shown by the violence of criticism and often the strength of personal antipathies found within organizations which, to the world, present a united front. The most effective unions are usually those in which members agree to differ up to a point just short of scission: the least useful are thus eliminated before, instead of at, the moment of crisis. If, for the purpose of concealing the disunion of Christendom, the Churches were to form the habit of discounting their differences, there would be grave danger that the spirit of compromise might lead them, or some of them, into the most embarrassing liaisons: this happened in Nazi Germany. It is frequently complained of coalitions that, once the common danger is removed, they break up. But that is what coalitions should do. We know from experience what a dismal spectacle they present if they do not. It is better that materialism and false spirituality should be combated by Christians as Christians, Moslems as Moslems, and Buddhists as Buddhists, than that the followers of these faiths should combine to speak in the name of some vague entity called Religion, or Idealism, or even the Perennial Philosophy.

These observations, which are designed to discourage false attempts at concord, should not be construed as an invitation to each of us to retire into his separate phalanstery, thereby abandoning the effort of mutual understanding. Such a proposal would appear strange at the conclusion of a book of this kind. On the contrary, we should redouble our efforts to study other forms of belief, particularly those which appear to differ most widely from our own. There is a regrettable tendency, even so, to roam far afield in search of enlightenment, while neglecting that which is near to hand. If, as we have suggested, the study of comparative religion leads us to believe that certain forms of thought have flourished, with local variations, over wide areas, thereby indicating that civilized mankind *tends*, in the absence of some specific revelation, to embrace a particular kind of faith, we may profitably enquire whether, apart from the examples we have already cited, such a tendency is visible in the philosophical speculations of the present day. To pursue such an enquiry may at first sight seem vain: first because we have already ascribed to oriental thought an indifference to the distinction between religion and philosophy, and secondly because academic philosophy in Europe seems, on a cursory inspection, to have so far divorced itself from religion as to exclude the possibility of such a tendency becoming manifest. The assumption is surely ill-founded; for a tendency can show itself just as effectively in a negative as in a positive fashion. And the impoverishment of much Western philosophy may be due precisely to lack of that form of alimentation from which, in previous centuries, it drew strength. Similarly, we may detect even in the etiolated systems or theories of the present day an impulse, often produced by debility, towards the kind of dogmatism hitherto associated with the "superstitions" of the past.

The theory—for it makes no claim to form a system—of Logical Positivism is a case in point. Logical Positivism, as propounded by different exponents not all of whom are in agreement, has enjoyed a vogue in England and to some extent in America which, given the aridity of its content, is nothing short of remarkable. This is not the place either to outline its history or to expound in detail its tenets; we must be content with a broad statement of its aims. The chief aim of Logical Positivism is to effect the "elimination of metaphysics". This is achieved by the application of a so-called Principle of Verifiability according to which all significant statements fall into two categories: either they represent statements that can be verified in fact or "in principle", or they are tautologies. All sentences containing statements, or apparent statements, which fall into neither of these categories are to be dismissed as nonsensical.

This, as we have said, is a bald summary of Logical Positivism theory. Even by its most enthusiastic propounders it has been recognized to contain ambiguities. For example, once verification in fact needs to be supplemented by verification "in principle", we have already taken off from the empiricist platform and may land anywhere. Nor is it easy to see what meaning can attach, on a theory which claims to have eliminated the concept of "truth", to the overworked word *veri*fication. The point to which we wish to draw attention, however, is the following. If the Logical Positivist standpoint is correct, it follows that almost all the ideas propounded from the beginning of time by the spiritual leaders of mankind have been meaningless. These ideas, in fact, represent not intelligible concepts but emotional noises.[1] And such indeed is the conclusion to which Logical Positivists willingly stand committed.

If the Logical Positivist standpoint were justified, it would follow not merely that metaphysics and theology were illegitimate forms of enquiry, but that all the traditional values of our civilized life were nothing more than fictions. But you cannot fight superstition except from some particular standpoint, whether it be Reason or even Truth; and it is clear that, in spite of its elimination of absolute values, Logical Positivism is all the time concealing some such "absolute" up its sleeve. Moreover, in declaring the statements of metaphysicians and theologians to be "emotive nonsense", the Logical Positivists (as the asperity of their polemic amply demonstrates) are not above firing off a good deal of emotive ammunition themselves. Affirmations such as "metaphysics is nonsense" produce their telling effect from the fact of their being

[1] Professor A. J. Ayer in his well-known *Language, Truth and Logic* (reprinted with a new Introduction in 1947) dismisses as nonsensical not merely the statements of metaphysicians and theologians, but such common ethical pronouncements as "stealing money is wrong". This, says Ayer, is "a sentence which has no factual meaning". Such a contention surely belongs to that class of fatuous theory which, as Professor C. D. Broad has remarked, can be entertained only in the philosophical lecture-room. It would be as interesting to observe whether, in the event of a Logical Positivist being summoned for petty larceny, this form of defence would impress a magistrate, as what would happen to judicial procedure if all magistrates became Logical Positivists.

"war-cries" in a crusade against obscurantism and clap-trap. Finally, the Logical Positivist, in combating dogma, is not guiltless of adopting a dogmatic manner quite as formidable as that of his traditional adversaries.

The concealed Absolute

The reader will perhaps by now have grasped the point of this digression. The Philosopher, as opposed to the Sophist or the Casuist or the Charvaka or the Dialectician, is concerned with (to use the title of a well-known modern book on philosophy) "interpreting the universe". His business is with the meaning and values of life. And even if, for purposes of display, he shirks this task, the responsibilities of his vocation will still lie heavy upon him. He will be dogged by the very problems he is endeavouring to disown. What he "eliminates"—what, like Mr. Podsnap in *Our Mutual Friend*, he "sweeps off the face of the earth"—will return to plague him. He is like a man who, transported on a misty day to the top of a mountain by a funicular railway or teleferic car, ridicules the exertions of those who painfully make the ascent on foot, and remains oblivious of the fact that the peak forms part of an impressive range of infinitely varied character. All he sees before him is a hand-made cairn of stones. What Bishop Berkeley called the "minute philosophers" always adopt this parochial view of philosophy. The neat, ordered, logical system of their own construction is the cairn. But just as this cairn reposes not on the plain below but on the summit of a mountain and is a symbol of achievement, so the "propositions" of our modern logicians represent the extreme abstraction from language in all its intellectual and emotional richness. They presuppose the existence of the "mountain" of philosophy, which men in the past have ascended with toil in order that the present vantage-point shall have been prepared, and the various means of ascent devised.

The controversies surrounding Logical Positivism, the iconoclastic effect of its theories, and above all the warmth with which its partisans leap to its defence, suggest that it partakes of the nature of a faith. And once we enter upon the realm of faith, an unfaith or "armed scepticism" is as significant and instructive as a plain affirmation of belief. A simple or ingenuous error, once exposed, deserves quiet interment: we do not need to rant and rage over its tomb. But the opponent of metaphysics and theology sees in these things a potent means of capturing the human spirit. He sees them as the "opium of the people". Hence the venom of his denunciation, for he believes himself likewise to be an intellectual leader to whom the masses will one day be persuaded to listen. And so we are not surprised to hear the familiar plea of disinterestedness, though upon what philosophical grounds such pure devotion can be justified we are not told.

The theory to which we have drawn attention represents the extreme position adopted by Western thought in its flight from the "idealism" of traditional philosophy in both West and East. The term "idealism" is admittedly unsatisfactory in many ways; it has been associated for too long with a particular theory of knowledge. But the term "spiritual" is not much better, and the term "supernatural" is, for our purpose, perhaps worst of all. It remains true that all the great thinkers of mankind have observed a distinction between spiritual and material reality, and that they have attempted to explain the latter by reference to the former and not the other way round. "We have tended to look to the lowest factor of explanation instead of the higher ones as the key to our problems. We explain mysticism in terms of medicine and pathology: the ancients explained the sensible by religion and by the highest philosophy of which they could think."[1] We have seen that such scepticism and materialism appear at specific moments in every philosophical tradition, in India, in China, in Greece, in 17th-century Europe: the author has described this impulse towards scepticism and finally nihilism as the *anti-philosophia perennis*. If modern Europe had nothing to show for itself except this provincial doctrine, our penury would be extreme; but no one prepared to give attention to such matters can ignore the influence of another philosophical theory of much greater profundity, that known as Existentialism. Here again the schools are numerous, the controversy violent, and the general theory enmeshed in obscurities. Within Existentialism, as within any broad doctrine that aims at understanding existence, all the major trends of philosophical enquiry are visible, from the most spiritual to the most material: in contrast to a hidebound system such as Logical Positivism, where the spiritual elements remain in large part *recessive*. This circumstance, while it may cause the student to become sidetracked, testifies to a general direction in thought: and as this direction is towards an understanding of the meaning of life, which may possibly involve its demonstration to be meaningless, we have no alternative but to follow.

In his essay *What I Believe*, Tolstoy drew attention to a fact of which students of modern philosophical, sociological, and psychological works must finally become painfully aware: namely the absolute poverty of thought which, once the ponderous bulk of surmise and speculation has been shovelled away, remains visible. Immense atolls of fact, towered over by fantastic pagodas of theory,

[1] *The Mind and Heart of Love*, by M. C. D'Arcy, S.J., p. 34.

may have served for many years to obscure this deficiency; but it must be admitted that the 19th century, with all its achievements in the technical sphere, bequeathed little to mankind in the way of wisdom. And its general optimism, its self-assurance, its promises of liberty and prosperity, have been followed by two international explosions which now promise to culminate in a third. To the more sensitive minds of the time, these facts were apparent. The *Autobiography* of John Stuart Mill is perhaps the most moving and tragic document of the age. Brought to the brink of despair and suicide by the calculating Utilitarianism in which he had been educated, Mill found nothing upon which to fall back but the poetry of Wordsworth, and in old age a vague melioristic religion. A similar emotional crisis, though with a different issue, afflicted Tolstoy himself. More significant for our time, however, was the lonely duel with despair fought by Sören Kierkegaard, the Danish thinker.

To Kierkegaard, the vague humanism of his time—and it is worth pointing out that he was born in 1813 and died in 1855—was rendered meaningless, deprived of all intelligibility even, by a single fact. This was the fact of death. To say that Kierkegaard was one of the few great thinkers to notice that men die would be to hold a strange view of what constitutes greatness. Other ages, and sometimes whole civilizations—such as Egypt and Babylon—have been preoccupied with the fact of death. But Kierkegaard's object—it would be too facile to say his desire—was to do more than confront his contemporaries with a *memento mori*; he was concerned to demonstrate that death, by constituting a full stop, made mockery of all the hopes and values upon which 19th-century civilization was based. In order to conceal the scandal of death, in fact, the 19th-century humanists and rationalists never ceased to hold out wild promises of an imminent triumph of science over mortality. This was to be achieved either by the manufacture of life itself or by the indefinite prolongation of human life; for next to the scandal of death, came, as we have already observed, the scandal of old age.

To realize the true nature of existence, said Kierkegaard, is to be confronted with despair: for the most obvious fact of existence, namely its more or less abrupt termination, is not intelligible on the existential plane.[1] In existence we belong to something—a family, a society, a profession, a country, the human species; but in death we belong only to ourselves. We are therefore compelled to live in

[1] Possibly these truths become most forcibly apparent to those of delicate constitution. One is reminded of the remark of Maine de Biran, "*Seuls les gens malsains se sentent exister.*"

a condition of perpetual anguish (*Angst*), serving the group of which we are a member until the day of our death, but knowing that such service is a matter of indifference to a society which, having registered our decease, will continue much as before. All the elaborate measures of social service, above all "cradle-to-grave" insurance, are illusory attempts of "man the citizen" to persuade himself that society cares for "man the individual". In reality society does not care, because society, having no personality, is incapable of solicitude. The social-service State, which modern social idealists believe to be the greatest achievement of our epoch, is simply the official Receiver of the bankrupt ideals of humanism.

It is not merely death which renders life meaningless. The same is true, as indeed Schopenhauer had pointed out, of desire. And here the Existentialist point of view approximates to that of the great oriental sages, particularly the Buddha. On the natural plane, all love, even nominally requited love, is hopeless love, because it creates an image and promotes aspirations to which no human object is adequate. It was because of the impossibility of such attainment and possession that there grew up in Europe that cult of Eros which, as several modern writers have shown,[1] made a virtue of frustration and despair. There comes a moment in every love-affair when possession, satisfaction, or what the American sex-statisticians give an even more unattractive name, becomes something irrelevant; when "no contact possible to flesh" can "allay the fever of the bone"; when the original object is almost forgotten or, if recalled, found to be scarcely recognizable. To refuse to face such facts, or to dismiss them as romantic humbug, will not do. The attempt to consider passion unsentimentally, whether as a "biological fact" or hygienic necessity, creates its own special anguish; for lust, with its terrible privacy, is a great deal less amenable to satisfaction than love. All lechers are solipsists.

Unlike most other contemporary apostles of despair, Kierkegaard found an answer to his problems in faith. Only in faith was the tension of existence rendered supportable or even intelligible; for men can learn to "support" life in a variety of ways —there is a short-term solution to everything. Even those modern philosophers for whom Kierkegaard's solution is unacceptable at least face these ultimate problems with resolution. To insist, with Jean-Paul Sartre, that "man is a useless passion" is at least to say something masculine, passionate, and therefore not wholly useless. It is not an accident that man alone can say these things; that he can affirm if only to deny; and that he can take the consequences of such

[1] E.g. C. S. Lewis: *The Allegory of Love*, and Denis de Rougemont: *Passion and Society* (translated by Montgomery Belgion).

affirmation and denial. In our survey, we have come upon thinker after thinker—the Egyptian Misanthrope, the sages Khekheperre-soneb, Ipuwer and Amenemope, Zoroaster, the Hebrew Psalmists and Prophets, and the great spiritual leaders of India and China—who, often against all reason and unaided by revelation, have preached the "divine connection", *Maat*, the *Tao*, the Way, with a unanimity impossible to confound with coincidence, and foolish to dismiss as illusion or poetry. It is not an accident that such men have been called Jainas, Nebiim, Buddhas, and Prophets, preachers of enlightenment and purveyors of wisdom; nor can we conceive of a time in which their teaching will have been rendered outmoded, unless men should at length choose to repudiate their humanity altogether. The Western World, having afforded the Orient some dubious specimens of its own wisdom, may well profit from deeper acquaintance with this great oriental tradition, thereby calling to mind the source of wisdom from which its own faith is derived. There are many to whom the apparent nihilism of oriental thought must always seem repulsive, and to whom the invitation to escape from nature and desire to a realm of spirit beyond conception is a fantastic example of human conceit and self-delusion. Every man must choose from this storehouse that which answers his individual needs. Perhaps the teaching most accessible and attractive to our Western minds is that contained in the *Bhagavad-Gita*, with its emphasis on *Bhakti*, or devotion to a personal God. For it is in the revelation of Sri Krishna to Arjuna that we find the noblest message ever to have issued from the oriental world: the summons to face the future and its perils with humility, with awe, even with a touch of anguish, but without fear.

INDEX

A

B

N

O

P

Q

R

S

T